LUTHER'S WORKS

American Edition

VOLUME 48

Published by Concordia Publishing House
and Fortress Press (formerly Muhlenberg Press)
in 55 volumes.
General Editors are Jaroslav Pelikan (for vols. 1-30)
and Helmut T. Lehmann (for vols. 31-55)

LUTHER'S WORKS

VOLUME 48

Letters

I

EDITED AND TRANSLATED BY

GOTTFRIED G. KRODEL

GENERAL EDITOR

HELMUT T. LEHMANN

FORTRESS PRESS / PHILADELPHIA

Library of Congress Catalog Card Number 55-9893

ISBN 0-8006-0348-6

Printed in the United States of America 1-348

GENERAL EDITORS' PREFACE

The first editions of Luther's collected works appeared in the sixteenth century, and so did the first efforts to make him "speak English." In America serious attempts in these directions were made for the first time in the nineteenth century. The Saint Louis edition of Luther was the first endeavor on American soil to publish a collected edition of his works, and the Henkel Press in Newmarket, Virginia, was the first to publish some of Luther's writings in an English translation. During the first decade of the twentieth century, J. N. Lenker produced translations of Luther's sermons and commentaries in thirteen volumes. A few years later the first of the six volumes in the Philadelphia (or Holman) edition of the *Works of Martin Luther* appeared. But a growing recognition of the need for more of Luther's works in English has resulted in this American edition of Luther's works.

The edition is intended primarily for the reader whose knowledge of late medieval Latin and sixteenth-century German is too small to permit him to work with Luther in the original languages. Those who can will continue to read Luther in his original words as these have been assembled in the monumental Weimar edition (*D. Martin Luthers Werke.* Kritische Gesamtausgabe, Weimar, 1883-). Its texts and helps have formed a basis for this edition, though in certain places we have felt constrained to depart from its readings and findings. We have tried throughout to translate Luther as he thought translating should be done. That is, we have striven for faithfulness on the basis of the best lexicographical materials available. But where literal accuracy and clarity have conflicted, it is clarity that we have preferred, so that sometimes paraphrase seemed more faithful than literal fidelity. We have proceeded in a similar way in the matter of Bible versions, translating Luther's translations. Where this could be done by the use of an existing English version—King James, Douay, or Revised Standard—we have done so. Where it could not, we have supplied our own. To indicate this in each specific instance would have been pedantic; to adopt a uniform procedure would have been artificial—especially in view of Luther's own inconsistency in this regard. In each volume the translator will be responsible primarily for matters of text and language, while the responsibility of the editor will extend principally to the historical and theological matters reflected in the introductions and notes.

Although the edition as planned will include fifty-five volumes, Luther's writings are not being translated in their entirety. Nor should they be. As he was the first to insist, much of what he wrote and said was not that important. Thus the edition is a selection of works that have proved their importance for the faith, life, and history of the Christian church. The first thirty volumes contain Luther's expositions of various biblical books, while the remaining volumes include what are usually called his "Reformation writings" and other occasional pieces. The final volume of the set will be an index volume; in addition to an index of quotations, proper names, and topics, and a list of corrections and changes, it will contain a glossary of many of the technical terms that recur in Luther's works and that cannot be defined each time they appear. Obviously Luther cannot be forced into any neat set of rubrics. He can provide his reader with bits of autobiography or with political observations as he expounds a psalm, and he can speak tenderly about the meaning of the faith in the midst of polemics against his opponents. It is the hope of publishers, editors, and translators that through this edition the message of Luther's faith will speak more clearly to the modern church.

J. P.
H. T. L.

CONTENTS

ABBREVIATIONS

ANF	—*The Ante-Nicene Fathers,* edited by Alexander Roberts and James Donaldson (Buffalo and New York, 1885-1896, American reprint of the Edinburgh edition).
ARG	—*Archiv für Reformationsgeschichte.*
CIC	—*Corpus Iuris Canonici,* edited by E. Friedberg (Graz, 1955).
C.R.	—*Corpus Reformatorum,* edited by C. G. Bretschneider and H. E. Bindseil (Halle/Saale, 1834-1860).
DRTA. JR	—*Deutsche Reichstagsakten unter Kaiser Karl V,* edited by Historische Kommission bei der Bayrischen Akademie der Wissenschaften (Gotha, 1893-).
EA Var. arg.	—*D. Martin Luthers Sämmtliche Werke.* Erlanger Ausgabe: Opera latina varii argumenti ad reformationis historiam imprimis pertinentia (Frankfurt/Erlangen, 1865-1873).
LCC	—*Library of Christian Classics.* John T. McNeill and Henry P. van Dusen, General Editors (Philadelphia, 1953-).
LW	—American Edition of *Luther's Works* (Philadelphia and St. Louis, 1955-).
MPL	—*Patrologia, Series Latina,* 221 vols., edited by J. P. Migne (Paris, 1884-1904).
O.C.D.	—*The Oxford Classical Dictionary,* edited by M. Cary *et al.* (2nd ed., Oxford University Press, 1950).
O.D.C.C.	—*The Oxford Dictionary of the Christian Church,* edited by F. L. Cross (2nd ed., Oxford University Press, 1958).

PE	–*Works of Martin Luther.* Philadelphia Edition (Philadelphia, 1915-1943).
PNF	–*The Nicene and Post-Nicene Fathers of the Christian Church.* First Series: edited by Philip Schaff. Second Series: edited by Philip Schaff and H. Wace (New York, 1886-1900).
S-J	–*Luther's Correspondence,* 2 vols., edited by Preserved Smith and Charles M. Jacobs (Philadelphia, 1913-1918).
St. L.	–*D. Martin Luthers sämmtliche Schriften,* edited by Johann Georg Walch. Edited and published in modern German, 23 vols. in 25 (2nd ed., St. Louis, 1880-1910).
WA	–*D. Martin Luthers Werke.* Kritische Gesamtausgabe (Weimar, 1883-).
WA, Br	–*D. Martin Luthers Werke.* Briefwechsel (Weimar, 1930-).
WA, DB	–*D. Martin Luthers Werke.* Deutsche Bibel (Weimar, 1906-1961).
WA, TR	–*D. Martin Luthers Werke.* Tischreden (Weimar, 1912-1921).

INTRODUCTION TO
Letters

Approximately 2,580 of Luther's letters are still in existence. It is certain that Luther himself wrote these. Naturally not all the letters of the Reformer have been preserved, and the number of letters written to him that are accessible is even smaller.

The text critical problems of Luther's letters are perhaps more complex and baffling than those of his other writings. Even today many problems are unsolved, and perhaps they never will be solved. Many of the letters and notes are available only as manuscript copies or in prints of the sixteenth century, while the original seems to be lost. Which of the copies is authentic? How are the various copies related to each other? If a message from Luther's hand is extant, yet in various drafts, which is the first and which the final draft? These are just a few of the questions that must be asked. It would have exceeded the working capacity of one man, even with the help of a research team, to clarify the text tradition for all of Luther's letters. As a result, Otto Clemen, the editor of Luther's correspondence in the Weimar Edition,[1] was forced to publish a text which in some places might be considered unsatisfactory as far as text criticism is concerned. In several instances the Enders edition of Luther's letters [2] is more adequate; nevertheless it, too, has its shortcomings.[3] The outstanding features of the Weimar Edition are the text critical apparatus (where the manuscript readings and the text of the printed editions are made available for comparison with the text which is offered) and the commentary. With the exception of Percy S. Allen, the editor of the Erasmus correspondence, there has never been a man—and

---

[1] *WA*, Br.

[2] E. L. Enders, G. Kawerau (eds.), *Dr. Martin Luthers Briefwechsel* (19 vols.; Frankfurt, Stuttgart, 1884-1932); hereinafter cited as Enders, *Briefwechsel.*

[3] For a detailed discussion of the problems involved, see *WA*, Br 1, xvi f., and the planned volume 11^{II} or 12.

perhaps never will be—with such profound knowledge of the people and events of the sixteenth century as was Otto Clemen, who once taught at the *Gymnasium* in Zwickau and was librarian of the famous *Ratsschulbibliothek* there.[4]

Several selections of Luther's letters are available in English; the most important of these is the one by Preserved Smith.[5] The merit of this work (incomplete and out-of-print) consists in the material Smith included with Luther's correspondence, such as letters of Humanists, of members of the Roman hierarchy, and of politically important figures, as well as contemporary reports on events with which Luther's name was connected. On the other hand, and this is one of the shortcomings of the Smith edition, Luther's letters seem to be lost among these additional documents, which frequently take more space than Luther's own writings. In addition many of the documents are not translated but only very freely summarized, so that the reader is hardly able to recognize the underlying original.

The text of Luther's letters is often unclear, more than is the case with his other writings. This is due either to corruption of the text tradition or to the fact that the letters were written in a great hurry and were not polished. As a result the translator of the present edition often had to be concerned more with a reproduction of Luther's thought than with literal fidelity. When essential this reproduction appears in brackets. At the same time the translator attempted to preserve Luther's style, which is of course more free and vivid in a letter than in a formal treatise. The reader will especially notice the effusive language Luther used in addressing secular and ecclesiastical dignitaries. Compared with the flowery language of the Humanists, however, Luther's wording was restrained; he was merely adhering to the polite forms of speech used in the sixteenth century. Luther's self-deprecation may

---

[4] This library is a treasury of sixteenth century material; Clemen dedicated his life to making it available to scholars.

[5] *S-J;* Vol. 1: 1507-1521; Vol. 2: 1521-1530. Smith published an earlier volume: *The Life and Letters of Martin Luther* (Boston, 1911). There also is a collection by M. A. Currie, *The Letters of Martin Luther* (London, 1908); this is a selection of five hundred very freely and often inaccurately rendered letters; since the text offers almost no commentary, this edition is of little value to the study of Luther.

also seem strange to the present-day reader. Such self-abasement was the custom of the day; yet in Luther's case it was more than a question of form. As a monk he was trained to minimize himself and to exalt his fellow-men.

An insight into Luther's personality can be gained only when one preserves the diversity of the material with which he dealt in any one letter and the way in which he did it. In relation to the specific circumstances under which it was written, a letter was a unity; it is therefore unfair to dissect it and offer only the "interesting" parts, as was done by Preserved Smith. Consequently in the present edition each letter is completely translated and set forth, including the address and signature.

Any selection made from a man's literary work can be questioned; this is especially true so far as a choice of his letters is concerned. The editor went through Luther's entire correspondence twice before deciding which letters should be translated. The selected letters should clearly show the environment in which the Reformer lived and the times he shaped. They are intended to be a companion to the study of the Reformation and they should enable the reader to see Luther in the context of the great political and intellectual controversies of the first part of the sixteenth century.

As they follow the major steps in Luther's life and career, the letters also portray Luther as a man. They present him as he was, without idealizing him. In reading Luther's letters one should keep in mind that except for official statements they were private documents reflecting the man's mood in a more direct way than any of his other literary works. The letters originated in the complex situation in which Luther found himself; yet they reveal insights which speak to men of today.

The letters in the American Edition of Luther's works are based on the text of the Weimar Edition. The dates are retained as they were established through the careful research of the editor of *WA*, Br. Each document is preceded by a short introduction, the necessary information regarding addressee and background of the letter, and the reference to the original in the Weimar Edition. Although the text critical apparatus of the *WA*, Br edition was consulted for the translation, text critical notes are added only when the editor considered them sufficiently important. This rather arbitrary procedure (which is, however, in keeping with the character of the *LW* edition) was especially necessary for the letters, in view of the text critical problems involved. It is perhaps superfluous to say that in compiling the explanatory notes the editor drew on the material presented by the *WA*, Br edition. Yet in many cases greater detail was necessary, especially for a clarification of the legal and political background of some of the letters. References to patristic material are given by book, chapter, and paragraph; this should enable the reader to locate them in any edition or translation he may have available.

G. G. K.

INTRODUCTION TO VOLUME 48

Volume 48 in *Luther's Works*[1] presents 119 letters written by Luther between 1507 and March, 1522, the time of his return from the Wartburg. They illustrate the period in Luther's life which is generally considered the most exciting: his monastic and academic careers, his attack on the Roman church, his trial for heresy, the Diet of Worms, and his exile at the Wartburg. The man who was taken to the Wartburg and the man who was called back from there faced totally different problems. "Externally speaking, Luther had reached the turning point of his career. The leader of the opposition was called to be the head of the government, albeit in a very restricted area. The demolisher was summoned to build. The change of course was not absolute because he had been constructive all along, and to the end he never ceased to flay the papacy. Nevertheless the change was vast between the role of railing against 'the execrable bull of Antichrist' and that of providing a new pattern of church, state, and society, a new constitution for the church, a new liturgy, and a new Scripture in the vernacular."[2] It is generally assumed that the Wartburg exile brought the first major period in Luther's life to a close.[3] It seemed only natural therefore to end the first volume of Luther's letters with this date. The letters eloquently give the highlights in the life of Luther, the man who irrevocably put the stamp of his name on the first quarter of the sixteenth century, in spite of his desire to live in seclusion and only "watch the splendid performance of the gifted people" of his age.[4]

It is impossible to give a complete bibliography of the publications which deal with Luther's life and work in general or with the period of his life which is covered by the letters of Volume 48 in particular. An investigation of any of the matters touched upon

---

[1] For the organization of the text, see pp. xv f.

[2] R. Bainton, *Here I Stand. A Life of Martin Luther* (Nashville, 1950), p. 215; hereinafter cited as Bainton.

[3] H. Bornkamm called the Wartburg period "the great breathing spell." ("Probleme der Lutherbiographie," V. Vajta [ed.], *Lutherforschung Heute* [Berlin, 1958], p. 19.) See also J. W. Doberstein, T. G. Tappert (trans.), H. Boehmer's *Road to Reformation* (Philadelphia, 1946).

[4] See p. 69.

in this volume has to begin with a careful study of the standard bibliographical work of Reformation history compiled by Karl Schottenloher.[5] More detailed information concerning persons and events may be found in general reference works.[6]

A history of the Reformation and Counter-Reformation, which relates Luther to the political and cultural situation in Europe, is provided by Harold J. Grimm.[7] B. J. Kidd has collected the most important primary sources concerning the Continental Reformation and added a short commentary to them.[8] Political events related to the church in Ducal Saxony at the time of Duke George are documented by the Duke's official papers.[9] The history of the University of Wittenberg in the first half of the sixteenth century is reflected in the official papers of the University.[10]

---

[5] *Bibliographie zur deutschen Geschichte im Zeitalter der Glaubensspaltung, 1517-1585* (6 vols.; Leipzig, 1933-1940). For bibliographies of the literature since 1940, see B. Gebhardt, *Handbuch der Deutschen Geschichte*, Vol. II: *Von der Reformation bis zum Ende des Absolutismus* (8th ed.; Stuttgart, 1955), and the bibliographical reviews offered periodically in *Church History* (1956, 1961), in *Archiv für Reformationsgeschichte*, and in the reports of the international congresses for Luther research: *Lutherforschung Heute* (Berlin, 1958); *Luther and Melanchthon* (Philadelphia, 1961). A general introduction to the modern historiography concerning Luther and the Reformation is offered by H. J. Grimm, "Luther Research Since 1920," *Journal of Modern History*, XXXII (1960); W. Pauck, "The Historiography of the German Reformation during the Past Twenty Years," *Church History*, IX (1940); W. P. Fuchs, "Forschungen und Darstellungen zur Geschichte des Reformationszeitalters," *Die Welt als Geschichte* (1956).

[6] *Allgemeine Deutsche Biographie* (45 vols., 11 supplementary vols.; Leipzig, 1875-1912); *Neue Deutsche Biographie* (München, 1953-); *New Schaff-Herzog Encyclopedia of Religious Knowledge* (13 vols.; New York, 1908-1912) and two supplementary volumes: *Twentieth Century Encyclopedia of Religious Knowledge* (2 vols.; Grand Rapids, 1955); *Die Religion in Geschichte und Gegenwart* (2nd ed., 6 vols.; Tübingen, 1927-1932; 3rd ed., Tübingen, 1957-); *Lexikon für Theologie und Kirche* (10 vols.; Regensburg, 1930-1938; 2nd ed.; Freiburg, 1957-).

[7] *The Reformation Era* (New York, 1954); hereinafter cited as Grimm.

[8] *Documents Illustrative of the Continental Reformation* (Oxford University Press, 1901); hereinafter cited as Kidd.

[9] F. Gess (ed.), *Akten und Briefe zur Kirchenpolitik Herzog Georgs von Sachsen* (2 vols.; Leipzig, 1905); hereinafter cited as *Akten und Briefe*.

[10] W. Friedensburg (ed.), *Urkundenbuch der Universität Wittenberg* (Geschichtsquellen der Provinz Sachsen, N.R. 3-5, 2 vols.; Magdeburg, 1926-1927); hereinafter cited as *Urkundenbuch*.

C. E. Förstemann (ed.), *Liber Decanorum Facultatis Theologicae Academiae Vitebergensis* (Leipzig, 1838); Förstemann (ed.), *Album Academiae Vitebergensis* (3 vols.; Leipzig, 1841).

A general history is provided by W. Friedensburg, *Geschichte der Universität Wittenberg* (Halle, 1917); hereinafter cited as Friedensburg, *G.U.W.*

Roland Bainton [11] and Ernest G. Schwiebert [12] have made the life and work of Luther the topic of profound, well-illustrated studies which complement each other. While Bainton's work is more concerned with the interpretation of Luther, Schwiebert, following the tradition of the great representatives of the historical school of the nineteenth and early twentieth centuries, focuses on the actual events. His work is an inexhaustible source of information. Luther's life up to the Wartburg period is the subject of special studies by Heinrich Boehmer [13] and Robert H. Fife.[14] Preserved Smith [15] has made a selection from Luther's letters and from documents which deal with events with which the Reformer was directly or indirectly related. Theodore G. Tappert [16] has selected material concerning spiritual counseling from Luther's writings. In this work Luther speaks to the reader through letters and table talks on such topics as "cheer for the anxious and despondent," "instructions to the perplexed and doubting," "encouragement to the persecuted and imprisoned," "counsel in questions of marriage and sex," and so on.

A valuable tool in working with Luther's correspondence is Georg Buchwald's *Luther Kalendarium*.[17] Though this work is rather difficult to use and certainly has many shortcomings, it is still the only chronological list of letters written by Luther. It also gives places he stayed at a particular time and activities he was engaged in at a particular time and place. Many of the assumptions concerning the place where Luther wrote a particular letter are based on this work.

A selection from the works [18] of Luther's co-worker Melanchthon

---

11 See note 2.

12 *Luther and His Times* (St. Louis, 1950); hereinafter cited as Schwiebert.

13 See note 3.

14 *The Revolt of Martin Luther* (New York, 1957); hereinafter cited as Fife.

15 S-*J*.

16 *Luther: Letters of Spiritual Counsel. LCC* 18; hereinafter cited as *Luther: Letters.*

17 G. Buchwald, *Luther Kalendarium* (*Schriften des Vereins für Reformationsgeschichte* 147; Leipzig, 1929).

18 R. Stupperich (ed.), *Melanchthon's Werke* (Gütersloh, 1951-); hereinafter cited as *Melanchthon*, Studienausgabe.

A selection of Melanchthon's writings is available in English: E. E. Flack, L. Satre (eds.), C. L. Hill (trans.), *Melanchthon: Selected Writings* (Minneapolis, 1962); hereinafter cited as *Melanchthon: S.W.*

now available in a modern edition is used instead of the text in the *Corpus Reformatorum* wherever possible.

Material on the theological background against which Luther has to be seen can be found in Henry Bettenson's *Documents* [19] and Heinrich Denzinger's *Enchiridion*.[20] Berthold Altaner's *Patrology* [21] and Johannes Quasten's *Patrology* [22] will introduce the reader to the patristic material he will encounter in this volume. The only history of the Augustinian Eremites in Germany in the fifteenth and sixteenth centuries is provided by Theodor Kolde; [23] it is outdated, however, in many respects.

Humanism, no less than Luther, shaped the sixteenth century. The works of the most important Humanist, Erasmus of Rotterdam, unfortunately are not yet available in a modern edition but only in an edition of the early eighteenth century.[24] His correspondence, however, is available in a masterpiece of modern editorial method.[25] Percy S. Allen's edition of the Erasmus correspondence, in addition to providing the text, is a wellspring of information about people and events of the first half of the sixteenth century.

The works of Humanists representing nationalistic opposition to Rome, especially those of Ulrich von Hutten,[26] document the *Zeitgeist*, the sentiment of the period which was ready for the great religious, social, and political revolution brought about by the Reformation.

G. G. K.

---

[19] *Documents of the Christian Church* (6th ed.; Oxford University Press, 1956); hereinafter cited as Bettenson.

[20] *Enchiridion Symbolorum Definitionum et Declarationum de Rebus Fidei et Morum* (31st ed.; Freiburg/Breisgau, 1957); R. J. Deferrari (trans.), *Sources of Catholic Dogma* (St. Louis, 1958); hereinafter cited as Denzinger.

[21] *Patrologie* (5th ed.; Freiburg/Breisgau, 1958); H. C. Graef (trans.) *Patrology* (Freiburg/Breisgau, 1960); hereinafter cited as *Patrology*.

[22] *Patrology* (Utrecht-Antwerp, Westminster, Md., 1950-).

[23] *Die deutsche Augustiner-Congregation und Johann von Staupitz* (Gotha, 1879); hereinafter cited as Kolde.

[24] J. Clericus (ed.), *Desiderii Erasmi Roterodami Opera Omnia* (10 vols.; Leyden, 1703-1706); hereinafter cited as Clericus.

A modern edition of some selected works has been prepared by H. Holborn in his *Desiderius Erasmus Roterodamus. Ausgewählte Werke* (München, 1933).

[25] P. S. Allen *et al.* (eds.), *Opus Epistolarum Desiderii Erasmi Roterodami* (12 vols.; New York, Oxford University Press, 1906-1958); hereinafter cited as Allen (vol., number of letter).

[26] E. Böcking (ed.), *Ulrich von Hutten, Opera Omnia* (5 vols.; Leipzig: 1859-1862; 2 supplementary vols.); hereinafter cited as Böcking.

Note on Scriptural References

In quoting Scripture, Luther cites only chapter, not verse, since chapters were not yet customarily divided into verses at that time. In the present translation Luther's own citations have been retained—except in the case of the Psalms—and supplemented or corrected as need be in brackets to conform to the versification in the RSV.

Citations from the Psalms present a special problem. Luther had not yet translated the Old Testament when he wrote the letters in the present volume; his citations are from the Vulgate. In the Vulgate—and in the modern Roman Catholic English versions based upon it—the Psalms are numbered differently than in the AV and RSV, though in both cases the total number of Psalms is 150. The difference parallels that between the Septuagint and the Hebrew in that for the greater part of the Psalter the numeration of the former is one behind that of the latter; only for Psalms 1-8 and 148-150 is the numeration identical. Further confusion arises from the fact that in modern Latin and German Bibles—following Hebrew precedent—the title or introductory statement attached to many of the Psalms is frequently given a verse number, a practice not followed in the RSV. In the present volume Luther's Psalm citations, if they were correct in terms of the Vulgate of his time, have been altered directly in the process of translation to conform to the chapter numbers of the RSV. The reference to the Vulgate found occasionally in parentheses suggests only that the quoted text is closer to the Vulgate translation than to the RSV.

LUTHER'S WORKS

VOLUME 48

1

To John Braun
Erfurt, April 22, 1507

Luther entered the monastery of the Augustinian Eremites in Erfurt on July 17, 1505. After his novitiate year he was allowed to take the vows and was designated for the priesthood. In this letter Luther invites an elderly friend to come to the celebration of his first mass. This is the oldest preserved letter of Luther.

See Bainton, pp. 39 ff.; Fife, pp. 97 ff.

Text in Latin: WA, Br 1, 10-11.

To the pious and venerable John Braun, a priest of Christ and Mary, a vicar at Eisenach,[1] my dearest friend in Christ

Greetings in Christ Jesus, our Lord. I would fear, kindest sir, to disturb your love with my burdensome letters and wishes, if I did not consider (on the basis of your gracious heart which is so generously inclined toward me) the sincere friendship I have experienced in so many ways and favors. Therefore I do not hesitate to write this little letter to you, trusting that in the closeness of our mutual friendship you will listen, and that it might find you easily approachable.

God, who is glorious and holy in all his works, has deigned to exalt me magnificently—a miserable and totally unworthy sinner—by calling me into his supreme ministry, solely on the basis of his bounteous mercy. Therefore I have to fulfil completely the office entrusted to me so that I may be acceptable (as much as dust can be acceptable to God) to such great splendor of divine goodness.

According to the resolution of my fathers, it is determined that I should begin this [holy office] with the help of God's grace on the fourth Sunday following Easter, which we call Cantate.[2] For this day was set aside to celebrate my first mass before God,

[1] John Braun, O.F.M., was vicar of the St. Mary's Chapter in Eisenach. Luther met him (perhaps in the home of one of the Schalbes, see note 6) when he attended school in Eisenach (1498-1501).

[2] May 2, 1507.

since it is convenient to my father.[3] To this then, kind friend, I invite you humbly, perhaps even boldly. I do this certainly not because I consider myself in a position, due to favors I may have granted you (there are none), to request you to inconvenience yourself with the trouble of such a journey to visit me, a poor and humble man; but I do so because I experienced your good will and your obvious kindness toward me when I visited you the other day,[4] and in great abundance on many other occasions.

Therefore, dearest Father, Sir, and Friar (the first title is due to your age and office, the second due to your merits, the third due to your Order), please honor me with your presence if time and your clerical or domestic duties in any way permit, and support me with your valuable presence and prayers, that my sacrifice may be acceptable to God. You may bring along my kinsman Conrad (who was once sacristan at St. Nicholas Church),[5] and anyone you may wish as a traveling companion, so long as he has freed himself from domestic obligations and will enjoy coming.

Finally I urge you to come right into our monastery to stay with us this little while (I am not afraid that you will settle down here!) and not to look elsewhere for quarters. You will have to become a *cellarius,* that is, an inhabitant of a monastic cell.

Farewell in Christ Jesus, our Lord.

Written at our cloister in Erfurt on April 22, the year of [*our*] *Lord 1507*

FRIAR MARTIN LUTHER
from Mansfeld

I do not dare to importune or burden those excellent people of the Schalbe Foundation, who certainly have done so much for me.[6] I am sure that it would not befit their social position and

---

[3] Luther was mainly interested in the presence of his father, who had violently opposed his son's entrance into the monastery (see pp. 301, 331 f.). His father did, however, honor him with his presence and the monastery with a nice sum of money; see *WA*, TR 2, No. 1558.

[4] Precise information concerning this visit is not available.

[5] Conrad Hutter was a relative of Luther on his mother's side; see *WA*, Br 1, 12, n. 10.

[6] Members of the Schalbe family were patrons of a small Franciscan monastery located at the foot of the Wartburg. Luther had received free board from one of the Schalbes.

prestige to be invited to such an unimportant and humble affair, or to be bothered by the wishes of a monk who is now dead to the world. In addition I am uncertain and somewhat dubious whether an invitation would please or annoy them. Therefore I have decided to be silent; but if there should be an opportunity, I wish you would express my gratitude to them. Farewell.

2

To the Augustinians at Erfurt
Wittenberg, September 22, 1512

After his ordination to the priesthood, Luther's superiors assigned him to the study of theology, at first in the studium generale (see p. 28, n. 3) of the Erfurt monastery. In the winter semester of 1508/09 hc was transferred to the monastery in Wittenberg. While pursuing his studies in the Theological Faculty of the University of Wittenberg, which had just been founded, he taught some philosophy courses on the Faculty of Liberal Arts. On March 9, 1509, Luther was graduated as Bachelor in Biblical Studies and was then recalled to the monastery in Erfurt. In the fall of 1509 he was graduated from the University of Erfurt as Master of the Sentences; following that he had to lecture on the Sentences of Peter Lombard, the standard theological work of that period (see O.D.C.C., pp. 1054 f.). At the same time he continued his studies, concentrating especially on the works of St. Augustine. Transferred permanently to Wittenberg in 1511 by von Staupitz, the vicar general of the Order, Luther was directed to complete the steps leading to the Doctorate in Biblical Theology. This degree would enable him eventually to occupy the Chair of Biblical Theology, then held by von Staupitz but unavoidably neglected by him due to the pressure of his administrative duties in the Order.

This letter is Luther's invitation to his old friends in the monastery in Erfurt to come to his graduation as Doctor of Theology. The graduation exercises and festivities were scheduled for October 18 and 19, 1512.

See Fife, pp. 104 ff.; Schwiebert, pp. 199 ff.· On Luther as a professor, see T. G. Tappert, "Luther in His Academic Role," The Mature Luther ("Martin Luther Lectures," Vol. III [Decorah, Iowa, 1959]), pp. 3 ff.

Text in Latin: WA, Br 1, 18.

To the reverend, venerable, and godly fathers,
to the Prior,[1] the Master,[2] and the seniors of
the monastery of the Order of the Eremites of
Bishop St. Augustine in Erfurt,[3]
my fathers, honored in the Lord

Jesus

Greetings in the Lord

Reverend, venerable, and beloved fathers: Pay attention, St. Luke's Day[4] is approaching! On that day, in obedience to the fathers and the Reverend Father Vicar,[5] I shall be solemnly graduated as a Doctor of Theology. I assume that you, my fathers, are already very well aware of this due to a letter from our Reverend Father

[1] It is not certain who was prior of the Erfurt monastery in 1512; it may have been Andrew Löhr, who we know was prior in 1514.

[2] John Nathin, one of Luther's former teachers in the ***studium generale*** (see p. 28, n. 3). He was a disciple of the Occamist Gabriel Biel (see *O.D.C.C.*, pp. 172, 1462 f.) and apparently had been graduated as Doctor of Theology from the University in Erfurt in 1493.

[3] The Eremites of St. Augustine, a mendicant order similar to the Franciscans and Dominicans, was founded in 1255 by the union of various groups of Italian hermits. According to tradition their Rule originated with St. Augustine, bishop of Hippo (see *O.D.C.C.*, pp. 106 ff.). At the beginning of the fifteenth century a number of Augustinian monasteries in Holland and Germany submitted to a strict reform in an attempt to restore the original purity of the Order. In a bitter struggle against other monasteries, these "Rule-observing" Augustinians formed the "Congregation of Reformed Augustinians" which was independent of the four provinces into which the German Augustinians were organized. This congregation was headed by a vicar general and divided into several districts. It was sometimes referred to as the "German" or "Saxon" congregation, although by no means all German Augustinians had joined it. Both the monastery in Erfurt (which Luther had entered in 1505) and that in Wittenberg belonged to the Reformed Augustinians. One of their distinguishing marks was the attention they paid to the study of the church fathers and the Scriptures.

[4] October 18, 1512.

[5] John von Staupitz; see p. 64, n. 1. Luther always stressed that he acquired his degree and thus the obligation to teach the gospel only out of obedience to his superiors and not out of his own desire. See pp. 146, 232, 274, 314 f.

Prior[6] here at Wittenberg. I omit all self-accusations, and do not mention my unworthiness, lest I seem to seek honor and praise by means of humility. God knows, and my conscience also knows, to what extent I am worthy of and grateful for such a bestowal of glory and honor.

Therefore I beseech you for the sake of Christ's mercy to commend me to God in your common prayers—you know, on the basis of the law of love, you are my debtors in this—so that God's will, gracious and blessed, may be with me. Further I beg you to honor me with your presence, if it can be done with any ease, and to partake in this my solemn "parade" (I am honest) for the sake of decorum and the honor of our Order, and especially of our district.[7] I would not presume, my fathers, to bother you with the inconveniences and expenses involved in such a journey, had the Most Reverend Father Vicar[8] not ordered it. In addition it would seem shameful, disgraceful, and even scandalous that I should ascend to such dignity without you in Erfurt knowing of it, or being invited to it. It would especially please me if the venerable Father Lector, George Leiffer,[9] would want to and would be able to come with you; however if this is not possible, the Lord's will be done. I pray and trust, as is fitting, that in this matter your fatherly love may show itself. I shall remember with gratitude your acceptance of my invitation.

Farewell in the Lord to all and each of you, as well as to our friars, to whom I and all of us commend ourselves in prayer.

Written at Wittenberg, September 22, 1512

Friar Martin Luther
Augustinian

---

[6] Wenceslas Link; see pp. 169 f.

[7] See note 3.

[8] John von Staupitz; see p. 64, n. 1.

[9] It was customary that during mealtimes one friar read aloud from Scripture or from the writings of the church fathers. George Leiffer was *lector*, or reader, in the Erfurt monastery. The term "*lector*" could also have meant a friar who was teaching in the *studium generale* (see p. 28, n. 3), or any person lecturing in an academic institution.

3

To George Spalatin
Wittenberg,[1] August 5, 1514

George Spalatin (1484-1545) studied liberal arts, some theology, and law at Erfurt and Wittenberg, and in 1503 received his Master's degree from the University of Wittenberg. After being ordained to the priesthood in 1508, he was called in 1509 to the Electoral Saxon court to educate Prince John Frederick (see pp. 181 f.). In 1511 he was appointed a canon at Altenburg, but remained at court in the personal service of Elector Frederick (see pp. 49 f.). He was made librarian (a position which made him responsible for the development of the library at the University of Wittenberg; see Schwiebert, pp. 245 f.), court chaplain, secretary, and private counselor; ultimately he became one of the most influential persons surrounding the Elector. He was the liaison man between the University of Wittenberg and the Electoral court. The date of the beginning of his friendship with Luther cannot be definitely established; however at the time this letter was written Spalatin and Luther were already well acquainted. The friendship between the two men, which withstood mutual criticism (see pp. 326 f., 382 ff.), lasted until Spalatin's death. Through Luther's influence Spalatin became deeply involved in biblical studies and developed into a wholehearted, though careful, supporter of the Reformation. When Elector Frederick died in 1525, Spalatin left the court and took over his own congregation in Altenburg. Yet he did not disappear from public affairs; his name was connected with almost every great political event of the twenties and thirties of the sixteenth century, as well as with the great developments in the territorial churches of the Reformation. His diplomatic shrewdness, his theological sensitivity, and his earnest struggle for truth made him one of the truly great, though little known, men of the Reformation. Virtually none of his letters is extant, although he carefully preserved letters ad-

[1] The sources of this and letters No. 6, 7, 9, 10, 14, 15, 17, 18, 20, 24, 29, 30, 33, 34, 35, 38, 39, 40, 44, 45, 46, 50, 51, 52, 54, 55, 58, 59, 60, 62 do not give the place from where Luther wrote; however, one can infer from their contents that it was Wittenberg.

dressed to him. Many of his writings and translations are still available, though difficult to obtain. See O.D.C.C., p. 1278.

In September, 1513, John Reuchlin, the most outstanding Humanist and Hebrew scholar of the early sixteenth century (see O.D.C.C., p. 1159), was put on trial by the Inquisition for his interest in Jewish literature. This was the result of a prolonged and bitter literary battle. In the spring of 1514 Ortwin Gratius, one of Reuchlin's enemies, published a book in which he slandered the Hebrew scholar. Highly indignant at this attack, Spalatin called it to Luther's attention. In this letter Luther expresses his opinion concerning this book and the entire controversy.

Text in Latin: WA, Br 1, 28-29; this is the oldest preserved letter in Luther's own handwriting.

To the most learned and highly esteemed priest in Christ,
George Spalatin, my dearest friend

Greetings. Up to this point, most learned Spalatin, I considered Ortwin,[2] that little "poet" in Cologne, to be an ass. But as you see he has [now] become a dog, even more, a ravenous wolf in sheep's clothing,[3] if not even a crocodile, as you sense so keenly. I assume that finally he himself "caught on" to his asininity (if I may use Greek in Latin),[4] since our John Reuchlin pushed his nose in it.[5] But since Ortwin has considered stripping off [his donkey skin] and clothing himself with the majesty of the lion, he has now instead ended up as a wolf or a crocodile due to an unfortunate leap, since he exceeded his ability in trying to accomplish this metamorphosis.[6] Good Lord, what can I say? I beg

---

[2] See the Introduction. Ortwin Gratius (1480?-1542), an editor of the Quentell Press in Cologne, was one of the most sarcastic opponents of John Reuchlin. He mocked the Hebrew scholar in a poem. Reuchlin replied, demonstrating that Gratius knew neither Greek nor Latin; therefore Luther calls him "little poet" and "ass." In 1514 Gratius published a collection of literary attacks on Reuchlin (see the Introduction) to which Luther is here referring. The Humanists took revenge in the *Epistolae obscurorum virorum* (*Letters of Obscure Men;* see *O.D.C.C.*, p. 459), in which they demonstrated once more the literary ineptitude of Gratius and his friends.

[3] Matt. 7:15.

[4] By "asininity" Luther means Greek gibberish.

[5] In the reply mentioned in note 2.

[6] Perhaps an allusion to Ovid's *Metamorphoses;* see *O.C.D.*, pp. 630 f.

you, let us learn on this one occasion how absolutely right are those who condemn envy.[7] I have in mind especially that envy which is the most senseless of all: it is so utterly eager to harm, yet unable to do so. Its licentiousness is without fear; its inability to damage is full of pain and disturbance. That Ortwin stupidly collects and twists ridiculous arguments which contradict each other. Such procedure surely should be bewailed and deplored, not so much because Ortwin heedlessly distorts the words and meanings of the definitely innocent Reuchlin,[8] but because through all this raving he increases the damage of blindness and obstinacy in his heart, as Scripture says, "He burdens himself with heavy mud."[9] In corresponding with you, I could laugh at many details if it were not that one should rather weep over than laugh at such great depravity of souls. I am afraid we shall have more of this. May God quickly end it.

One thing, however, pleases me: namely, that this matter reached Rome and the Apostolic See[10] rather than that permission of far-reaching consequence would be granted to these jealous people of Cologne to pass judgment.[11] Since Rome has the most learned people among the cardinals, Reuchlin's case will at least be considered more favorably there than those jealous people of Cologne—those beginners in grammar!—would ever allow. They are unable to distinguish between what an author [only] reports and what he himself believes; they cannot even understand what he says, or—I should more correctly say—they do not want to understand it.

---

7 Literally: ". . . how absolutely right, just, and sound is the opinion on envy of all who have ever written or spoken, of all who presently are writing and speaking, and of all who will write and speak [on this subject]."

8 Luther wrote *Capnio*, i.e., Reuchlin's Hellenized name, the root of the word which refers to smoke.

9 Hab. 2:6 (Vulgate).

10 Both Reuchlin and his enemies had appealed to Rome and both were summoned there.

11 Luther wrote *in partibus latius . . . licentiam iudicandi;* this is a technical term for referring a case to judges and granting them the authority to deal with it. The University of Cologne and the Dominican monastery there was the center of the agitation against Reuchlin. Jakob of Hochstraaten, O.P., prior of the Cologne monastery, was inquisitor. He possessed wide powers of censorship, which in Reuchlin's case were greatly restricted through the appeal to Rome; see note 10.

Farewell and pray for me, and let us pray for our Reuchlin.[12]
From the monastery, August 5, [15]14

FRIAR MARTIN
Augustinian

4

To George Spenlein
Wittenberg, April 8, 1516

George Spenlein was an Augustinian friar in the monastery at Wittenberg who had recently been transferred to Memmingen. In this letter Luther is reporting on the disposal of some of Spenlein's possessions. It gives an insight into Luther's understanding of justification and its implication for the Christian life prior to his controversy with Rome.

Text in Latin: WA, Br 1, 35-36. The following translation, with minor changes, is by Theodore G. Tappert and is used by permission from Luther: Letters. LCC 18, 109-111. Published 1955, The Westminster Press.

To the godly and sincere Friar George Spenlein,
Augustinian Eremite[1] in the monastery at Memmingen,
my dear friend in the Lord

Jesus Christ

Grace and peace to you from God the Father
and from the Lord Jesus Christ

My dearest Friar George: I wish you to know that I sold some of your things for two-and-a-half gulden,[2] namely, the coat of Brussels for one gulden, the larger work of the Eisenach theolo-

[12] See note 8.
[1] See p. 6, n. 3.
[2] For various reasons it is difficult to give the gulden's exact dollar value. One may assume that Luther used the so-called "Rhenish gulden," which seems to have been the common currency of the University of Wittenberg as well as of Electoral Saxony. According to Schwiebert, pp. 257 ff., the Rhenish gulden of 1536 had the buying power of approximately $13.40 in terms of 1913 values.

gian[3] for half a gulden, and the cowl and some other things for one gulden. Some things are left, such as the *Eclogues* of Baptista Mantuanus[4] and your collections [of other literary materials]. These you must consider a loss, for we have not been able to dispose of them. The two-and-a-half gulden which you owe to the Most Reverend Father Vicar[5] we gave him in your name. The other half gulden which you still owe him you must either try to pay or get him to cancel. I felt that the Most Reverend Father was so well disposed toward you that he would not object to doing so.

Now I should like to know whether your soul, tired of its own righteousness, is learning to be revived by and to trust in the righteousness of Christ. For in our age the temptation to presumption besets many, especially those who try with all their might to be just and good without knowing the righteousness of God, which is most bountifully and freely given us in Christ. They try to do good of themselves in order that they might stand before God clothed in their own virtues and merits. But this is impossible. While you were here, you were one who held this opinion, or rather, error. So was I, and I am still fighting against the error without having conquered it as yet.

Therefore, my dear Friar, learn Christ and him crucified. Learn to praise him and, despairing of yourself, say, "Lord Jesus, you are my righteousness, just as I am your sin. You have taken upon yourself what is mine and have given to me what is yours. You have taken upon yourself what you were not and have given to me what I was not."[6] Beware of aspiring to such purity that

[3] *Summulae totius logicae . . . per Iodocum Trutvetter Isenachcensem Theologum* (Erfurt: W. Schenck, August, 1501). The author, Jodocus Trutvetter of Eisenach, was one of Luther's teachers in philosophy and Scholastic theology at the University of Erfurt (see p. 5; p. 59, n. 19), and this was his major work on logic.

[4] Poetical work of Baptista Mantuanus, a Carmelite who died in 1516?; modern edition by W. P. Mustard, *The Eclogues of Baptista Mantuanus* (The John Hopkins University Press, 1911).

[5] John von Staupitz; see p. 64, n. 1.

[6] This is one of the main ways Luther tried to express the mystery of salvation. In his *First Lectures on the Psalms* (see p. 18, n. 3) he made the following statement: through faith Christ and the sinner are, so to speak, initiated into a marriage. The sinner is described as the prostitute who had been cleansed and rehabilitated through this marriage; see *WA* 4, 130 f.; *WA* 3, 141. Later Luther developed this idea; in the 1520 treatise, *The Freedom of a Christian* (see p. 180, n. 2), he gave this understanding of faith its finest

you will not wish to be looked upon as a sinner, or to be one.[7] For Christ dwells only in sinners. On this account he descended from heaven, where he dwelt among the righteous, to dwell among sinners. Meditate on this love of his and you will see his sweet consolation. For why was it necessary for him to die if we can obtain a good conscience by our works and afflictions? Accordingly you will find peace only in him and only when you despair of yourself and your own works. Besides, you will learn from him that just as he has received you, so he has made your sins his own and has made his righteousness yours.

If you firmly believe this as you ought (and he is damned who does not believe it), receive your untaught and hitherto erring brothers, patiently help them, make their sins yours, and, if you have any goodness, let it be theirs. Thus the Apostle teaches, "Receive one another as Christ also received you to the glory of God."[8] And again, "Have this mind among yourselves, which you have in Christ Jesus, who, though he was in the form of God, [did not count equality with God a thing to be grasped], but emptied himself," etc.[9] Even so, if you seem to yourself to be better than they are, do not count it as booty, as if it were yours alone, but humble yourself, forget what you are and be as one of them in order that you may help them.

Cursed is the righteousness of the man who is unwilling to assist others on the ground that they are worse than he is, and who thinks of fleeing from and forsaking those whom he ought now to be helping with patience, prayer, and example. This would be burying the Lord's talent and not paying what is due.[10] If you are a lily and a rose of Christ, therefore, know that you will live among thorns. Only see to it that you will not become a thorn as a result of impatience, rash judgment, or secret pride. The rule of Christ is in the midst of his enemies, as the Psalm puts it.[11] Why, then, do you imagine that you are among friends?

formulation; see *WA* 7, 22 ff., 49 ff.; *LW* 31, 343 ff. See also *WA* 2, 742 ff.; *LW* 35, 49 ff.

[7] For a similar statement, see p. 282.

[8] Rom. 15:7 (Vulgate).

[9] Phil. 2:5-7.

[10] Matt. 25:18; 18:28.

[11] Ps. 110:2. See also p. 252, n. 12.

Pray, therefore, for whatever you lack, kneeling before the face of the Lord Jesus. He will teach you all things. Only keep your eyes fixed on what he has done for you and for all men in order that you may learn what you should do for others. If he had desired to live only among good people and to die only for his friends, for whom, I ask you, would he have died or with whom would he ever have lived? Act accordingly, my dear Friar, and pray for me. The Lord be with you.

Farewell in the Lord.

From Wittenberg, April 8, 1516

Yours,
FRIAR MARTIN LUTHER
Augustinian

5

To John Lang
Langensalza, May 29, 1516

During the years 1513-1517, Luther gained fame as an academic lecturer; his reputation rose correspondingly in his Order and in 1515 he was elected district vicar of the Congregation of the Reformed Augustinians of central Germany (see p. 6, n. 3). In the performance of his duties he had to inspect the monasteries in his district and check on their administration, as well as on the conduct of the friars. During one of his inspection journeys in the spring of 1516 he visited the monastery in Erfurt. Later, while still traveling from one monastery to another, he wrote this letter, seeking to clarify some budget matters of the monastery in Erfurt.

John Lang (1488?-1548), an Augustinian of Erfurt, pursued his academic career with Luther at Erfurt and Wittenberg. In 1516 he was transferred to the Erfurt monastery where he was made prior, and in April of 1518 he succeeded Luther as district vicar (see p. 61, n. 6). An adherent of Luther's teaching, he introduced the Reformation in Erfurt about 1520.

Text in Latin: WA, Br 1, 41-42.

TO JOHN LANG, MAY 29, 1516

To the venerable and godly Father John Lang,
Bachelor of Theology, prior of the Augustinian Eremites [1] at Erfurt,
always dear to me in the Lord

Jesus

May grace and peace be multiplied to you

Excellent Father, and my faithful co-worker in the Lord's work: now that I am gone something comes to my mind of which I had not thought during my last visit, nor had I thought of it, would I have considered it important or formed a clear idea of it. The point is that the guest quarters (which I have always considered a big danger to our monasteries if abused, although they can be a God-pleasing service if administered in responsibility to the Lord) cannot be better handled and managed unless one carefully watches what and how much is spent for them. Therefore with confidence in you (in which I believe that you will do more than I wish), I do not order but rather admonish you in the Lord to draw up a special list, in which you record daily how much beer, wine, bread, meat, and, in short, how much of anything else may have been used in the guest house. Of course do not list your official expenses and those of the other friars,[2] but only those incurred because of the usual guests. If you do not find a more efficient form, then organize this list so that you write in different columns the following: on the day of this saint, or on this week-day, so much was consumed—for instance, so much wine, so much bread, etc., by this or that guest. Please do not consider this a tedious or superfluous undertaking; otherwise I would have to order you to do it. Perhaps you do not know what my thinking is. Through such organization (unless I am totally wrong) you will be able to see whether the monastery is a monastery rather than a tavern or hotel. For through this method you will be able to know not only how much was used up but also to whom and on which days you have shown hospitality and, finally, to what guests you extended the honor of such hospitality. In addition

[1] See p. 6, n. 3.
[2] Perhaps Luther was thinking of expenses incurred for graduations and ordinations.

you can thus counter the dissatisfaction of the brethren and give an accounting if, for instance, you should be blamed for mismanagement—and also accomplish many other things which I do not mention now.

I also want you to prepare a separate list enumerating the comings and goings of mendicant friars and their hangers-on. Then you can oppose those restless and insatiable people who are so proud of their great usefulness and of the multitude of their good works by telling them instead how profusely they imbibe.

Farewell, be firm and the Lord will be with you. Remember that you are placed as a sign which will be spoken against: [3] for some a blessed life-giving fragrance, for others, truly a scent causing death.[4] Do pray for me.

From Langensalza, May 29, 1516

FRIAR MARTIN LUTHER

I found no monasteries in this district [5] which are in as good order as, by God's grace, the one at Gotha and this one at Langensalza. The latter we examined in one hour, the former in about two, and therefore we finished quickly. God willing, we shall go tomorrow to Nordhausen. I hope the Lord works even without me in these places and governs their spiritual and temporal affairs in spite of the devil. Some kind of illness has attacked me; if the Lord does not prevent it I shall end up with a fever. Please pray for me that God's most glorious will toward me may always be praised. Amen.

---

[3] Luke 2:34.
[4] II Cor. 2:15-16.
[5] See the Introduction to this letter.

6

To George Spalatin
Wittenberg, August 24, 1516

Luther hastily seeks the help of Spalatin, librarian of the Electoral library, in obtaining some information on the Apostle Bartholomew.

On George Spalatin, see pp. 8 f. On the date of this letter, see WA, Br 1, No. 19, Introduction.

Text in Latin: WA, Br 1, 50.

To my friend George Spalatin, servant of God

Jesus

Greetings. I seek a service, dearest Spalatin, requiring your love and faithfulness. Please loan a copy of St. Jerome's letters[1] to me for an hour, or at least (and this I would like even more) copy for me as quickly as you can what that saint has written about St. Bartholomew the Apostle in the little book *On Famous Men*.[2] I should have it before noon, since I will then be preaching to the people.[3] I am quite annoyed with the nonsense and the lies to be found in the *Catalogue*[4] and the *Golden Legend*.[5] Farewell, excellent Brother.

From our little monastery

Friar Martin Luder[6]
Augustinian

Don't be surprised that I, a theologian, don't have Jerome's

[1] St. Jerome's letters: see *Patrology*, pp. 471 f. For the text, see *MPL* 22; for an English translation, see *PNF*[2] 6.

[2] *De viris illustribus* (*On Famous Men*), 36, and *De vitis apostolorum* (*On the Lives of the Apostles*); see *MPL* 23, 683 and 762.

[3] This sermon is printed in *WA*, 1, 79 ff.; see also *WA* 4, 683 ff.

[4] Peter de Natalibus, *Catalogus sanctorum* (*Catalogue of Saints*) (Lyons: G.L. [?], 1508).

[5] *Legenda aurea* (*Golden Legend*) by Jacob of Voragine; published in several editions, this is a popular thirteenth-century handbook of the lives of the saints. See *O.D.C.C.*, pp. 569 f. It is not quite clear to what "lies" concerning St. Bartholomew Luther is referring.

[6] This is a variation of the spelling of Luther's name; we do not know why he used it, but it appears in several of his early letters.

works. I am waiting for the edition by Erasmus.[7] John Lang[8] has taken with him the edition[9] I generally had used, [and he has even] sold it.

7

To George Spalatin
Wittenberg, September 9, 1516

Luther reports in this letter on his academic work, especially on the publication of the First Lectures on the Psalms.

On the controversial date of this letter, see S-J 1, 48, n. 2, and WA, Br 1, 53 ff. On George Spalatin, see pp. 8 f.

Text in Latin: WA, Br 1, 56.

To the most learned George Spalatin, a priest of Christ, whom I venerate in the Lord

Jesus

Greetings. When I finally returned yesterday[1] late in the day, I found your letter, best Spalatin. Please answer Martin Mercator[2] on my behalf that he cannot expect my lecture notes on the Psalms.[3] Although I am not at all eager that they be published

[7] This nine-volume edition was published in the summer of 1516 by John Froben in Basel. Erasmus edited only the first four volumes, which contained the letters.

[8] John Lang had recently been transferred to Erfurt; see p. 14.

[9] This edition of Jerome's works cannot be identified exactly. The first edition of Jerome's letters (and of some of his treatises) was published in Rome in 1470. For more details on the early editions of Jerome's works, see *PNF*[2] 6, xxvi.

[1] Perhaps from another visitation journey; see p. 14.

[2] The identity of this Martin Mercator could not be established. Perhaps Mercator is a professional name and one would then have to read "the merchant" (or businessman) Martin. But this, too, does not give any real clue to his identity.

[3] This is a reference to Luther's famous first exegetical lecture, the *Dictata super Psalterium* (*First Lectures on the Psalms*). This series of lectures was delivered from August, 1513, to October?, 1515, and is reproduced in WA 3–4. See Fife, pp. 190 ff.

at any place or time, yet I am forced by an order[4] I have not yet fulfilled. Now, however, having finished lecturing on Paul,[5] I shall devote myself wholeheartedly to this one task.[6] But even after completion the manuscripts will not be in such a condition that they could be printed without my supervision.[7] Further, our Liberal Arts Faculty wish them to be printed by our printer;[8] this [work] could not be started before Lent. [Were they printed here] this would please me too—if they must be published at all—primarily because they would then be printed in a rougher type face. I am not impressed with publications printed in elegant type by famous printers. Usually they are trifles, worthy only of the eraser.

Farewell.

Written in haste from the monastery, at noon, the day after the Nativity,[9] *1516*

FRIAR MARTIN LUDER[10]
Augustinian

[4] Perhaps by von Staupitz; see p. 64, n. 1.
[5] Lectures on St. Paul's Epistle to the Romans; see *WA* 56; 57. Luther ended this course on September 7, 1516.
[6] Luther never edited these lectures; in the spring of 1517, however, he published a commentary on the *Seven Penitential Psalms* (see *WA* 1, 158 ff.; *LW* 14, IX f., 138 ff.), in which he used some of the material of his *First Lectures on the Psalms*.
[7] The printing would therefore have to be done by the local press.
[8] John Grünenberg, who had settled down in Wittenberg in 1508. He printed the commentary on the *Seven Penitential Psalms* (see notes 6 and 7). His type faces and his work must have been far from the best, since Luther repeatedly complained about them; see pp. 75, 81, 150, 255, 288, 292. Grünenberg used small type faces and many abbreviations, a style of printing commonly called *Antiqua*. On printing books in Wittenberg, see W. Mejer, *Der Buchdrucker Hans Lufft zu Wittenberg* (Leipzig: K. Hiersemann, 1923); O. Clemen, *Die lutherische Reformation und der Buchdruck* ("Schriften des Vereins für Reformationsgeschichte," 167 [Leipzig: Heinsius, 1939]). On Grünenberg, see G. Wustmann, *Aus Leipzigs Vergangenheit* (Leipzig, 1885), pp. 39 f.; Friedensburg, *G.U.W.*, p. 78; *Urkundenbuch* 1, 72.
[9] "Nativity" can refer to the Nativity of the Virgin (September 8) or to the Nativity of Our Lord, but the reference to the end of the lectures on St. Paul's Epistle to the Romans (see note 5) suggests the former.
[10] See p. 17, n. 6.

8

To Michael Dressel
Wittenberg, September 25, 1516

In this letter Luther, as district vicar, deposes Michael Dressel, the prior of the Augustinian monastery in Neustadt/Orla, and arranges for the election of the new prior. He reports on other monasteries and on the plague in Wittenberg.

Text in Latin: WA, Br 1, 57-59.

To the venerable and godly fathers, to Friar Michael Dressel,
prior of the monastery of the Eremites of St. Augustine[1]
in Neustadt,
and also to the seniors and officers of that monastery,
my beloved in the Lord

Jesus

Greetings in the Lord. I hear with sorrow—as I ought to be sorrowful about hearing such news—excellent fathers and friars, that you live without peace and unity. You live in one house, but you are not of one mind, and you are not of one heart and one soul in the Lord,[2] as required by the Rule.[3] That way of miserable and useless living comes either from the weakness of your humility—because where there is true humility, there is peace—or it originates in my negligence. As a matter of fact, it must be both your fault and mine, because we do not weep aloud before the Lord who has created us and we do not pray that he

---

[1] See p. 6, n. 3.
[2] Acts 4:32.
[3] Luther refers to Chapter 1 of the *Regula Augustini*, i.e., the constitution of the Augustinian Eremites. This is the so-called *Regula tertia*, or *Third Rule*, which is a summary and explanation of the *Second* and *First Rule*. According to tradition all three Rules were drawn up by Augustine himself, but this assumption is highly controversial. When Luther quotes the Rule he refers to the *Regula Augustini* in the edition prepared by von Staupitz and published in 1504. For the text of the Rule, see *Lucae Holstenii codex regularum monasticorum et canonicorum* (Wien, 1759), II, 123 ff. See also E. A. Foran, O.S.A., *The Augustinians from St. Augustine to the Union, 1256* (London: Oates and Washburne, Ltd., 1938); *O.D.C.C.*, p. 109.

make our way straight in his sight and lead us in his righteousness.[4] He errs, he errs, he errs who presumes to guide himself by his own wisdom—not to speak of guiding others. But guidance must be obtained from God by humble prayer and a devout mind, as the Psalm says, "Direct my steps according to your word."[5] And Tobias teaches his son: "At all times praise the Lord and plead with him to guide your ways."[6] Because you have not done this, or you have not done it properly, it is no wonder that you were not directed but rather hindered. What now? Life without peace is dangerous because it is without Christ, and it is death rather than life.

Therefore I am forced to do in my absence what I did not want to do while present.[7] Of course I would by far prefer being with you now, but I cannot be. For that reason, receive my order in salutary obedience, if by chance the Lord of peace will deign to work with us. The entire trouble, or rather the root of your disorder, is that you are not in concord with your head, the prior; this is more harmful than if one friar disagrees with another. Therefore, by authority of this office,[8] I order you, Friar Michael Dressel, to resign from your office and [surrender] the seal. By the same authority I release you from the office of prior in the name of the Father and of the Son and of the Holy Ghost. Amen. And since I am absent this letter should have the same effect upon you as I would, were I present.[9]

I do not want you to complain that I have judged you without a hearing, or that I have not accepted your defense. I am completely convinced that everything you did, you did with the best of intentions. Under no circumstances could I think that you have done anything intentionally or maliciously from which disturbance might have arisen. You have done as much as you

---

[4] Ps. 5:8.
[5] Ps. 119:133 (Vulgate).
[6] Tob. 4:20 (Vulgate).
[7] Perhaps during the visitation journey mentioned on p. 18.
[8] Luther in his position as district vicar (see p. 14) was superior of the monastery in Neustadt.
[9] Literally: "And being absent, I want this letter to do to you, who are not available to me now, [precisely] what I would have done to you, could I be with you."

had grace to do. I thank you for this, and if any of your friars should not show you their gratitude I should be most displeased.

The following should console you. It is not enough that a man be good and pious by himself. Peace and harmony with those around him are also necessary. For the sake of preserving peace, the best undertakings must often be deemed unsatisfactory and be rightly condemned. How much less, then, can undertakings which have not led to peace, though done with good intentions and complete devotion, be considered preferable to peace!

Since the prior is now released from his office, I ask you for the sake of Christ's mercy to plan immediately and unanimously [the election of the new prior]. Choose three candidates in order of preference, according to the Rule.[10] I have often found elections to be useless and votes cast in vain. As a result, [I urge you] to conduct this business sensibly and not to elect anyone who is not eligible [for this office], or have anyone of you even cast his vote for such a man; by this I mean someone who may already have an office or who for other reasons is not eligible. In voting this way one wastes time and effort and the votes are cast in vain. Therefore I would like you to list publicly, before the election, all who are not eligible, so that everyone may know for whom he cannot vote. It would not be wrong if you would also list some [friars] qualified for election for the benefit of any who perhaps do not know who is eligible.

Whomever you might elect, my excellent friars, do this with all deliberation so that you do not search [for the right candidate] by means of your own ability, but as I have already said, ask with constant prayers for the Lord's guidance. Scripture states, namely, in Jeremiah, "I know, O Lord, that a man's way is not his own, nor are the steps in which he walks his own."[11] For behold, I declare to you and I predict by this letter that if you will not maintain your Rule by prayers as a trust of God, you will not have peace and favorable results, even if St. John the Baptist were your prior. Everything rests in the hand of the Lord. He who does not believe this will suffer distress and restlessness until he finds out by experience.

[10] See note 3. On the way in which a prior was elected, see Kolde, pp. 224 f.
[11] Jer. 10:23 (Vulgate).

I ask you to be diligent and faithful in the training of novices. This is, of course, the first and most important task of the whole monastery, as I have said and stressed during my visit with you.

Farewell, and pray for me and for all of us.

In the monastery at Magdeburg, Friar John Busch, the subdeacon, passed away; at Dresden, the Father Senior, John Kunzel. The plague roars around us, and we daily expect the fate the people of Magdeburg suffer. Therefore pray for us and the brethren at Magdeburg, that the Lord may in mercy call whom he intends to call.

Farewell in the Lord.

From Wittenberg, September 25, 1516

FRIAR MARTIN LUDER[12]
District vicar of the Augustinians

9

To George Spalatin
Wittenberg, October 19, 1516

In 1515/16, Luther lectured on Romans, basing his work on the Vulgate. But as soon as Erasmus published his Greek text of the New Testament, Luther used this edition, which introduced him to Erasmus' theology. Although Luther appreciated Erasmus' scholarship, he realized the gulf separating him from Erasmus' theology. At issue were justification and the interpretation of Scripture. Here Luther criticizes Erasmus and asks Spalatin to tell Erasmus of his opinion.

On Luther's relationship to Erasmus, see pp. 116 f. See also pp. 5 f., 18 f., 52 ff. On George Spalatin, see pp. 8 f.

Text in Latin: WA, Br 1, 70-71.

To the servant of Christ and priest of the Lord,
George Spalatin, a most learned Master [of Arts],
my sincere friend and upright brother

Jesus

[12] See p. 17, n. 6.

Greetings. What disturbs me about Erasmus, that most learned man, my Spalatin, is the following: in explaining the Apostle [Paul], he understands the righteousness which originates in "works" or in "the Law" or "our own righteousness" (the Apostle calls it that)[1] as referring to those ceremonial and figurative observances [of the Old Testament]. Moreover he does not clearly state that in Romans, chapter 5, the Apostle is speaking of original sin, although he admits that there is such a thing. Had Erasmus studied the books Augustine wrote against the Pelagians (especially the treatises *On the Letter and the Spirit, On Merits and Forgiveness of Sinners, Against the Two Letters of the Pelagians,* and *Against Julian,*[2] almost all of which can be found in the eighth volume of his works),[3] and had he recognized that nothing in Augustine is of his own wisdom but is rather that of the most outstanding Fathers, such as Cyprian, [Gregory of] Nazianzus, Rheticus, Irenaeus, Hilary, Olympius, Innocent, and Ambrose,[4] then perhaps he would not only correctly understand the Apostle, but he would also hold Augustine in higher esteem than he has so far done.

I definitely do not hesitate to disagree with Erasmus on this point, because in Bible exegesis I esteem Jerome[5] in comparison to Augustine as little as Erasmus himself in all things prefers Jerome to Augustine. Devotion to my Order does not compel me to approve of the blessed Augustine; before I had stumbled upon his books I had no regard for him in the least.[6] But I see that the

[1] Rom. 9:31-32; 10:3.

[2] For the bibliography of St. Augustine's writings against the Pelagians, see *Patrology*, pp. 508 f.; *O.D.C.C.*, pp. 107 f.; for the text, see *MPL* 44, 45; for an English text, see *PNF*[1] 5. The Pelagians were opponents of Augustine who maintained the concept of absolute free will against his determinism.

[3] Luther refers to the edition of St. Augustine's works published in 1506 by John Amerbach in Basel.

[4] On the lives and works of these church fathers, see *O.D.C.C.* and *Patrology;* which of their works Luther had actually studied cannot be determined exactly. The works of Rheticus, bishop of Autun at the time of Constantine (early fourth century), and of Olympius, a bishop in Spain also at the time of Constantine, were known to Luther only from quotations in Augustine's works. A similar list of church fathers is in *WA* 1, 607; *LW* 31, 214 f.

[5] On the importance of St. Jerome as a biblical scholar, see *O.D.C.C.*, pp. 719 f., and *Patrology*, pp. 466 ff.

[6] Luther certainly had become familiar with some of Augustine's works in the *studium generale* (see p. 28, n. 3). However it is generally agreed that he did not study them carefully before 1509. See p. 42.

blessed Jerome emphasizes and puts great weight on the historical meaning of Scripture. How amazing that he interprets Scripture better when he skims over the surface—as for instance in his letters [7] —than when he labors over it, as in his minor works.[8]

The "righteousness based upon the Law" or "upon deeds" is, therefore, in no way merely a matter of [religious] ceremonial but rather of the fulfilment of the entire Decalogue. Fulfilment without faith in Christ—even if it creates men like Fabricius, Regulus,[9] and others who are wholly irreproachable in the sight of man—no more resembles righteousness than sorb apples resemble figs. For we are not, as Aristotle believes, made righteous by the doing of just deeds,[10] unless we deceive ourselves; but rather—if I may say so—in becoming and being righteous people we do just deeds. First it is necessary that the person be changed, then the deeds [will follow]. Abel pleases [God] before his gift does.[11] But more of this at another time.

I ask you, therefore, to do the service of a friend and Christian and inform Erasmus of my thoughts.[12] I hope and desire that he will be highly esteemed. But I am afraid that because of his fame many will take up the defense of the literal, that is, the dead,[13]

---

7 Luther must have studied them quite carefully; see pp. 17 f.

8 I.e., his commentaries on various books of the Bible; for an evaluation of these, see *Patrology*, p. 470.

9 Two heroes of Roman history: Gajus Fabricius Luscinus (see *O.C.D.*, p. 355) and Marcus Atilius Regulus (see *O.C.D.*, p. 757).

10 This is a reference to Aristotle's *Nicomachean Ethics*, II, 1-7. For Luther's evaluation of Aristotle, see pp. 37 f., 41 f.

11 Gen. 4:4.

12 On December 11, 1516, Spalatin did write to Erasmus, as requested. His letter reproduced the greater part of Luther's letter; however it does not mention Luther's name; see Allen 2, 501. It seems that Erasmus never acknowledged this letter in spite of Spalatin's reminder of November 13, 1517; see Allen 3, 711. Spalatin's first letter may have been lost, or perhaps Erasmus was indignant and did not want to answer.

13 Luther placed "literal," "historical," or "dead" understanding of Scripture over against "spiritual" understanding, in which the reader not only looks "objectively" at the text but applies it to his own situation before God; thus the reader enters into a personal relationship with God in which the Holy Spirit is active. This differentiation in the understanding of Scripture must be viewed against the background of Paul's distinction between "the letter which kills" and "the spirit which gives life" (II Cor. 3:3-6), as interpreted by Augustine in his *De spiritu et litera* (*On the Spirit and the Letter*); see p. 54, n. 7. Augustine understood this passage as applying to the difference

understanding [of Scripture], of which the commentary of Lyra,[14] and almost all the commentaries written since St. Augustine, are so full. Even Stapulensis,[15] a man otherwise spiritual and most sound—God knows—lacks spiritual understanding in interpreting divine Scripture; yet he definitely shows so much of it in the conduct of his own life and the encouragement of others.

You could call me rash for bringing such famous men under the whip of Aristarch,[16] if you would not know that I do this out of concern for theology and the salvation of the brethren.

Farewell, my Spalatin, and pray for me.

In great haste, from a corner in our monastery, October 19, 1516

Friar Martin Luder [17]
Augustinian

---

between the Law of God and the Spirit of God. The Law commands obedience but cannot evoke it and, therefore, has to condemn or kill man; hence "dead" understanding. The Spirit gives life because he moves the heart of man and enables him to fulfil God's commandments. For further details, see Jaroslav Pelikan, *Luther the Expositor* (companion vol. to *LW* 1-30), pp. 5 ff.; Gordon Rupp, *The Righteousness of God: Luther Studies* (New York, 1953), pp. 81 ff.; W. A. Quanbeck, "Luther's Early Exegesis," *Luther Today* ("Martin Luther Lectures," Vol. I [Decorah, Iowa, 1957]), pp. 37 ff.; *LCC* 15, xxiv ff.

14 Nicholas of Lyra, O.F.M. (1270?-1340?), wrote a Bible commentary, the *Postillae perpetuae in Vetus et Novum Testamentum;* it was the exegetical handbook of the later Middle Ages. "As against the current allegoristic interpretations of the Bible, he set himself to arrive at the exact and literal sense . . ." (*O.D.C.C.*, p. 957). In the *First Lectures on the Psalms* (see p. 18, n. 3), Luther made great use of Lyra's commentary; see Fife, pp. 193 f. Luther's statement here should be compared with his later comment (recorded by A. Lauterbach) in which Luther apparently highly recommended Lyra's work as work of an outstanding historian; see *WA*, *TR* 4, No. 4673.

15 Stapulensis is the Latinized name of the famous French Humanist Lefevre d'Etaples (1455?-1536); see *O.D.C.C.*, p. 489. In 1509 he published a commentary on the Psalms (*Psalterium Quincuplex*) and in 1512 a commentary on the Pauline epistles. Luther made great use of the former work in his *First Lectures on the Psalms* (see p. 18, n. 3; Fife, pp. 190 ff.), and his desk copy with many marginal notes is available; see *WA* 4, 466 ff. On the importance of Lyra and Faber for the development of Luther's hermeneutics, see the literature mentioned in note 13; see also Schwiebert, pp. 275 ff.; Fife, pp. 179 ff.; K. Bauer, *Die Wittenberger Universitätstheologie und die Anfänge der Deutschen Reformation* (Tübingen: J.C.B. Mohr, Paul Siebeck, 1928).

16 Cicero (*Ep. ad Atticum* I, 14, 3), Horace (*Ars poetica* 450), and other classical authors considered Aristarch of Samothrace (215?-143? B.C.) the most biting critic who had ever lived; see *O.C.D.*, p. 89. Luther may have learned of Aristarch through the works of Erasmus; see Clericus 2, 205, A.

17 See p. 17, n. 6.

10

To John Lang
Wittenberg, October 26, 1516

This letter gives us insight into the daily routine of Luther's life. Complaining about the size of his correspondence, Luther reports on his duties in the monastery and as a vicar of a district. In addition there were his academic responsibilities. Commenting on the transfer of friars from Erfurt to Wittenberg, either already completed or still contemplated by Lang, Luther tells briefly of the situation in the Wittenberg monastery and in the plague-infested city. In the last paragraphs Luther gives the Prior of the Erfurt monastery an almost official-sounding report on current business within the German Congregation of the Augustinians: Father Spangenberg is on an official journey through the Netherlands; Father Henry of Zütphen is prior at Dortrecht, and Father Henry Zwetzen is prior at Neustadt; Lector Fug has sent encouraging news concerning Reuchlin's case; Father Wenceslas Link is in Munich; Father Fladenstein in Culmbach and Father Dressel in Neustadt are relieved of their offices; the Vicar General plans to spend the winter in Munich. One item of business has to remain unsettled for the moment, since Luther cannot read Lang's last letter.

On John Lang, see p. 14.

Text in Latin: WA, Br 1, 72-73.

To the venerable Father John Lang, Bachelor [of Theology], prior of the Augustinians [1] at Erfurt, my friend

Jesus

Greetings. I nearly need two copyists or secretaries. All day long I do almost nothing else than write letters; therefore I am sometimes not aware of whether or not I constantly repeat myself, but you will see. I am a preacher at the monastery, I am a reader during

[1] See p. 6, n. 3.

mealtimes,[2] I am asked daily to preach in the city church, I have to supervise the study [of novices and friars],[3] I am a vicar (and that means I am eleven times prior),[4] I am caretaker of the fish [pond] at Leitzkau,[5] I represent the people of Herzberg at the court in Torgau,[6] I lecture on Paul,[7] and I am assembling [material for] a commentary on the Psalms.[8] As I have already mentioned, the greater part of my time is filled with the job of letter writing. I hardly have any uninterrupted time to say the Hourly Prayers[9] and celebrate [mass]. Besides all this there are my own struggles with the flesh, the world, and the devil.[10] See what a lazy man I am!

---

[2] On this office, see p. 5, n. 9.

[3] Usually each monastery had its own *studium generale* (see p. 7) supervised by one of the theologically-trained friars. Here novices and friars were instructed in the history of the Order and the theology of the Order's patron, St. Augustine. If preparing for the priesthood, the friars were also supposed to study liturgy and Scholastic theology, especially the *Sentences* of Peter Lombard (see *O.D.C.C.*, pp. 1054 f.), which was the dogmatic handbook of the time.

[4] As district vicar, Luther had eleven monasteries under his jurisdiction; see p. 14.

[5] A fish pond in Leitzkau, near Magdeburg, belonged to the monastery in Wittenberg; Luther had to collect the rent for it.

[6] The city council of Herzberg was then involved in a controversy with the Electoral court in Torgau with regard to the parish church. In 1492 Elector Frederick had incorporated it into the Herzberg monastery. In 1515 the Elector tried to return it to the city, an intention with which the monastery was highly displeased. It seems that Luther tried to mediate between the three parties. The text does not make it clear which side he defended.

[7] Luther is referring to his lectures on St. Paul's Epistle to the Galatians (see *WA* 57), which he had just started; see note 17.

[8] See p. 18, n. 3; p. 19, n. 6.

[9] These are the prayers for the canonical Hours as laid down in the *Breviary*. The western church recognizes seven Hours: Matins and Lauds, Prime, Terce, Sext, None, Vespers, Compline; see *O.D.C.C.*, p. 659. In a later comment on his life as a monk, Luther stated that he had been kept so busy during the week that he had to neglect the Hourly Prayers; he had tried to make up for his neglect by abstaining from meals and by praying all day Saturday; see *WA*, TR 4, No. 5094.

[10] This refers to Luther's *geistliche Anfechtung*, a term "for which there is no English equivalent. It may be a trial sent by God to test man, or an assault by the devil to destroy man. It is all the doubt, turmoil, pang, tremor, panic . . . and desperation which invade the spirit of man." Bainton, p. 42. For this element basic to Luther's religious make-up, see J. von Rohr, "A Study of the Anfechtung of Martin Luther to the Time of His Evangelical Awakening with Special Reference to the Problem of Salvation" (Ph. D. dissertation, Yale University, 1947); F. H. Littel (ed.), *Reformation Studies. Essays in Honor of Roland H. Bainton* (Richmond, Va., 1962), pp. 46 ff.; G. Rupp, *The Righteousness of God: Luther Studies*, pp. 81 ff.; L. Pinomaa, *Der*

I think that in the meantime my decision and answer regarding Friar John Metzel has reached you.[11] I shall see, however, what I can do. How do you think I can house your *Sardanapales* and *Sybarites?*[12] If you have trained them poorly then you must sustain those poorly trained people. I have enough useless friars around here—if anyone is useless to a suffering soul. I have become convinced that those who are no good at all are more useful than the most useful ones; therefore for the time being, keep them.

With regard to the friars who have been sent to me, I believe (yet I am not sure) that I have written to you recently. I have sent the lay brother, together with a younger friar, to Master Spangenberg's place;[13] they wished to go there so that they would

---

existenzielle Charakter der Theologie Luthers: Das Hervorbrechen der Theologie der Anfechtung und ihre Bedeutung für das Luther Verständnis ("Annales Ac. Scient.," Finnicae XLVII [Helsinki, 1940]). For similar statements, see pp. 143, 257, 319, 323 f., 357.

[11] The background of this statement is not known. Earlier in October Luther had informed Lang that he would "give" him a certain John Metzeler. This friar must be the one mentioned here; see *WA*, Br 1, 65.

[12] *Sybarites* were the inhabitants of the old Greek city Sybaris (located in southern Italy) who enjoyed luxurious living; see *O.C.D.*, p. 870. *Sardanapales* were the followers of the Assyrian king Sardanapulus (7th century B.C.). Luther meant that he could not house Lang's friars who behaved like Sybarites and Sardanapales. Lang must have intended to transfer more friars to Wittenberg. In the first sentence of the following paragraph Luther refers to a "recent" letter. This is *WA*, Br 1, No. 26, of the middle of October, 1516, in which Luther agreed to keep the friars whom Lang had sent (see *WA*, Br 1, 66), although originally he had not wanted to do so; see *WA*, Br 1, 52 (to John Lang: August 30, 1516). Now, in this letter of October 26, he wanted to put a halt to further transfers of friars to Wittenberg. Luther's reasons for this refusal were the poverty of the Wittenberg monastery and the plague in the city. In addition he had enough useless friars!

[13] Two of Lang's transferees (see note 12) were sent by Luther to the Augustinian monastery of Eschwege, where John Bethel of Spangenberg was staying. Spangenberg was graduated as Licentiate of Theology (see p. 264, n. 3) from the University of Wittenberg in 1511 and then transferred to the Eschwege monastery. In 1516 the vicar general of the Order, John von Staupitz, sent him on a special mission to Dordrecht (see below). Spangenberg was successful in gaining the Dordrecht monastery for the Reformed Congregation (see p. 6, n. 3). While prior of the Eschwege monastery from 1518 to 1523, Spangenberg tried hard to stop the influence Luther's ideas had on monastic life. In 1522, when it seemed that the German Augustinians were doomed to lose their identity and when Wenceslas Link resigned from the office of vicar general (see pp. 169 f.; p. 171, n. 7), Spangenberg was elected vicar general. In this position he marshaled the few traditional-minded German Augustinians to the cause of maintaining the Order. Yet he realized his efforts were fruitless and resigned in 1529. In 1530 he was reported to be a pastor in Eschwege.

not remain in this climate, which is not good for their health.[14] I have kept two other friars, together with the two from Cologne.[15] I felt so sorry about their "aptitude" that even considering the loss involved I would prefer to keep them rather than send them back. Twenty-two priests, twelve novices, and in all, forty-one persons live on our more than meager supplies; but the Lord will provide for us.

You write that yesterday you started to lecture on the second book of the *Sentences*.[16] Tomorrow I shall begin with the Epistle to the Galatians.[17] I am afraid, however, that the plague may not allow the course to be continued. Around us the plague takes at the most three or two [in a day]—though not yet daily. Today a son of the craftsman (a neighbor living across from us) was buried; yesterday he was still healthy—and another son also suffers from the epidemic. What am I to say? The plague is here and attacks quite cruelly and suddenly, especially the younger generation. You, together with Master Bartholomew, advise me to escape.[18] Whereto should I flee? I hope the world will not fall to pieces when Friar Martin tumbles down. Of course I shall disperse the friars across the whole countryside if the plague increases.

[14] For a similar statement, see p. 78.

[15] In the middle of October Luther reported to Lang the arrival of these two students from Cologne; see *WA*, Br 1, 67. They were a certain John of Neuss and a certain Himmel, or perhaps Hummel, of Emmerich; the latter was graduated as Master of Arts in February, 1518. In 1521 Himmel became instructor at the University of Cologne but soon ran into trouble, perhaps because he supported Luther. In 1527 he was in Wittenberg again; in 1557 he died a faithful follower of Luther; see *WA*, Br 1, 69, n. 25.

[16] During the summer of 1516 Lang was made supervisor of the *studium generale* (see note 3) of the Erfurt monastery (see p. 5); he was then also appointed *sententiarius*, a position in which he had to lecture on the *Sentences* of Peter Lombard.

[17] Luther began to lecture on St. Paul's Epistle to the Galatians on October 27, 1516, and ended this course on March 13?, 1517; see also note 7.

[18] This apparently is Bartholomew Arnoldi of Usingen (1465?-1532), one of Luther's former teachers at the University of Erfurt. Following matriculation in the University of Erfurt in 1484, Arnoldi became a member of its Philosophical Faculty in 1491 and was graduated as Doctor of Theology in 1514. He was a moderate Nominalist who criticized Occam's doctrine of justification and replaced it with that of Thomas Aquinas and Albert the Great. Due to the Reformation Arnoldi had to leave Erfurt in 1525. He became theological advisor to Conrad of Thüngen, the bishop of Würzburg, a position he held for the rest of his life. For other interpretations of this sentence and its rather unclear structure in the original, see *WA*, Br 1, 74, n. 16.

My place is here, due to obedience. It would not be proper for me to leave until the Reverend Father Vicar will for the second time order me to leave.[19] It is not that I am not afraid of death (I am not the Apostle Paul but only a lecturer on the Apostle Paul!), but I hope the Lord will rescue me from my fears.

The Reverend Father Master John Hirschen, the prior at Cologne, wrote me that Father Master Spangenberg[20] was received with great honor and love by the citizens of Dortrecht, and that the monastery there will shortly be more distinguished than any other. Lector Henry,[21] who was once my classmate—as they say—is prior there; before that he was sub-prior at Cologne. Lector Fug reports that Reuchlin's case is developing favorably, and that [Reuchlin] conducts himself admirably.[22] With regard to the "letter of order or permission" would you please also send along an interpreter! I am unable to make out what those pages contain.[23] Give my greetings to all who should be greeted; I cannot write just now to the masters. I shall write more at another time. If you wish you may read this letter to them.

Master Wenceslas has been released from his office and has become a preacher at Munich.[24] Bachelor Fladenstein has also been released from his office at Culmbach.[25] In Neustadt Friar Michael has been released from office and Friar Henry Zwetzen is now prior

[19] John von Staupitz; see p. 64, n. 1. In his (no longer extant) letter of October 8 (see p. 32), he must have ordered Luther to leave the plague-infested city; Luther apparently felt he should wait to hear further from the Vicar General.

[20] John of Spangenberg; see note 13.

[21] Henry of Zütphen had matriculated in Wittenberg in 1508, while Luther was a student there; see p. 5. On the office of lector, see p. 7, n. 9. On Luther's tribute to Henry, one of the first martyrs of the Reformation, see *LW* 32, 263 ff.

[22] On John Reuchlin's trial, see p. 10, n. 11. John Fug, wholeheartedly devoted to Reuchlin's case, was sub-prior of the Cologne monastery and a theologian of some stature. On the office of lector, see p. 7, n. 9.

[23] The background of this statement is not known.

[24] Wenceslas Link; see pp. 169 f. One cannot verify exactly the office from which he had been released. In 1512 Link was dean of the Theological Faculty of the University of Wittenberg and in 1515 prior of the Wittenberg monastery (see p. 7). An Augustinian would frequently be "city preacher," that is, the main and perhaps only preacher. Link's new position could, however, also mean that he had become a preacher of the Munich monastery.

[25] Little is known of Fladenstein; in the summer semester, 1503, he had matriculated in Wittenberg; see *WA*, Br 1, 75, n. 23. Bachelor is used here as an academic title.

there.[26] I have made this change because I hoped to be in charge there myself for half a year.[27] That place desperately needs some one to rule it. On October 8 the Reverend Father Vicar wrote to me again from Alberkirchen, that is, from the house of Pfeffinger,[28] where Pfeffinger and his Sarah are now raising a Bavarian pig.[29] He writes that he plans to enjoy a quiet winter in Munich.

In haste, farewell, and remember us in this time of the Lord's visitation; to him be glory. Amen.

October 26, 1516

FRIAR MARTIN
Augustinian vicar [30]

11

To George Spalatin
Wittenberg, December 14, 1516

Luther expresses his appreciation for some cloth given to him by Elector Frederick. He reports on a trip of von Staupitz through the Rhineland and recommends to Spalatin the German Theology and sermons by John Tauler.

On George Spalatin, see pp. 8 f.

Text in Latin: WA, Br 1, 77-79.

To the servant of Christ and priest of the Lord,

[26] See p. 20.

[27] Just how—and at what date—Luther intended to be "in charge" there is not clear.

[28] In the fall of 1516 John von Staupitz (see p. 64, n. 1) stayed at a farm of Deginhard Pfeffinger (the thrifty Electoral Saxon treasurer; see pp. 50 f., 78, 121) in Salmannskirchen (not Alberkirchen, as Luther wrote) in Upper Bavaria; see *WA*, Br 1, 75, n. 24. The Vicar's letter is no longer extant; see note 19.

[29] "Pig" was a nickname for the Bavarians, since they raised the greatest supply of pigs in Germany. The name of Pfeffinger's wife was Ehrentraut; she was a member of the old Bavarian family Seiboldsdorf at Schenkenau. When Luther calls her by the Jewish name "Sarah," he is trying to be humorous: the Jews were not supposed to have anything to do with pigs, but "Sarah" Pfeffinger was raising a pig anyhow. How much of a joke this actually was is another matter; see *WA*, Br 1, 75, n. 26.

[30] On the office of district vicar, see p. 6, n. 3, and p. 14.

George Spalatin, Master of Arts, my most learned and sincere friend and upright brother

Jesus

Greetings. Your letter, excellent Spalatin, was delivered to me exactly on St. Lucia's Day.[1] This is the letter in which, among other things, you were rightly concerned [about the mail service] and admonished me to forward my mail via the Wittenberg carrier if I want to send something to you or to Hirschfeld.[2] I, too, have wished nothing so much as a safe carrier or reliable agent for [my letters]. I have indeed written two letters[3] to the venerable Minorite Father James, the Sovereign's[4] father confessor.[5] I asked him both to thank the Sovereign in my behalf for so generously providing me with cloth to wear that is perhaps better than is fitting for a cowl, were it not a sovereign's present, and to report to the Elector on the relics which the Sovereign had commissioned our Reverend Father Vicar[6] to take care of in the Rhineland. But

---

[1] December 13, 1516; Spalatin's letter does not seem to be extant.

[2] Bernhard von Hirschfeld (1490-1551), Electoral Saxon councilor, went in his early youth as a page to the Electoral Saxon court. In 1517 he undertook a pilgrimage to the Holy Land. While in the service of the Saxon Elector he worked primarily in the department of revenue. His abilities in financial matters made him valuable to the church visitation of 1529. From 1529 to 1533 he was *Amtmann*, i.e., high constable, at Schleibe, and at the same time a member of the Electoral court at Wittenberg. During the Smalcaldic War (1546/47) he was commandant of Wittenberg. After the Smalcaldic War he joined the administration of Maurice of Saxony. See *ARG* 8 (1911), 10 ff.

[3] These letters seem to be lost.

[4] Elector Frederick; see pp. 49 f.

[5] James Vogt, or Voigt, O.F.M., a man of sincere piety, was prior of various Franciscan monasteries in Saxony and Thuringia. He served Elector Frederick as a father confessor, preacher, and counselor, and so had a deep influence on the Elector's religious life. In 1493 Vogt accompanied the Elector to the Holy Land. The collection of relics in the Castle Church in Wittenberg was the object of his special love and care. He sympathized with the Reformation at the beginning, being impressed especially with the zeal and integrity of Luther. However, after the Wittenberg disturbances of 1521/22 (see p. 386, n. 1) he rapidly withdrew from the cause of the Reformation. He died in April, 1522. See ARG 6 (1909), 316, n. 2.

[6] As vicar general, John von Staupitz (see p. 64, n. 1) visited the Reformed Augustinian monasteries in the Rhineland (see p. 61, n. 3) in the summer of 1516. Elector Frederick had commissioned him to obtain from the Mother Superior of the St. Ursula monastery in Cologne the relics of the famed "Eleven Thousand Virgins." According to tradition sometime in the fifth

I do not know whether my letters ever arrived or ever will. Therefore I also want to inform you of the current status of this matter.

The Reverend Father Vicar has succeeded in getting permission from the Archbishop of Cologne [7] to secure the relics for the Sovereign and also in having an agent or (as he is called) official commissioner of the Archbishop appointed. The Sub-prior of our monastery at Cologne [8] was commissioned by both the Sovereign and the Vicar to seek out the relics and negotiate their surrender. Yet after the departure of the Reverend Father Vicar, the Mother Superior of St. Ursula (who was approached for the relics by said agents)[9] took shelter behind a papal prohibition; she argued that she could not with good conscience consent to release the relics without papal mandate or permission. Although a copy of the papal permission [to obtain relics][10] was shown to her, she has thus far refused [to surrender them], since the copy was not attested and sealed. So, if you wish, you may inform the Elector that he should either send there a well-authorized copy of the papal permission or else free the Reverend Father Vicar [from further obligations in this regard].

You write that the Most Illustrious Sovereign refers to me often and with great respect; this does not make me particularly happy, yet I pray that the Lord God may reward his humility with glory. Certainly I am not worthy that anyone should think of me, not to mention a sovereign, and in addition one of such high rank. Daily I see and realize that those people who have the worst opinion of me benefit me most. Nevertheless I ask you to let me extend my gratitude through you for the good will and kindness of our ruler, even though I do not want to be praised by you or anyone else, since the praise of man is always vain. Only praise from God is genuine, as it is written, "My soul will be glorified

---

century these virgins left Britain, led by a chieftain's daughter named Ursula; they landed somewhere on the coast of the Netherlands, where they were slaughtered by pagan Huns; see *O.D.C.C.*, p. 1399.

[7] Hermann von Wied, who later played an important role in the Reformation; see *O.D.C.C.*, p. 629.

[8] A certain John Ferber was then sub-prior of the Cologne monastery; see *WA*, Br 1, 80.

[9] The Sub-prior as the Elector's agent and a certain Martin Oed as the Archbishop's agent.

[10] Issued by Pope Julius II in 1507 to Elector Frederick; see *WA*, Br 1, 80.

not in man but in God."[11] And again, "Not in your name but in his holy name you find your glory."[12] It is not that we feel that people who praise us should be reproved for that, but the trouble is that they praise men rather than God, to whom alone be praise, honor, and glory. Amen.

You request my judgment regarding your plan to translate some little writings into German. That is beyond my competence. Who am I to judge what will appeal to the general public and be of profit to them? Whatever pleases and is useful is so only by the grace of God. Don't you know that the more wholesome something is, the less it is popular and the less it gains ground? What is more wholesome than the gospel and Christ? Yet the people treat them lightly; for most people [the gospel and Christ] are a deadly fragrance, causing death, and only for a very few are they a fragrance of life, bringing life.[13] You may say that you want to be of help only to those who like good things. If this is the case then you do not need my opinion any more. The sheep always listen to every word of the shepherd.[14] They resent and flee only from the word of strangers. Whatever you do, as long as it is good and [according to] the word of Christ, do not doubt that it will find acceptance and prove beneficial, but only in the case of a very few souls, because sheep are very seldom found in this kingdom of wolves. Yet above all, seek Christ's counsel and will through a brief humble prayer, for even good projects do not please him if they are done without his command and will. So says Isaiah 30 [:1], "Woe, rebellious sons, that you work out a plan, but not mine, that you make a league, but it is not of my Spirit." Therefore do not follow your own good and pious intention (the way the great mass of monks and priests repeatedly and hopelessly err), but ask for permission, or rather, for a directive [from God], not only especially in this but also in all your work, unless you want your work to become nothing but stubble.[15]

Nevertheless I shall add my advice: if reading a pure and solid theology, which is available in German and is of a quality closest

[11] Ps. 34:2 (Vulgate? but RSV numbering).
[12] Ps. 105:3 (Vulgate? but RSV numbering).
[13] II Cor. 2:15-16; see p. 16.
[14] John 10:3.
[15] See Isa. 47:14; I Cor. 3:12-13.

to that of the Fathers, might please you, then get for yourself the sermons of John Tauler, the Dominican.[16] I am enclosing for you, so to speak, the essence of them all.[17] I have seen no theological work in Latin or German that is more sound and more in harmony with the gospel than this. Taste it and see how sweet the Lord is [18] after you have first tried and realized how bitter is whatever we are.

Farewell, and pray for me.

From our monastery in Wittenberg, December 14, 1516

FRIAR MARTIN LUDER [19]
Augustinian

12

To John Lang
Wittenberg, February 8, 1517

This is a covering letter for Luther's (not extant) letter to his former teacher Jodocus Trutvetter, whom Luther tries to dissuade from adhering to Aristotelian principles. Luther takes this opportunity to set forth his position on Aristotle and Scholastic theology.

On John Lang, see p. 14.

Text in Latin: WA, Br 1, 88-89.

To the venerable Father John Lang, Bachelor of Theology, prior of the Eremites [1] at Erfurt, dear to me in the Lord

---

[16] John Tauler, O.P. (d. 1361), was one of the most prominent representatives of German mysticism; see *O.D.C.C.*, pp. 1323 f. Luther studied the mystics, perhaps upon the suggestion of John von Staupitz; he was deeply attracted by them and to a certain degree was influenced by their thoughts; see Bainton, pp. 56 f. In the summer and fall of 1516, John Lang and Luther together thoroughly studied an edition of Tauler's sermons published in Augsburg in 1508; see *WA*, Br 1, 65. See also in this volume, pp. 366 f.

[17] In December of 1516 Luther published in Wittenberg an anonymous treatise, entitled *Theologia Deutsch* (see *O.D.C.C.*, pp. 1343 f.; *WA* 1, 152; *LW* 31, 73 ff.), which he considered the essence of Tauler's sermons.

[18] Ps. 34:8.

[19] See p. 17, n. 6.

[1] See p. 6, n. 3.

Jesus

Greetings. I am enclosing this letter, my Father, for the distinguished Mr. Jodocus from Eisenach.[2] This letter is filled with serious questions regarding logic, philosophy, and theology; that is, it is full of blasphemies and revilings against Aristotle,[3] Porphyry,[4] the masters of the *Sentences*,[5] or in other words against the hopeless studies which characterize our age.[6] This is the way it will be understood by those for whom it is an established fact that one must be silent, not only as a five-year-old (as the Pythagoreans[7] believe) but also perpetually and to all eternity, as the dead. We are to believe everything, always obediently to listen and not even once, by way of a mild introduction, wrangle or mutter against Aristotle and the *Sentences*. What will they not believe who have taken for granted everything which Aristotle, this chief of all charlatans, insinuates and imposes on others, things which are so absurd that not even an ass or a stone could remain silent about them!

So by all means forward this letter to that excellent gentleman and trace out quite carefully what he himself and all the others

---

[2] Jodocus Trutvetter (see p. 12, n. 3) of Eisenach and Bartholomew Arnoldi of Usingen (see p. 30, n. 18) had been Luther's teachers in the monastery and at the University of Erfurt (see p. 5; p. 59, n. 19). They must have been rather shocked by this onslaught of their former pupil. Apparently Luther had to wait longer for an answer than he had hoped; see p. 41. The letter Luther enclosed is not extant. In a letter of February 22, 1518, Luther also mentioned a letter to Trutvetter and reports on its content; see p. 57. Perhaps these two letters were identical; if not, they must have been of similar content.

[3] Next to Plato, Aristotle (384-322 B.C.) is considered the most important Greek philosopher. Some of his philosophical ideas became the basis for Scholastic theology and were thus incorporated into Christian thought. See *O.D.C.C.*, pp. 83 f., 1225 f.

[4] Porphyry (A.D. 232?-303?) was an outstanding representative of Neo-Platonism. He collected and edited the works of Plotinus; he also wrote an introduction to Aristotle's *Categories;* see p. 57, n. 10; *O.D.C.C.*, pp. 1091 f.

[5] The *Sentences* of Peter Lombard (see p. 28, n. 3; p. 30, n. 16) presented the Christian faith in a systematic way. It was the standard textbook for theology in the Middle Ages and was commented upon by the masters of the *Sentences* in their classroom lectures.

[6] Luther agreed with the Humanists, who did everything they could to replace these "hopeless studies," that is, the study of Aristotle and the Scholastics. with the study of the Bible and classical languages. See p. 41.

[7] Disciples of the Greek philosopher Pythagoras (580?-500? B.C.).

think of me in this respect and report it to me. I wish nothing more fervently than to disclose to many the true face of that actor [8] who has fooled the church so tremendously with the Greek mask, and to show to them all his ignominy, had I only time! I am working on short notes on the *First Book of Physics* [9] with which I am determined to enact the story of Aristaeus against this, my Protheus.[10] He is the most subtle seducer of gifted people, so that if Aristotle had not been flesh, I would not hesitate to claim that he was really a devil. Part of my cross, indeed its heaviest portion, is that I have to see friars born with the highest gifts for fine studies spending their lives and wasting their energies in such play-acting; in addition universities do not cease burning and condemning good books [11] but produce, or rather dream up, bad ones.

I wish that both Master Usingen and the gentleman from Eisenach [12] would stay away from such work and one day no longer pursue it at all. All my files are filled with material against [the schoolmen's] books, which I consider absolutely useless. All others could see that too, if they would not be bound by the eternal law of silence, as I have mentioned.

Farewell, and pray for me.

From Wittenberg, February 8, 1516[13]

FRIAR MARTIN LUTHER
Augustinian

---

[8] Aristotle.

[9] These notes on the first book of Aristotle's *Ta peri physeos* (*On Physics*) are lost. The theses of September, 1517, against Scholastic theology (see *WA* 1, 224 ff.; *LW* 31, 9 ff.), however, are the results of this work on Aristotle and present Luther's criticism of the infiltration of theology by Aristotelian philosophy.

[10] Aristaeus, the son of the gods Apollo and Cyrene, captured and bound the sea god and magician Protheus (see *LW* 31, 277, n. 26), in spite of the magician repeatedly changing himself into animals, fire, and water; see Vergil *Georgica* IV, 387 ff.; *O.C.D.*, p. 89. Luther identified Aristotle with Protheus.

[11] Luther is perhaps thinking of the role of the University of Cologne in the campaign against John Reuchlin; see p. 10, n. 11.

[12] See note 2.

[13] This date, although appearing in the extant manuscript copy of this letter and most printed editions, is wrong. In February, 1516, Luther could not have addressed Lang as "prior of the monastery in Erfurt," since Lang was not appointed to this position before May, 1516; see p. 14; *WA*, Br 1, 41. In addition in letter No. 13 Luther refers to this letter, and No. 13 is dated 1517.

13

To John Lang
Wittenberg, March 1, 1517

Luther transfers Gabriel Zwilling to the monastery in Erfurt; he reports on his work on the Seven Penitential Psalms and also gives his opinion of Erasmus.

On John Lang, see p. 14.

Text in Latin: WA, Br 1, 90.

To the venerable teacher of true godliness, John Lang, Bachelor of Theology, prior of the Augustinian Eremites [1] at Erfurt, esteemed by me in the Lord

Jesus

Greetings. By order of the Reverend Father Vicar,[2] I am sending to you, venerable Father, our Friar Gabriel.[3] According to the same order you should take good care that he and the others behave in the best way, that is, as Christians. It has been decided, and will be good for him, that he should live in all things according to the monastic discipline. You know that he is not yet familiar with or trained in the regulations or customs of the Order. Finally, as soon as possible release (together with this Friar Leonard)[4] that

[1] See p. 6, n. 3.

[2] John von Staupitz; see p. 64, n. 1.

[3] Gabriel Zwilling, an Augustinian, studied at the University of Wittenberg from 1512 until 1517, when he was transferred to Erfurt. In the fall of 1521, while Luther was at the Wartburg, Zwilling introduced the first major reform in the monastery in Wittenberg. He abandoned the celebration of the mass in its traditional form and undertook steps to shape a new communion liturgy (see pp. 324 f.). Together with Karlstadt and the "Zwickau prophets" (see p. 364, n. 28), he tried to push the Reformation to a complete separation from the Roman church. His zeal for breaking with everything old subsided upon Luther's return from the Wartburg in the spring of 1522. Unlike Karlstadt, Zwilling was able to work out his differences with Luther and regain the Reformer's friendship. Zwilling later worked as a pastor in Torgau, where he died in 1558.

[4] The letter carrier; "Leonard" is missing in the manuscript copy of this letter but can be found in the earliest printed edition. The *WA*, Br editor suggests that this was Leonard Beier, an Augustinian of Munich (1495?-1552?). Beier was graduated from Wittenberg University as Bachelor of

friar whom you have promised to send to us in his stead. We do need a friar to replace Gabriel.

I have translated the Psalms and explained them in German;[5] even if they should please no one else, nonetheless they please me exceedingly well. John, the printer,[6] is waiting for you to release those[7] I have sent to you, however.

I am reading our Erasmus[8] but daily I dislike him more and more. Nevertheless it pleases me that he is constantly yet learnedly exposing and condemning the monks and priests for their deep-rooted and sleepy ignorance. I am afraid, however, that he does not advance the cause of Christ and the grace of God sufficiently; here he knows even less than Stapulensis.[9] Human things weigh more with him than the divine. Although I pass judgment upon him reluctantly, nevertheless I do it to warn you not to read everything, or rather, not to accept it without scrutiny, for we live in perilous times. I see that not everyone is a truly wise Christian just because he knows Greek and Hebrew. St. Jerome with his five languages cannot be compared with Augustine, who knew only one language.[10] Erasmus, however, is of an absolutely different opinion on this. But the discernment of one who attributes weight to man's will is different from that of him who knows of nothing else but grace. I definitely wish to keep this opinion a secret so that I do not strengthen the conspiracy of his enemies.[11]

Arts in October, 1516, and as Master of Arts in February, 1518. He accompanied Luther to Heidelberg in April, 1518 (see p. 60), and in the fall of 1518 he also accompanied Luther to Augsburg (see p. 90, n. 4).

[5] These are the *Seven Penitential Psalms;* see p. 19, n. 6.

[6] John Grünenberg; see p. 19, n. 8.

[7] "Those" refers either to certain pages of the manuscript of the Psalm commentary (which Luther probably had sent to his friends in Erfurt for critical appraisal), or to some friars apparently sent to Erfurt by Luther for reasons unknown to us. In either case Lang was to release them and send them back to Wittenberg—if pages, to be set in type, if friars, to aid in the typesetting.

[8] See pp. 23 ff., 52 ff.

[9] Lefevre d'Etaples; see p. 26, n. 15.

[10] St. Jerome (see *Patrology*, pp. 466 f.) was famous for his knowledge of Latin, Greek, Hebrew, and Aramaic. According to a letter of St. Augustine, he knew the languages of almost all the nations (Jews, Greeks, Chaldees, Persians, Medes, and Arabs) as if he were one of them. St. Augustine, on the other hand, could use only Latin.

[11] For a similar statement, see p. 53.

Perhaps the Lord will give him, in His own good time, a true understanding.

Farewell, and greet the masters and the Lector;[12] find out whether Doctor Jodocus will be kind enough to answer me.[13]

From our hermitage in Wittenberg, March 1, 1517

FRIAR MARTIN LUTHER
Augustinian vicar[14]

14

To John Lang
Wittenberg, May 18, 1517

Luther reports briefly on the prosperous development of "our" theology, based on St. Augustine and the Bible, which is rapidly superseding Scholasticism at the University of Wittenberg.

On the University reorganization, see pp. 37 f., 63, 82, 95 f., 111 f., 123, 165 f.; see also Schwiebert, pp. 293 ff. On John Lang, see p. 14.

Text in Latin: WA, Br 1, 99.

To my friend, Father John Lang, prior of the Eremites[1]
of St. Augustine at Erfurt

Jesus

Greetings. I really had no other reason for writing to you except that I thought this father[2] should not leave without a letter and greetings. I am relieved, thanks to God, that Friar John Gumann[3] has returned home safely. The Reverend Father Vicar[4] writes that he intends to come to see us very soon.

---

[12] George Leiffer, whom Luther had especially invited to his graduation; see p. 7.
[13] See p. 37, n. 2.
[14] On the office of district vicar, see p. 6, n. 3; p. 14.
[1] See p. 6, n. 3.
[2] This Augustinian is not known to us.
[3] An Augustinian from Nürnberg who had matriculated in Wittenberg in 1506; see WA, Br 1, 99, n. 1.
[4] John von Staupitz; see p. 64, n. 1.

Our theology and St. Augustine are progressing well, and with God's help rule at our University. Aristotle is gradually falling from his throne, and his final doom is only a matter of time.[5] It is amazing how the lectures on the *Sentences*[6] are disdained. Indeed no one can expect to have any students if he does not want to teach this theology, that is, lecture on the Bible or on St. Augustine or another teacher of ecclesiastical eminence.[7]

Farewell, and pray for me.

May 18, 1517

FRIAR MARTIN LUTHER

Greetings from Master Christian Goldschmidt,[8] who is visiting me right now.

15

To George Spalatin
Wittenberg, the end of August, 1517[1]

This is a dinner invitation extended to Spalatin and some friends.

On George Spalatin, see pp. 8 f.

Text in Latin: WA, Br 1, 103.

To my friend Spalatin, at the castle

[5] For Luther's opinion of Aristotle and the Scholastic theologians, see pp. 37 f., 59.

[6] See p. 37, n. 5.

[7] About one year later Luther wrote to John Lang with reference to the changes in the curriculum: Wittenberg University "is getting ahead. We expect before long to have lectures on the two or rather three [classical] languages, on Pliny, mathematics, Quintilian, and other excellent subjects, after the absurd courses in Petrus Hispanus and Tartaretus [Scholastic logicians] and in Aristotle are dropped." See *WA*, Br 1, 155; Schwiebert, p. 297.

[8] This was actually Christian Düring (d. 1533), who was often called Aurifaber or Goldschmidt because of his profession. He also owned a restaurant and one of the major "trucking businesses" in Wittenberg, as well as being in the publishing business. Over the years he became a very close friend of Luther; see p. 202, n. 13.

[1] The approximate date of this note can be established from Scheurl's (see note 5, below) letters; see *WA*, Br 1, No. 44, Introduction.

Jesus

Greetings. Come with the Father Confessor[2] and his friend[3] after nine o'clock.[4] If Sir Christopher, the ambassador,[5] is staying with you, he may come with you; otherwise our friend Otto[6] has been told to invite him. Farewell. See to it that you also get some wine for us, because as you know you will come from the castle to the monastery and not from the monastery to the castle.

FRIAR MARTIN LUTHER

16

To Cardinal Albrecht, Archbishop of Mainz Wittenberg, October 31, 1517

According to the officially approved practice of the medieval church, absolution of sin was granted to the sinner who had repented, upon his confession and satisfaction; the latter consisted of punishments (such as fasting, prayers, pilgrimages, or even exclusion from the Eucharist) imposed on the penitent sinner by the bishop or the priest on the basis of certain ecclesiastical regulations. Yet the sinner who was reconciled with God through absolution still had to experience purgatory. This was considered a place and state of temporary punishment where the sinner would expiate his venial sins and experience such punishment as was still due, so to speak, for mortal sins already forgiven. Having thus com-

[2] James Vogt; see p. 33, n. 5.
[3] Unknown to us.
[4] Luther did not make it clear whether he was inviting his friends to a late morning or pre-midnight gathering. It may have been the former since the monks arose at four or five A.M. and had their main meal well before noon; see *S-J* 1, 60, n. 30. It may have been this main meal to which Luther was inviting his friends.
[5] Christopher Scheurl had been a professor of law at the University of Wittenberg. After 1512, however, he was a legal counselor and special envoy of his native city of Nürnberg.
[6] This was apparently the Augustinian friar Otto Beckmann of Westphalia. According to *WA*, Br 1, No. 45, Introduction, Luther sent him to Erfurt in September, 1517. On Beckmann, who in later years turned against Luther, see *ARG* 7 (1910), 195 f.; *S-J* 1, 51, n. 2.

pletely atoned for his guilt he would be admitted to the Beatific Vision of God.

Indulgences relaxed or even commuted the punishment the penitent would have to undergo both in this world and in purgatory. Indulgence letters were granted for certain religious works (such as participation in a crusade, the visiting of certain shrines, praying in sanctuaries where relics of saints were kept, ordering and paying for the celebration of masses) or simply for the payment of money to the church, a practice which became extremely popular in the later Middle Ages. The treasury of the merits of Christ, of the Blessed Virgin, and of all the saints was considered to make available benefits sufficient to compensate for all the sinner's punishments. The treasury of merits was entrusted to and administered by the church, which made it available to the faithful by the granting of indulgences. There were two types of indulgences: a partial one, available only at specific times and places, and a general or plenary one, which was periodically granted by the popes. During the later Middle Ages indulgences came to be thought of mainly as a means of shortening the time a sinner would have to spend in purgatory. The church went so far as to assure the faithful that they could shorten not only their own suffering but also that of their loved ones already in purgatory. Since purgatory was to cleanse the sinner of any guilt as yet unatoned, people increasingly considered indulgences to be a means of canceling their guilt. When Luther first began to deal with this problem the papacy had issued various decrees concerning the understanding and handling of indulgences, but it had not yet promulgated a general dogma on this matter. See O.D.C.C., pp. 688 f., 1125 f.

In 1506 Pope Julius II proclaimed a plenary indulgence which was renewed by Pope Leo X; the proceeds were to go toward the construction of the Church of St. Peter in Rome. In 1515 Albrecht of Brandenburg (1490-1545) was put in charge of the administration of this plenary indulgence in the ecclesiastical provinces of Mainz and Halberstadt. He had become archbishop of Magdeburg in 1513 and at the same time administrator of the diocese of Halberstadt. In 1514 he was elected archbishop of Mainz, thus becoming the highest church dignitary in the Empire. This accumulation of offices was altogether contrary to ecclesiastical custom. To acquire the necessary dispensation and the chair of Mainz, Albrecht had to pay a huge sum of money, which was advanced by the Fuggers, one of the biggest banking concerns of the sixteenth century. The sale of indulgences in the Archbishop's territories was to provide the means of reimbursing the Fuggers. One-half of the income was designated for the Curia, and the other half for the Fuggers. The actual promotion of the indulgences was entrusted to sub-commissioners and preachers (one of them being the Dominican John Tetzel, see O.D.C.C., p. 1336), for whose guidance Albrecht's chancellery had published an Instruction, listing the various benefits of the indulgences offered to the people.

Moved by a deep pastoral concern, Luther nailed his Ninety-five Theses (see WA 1, 233 ff.; LW 31, 25 ff.) to the door of the Castle Church in Wittenberg on October 31, 1517. In these theses, intended for a public academic disputation, Luther protested against the sale of indulgences—"the bingo of the sixteenth century" (Bainton, p. 72)—as an institution which undermined the individual's religious responsibility, the majesty of God's law, and the biblical understanding of repentance. This letter was written the same day and is a covering letter for a copy of the Ninety-five Theses; in it Luther requests that the indulgence traffic be halted and the Instruction to the indulgence agents be withdrawn.

See LW 31, 19 ff.; Bainton, pp. 71 ff.; Fife, pp. 245 f.

Text in Latin: WA, Br 1, 110-112.

To the Most Reverend Father in Christ, the Most Illustrious Lord, Sir Albrecht, archbishop of the churches of Magdeburg and Mainz, primate, margrave of Brandenburg, etc., my lord and shepherd in Christ, esteemed in respect and love

Jesus

Grace and mercy from God, and my complete devotion

Most Reverend Father in Christ, Most Illustrious Sovereign: Forgive me that I, the least of all men, have the temerity to consider writing to Your Highness. The Lord Jesus is my witness that I have long hesitated doing this on account of my insignificance and unworthiness, of which I am well aware. I do it now impudently, and I am motivated solely by the obligation of my loyalty, which I know I owe you, Most Reverend Father in Christ. May Your Highness therefore deign to glance at what is but a grain of dust and, for the sake of your episcopal kindness, listen to my request.

Under your most distinguished name, papal indulgences are offered all across the land for the construction of St. Peter. Now, I do not so much complain about the quacking of the preachers, which I haven't heard;[1] but I bewail the gross misunderstanding among the people which comes from these preachers and which they spread everywhere among common men. Evidently the poor souls believe that when they have bought indulgence letters they are then assured of their salvation.[2] They are likewise convinced that souls escape from purgatory as soon as they have placed a contribution into the chest.[3] Further, they assume that the grace obtained through these indulgences is so completely effective that there is no sin of such magnitude that it cannot be forgiven—even if (as they say) someone should rape the Mother of God, were this possible.[4] Finally they also believe that man is freed from every penalty and guilt by these indulgences.[5]

O great God! The souls committed to your care, excellent Father, are thus directed to death. For all these souls you have the heaviest and a constantly increasing responsibility.[6] Therefore I can no longer be silent on this subject. No man can be assured of his salvation by any episcopal function. He is not even assured of his salvation by the infusion of God's grace,[7] because the Apostle [Paul] orders us to work out our salvation constantly "in fear and trembling."[8] Even "the just will hardly be saved."[9] Finally the

---

1 The indulgence agents were not allowed to enter the territory of Electoral Saxony, since the Elector did not want to lose the income from the indulgences which could be obtained at the All Saints' Chapter in Wittenberg (see p. 338, n. 8).
2 See Thesis 32. *WA* 1, 234; *LW* 31, 28.
3 See Thesis 27. *WA* 1, 234; *LW* 31, 27 f.
4 See Thesis 75. *WA* 1, 237; *LW* 31, 32. Tetzel denied having made such a claim.
5 See Thesis 21. *WA* 1, 234; *LW* 31, 27.
6 See Thesis 80. *WA* 1, 237; *LW* 31, 32.
7 On the term "infusion of grace," see pp. 156 ff., 367 ff.
8 Phil. 2:12-13.
9 I Pet. 4:18.

way that leads to life is so narrow[10] that the Lord, through the prophets Amos[11] and Zechariah,[12] calls those that will be saved "a brand plucked out of the fire." And everywhere else the Lord proclaims the difficulty of salvation. How can the [indulgence agents] then make the people feel secure and without fear [concerning salvation] by means of those false stories and promises of pardon? After all, the indulgences contribute absolutely nothing to the salvation and holiness of souls; they only compensate for the external punishment which—on the basis of Canon Law—once used to be imposed.[13]

Works of piety and love are infinitely better than indulgences;[14] and yet [the indulgence preachers] do not preach them with an equally big display and effort. What is even worse, [the preachers] are silent about them because they have to preach the sale of the indulgences. The first and only duty of the bishops, however, is to see that the people learn the gospel and the love of Christ. For on no occasion has Christ ordered that indulgences should be preached, but he forcefully commanded the gospel to be preached. What a horror, what a danger for a bishop to permit the loud noise of indulgences among his people, while the gospel is silenced, and to be more concerned with the sale of indulgences than with the gospel! Will not Christ say to [such bishops], "You strain out a gnat but swallow a camel"?[15]

Added to all this, my Most Reverend Father in the Lord, is the fact that in the *Instruction*[16] for the indulgence agents which is published under Your Highness' name, it is written (certainly without your full awareness and consent, Most Reverend Father)[17] that one of the principal graces [bestowed through the indulgences] is that inestimable gift of God by which man is reconciled with God and by which all the punishments of purgatory

[10] Matt. 7:14.
[11] Amos 4:11.
[12] Zech. 3:2.
[13] See Thesis 5. *WA* 1, 233; *LW* 31, 26.
[14] See Thesis 43. *WA* 1, 235; *LW* 31, 29.
[15] Matt. 23:24.
[16] For the Archbishop's *Instruction*, see Kidd, No. 6; *St. L.* 15, 301 ff.; Bettenson, pp. 260 ff.
[17] This statement should be compared with Luther's letter of December 1, 1521, to the Archbishop; see pp. 339 ff.; see also pp. 326, 376 ff.

are blotted out.[18] It is also written there that contrition is not necessary on the part of those who buy off their souls [19] or acquire *confessionalia*.[20]

What can I do, excellent Bishop and Most Illustrious Sovereign? I can only beg you, Most Reverend Father, through the Lord Jesus Christ, to deign to give this matter your fatherly attention and totally withdraw that little book [21] and command the preachers of indulgences to preach in another way. If this is not done, someone may rise and, by means of publications, silence those preachers and refute the little book. This would be the greatest disgrace for Your Most Illustrious Highness. I certainly shudder at this possibility, yet I am afraid it will happen if things are not quickly remedied.

I beg Your Most Illustrious Grace to accept this faithful service of my humble self in a princely and episcopal—that is, in the most kind—way, just as I am rendering it with a most honest heart, and in absolute loyalty to you, Most Reverend Father. For I, too, am a part of your flock. May the Lord Jesus protect you, Most Reverend Father, forever. Amen.

From Wittenberg, October 31, 1517

Were it agreeable to you, Most Reverend Father, you could

---

[18] The *Instruction* stated: "The first grace is the complete remission of all sins; and nothing greater than this can be named, since sinful man, deprived of the grace of God, obtains complete remission by these means and once more enjoys God's grace; moreover through this remission of sins the punishment which one is obliged to undergo in purgatory on account of the affront of the Divine Majesty is all remitted and the pains of purgatory completely blotted out." See Bettenson, p. 260; *WA*, Br 1, 113, n. 19.

[19] The *Instruction* stated: "The fourth important grace is for those souls in purgatory, and is the complete remission of all sins, which remission the pope brings to pass through his intercession . . . in this wise: that the same contribution shall be placed in the chest by a living person as one would make for himself. . . . It is furthermore not necessary that the persons who place their contributions in the chest for the dead should be contrite in heart and have orally confessed. . . ." See Bettenson, pp. 262 f.; *WA*, Br 1, 113, n. 19.

[20] Confessional letters. The *Instruction* stated: "The second principal grace is a 'confessional' [confessional letter] replete with the greatest, most important, and hitherto unheard of privileges. . . ." See Bettenson, p. 261. Among these privileges were the individual's right to choose his own father confessor (thus avoiding parochial discipline) and the power given to this father confessor to forgive sins, even in cases usually reserved for the Holy See.

[21] The *Instruction*; see note 16.

examine my disputation theses,[22] so that you may see how dubious is this belief concerning indulgences, which these preachers propagate as if it were the surest thing in the whole world.

Your unworthy son,
MARTIN LUTHER
Augustinian,
called Doctor of Sacred Theology[23]

17

To Elector Frederick
Wittenberg, about November 6, 1517

Luther is reminding the Elector of the promise to give him a new cowl. He is also trying to remove an apparent misunderstanding between the Elector and von Staupitz, and thus restore a good relationship between the two men. In addition he advises against a new tax.

Frederick the Wise (1463-1525; after 1486 one of the seven electors of the Holy Roman Empire) was a member of the Ernestine branch of the ruling family in Saxony and one of the most outstanding and capable rulers of the first quarter of the sixteenth century. He reorganized the government of his territory and promoted the Reichsreform, which was intended to provide a new order for the administration of the Empire. He was a pious man, who was more sincere in this regard than many of his contemporaries. Although he was quite thrifty, he was willing to spend

22 *The Ninety-five Theses.* *WA* 1, 233 ff.; *LW* 31, 25 ff. On the events of October 31, 1517, in Wittenberg, see H. Volz, *Martin Luthers Thesenanschlag und dessen Vorgeschichte* (Weimar, 1959); H. Bornkamm, "Der 31. Oktober als Tag des Thesenanschlags," *Deutsches Pfarrerblatt*, 61 (1961); E. Iserloh, *Luthers Thesenanschlag: Tatsache oder Legende?* (Institut für Europäische Geschichte in Mainz, Vorträge No. 31; Wiesbaden: F. Steiner, 1962).

23 Luther justified his attacks on the indulgences on the basis of his responsibility as an officially called Doctor of Sacred Theology. During his graduation as doctor (see p. 5) he had sworn an oath of loyalty to the Roman church (see Schwiebert, p. 195), and, argued Luther, this oath compelled him to speak. See also p. 6, n. 5; P. Steinlein, "Luthers Doktorat," *Neue kirchliche Zeitschrift* (*Luthertum*), XXIII (1912).

great sums of money to add to the collection of relics at the Wittenberg Castle Church. In his attitude toward Luther, Elector Frederick was guided by his piety, a responsible conscience, and a feeling for justice; contrary to the opinion of many scholars, he was not influenced by political reasons (such as territorial antagonism to the Emperor) or by any economic considerations (such as confiscation of the property of churches that had gone over to the evangelical party). He supported Luther in a careful yet effective way, and on the basis of his key role in Imperial politics he was in a very good position to protect the Reformer. Elector Frederick deliberated over every move he made, but once he had come to a decision, he proceeded with determination. He was probably the last of the men around Luther (whom, incidentally, he apparently never met, and with whom he usually communicated through Spalatin) to gain an insight into and understanding of the Reformer's thought. Finally in his dying hour he publicly professed his adherence to the Reformation by receiving the Lord's Supper with bread and wine. This was the deed of a man who was slow to decide and act, but once convinced of the right of what he undertook, was willing to assume full responsibility for his action. See O.D.C.C., p. 526.

Text in German: WA, Br 1, 119-120.

To my most gracious and dear Lord, Duke Frederick,
elector of Saxony

To His Grace: *Personal*

Jesus[1]

Most Gracious Lord and Sovereign: Since Your Grace promised me a new cowl a year ago, as Hirschfeld[2] told me, I now come and ask Your Grace to remember this promise.[3] I beg, however, gracious Lord, if Pfeffinger[4] is again to make the arrangements,

---

[1] This word is written in Latin.
[2] Bernhard von Hirschfeld; see p. 33, n. 2.
[3] It seems that on December 14, 1516, Luther had somewhat prematurely expressed his gratitude for the cowl; see p. 33; p. 121, n. 5.
[4] Deginhard Pfeffinger; see p. 32, n. 28.

that he do so now in deed and not just with a friendly promise. He is very good at spinning fine words, but these do not produce good cloth.

Most Gracious Lord, I have been told by the prior at Erfurt[5] (who had learned of it from Your Grace's father confessor)[6] that Your Grace is annoyed at Doctor Staupitz, our esteemed and dear father, because of a certain letter.[7] Therefore when [Doctor Staupitz] was here and sought Your Grace at Torgau,[8] I talked to His Honor and declared that I would not like to see Your Grace's displeasure come upon His Honor. Truthfully, from the long conversation in which we discussed Your Grace all evening, I found out nothing else than that he has Your Grace in his inmost heart, that the Elector of Saxony is his dear sovereign, and that he is more than well disposed toward Your Grace. This was so much the case that he finally stated: I do not know how I have ever provoked my Most Gracious Lord, unless it be that I held His Grace in too high a regard(!). Therefore, Most Gracious Lord, I plead on his behalf—as he has suggested to me several times—that Your Grace continue to favor and to be loyal to him, just as Your Grace has undoubtedly experienced his loyalty many times.

Most Gracious Lord, that I too may show my faithfulness toward Your Grace, and may earn my courtly cowl, let me add the following: I have heard that Your Grace plans, at the end of this tax period, to impose another and perhaps even heavier tax.[9] If Your Grace will not scorn the plea of a poor beggar, I beg that for the sake of God you will not let it come to that. I and many others who mean well with Your Grace are sincerely sorry that even the last taxation has reduced Your Grace's reputation, name, and good will. Of course God has provided Your Grace with so much intelligence that sees further in such things than I, or maybe all of Your Grace's subjects. But it may well be, indeed, God wills it so, that even great wisdom sometimes be guided by the

---

[5] John Lang; see p. 14.
[6] James Vogt; see p. 33, n. 5.
[7] John von Staupitz; see p. 64, n. 1. This letter is not available.
[8] Von Staupitz, who stayed in Nürnberg at that time, must have traveled to the Electoral residence in Torgau in an attempt to clarify this matter; he must have been unable to do so; see *WA*, Br 1, 116.
[9] This was another tax on beverages; see *WA*, Br 1, No. 51, Introduction.

lesser, so that no one may depend upon himself but only upon God, our Lord. May he preserve Your Grace in good health for our benefit, and thereafter Your Grace's soul to salvation. Amen.

Your Grace's dedicated priest,
DOCTOR MARTIN LUDER [10]
at Wittenberg

18

To George Spalatin
Wittenberg, January 18, 1518

Luther answers Spalatin's question concerning the best way of studying Scripture. As he expresses his opinion of Erasmian hermeneutics Luther develops and states his own exegetical and hermeneutical rules.

See pp. 23 ff. On George Spalatin, see pp. 8 f.
Text in Latin: WA, Br 1, 133-134.

To my honest friend George Spalatin,
truly a disciple of Christ and a brother, etc.

Jesus

Greetings. Excellent Spalatin: You have previously asked me questions that were within my power—or at least my temerity—to answer; but now, when you demand to be directed in those things which pertain to a thorough knowledge of Scripture, you require something far beyond the limit of my abilities, especially as I have not been able to find a guide for myself in this matter.

Certainly different men think differently on this subject; even the most learned and gifted do not agree. You have Erasmus, who plainly asserts that blessed Jerome is such a great theologian in the church that he alone deserves to be considered. If I should place blessed Augustine over against him, I would seem to be

[10] See p. 17, n. 6.

quite a biased and unreliable judge, not only because I am a member of the Augustinian Order[1] but also on account of the widespread and long-accepted opinion of Erasmus that it would be impudent even to compare Augustine with Jerome.[2] Still other men have other opinions. Among such famous judges I would not venture to decide anything concerning these weighty matters on account of the limitation in my learning and gifts. But in the face of all who either passionately hate or slothfully neglect good learning—and that is before all men—I always give Erasmus the highest praise and defend him as much as I can; I am very careful not to air my disagreements with him lest by chance I too would confirm [his enemies] in their hatred of him. Yet, if I have to speak as a theologian rather than as a philologian, there are many things in Erasmus which seem to me to be completely incongruous with a knowledge of Christ. Otherwise there is no man more learned or ingenious than he, not even Jerome, whom he extols so much. Now if you should disclose my opinion of Erasmus to someone else, you will have violated the principles of friendship. I am not warning you without good reason. There are many, as you know, who are eager to find an occasion to slander good learning. Therefore let what I have told you remain a secret.[3] Of course do not accept my judgment until you yourself have established it by [your own] reading. Yet if you insist on learning my method of studying [Scripture], I shall of course hide nothing from you as my closest friend, but only on the condition that you will not follow me without discretion.

To begin with, it is absolutely certain that one cannot enter into the [meaning of] Scripture by study or innate intelligence. Therefore your first task is to begin with prayer. You must ask that the Lord in his great mercy grant you a true understanding of his words, should it please him to accomplish anything through

---

1 See p. 24.

2 In previous months Luther must have carefully studied Erasmus' introduction to the works of St. Jerome; see p. 18, n. 7. In this introduction, as well as in his edition of the New Testament (see p. 23), Erasmus expressed his preference for St. Jerome. See Allen 2, 326, 396; 3, 844.

3 See pp. 40, 184 f. Luther was caught between his admiration for the linguistic ability of Erasmus and his criticism of the theological views of the great Humanist. Were he publicly to attack the latter, Luther feared he would lend support to the Scholastic opponents of Humanistic studies.

you for his glory and not for your glory or that of any other man. For there is no one who can teach the divine words except he who is their author, as he says, "They shall all be taught by God."[4] You must therefore completely despair of your own diligence and intelligence and rely solely on the infusion of the Spirit. Believe me, for I have had experience in this matter.

Then having achieved this despairing humility, read [the books of] the Bible in order from beginning to end, so that you first get the simple story in your mind (as I believe you have already done long since). Blessed Jerome, in his letters and commentaries, will be of great help to you in this.[5] But for an understanding of Christ and the grace of God (that is, for the more hidden understanding which is given by the Spirit), Augustine and Ambrose seem to me to be far better guides, especially because it appears to me that blessed Jerome "Origenizes" (that is, allegorizes)[6] too much. I say this aside from the judgment of Erasmus—but you asked for my opinion and not for his.

If you like my course of study, begin by reading Augustine's *On the Spirit and the Letter,* which our Karlstadt, a man of incomparable zeal, has now edited and explained with remarkable annotations.[7] Then take the book *Against Julian* and likewise the book *Against the Two Letters of the Pelagians.*[8] Add blessed Ambrose's work on the calling of all heathen, although this book appears from its style, character, and chronology to have been written by someone other than Ambrose; it is, nevertheless, a

[4] John 6:45.

[5] See pp. 17, 24 f., 40.

[6] "Origenizes" refers to Origen (d. A.D. 253?), a great biblical scholar of the early church who developed the allegorical method of biblical exegesis. Corresponding to the human body, soul, and spirit, he recognized a literal, moral, and allegorical sense of a text, of which he preferred the last; see *O.D.C.C.*, pp. 36 f., 992 f.; *Patrology*, pp. 226 f., 231 f.

[7] In the spring of 1518 Andrew Karlstadt (see p. 79, n. 12) published St. Augustine's *De spiritu et litera* (*On the Spirit and the Letter*); modern edition: E. Kähler (ed.), *Karlstadt und Augustin. Der Kommentar des Andreas Bodenstein von Karlstadt zu Augustins Schrift De Spiritu et Litera* (Hallische Monographien 19 [Halle/Saale: Max Niemeyer Verlag, 1952]). This treatise (see *Patrology*, p. 508), already mentioned by Luther in October, 1516 (see p. 25, n. 13), was important for Luther and for the development of the Theological Faculty of the University of Wittenberg; see Schwiebert, pp. 293 ff.; Fife, pp. 203 ff.

[8] On these writings of St. Augustine, see p. 24, nn. 2, 3.

very learned book.[9] If these suggestions appeal to you, I shall send you more later on. Forgive my temerity that in such a difficult subject I dare to set forth my ideas over and above those of such famous men.

In closing I shall say nothing on Erasmus' *Defense,*[10] but I am very sorry that such a conflict should have broken out between these great princes of learning. Erasmus is certainly by far the superior of the two, and he is a greater master of language. However he is also more violent, though he makes a great effort to preserve friendship.

Farewell, my Spalatin.

From our monastery, January 18, 1518, the day on which you had sent your letter[11]

FRIAR MARTIN ELEUTHERIUS[12]

Father Staupitz[13] is staying in Munich, Bavaria, from where he has recently sent me a letter.

---

[9] *De vocatione omnium gentium* (*On the Call of All the Heathen*). *MPL* 17, 1167 ff. St. Ambrose's authorship of this work is indeed a controversial matter; see *Patrology*, p. 536.

[10] Erasmus and Lefevre d'Etaples (Faber Stapulensis; see p. 26, n. 15) were engaged in a sharp controversy over Heb. 2:7. Luther is referring to Erasmus' *Defense* against Lefevre d'Etaples: *Apologia ad Jacobum Fabrum Stapulensem* (Louvain: D. Martens, 1517). Clericus 9, 17 ff.

[11] Spalatin must have been in Wittenberg for his letter to have reached Luther the same day; this letter is not extant.

[12] After October 31, 1517, Luther occasionally signed his letters "Eleutherius." Among Humanists the custom of turning one's name into Latin or Greek on the basis of either meaning or sound was prevalent. For instance, Melanchthon's (see p. 77, n. 3) name was originally *Schwarzerd*, which means black earth. Luther derived "Eleutherius" from the Greek word for "free." Perhaps he wanted to demonstrate that he was now—after nailing the *Ninety-five Theses* to the door of the Castle Church in Wittenberg—a free man; he had liberated himself from the nonbiblical understanding of penance and had become a free man in Christ, no longer enslaved by human institutions (such as indulgences) but subject only to Christ. This supposition seems to be corroborated by the fact that Luther signed a letter to Lang (November 11, 1517; the covering letter for the *Ninety-five Theses*): "Friar Martin Eleutherius, or rather a slave and very much a captive." See *WA*, Br 1, 122.

[13] John von Staupitz; see p. 64, n. 1; this letter is not extant.

19

To George Spalatin
Wittenberg, February 22, 1518

Luther mentions his fear that the controversy on indulgences stirred up by his Ninety-five Theses may cause hostility between the Elector of Brandenburg and the Elector of Saxony. In answer to certain questions Luther denies the usefulness of dialectic for the work of a biblical theologian.

See pp. 37 f. On Spalatin, see pp. 8 f.

Text in Latin: WA, Br 1, 149-150.

To my friend George Spalatin, a servant of Christ
and secretary to the Elector [1]

Jesus

Greetings. I am not distressed, excellent Spalatin, that [my enemies] are speaking so badly of me, or that they stamp our Elector as the author of my theses.[2] I fear only that this affair might create hostility between our great rulers, should perhaps the Sovereign of Brandenburg,[3] out of vengeance, permit something similar to happen as we have recently heard about *Schencke*.[4]

Moreover you ask to what extent I (!) consider dialectic[5] useful for a theologian. Honestly, I do not see how dialectic would

[1] Elector Frederick; see pp. 49 f.
[2] *The Ninety-five Theses;* see p. 49, n. 22.
[3] Elector Joachim I of Brandenburg (1499-1535) was a brother of Albrecht of Mainz (see pp. 44 f.) and a bitter foe of Luther (see pp. 217, 220).
[4] This word is written in German. Luther might have been referring to the fate of a certain knight who had turned to robbery and was captured and decapitated. Luther's remark is far from clear; see *WA*, Br 1, 150, n. 2.
[5] Dialectic was one of the seven liberal arts taught during the Middle Ages. Consisting of the art and practice of discussion, it is logic which examines the truth of a theory by investigating its premises and consequences. It is concerned with the meaning of words, with definitions, with the logical organization of statements, and with their implications for philosophy and theology. In the dialectic process of thought, contradictory statements about the same object are reduced to absurdity and thus shown to be logically untenable; truth is held to be established by arriving at a statement which can no longer be logically opposed. The dialectic process of thought could also lead to a syllogism, a conclusion logically drawn from a major and a minor premise.

not be rather harmful for a true theologian. Maybe it could be play and exercise useful for the minds of youngsters, but in Bible study, where only faith and enlightenment from above are desired, all syllogism has to be left behind; this does not differ from Abraham's leaving his servants behind with the asses when he set out to sacrifice.[6] John Reuchlin affirms this sufficiently in the second book of his *Cabala*.[7] If any dialectic is necessary, then the inborn, instinctive one will suffice. By this, man is enabled to compare objects of faith with one another and thus to draw true conclusions. I have often discussed with friends what might be the advantage of all this painful study of philosophy and dialectic. All of us were certainly astonished, indeed, we bewailed the state of our minds. We found no usefulness but a flood of harm [in these studies].

Regarding this problem, I have finally written to the gentleman from Eisenach,[8] who seems to be king of dialectic philosophers in our day. I mainly argued that—and this cannot be denied—dialectic, instead of being useful to theology, is rather an obstacle to theological studies, because theology uses the same vocabulary in a manner quite different from that of dialectic. In what way therefore, I asked, can dialectic be of use, since once I begin to study theology I am forced to reject the dialectic meaning of a word and have to accept its [theological] meaning?[9] In order that I might not be just juggling with words, I added some examples, as, for instance, the following: in the *Porphyrian Tree*[10]

6 Gen. 22:5.

7 Here Luther gives a general reference to the second book of *De arte cabbalistica, Libri tres* (*Three Books on the Cabala*) by John Reuchlin (Hagenau: T. Anshelm, 1517). On John Reuchlin, see p. 9. On the *Cabala*, see *O.D.C.C.*, pp. 213, 1159.

8 Jodocus Trutvetter; see p. 12, n. 3. This letter is not extant. It can be assumed, however, that it was similar in content to the letter mentioned on p. 37.

9 In the medieval university, dialectic was studied before theology, for which it was intended to serve as a tool.

10 *Arbor Porphyriana* (*The Porphyrian Tree*) is the name given to a list of categories Porphyry (see p. 37, n. 4) furnished in his *Eisagoge eis tas Aristotelous kategorias* (*Introduction to Aristotle's Categories*); see A. Busse (ed.), *Porphyrii Isagoge et in Aristotelis Categorias Commentaria* (Commentaria in Aristotelem Graeca 4, I [Berlin: Akademieverlag, 1887]). In the Middle Ages, Boethius' Latin translation and commentary on Porphyry's *Introduction* was the most widely used textbook on logic; early edition: Boethius *Opera*

the word "body" means something which consists of "matter" and "form." [11] But such a body cannot be attributed to man, because in Scripture our "body" only stands for the "matter" and does not include the "form." For example, "Do not fear those who kill the body but cannot kill the soul." [12] I mentioned further that it is absurd to state that an angel is neither a rational nor an irrational being; [13] and also that regarding [the understanding] of Scripture, it would be useless to define man as being "sensitive," "rational," "corporeal," [and] "animate." [14] In short I said, and I

---

ommnia (Venice: Joannes and Gregorius de Gregoriis, 1483; 2nd ed. 1497-1499); modern edition in *Corpus scriptorum ecclesiasticorum latinorum* XXXXVIII.

[11] See *Corpus scriptorum ecclesiasticorum latinorum* XXXXVIII, 206, 1 f., 267, 3 f.

[12] Matt. 10:28. Aristotle and medieval thinkers used the term "*eidos*" or "*forma*" ("form") to describe the unchanging element which specifies matter as a thing and gives it its specific character and being. According to Thomistic teaching, approved by the Council of Vienne in 1312 and the Fifth Lateran Council in 1513, the soul is the form of the human body which gives it human existence; see *O.D.C.C.*, p. 513. Luther feels that it is impossible to speak of the "body" as consisting of "matter" and "form," since the term "body" would then have to include the notion of "soul." This, Luther claims, would be against Scripture as seen in the example he takes from Matt. 10:28, in which "body" and "soul" are designated as two separate "entities." Therefore, Luther concludes on the basis of Scripture, Porphyry's definition of the term "body" (which is based on Aristotelian thought) must be rejected. Here Luther confused the definition of the term "body" as given by Porphyry in his *Introduction* with that given by Porphyry's translator and commentator Boethius (see note 10). Porphyry defined *man* as consisting of matter and form (see *Corpus scriptorum ecclesiasticorum latinorum* XXXXVIII, 265, 13-20), a statement to which Luther certainly would not have objected. In his commentary on Porphyry's *Introduction*, Boethius explained Porphyry's definition in statements which, if considered apart from their context, might furnish the basis for Luther's criticism; see *Corpus scriptorum ecclesiasticorum latinorum* XXXXVIII, 265, 13–275, 2.

[13] *Corpus scriptorum ecclesiasticorum latinorum* XXXXVIII, 269-271. In Thomistic Scholasticism the term "*rationalis*" ("rational") referred to the deductive process of thought by which knowledge of truth is acquired. "Irrational" on the other hand designated the inability to obtain truth at all or to express it logically. Since angels, like God, apprehend truth intuitively (*intellectualis*) their perception of truth cannot be called rational but only "intuitive." See L. Schütz, *Thomas Lexicon* (2nd ed.; Paderborn, 1895): "*intellectualis*," "*rationalis*." Luther rejects the notion that angels' perception of truth is not rational (in the said way) and that angels are irrational beings, and states that their perception of truth has to be called *intellectualis*. Luther, however, does not give his own understanding or the scriptural basis for his argument.

[14] "Sensitive": capable of sense perception, receiving impressions through the senses. See L. Schütz, *op. cit.*: "*sensitivus*." This definition seems to be a

still maintain, that the whole fiction of the *Porphyrian Tree* is nothing less than tales of old women, or dreams of the sick; it is rightly called "porphyrian"[15] (that is, "bloodthirsty") because of the Christian souls it would murder. Finally I tore to pieces the categories[16] and some other subjects in philosophy and theology. The man didn't like this at all, and maintained that my arguments were not convincing[17] and I myself should not regard them as such. Yet these people are captives of Aristotle and Porphyry,[18] and pay attention not to what [these philosophers] say, but to the fact that they say something. That is the reason they cannot catch on to the meaning of even a single chapter of Scripture, much less teach it. Therefore if you trust my judgment, let dialectic be of use to you wherever it can; in Bible study, however, it will only do harm. I used to practice the teachings and rules of Scholastic theology.[19] By all means I wanted to handle Holy Scripture according to these rules. I was afraid (may God destroy me if I lie!) more of the Fathers of the church than of the terrors of hell. At that time I saw what good such studies had done! When you visit me sometime, I shall test this further with you and make you see for yourself what you now only hear.

Farewell, and pray for me.

Wittenberg, February 22, 1518

Friar Martin Eleutherius
Augustinian

---

reference to Porphyry's definition of man given in his *Introduction* (see note 10).

15 *Porphyreos*, or "purple," is a Greek word used by Homer to describe blood and death.

16 Categories are the fundamental conceptions to which all knowledge can be reduced. The Greek philosopher Archytas (4th century B.C.) classified them in ten topics; this classification was adopted by Aristotle and handed down to the Middle Ages by Porphyry and Boethius (see note 10). In the medieval curriculum the categories were basic to the study of dialectic.

17 Literally: "Achillean," like the powerful Greek hero in the Trojan war; see *O.C.D.*, pp. 3 f.

18 For similar statements, see pp. 37 f.

19 As an undergraduate at the University of Erfurt and later as a theological student and lecturer both in Erfurt and Wittenberg (see p. 5), Luther pursued his studies in the Nominalistic school of Scholasticism and became a follower of the *via moderna* (see p. 96, n. 8; *O.D.C.C.*, pp. 962 f.). He concentrated on the philosophy and theology of William of Occam (see *O.D.C.C.*, pp. 1462 f.) and the late medieval schoolmen; he studied the works of Pierre d'Ailly (see *O.D.C.C.*, pp. 368 f.) and of Gabriel Biel (see

20

To George Spalatin
Wittenberg, May 18, 1518

As a district vicar, Luther was expected to attend the triennial chapter meeting of his Order, scheduled to open April 25 in Heidelberg. Luther was in charge of a disputation to be conducted at this meeting, in which he was to present the theses and over which he was to preside. His Wittenberg student, Leonard Beier, a fellow Augustinian (see p. 39, n. 4), was to defend the theses. Like Luther's theses against Scholastic theology, which had been debated in Wittenberg on September 4, 1517 (see WA 1, 224 ff.; LW 31, 9 ff.), these "Heidelberg Theses" (see WA 1, 353 ff.; LW 31, 39 ff.) dealt with man's inability to know and to do by his own power God's will.

This letter is Luther's report on the meeting in Heidelberg. In addition Luther expresses his concern for establishing professorships in Greek and Hebrew at the University of Wittenberg.

On George Spalatin, see pp. 8 f.

Text in Latin: WA, Br 1, 173-174.

To my most learned and kind friend Spalatin

Jesus

Greetings. At last, my Spalatin, by the grace of Christ I have returned to our hearth.[1] I arrived at Wittenberg on the Saturday after Ascension Day.[2] I, who left on foot, returned by wagon. My superiors made me ride almost up to Würzburg with the delegation from Nürnberg. From there I traveled with the Erfurt delegation and from Erfurt on, with the party from Eisleben; and they finally brought me, both at their own expense and with their

p. 65, n. 3), the two most outstanding theologians of the *via moderna* in the later Middle Ages. In later years Luther stated that he was an Occamist; see WA 6, 195. These studies in Scholasticism were, however, replaced by those in St. Augustine, the mystics, and the Bible.

[1] Literally: "to our *penates*," i.e., the Roman gods of the hearth.

[2] May 15, 1518.

horses, to Wittenberg. I certainly have been quite safe during the whole trip. Food and drink agreed wonderfully with me, so much so that several people think I have become more settled and slightly more rotund. The Most Illustrious Sovereign Wolfgang,[3] the count palatine, and Master James Simler gave me an outstanding reception; so did Hazius, the master of the court.[4] He invited us, that is, the Father Vicar Staupitz[5] and our friend Lang, who is now vicar of the district[6] [and me]; we enjoyed ourselves in pleasant and delightful conversation while we dined and wined. We viewed all the treasures of the castle chapel,[7] and saw the armory, and just about every precious object with which this truly royal and extraordinarily famous castle sparkles. Master James [Simler] could not praise highly enough the letter our Sovereign had written in my behalf;[8] he said, in his Neckar dialect, "By God, you have excellent credentials!"[9] I was given every possible courtesy.

The doctors[10] willingly allowed my disputation[11] and debated with me in such a fair way that they have my highest esteem. Theology seemed to be some strange thing to them; nevertheless they fought it keenly and with finesse. There was one exception: he was the fifth doctor [who spoke] and a junior in rank.[12] He aroused the laughter of the whole audience by saying, "If farmers would hear this, they would certainly stone you to death." My

[3] Count Palatine Wolfgang (1494-1558); he had studied in the summer of 1515 at the University of Wittenberg; see *WA*, Br 1, 174, n. 2.

[4] James Simler was a former tutor and traveling companion of Count Wolfgang; Hazius is unknown if one does not assume—with *WA*, Br 1, 174, n. 4—that he is the future Chancellor Heinrich Hase.

[5] John von Staupitz; see p. 64, n. 1.

[6] John Lang; see p. 14. Luther's own term in this office (see p. 14) had expired; according to the bylaws of the Rule (see p. 20, n. 3), a district vicar could not be re-elected right away. In addition through his *Ninety-five Theses* Luther had become a controversial figure in the Order. Therefore it seemed wise not to elect him to any other high administrative office.

[7] Among them was said to be a splinter from Christ's cross and a small piece of his robe.

[8] Elector Frederick; see pp. 49 f. Because Luther was a controversial figure, Spalatin had provided him with several official letters commending Luther to the magistrates and rulers of the territories in which he would be.

[9] The quotation is written in colloquial German.

[10] The doctors of the Theological Faculty of the University in Heidelberg.

[11] See the Introduction.

[12] A certain George Niger, who had recently acquired the doctor's degree; therefore Luther calls him "junior." See *WA*, Br 1, 174, n. 8.

theology is like rotten food to the people from Erfurt.[13] Especially the Doctor from Eisenach[14] has condemned[15] all my statements; he has written me a letter[16] in which he has accused me of being an ignoramus in dialectic, not to speak of theology. I would have held a disputation at Erfurt, too, had the May prayer days[17] not interfered with it. Nevertheless I did have a face-to-face conference with the Doctor from Eisenach.[18] I was at least able to make him realize that he could neither substantiate his position nor refute mine; on the contrary, his propositions were like that beast which is supposed to have devoured itself.[19] But it is vain to tell a story to someone who is deaf.[20] They obstinately cling to their neat little distinctions, even when they confess that these are confirmed by no other authority than what they call the wisdom of natural reason, which for us is the same as the abyss of darkness. We preach no other light than Jesus Christ, the true and only light. I worked harder with Doctor Usingen[21] than with anyone else in order to persuade him (for he was my traveling companion in the wagon). But I don't know if I ac-

[13] Literally: ". . . is twice-deadly cabbage"; this is a Greek idiomatic saying, recorded in Erasmus' *Adagia;* see Clericus 2, 196, E f. Luther's attack against the Scholastic approach in theology and his denial that man can take any initiative in the process of salvation seemed to his former teachers, fellow students, and some of the Augustinians of Erfurt to be an utter rejection of the training he had received in their midst.

[14] Jodocus Trutvetter; see p. 12, n. 3.

[15] Literally: ". . . marked all my statements with a black *theta,*" that is, the eighth letter in the Greek alphabet, usually transcribed as "th." If during a trial in Athens someone voted for death, he engraved a *theta* on his voting tablet, since the Greek word for death (*thanatos*) begins with this letter. See Erasmus' *Adagia.* Clericus 2, 203, E f.

[16] This letter is not available; it must have been an answer to Luther's letter mentioned on p. 37; or it was Trutvetter's communication mentioned on p. 59.

[17] The three days of prayer and abstinence preceding the Feast of Ascension; they begin with Rogate Sunday which in 1518 fell on May 9; see *WA,* Br 1, 175, n. 11.

[18] On his return trip Luther had tried in vain to visit with Trutvetter on the evening of May 8; as a result he wrote *WA,* Br 1, No. 74, explaining why he wanted to see Trutvetter. It could not be determined when the conference to which Luther is referring took place; on the basis of Luther's remark here, and another one in a letter of July 10, 1518 (see *WA,* Br 1, 186), it can be assumed that Luther had been able to see Trutvetter after all.

[19] Perhaps an allusion to Revelation 17.

[20] An allusion to a classical saying which is recorded in Erasmus' *Adagia;* see Clericus 2, 178, C.

[21] Bartholomew Arnoldi of Usingen; see p. 30, n. 18.

complished anything. I left him pensive and wondering. How terrible, to grow old in false suppositions! On the other hand the thinking of the young men—in fact, of all youth—differs by two whole octaves [22] from the old. I have great hope that as Christ went over to the Gentiles when he was rejected by the Jews, so now too his true theology (which those opinionated old men reject) may pass over to the younger generation. This much concerning me.

Finally I hope and ask of you not to forget our University; that is, that you be concerned for the establishment of a chair in Greek and a chair in Hebrew.[23] I believe you have seen the announcement of the University of Leipzig; as usual, they imitate us. In the announcement they brag of many lectures; but I do not believe they all will be held.[24] I couldn't possibly direct the letter to the Most Illustrious ruling Bishop at Naumburg [25] by a person more appropriate than you. Therefore please do what your best friends ask of you.

Farewell in the Lord.

From our monastery, May 18, 1518

FRIAR MARTIN ELEUTHERIUS [26]
Augustinian

---

[22] A classical saying indicating an enormous gulf between two things. Luther's source of this expression is, again, Erasmus' *Adagia;* see Clericus 2, 94, F f.

[23] See p. 37, n. 6; p. 41; p. 96, n. 8. Luther was deeply concerned that these chairs be established and filled with excellently qualified men. Melanchthon (see p. 77, n. 3) was one of the professors who was called as a result of this plea; he took the Chair of Greek. On the professor of Hebrew, see p. 123, n. 4.

[24] At the beginning of the sixteenth century, strong rivalry existed between the University of Leipzig and the University of Wittenberg. Leipzig University had been founded at the beginning of the fifteenth century in a geographic as well as industrial and cultural center and was proud of its large student body and famous faculty. It looked down on provincial Wittenberg and the University founded there in 1502. Between 1516 and 1521, this situation developed into open hostility on the part of Leipzig when Wittenberg suddenly became famous for its Humanistically-oriented curriculum (see p. 41) which attracted an increasing number of students. But the tensions were religious as well as academic: until 1539 the University of Leipzig sided officially with the Roman church and did everything to undermine Wittenberg's stature. See also p. 78; p. 134, n. 3; pp. 138, 149, 160, 164.

[25] Count Palatine Philip; the letter is not extant.

[26] See p. 55, n. 12.

21

To John von Staupitz[1]
Wittenberg, May 30, 1518

Luther's Ninety-five Theses against indulgences were originally intended as the basis for an academic disputation which, however, never took place. When Luther realized how widely they had been spread and how they were interpreted, he decided to publish explanations of these theses to clarify their purpose and substantiate them with detailed material. After some difficulty he was finally granted permission to do this by his bishop Jerome Sculteus of Brandenburg, who was also the ecclesiastical superior of the University of Wittenberg. Luther's Explanations of the Theses Concerning the Value of Indulgences (see WA 1, 530 ff.; LW 31, 83 ff.) was an appeal to Pope Leo X (to whom Luther dedicated it in a special letter) to look into the indulgence matter and was intended to serve as Luther's defense against the attacks of his opponents.

This letter—the covering letter for the Explanations, requesting von Staupitz to forward both documents (the Explanations and the

[1] John von Staupitz, a member of an old Saxon aristocratic family, had already earned his Master of Arts degree when he entered the Augustinian monastery of Tübingen in 1497. In 1500 he received his Doctorate in Biblical Theology from the University of Tübingen, and in 1503 he was elected vicar general of the German Congregation of Reformed Augustinians (see p. 6, n. 3). He assisted Elector Frederick in organizing the University of Wittenberg and brought many of the teachers the new faculty required; he himself took over the Chair of Biblical Theology. It is generally assumed that von Staupitz met Luther in the Wittenberg monastery in 1508 or 1509 (see p. 5). Over the years the Vicar General became Luther's spiritual confidant and exercised great influence on him; this can especially be seen in this letter. Because of his time-consuming responsibilities within the Order, von Staupitz resigned his professorship in 1512, designating Luther as his successor. Although he stood by Luther during the early stages of the trial for heresy (see p. 86), he was unable to follow him all the way, and after 1519 he and Luther became estranged. Nevertheless the Reformer retained a deep gratitude and admiration for his former superior. In 1520 von Staupitz resigned as vicar general of the Augustinians because the Order had become so heavily infiltrated by Reformation followers and became an abbot of a Benedictine monastery (see *WA*, Br 2, 567; S-J 2, 129). By this step he affirmed his strong feeling for the traditions in which he was nurtured. However his deep and warm concern for the revival of an evangelical piety and his opposition to the secularized ways of the Roman church made him highly suspect in the eyes of the Inquisition. He died a lonely man in 1524.

letter of dedication) to Rome—gives a detailed account of the development of Luther's understanding of penitence, which led him finally to the attack on indulgences. Luther also gratefully acknowledges the help von Staupitz extended to him in his struggles for the biblical understanding of penitence.

On Luther's difficulties with the penitential system of his day, see Bainton, pp. 54 ff.

Text in Latin: WA 1, 525-527.

To my reverend and true father, John Staupitz,
Professor of Sacred Theology, vicar of the Augustinian Order,
Friar Martin Luther, your pupil, sends greetings and
dedicates himself

Reverend Father: I remember that during your most delightful and helpful talks, through which the Lord Jesus wonderfully consoled me, you sometimes mentioned the term "*poenitentia.*"[2] I was then distressed by my conscience and by the tortures of those who through endless and insupportable precepts teach the so-called method of confession. Therefore I accepted you as a messenger from heaven when you said that *poenitentia* is genuine only if it begins with love for justice and for God and that what they consider to be the final stage and completion[3] is in reality rather the very beginning of *poenitentia.*

---

[2] *Poenitentia* means either the remorse of the sinner or the penance imposed on the sinner by the church. The penitential system of the early and medieval church (see pp. 43 f.) fused both meanings in the term "do penance" (which meant both a contrite heart on the part of the sinner and his fulfilling of satisfactions), basing this on the translation of Matt. 3:2 in the Vulgate (see note 15). See *O.D.C.C.*, pp. 1041, 1154. Luther's desperation in the monastery was partially caused by this understanding of *poenitentia:* on the one hand he realized that he could never completely atone for his sins, despite his constant desperate struggle to do his penance properly; on the other hand he knew that without *poenitentia* no man could stand before God free of guilt.

[3] So taught, e.g., Gabriel Biel (1420?-1495; see p. 59, n. 19; *O.D.C.C.*, p. 172), one of the Nominalistic theologians whose works Luther had studied. According to Biel, man constantly fears to transgress God's holy will and to become guilty and the object of God's wrath. This servile fear has to be transformed into love for God, if the sinner is to be absolved. Man should be able to attain such love by an intense training of his mind and will and by keeping God's commandments. Ostensibly this would create a truly

Your word pierced me like the sharp arrow of the Mighty.[4] As a result, I began to compare your statements with the passages of Scripture which speak of *poenitentia.* And behold—what a most pleasant scene! Biblical words came leaping toward me from all sides, clearly smiling and nodding assent to your statement. They so supported your opinion that while formerly almost no word in the whole Scripture was more bitter to me than *poenitentia* (although I zealously made a pretense before God and tried to express a feigned and constrained love for him), now no word sounds sweeter or more pleasant to me than *poenitentia.* The commandments of God become sweet when they are read not only in books but also in the wounds of the sweetest Savior.[5]

After this it happened that I learned—thanks to the work and talent of the most learned men who teach us Greek and Hebrew with such great devotion[6]—that the word *poenitentia* means *metanoia* in Greek;[7] it is derived from *meta* and *noun,* that is, from "afterward"[8] and "mind." *Poenitentia* or *metanoia,* therefore, means coming to one's right mind and a comprehension of one's own evil after one has accepted the damage and recognized the error.[9] This is impossible without a change in one's disposi-

contrite heart, thus completing *poenitentia;* see R. Seeberg, *Lehrbuch der Dogmengeschichte* (4th ed.; Leipzig: Verlag A. Deichert, 1933), III, 538 f. Under the influence of von Staupitz, Luther learned that *poenitentia* begins with love for God, that is, with a heart turned to God. He also learned that a heart may be brought to this love (that is, to repent) only by the God of grace and love who reveals himself in Jesus Christ (therefore Luther's reference to Christ's wounds at the end of the following paragraph), and not by servile fear of breaking the commandments and thus becoming guilty and deserving God's wrath. When this change in the understanding of *poenitentia* took place in Luther's life is highly controversial and is assumed by various scholars to have been sometime between 1508 and 1517. As a result the individual stages of development in this change, described by Luther in this letter, cannot be pinpointed.

[4] Ps. 120:4.

[5] For similar statements, see *WA,* TR 2, Nos. 1490, 1820, 2654 a.

[6] Luther is thinking mainly of Erasmus, who published the Greek text of the New Testament with notes in 1516 (see p. 23).

[7] Luther transliterates the Greek word *metanoia* in various ways, for instance: *metanoea, metanea,* or *metania.*

[8] *Meta* does not only mean "afterward," but it is also a prefix indicating change or transition, or movement from one place or state to another; see the following paragraph.

[9] Here Luther is apparently drawing on the explanation of the Greek word *metanoeite,* "repent," given by Erasmus in the *Annotations* to Matt. 3:2 in the 1516 edition of the Greek text of the New Testament (see note 6).

tion and [the object of one's] love. All these definitions agree so well with Pauline theology that, at least in my opinion, almost nothing could illustrate Paul's theology better than the way they do.

Then I progressed further and saw that *metanoia* could be understood as a composite not only of "afterward" and "mind," but also of the [prefix] "trans" and "mind" (although this may of course be a forced interpretation), so that *metanoia* could mean the transformation of one's mind and disposition. Yet it seemed to express not only the actual change of disposition but also the way by which this change is accomplished, that is, the grace of God. Such transition of the mind, that is, the most true *poenitentia,* is found very frequently in Holy Scripture: the old Passover foreshadowed it,[10] and Christ made it a reality;[11] it was also long before that time prefigured in Abraham, when (according to the learned exegesis of Paul of Burgos)[12] he began to be called "he who passes over," that is, a "Hebrew," evidently because he had come across into Mesopotamia.[13] The title of the Psalm likewise [suggests] it when it calls the singer "Idithun," which means "he who jumps over."[14]

Continuing this line of reasoning, I became so bold as to believe that they were wrong who attributed so much to penitential works that they left us hardly anything of *poenitentia,* except some trivial satisfactions on the one hand and a most laborious confession on the other. It is evident that they were misled by the Latin term, because the expression *poenitentiam*

---

[10] Exod. 12:11.
[11] I Cor. 5:7.
[12] Paul of Burgos (1353?-1435?) was the converted Jew Salomon ben Levi. He became bishop of Cartagena in 1405, bishop of Burgos in 1415, and chancellor of Castile in 1416?. The *Additiones,* his most important work, consists of critical additions to the *Postil* of Nicholas of Lyra (see p. 26, n. 14). Luther used both commentaries, especially in his *First Lectures on the Psalms;* see p. 18, n. 3. Here he is referring to the *Additio* 1 of the explanation of Gen. 12:6, or Matthew 21 in *Postilla Fratris Nicolai de Lyra . . . cum Additionibus Pauli Episcopi Burgensis* . . . (Nürnberg: J. Koberger, 1493).
[13] Gen. 12:6. Luther understands the noun "Hebrew," *ibri* in Hebrew, as being derived from the Hebrew verb *ibari,* meaning to pass over or through.
[14] Psalm 39, the heading in Hebrew.

agere[15] suggests more an action than a change in disposition; and in no way does this do justice to the Greek *metanoein.*[16]

While this thought was still agitating me, behold, suddenly around us the new war trumpets of indulgences and the bugles of pardon started to sound, even to blast, but they failed to evoke in us any prompt zeal for the battle. In short, while the doctrine of the true *poenitentia* was neglected, they[17] even dared to magnify not *poenitentia*—not even its least important part, which is called satisfaction[18]—but only the remission of this least important part, so that one has never heard of a similar "glorification" of *poenitentia.* Finally they taught impious, false, and heretical things with so much authority—temerity, I wanted to say—that if anyone muttered anything in protest he was immediately a heretic destined for the stake and guilty of eternal damnation.

Since I was not able to counteract the furor of these men, I determined modestly to take issue with them and to pronounce their teachings as open to doubt.[19] I relied on the judgment of all the doctors and of the whole church that it is better to perform the satisfactions than to have them remitted by buying indulgences. There is no one who has ever taught differently. This is why I entered the disputation; that is, I have provoked all the people, the great, the average, the mediocre, to hate me thoroughly, at least as much as could be engineered and accomplished by these men who have such great zeal for money (oh, no, I should have said for souls!). Since these "lovely" people cannot refute what I have said, they arm themselves with the greatest cunning and pretend that I violated papal authority by my theses.[20]

---

15 The Vulgate translation of *metanoeite* in Matt. 3:2 is *poenitentiam agite.* This could mean both the attempt to attain a penitent heart and the fulfilment of the satisfactions imposed by the church upon the penitent (see pp. 43 f.). In his *Annotations,* Erasmus has demonstrated (see notes 6, 9) how the word *poenitentia* came to be applied to the satisfactions and why he considered *poenitentiam agite* to be an unsatisfactory translation of *metanoeite.* See Clericus 6, 17, E f.

16 Luther transliterates this Greek verb as *metanoin.*

17 The agents and preachers of the indulgences; see pp. 45 ff.

18 See pp. 43 f.

19 By means of the *Ninety-five Theses;* see p. 49, n. 22.

20 In April/May, 1518, John Tetzel, one of the indulgence commissioners of Albrecht of Mainz, had issued theses in which he charged Luther with viola-

This is the reason, Reverend Father, why I now, unfortunately, step out into public view. I have always loved privacy and would much prefer to watch the splendid performance of the gifted people of our age than become a part of the show and be ridiculed. But I know that weeds are to be found among the useful greens, and white has to be interspersed with black for the sake of decor and beauty.

And so I am asking you to receive this poor writing of mine[21] and to forward it with whatever speed is available to you to our excellent Pope Leo X,[22] so that it may serve me there as an advocate, so to speak, in the face of the contrivings of the evil-minded. I ask this not because I want to get you involved in my danger; I prefer to take all the risk myself. Christ will know whether my words are his or my own. Without Christ's command not even a pope can speak, nor is the heart of a king in his own hand.[23] This Christ is the judge whose verdict I am awaiting through the Roman See.[24]

Besides this, I have no other answer to my threatening friends than the word of Reuchlin, "He who is poor has nothing to fear; he has nothing to lose."[25] I have no property, and desire none. If I possessed any prestige and honor—well, he who loses them now will simply continue to lose them. There is only one thing left: my poor worn body, which is exhausted by constant hardships.[26] If they take this away by force or guile (in order to

---

tion of the papal authority. For the text, see *EA Var. arg.* 1, 296 ff.; *St. L.* 18, 94 f.

[21] *Resolutiones disputationum de indulgentiarum virtute* (*Explanations of the Theses Concerning the Value of Indulgences*) (Wittenberg: J. Grünenberg, August, 1518). *WA* 1, 529 ff.; *LW* 31, 83 ff. With his letter Luther is enclosing a copy of the manuscript; a printed copy was not available before August 21, 1518; see p. 75; see also *WA* 1, 522.

[22] See p. 100.

[23] Prov. 21:1.

[24] When Luther made this statement he obviously was still willing to acknowledge the authority of the Papal See. In the following months his view underwent a rapid change until, during the Leipzig Disputation, 1519 (see p. 126), he challenged this authority and made acceptance of any papal verdict dependent upon its agreement with Scripture. See also p. 74, n. 7; pp. 88 f.

[25] This statement of Reuchlin could not be traced; on Reuchlin, see p. 9.

[26] Luther's health had been drastically impaired by the severity of his ascetic exercises and the almost superhuman load of work he had been carrying (see pp. 27 f.). "I almost met death by my fasting, abstinence, and austerity in labor

serve God), then they will deprive me of perhaps only one or two hours of life. It is enough for me to have the dear Savior and Redeemer, my Lord Jesus Christ. I shall sing praise to him as long as I live.[27] What do I care if someone does not want to join me in this hymn of praise? He may howl, even all by himself, if he wishes to do so.

My dearest Father, the Lord Jesus keep you unto eternity.

Wittenberg, May 30, 1518[28]

22

To George Spalatin
Wittenberg, August 8, 1518

Archbishop Albrecht of Mainz received Luther's Ninety-five Theses, but did not wish to get entangled in the matter. Therefore he had the theses forwarded to the Curia with the indictment that Luther was spreading new doctrines. The Curia did not take the case very seriously until the indulgence commissioner John Tetzel and his Dominican Order implied Luther was a heretic. Under Dominican pressure the Curia then began in mid-June, 1518, to try Luther for heresy and summoned him to appear before the papal court. In this letter Luther asks Spalatin to have the Electoral and Imperial governments intervene at the Papal See so that his case would be heard in Germany by impartial judges.

See Bainton, pp. 90 ff.; Schwiebert, pp. 338 ff. On George Spalatin, see pp. 8 f.

Text in Latin: WA, Br 1, 188.

To my most learned and friendly George Spalatin,
presently at Augsburg,[1] my friend, sincerely loved in Christ

and clothing; by all this my body was terribly weakened and exhausted"; see *WA* 44, 705. See also pp. 16, 88, 188, 198; p. 217, n. 15.

27 Ps. 146:2.

28 The signature is missing since the translation is based on a printed edition of the text of the *Explanations* (see note 21), where the letter appears as a preface.

1 Spalatin was accompanying Elector Frederick to the *Reichstag* (diet) which

TO GEORGE SPALATIN, AUGUST 8, 1518

Jesus

Greetings. My Spalatin, I now need your help more than ever, or rather, it is the honor of almost our whole University that needs it along with me. This means that you should use your influence with the Most Illustrious Sovereign [2] and Doctor Pfeffinger [3] that our Sovereign and His Imperial Majesty [4] obtain for me from the Pope the return of my case, so that it is tried before German judges [5]—as I have already written to our Sovereign.[6] For you can see how subtly and maliciously those murderous Dominicans [7]

was in session in Augsburg in the summer of 1518. Not until 1663 did the diet meet at fixed times and places. It was composed of the *Reichsstände* (Imperial Estates) and their representatives, which were organized into the Electoral college (the Duke of Saxony was one of its seven members), the college of the other secular and ecclesiastical peers, and the college made up of representatives of the free Imperial cities. The diet was the political platform of the Empire, which was in reality a loose confederation of sovereign territories. The *Reichstagsabschied* (Resolution of the Diet) was binding upon the emperor and the Estates as a contract between sovereign parties. Based on this resolution, the emperor and the Imperial chancellory (over which the grand-chancellor presided) directed the affairs of the Empire. In case of the emperor's inability to act, he was replaced by the *Reichsregiment* (Council of Regency), which then took charge of the daily duties of administration. Between 1500 and 1520, Elector Frederick of Saxony had been president of this council several times. Therefore in this letter Luther is approaching one of the highest dignitaries of the Imperial government. To understand Luther's request for help as well as the procedure of his trial, one has to look at the legal environment of his case. No subject of an Electoral territory could be tried before an extraterritorial court except members of the clergy and monastic orders. Luther was, therefore, subject to the jurisdiction of the church. No ecclesiastical sentence which went beyond the purely spiritual sphere could be legally executed, however, if the secular authorities refused to co-operate. In this letter Luther is appealing to these secular authorities for help, and he eventually received it; in addition, since Elector Frederick was determined to hold his protecting hand over Luther, the jurisdiction of the church would obviously be hampered. The church could prosecute and sentence Luther, but difficulties would arise in carrying out the sentence; to lay hold of Luther and enforce it, the church would have to deal with the Imperial or Electoral governments.

[2] Elector Frederick; see pp. 49 f.

[3] Deginhard Pfeffinger; see p. 32, n. 28.

[4] Maximilian I, emperor from 1493 to 1519.

[5] Pope Leo X; see p. 100. Luther wrote: ". . . *remissionem seu commissionem causae meae ad partes* . . . ." This is a technical term similar to the one he used in his letter of August 5, 1514; see p. 10, and note 1 there.

[6] This letter to Elector Frederick seems to be lost; the letter to Spalatin was a companion letter to it, sent by the same messenger.

[7] Especially John Tetzel and Sylvester Prierias. The latter was a father confessor of Pope Leo X and papal censor of publications; see *O.D.C.C.*, p. 1103.

carry on with a view to my ruin. I would have written about this to Doctor Pfeffinger, with the request that he and his friends use their influence and obtain this favor for me from His Majesty and the Sovereign; but this affair has to be handled in a great hurry. They have given me only a short time, as you can see and read in the *Summons*,[8] that Lernaean swamp full of hydras and other monsters.[9] Therefore if you love me and hate iniquity,[10] take care of this and ask for the Sovereign's advice and help soon. Let me know what you find out, or what is even more important, let our Most Reverend Father Vicar John Staupitz[11] know; he is probably already with you at Augsburg, or will soon arrive. He is staying at Salzburg, but he has promised the Nürnbergers to be with them for the Assumption Festival.[12] Finally please do not be disturbed or sad in my behalf. The Lord will provide with the trial a way out.[13]

I am already replying to the *Dialogue of Sylvester*,[14] which is exactly like a wild, entangled jungle.[15] You will soon have the whole work, when it is completed. That "sweetest" man is simultaneously my accuser and my judge,[16] as you can see from the *Summons*.

---

[8] The *Summons* was issued by the papal court and demanded that Luther appear in Rome within sixty days. The original of the *Summons* does not seem to be extant; we know of its content only by the information Luther gives us in his *Acta Augustana* (*Proceedings at Augsburg*). *WA* 2, 25 f.; *LW* 31, 290.

[9] Lerna, a marsh near Argos, was the abode of the mythical Lernaean hydra, which was slain by Hercules and Iolaus; see *O.C.D.*, p. 413; Erasmus, *Adagia;* see Clericus 2, 122, D f. See also Clericus 2, 197, C.

[10] See Ps. 45:7.

[11] See p. 64, n. 1.

[12] Assumption of the Virgin Mary, August 15.

[13] I Cor. 10:13 (Vulgate).

[14] Luther is referring to Sylvester Prierias' *Dialogue Concerning Papal Authority;* this was a refutation of the *Ninety-five Theses* and was to be the core of the charge against Luther. For the text, see *EA*, *Var. arg.* 1, 344 ff. Its tone of slander set the pace for the atmosphere in which the Curia planned to deal with Luther. Luther answered it immediately with his *Ad Dialogum Silvestri Prieritatis de Potestate Papae Responsio* (*Answer to the Dialogue of Sylvester Prierias Concerning Papal Authority*) (Leipzig: M. Lotther, August, 1518). *WA* 1, 647 ff.

[15] This is a pun; the Latin *silvester* means overgrown with woods.

[16] As papal censor of books, Prierias (see note 7) examined Luther's teachings for heresy, and on the basis of his findings condemned Luther (see note 14).

Farewell. I am occupied with so much writing that I cannot go into details.

Wittenberg, August 8, 1518

FRIAR MARTIN ELEUTHERIUS [17]
Augustinian

23

To George Spalatin
Wittenberg, August 28, 1518

This letter is Luther's reaction to the maneuvers of the Papal Legate to the German diet which was meeting at Augsburg during the summer of 1518; he reveals a plan to avoid the danger caused by the Summons to Rome (see p. 72). Luther also comments on some of his writings.

On George Spalatin, see pp. 8 f.

Text in Latin: WA, Br 1, 190-191.

To my friend George Spalatin, priest of Christ, chaplain to Duke Frederick of Saxony, a learned friend, presently at Augsburg [1]

Jesus

Greetings. The messenger I sent to the Most Illustrious Sovereign Frederick has not yet returned,[2] and so I am still waiting to see what the Lord will do through you people with regard to my case. I have heard, however, that the Most Reverend Cardinal Cajetan [3]

---

[17] See p. 55, n. 12.

[1] See p. 70, n. 1.

[2] Evidently with the answer to the letter mentioned on p. 71, n. 6. On Elector Frederick, see pp. 49 f.

[3] Jacopo de Vio of Gaeta (1468?-1534) assumed the names "Thomas" in honor of St. Thomas Aquinas and "Cajetan," which he derived from his birth place Gaeta. Cajetan, O. P., was the most outstanding Thomistic theologian of the early sixteenth century. He studied at Naples, Bologna, and Padua, and taught theology and philosophy in Padua, Pavia, and Rome. In 1517 he was elevated to cardinal. In 1518/19 he served as legate, or ambassador, of the Papal See to Germany. After 1519 he was engaged in various dip-

has particular orders from the Pope[4] to exert every effort to turn the Emperor[5] and the sovereigns against me. So afraid are the consciences of even such great bishops, or rather, so immense and unbearable is the power of truth over works done in darkness! In all this I fear nothing, as you know, my Spalatin. Even if their flattery and power should succeed in making me hated by all people, enough remains of my heart and conscience to know and confess that all for which I stand and which they attack, I have from God, to whom I gladly and of my own accord entrust and offer all of this. If he takes it away, it is taken away; if he preserves it, it is preserved. Hallowed and praised be his name forever. Amen.

Thus far I do not see clearly enough how I can avoid those punishments intended for me unless the Sovereign[6] extends his help to me. On the other hand I would rather constantly suffer punishments than have the reputation of the Sovereign hurt because of me. Believe me, I am still ready to present myself, as I have been previously;[7] convince those whom you wish of this, or those whom you consider necessary. I shall never be a heretic. I can err in a debate, but I do not desire to settle anything, nor am I, on the other hand, bound by human opinions.[8]

---

lomatic missions of the Curia. From 1525 on he functioned as an adviser of the Curia. In this position he prepared some of the theological and legal weapons which Rome used in the battle against the Reformation between 1524 and 1534. See *O.D.C.C.*, p. 216. For the instructions to Cardinal Cajetan, see p. 91, n. 13; *St. L.* 15, 523 ff.; 539 f.; *WA* 2, 23 f.; *LW* 31, 286 f.

[4] Pope Leo X; see p. 100.

[5] Maximilian I, emperor from 1493 to 1519.

[6] Elector Frederick.

[7] Throughout his whole struggle with Rome—as a matter of fact, throughout his life—one of Luther's strong arguments against the Roman church was that from the beginning he had been willing to listen and to be taught, and that *if* convicted of heresy he would be willing to suffer the consequences; he always pointed out that he made himself available but Rome was unwilling to "teach" him.

[8] The doctrine of indulgences had not yet received an official dogmatic definition (see p. 44). Claims concerning the indulgences could, therefore, be regarded as mere human opinions, and Luther could hold a different opinion without being thereby a "heretic." Because the indulgence case was an open one, Luther felt that arguments on the basis of Scripture and tradition rather than indictments were in order.

It seems wise to our learned and well-meaning friends[9] that I request from our Sovereign Frederick a so-called safe-conduct through his domain. They say that if he should refuse it to me, as I know he will, then I would have the most legal restriction and excuse not to appear in Rome. You would do me a great favor if you were willing to acquire in my name a written statement from the Most Illustrious Sovereign in which he would refuse to issue a safe-conduct to me and would leave it to my own risk, should I want to go anyway.[10] Fast action is necessary here. The days fly by and the appointed day draws near.[11] Too great a distance separates us, and daily business takes up much time.

I am sending the *Explanations* of my theses,[12] but the print is done badly, on account of my long absence.[13] My *Reply to the Dialogue of Sylvester*[14] is now being printed at Leipzig,[15] along with the *Dialogue* itself; I shall send it to you shortly.

I deeply regret that my name and case have risen to such a height and have gotten to such a stage that they have even become the concern of such outstanding sovereigns, and that the great splendor of these important men has to deal with such an insignificant person as myself. I have too small an opinion of myself, especially as a debater, to disturb those of my own kind, not to speak of the nobility.

---

[9] It is not known who these friends were. One of them might have been Jerome Schurf, a lawyer in Wittenberg who also taught at the University and was Luther's legal counsel at the Diet of Worms; see p. 219, n. 2.

[10] Elector Frederick refused this request; see Spalatin's letter to Luther: Augsburg, September 5, 1518. *WA*, Br 1, 201. In the meantime the Elector was able to arrange for a hearing to be conducted in Augsburg, or at least to gain strong diplomatic support for it, so that for the time being, at least, the *Summons* (see p. 72) was void.

[11] Luther was due to appear in Rome within sixty days after receiving the *Summons* (see p. 72). Since he had received the *Summons* on August 7, he was due in Rome on October 7; see *WA*, Br 1, 188; *WA* 2, 25; *LW* 31, 290.

[12] See p. 69, n. 21.

[13] In July, 1518, Luther visited Dresden; see *WA*, Br 1, 194. Because of his absence Luther could not supervise the printing. For Luther's evaluation of the printer's work, see p. 19, n. 8.

[14] See p. 72, n. 14.

[15] Luther's usual printer in Wittenberg, John Grünenberg, could not keep pace with Luther's writing activities.

Farewell, always in the Lord.
Wittenberg, August 28, 1518 [16]

FRIAR MARTIN ELEUTHERIUS [17]
Augustinian

Friends also suggest that care should be taken that the statement be, as they say, predated. That means it should be dated as if it were written on the Eve of St. Bartholomew.[18] They say this would not be a lie, since it is sure and obvious that up to now the Sovereign's heart and mind always wanted to refuse the safe-conduct, or permit.

24

To George Spalatin
Wittenberg, August 31, 1518

While Luther's trial for heresy dragged on, he continued to be deeply involved in his academic work. In this letter he reports on his treatise about excommunication and his reply to Prierias. He evaluates the inaugural address of Philip Melanchthon and expresses his concern about Melanchthon's salary.

On George Spalatin, see pp. 8 f.

Text in Latin: WA, Br 1, 191-192.

To the most learned and kind George Spalatin,
chaplain to the Duke of Saxony, my faithful friend in Christ

---

16 On the dating of this letter, see *WA*, Br 1, 189 f.

17 See p. 55, n. 12.

18 The day before any great feast, including the Apostles' days, is called the "eve" of the feast because a preparatory vigil service is observed on that day. In the western church, St. Bartholomew's Day is celebrated on August 24 (only in the city of Rome is it celebrated on August 25). Luther suggests that the letter be signed the Eve of St. Bartholomew, that is, August 23. He wanted to pretend that upon receipt of the *Summons* (see p. 72), he had at once undertaken the necessary preparations for the trip to Rome, which included a request for a safe-conduct, and that it was only due to the Elector's refusal that he could not obey the *Summons*.

Jesus

Greetings. The *Treatise on Excommunication* [1] was already published, my Spalatin, before your letter [2] arrived. Written with so much moderation, however, and supported by such strong arguments for truth, the treatise I hope not only will not be disapproved of by those who love truth, but may even be received with great favor by those whom tyranny itself pleases. Although troubled about it, I praised this sacred power highly but without flattery. I have set forth in it only what they themselves have taught and still teach.

With regard to what you write and urge concerning our Philip Melanchthon,[3] all has been done and ought to be done. Do not

---

1 Excommunication (see *O.D.C.C.*, p. 481) was a frequent punishment in Luther's time. The sacraments were even withheld from the faithful if they failed to pay the required church tithes—regardless of whether or not they were able to pay them. Excommunication was an immense pastoral problem. As a pastor Luther was often confronted by it, and finally in May, 1518, he preached quite openly on this sensitive subject. Either enemies or well-meaning but ill-informed friends circulated theses which were allegedly based on this sermon but misrepresented Luther's position. These theses even reached the diet, then in session in Augsburg (see p. 70, n. 1), and caused a major storm. Yet before Luther was informed of this situation, he had already decided to publish his own version in order to clarify his stand on the matter. He did this with his *Sermo de virtute excommunicationis* (*Treatise on the Power of Excommunication*) (Wittenberg: J. Grünenberg, end of August, 1518). *WA* 1, 636 f.; *PE* 2, 37 ff.

2 This letter is not extant, but in it Spalatin must have tried, most certainly upon orders of Elector Frederick, to prevent the publication of the *Treatise on the Power of Excommunication*. The Elector must have been afraid that this treatise would not only unnecessarily antagonize the Curia but also lessen the chance that the Imperial government might intervene in Luther's behalf; see pp. 70 ff.; p. 75, n. 11.

3 Philip Melanchthon (1497-1560), a brilliant young Humanist and Greek scholar, was a grandnephew of John Reuchlin. In 1514 he was graduated as Master of Arts from the University of Tübingen. In 1516 he became one of the close friends and admirers of Erasmus of Rotterdam (see pp. 116 f.). Upon Reuchlin's recommendation, Melanchthon was called in the summer of 1518, at the age of twenty-one, to the University of Wittenberg as professor of Greek. Soon after his arrival a close friendship developed between him and Luther, which lasted until the Reformer's death. Melanchthon absorbed Luther's theological thought and soon became deeply engaged in theological writing and lecturing. He became Luther's most capable co-worker, at least in the academic field. By the time of the Wittenberg disturbances of 1521/22 (see p. 386, n. 1), however, it was quite clear that Melanchthon could not supply the dynamic leadership Luther had been giving the Reformation. It seems tragic that Melanchthon was again and again called away from his academic work to carry out diplomatic missions,

doubt it. Four days after he had arrived, he delivered an extremely learned and absolutely faultless address.[4] All esteemed and admired him greatly, so you need not worry on what grounds you should recommend him to us. We very quickly turned our minds and eyes from his appearance and person to the man himself. We congratulate ourselves on having this man and marvel at what he has in him. We thank the Most Illustrious Sovereign,[5] as well as you, for your efforts. You ought, however, to exercise special care as to how you may present him in the most favorable light to our Sovereign. I certainly do not wish to have a different Greek instructor as long as he is alive. I only fear that perhaps his constitution is not sturdy enough for the rough way of life in our region.[6] I am also afraid that he has been hired for far too scanty a salary, as I hear. On this basis, the already exulting Leipzig Faculty may be hoping to snatch him away from us as soon as possible, for they tried to lure him shortly before he arrived here.[7] I and many with me suspect that Doctor Pfeffinger,[8] as is his way, also wanted in this case to be too good a steward of the Sovereign's

---

a task for which he was not well qualified. His main interest lay in shaping the field of education, in both theology and liberal arts. His greatest gift was his ability to state complicated issues with clarity and simplicity. The *Augsburg Confession* and the *Apology* are among his most outstanding and permanent contributions to the Reformation. Yet during the Diet of Augsburg (1530) Melanchthon's weak side became evident: to preserve the unity of the church he was too ready to compromise, thus endangering the very principles of the Reformation. As Melanchthon's ideas matured, their Humanistic basis increasingly penetrated and jeopardized Luther's influence. Melanchthon's theological position finally became clear in his stand in the Eucharistic controversy and in the later struggles within the Lutheran church after the Reformer's death. In these controversies Melanchthon moved rather close to Calvinism, and by doing so called forth violent opposition from those who considered themselves the true heirs of Luther's thoughts (whether they were right is another matter). See C. L. Manschreck, *Melanchthon: The Quiet Reformer* (New York, 1958); *O.D.C.C.*, pp. 882 f.

[4] Melanchthon had arrived in Wittenberg on August 25. His inaugural address of August 29 dealt with reshaping the curriculum; see *C.R.* 11, 15 ff.

[5] Elector Frederick (see pp. 49 f.), the secular supervisor of the University.

[6] For a similar statement, see pp. 29 f.

[7] In the autograph the last part of the sentence (from "for" on) is added in the margin. On the rivalry between Leipzig and Wittenberg, see p. 63, n. 24. When Melanchthon went through Leipzig on August 20 on his way to Wittenberg, the Leipzig Faculty gave him a royal reception and tried to induce him to stay at Leipzig; see *WA*, Br 1, 193, n. 4.

[8] Deginhard Pfeffinger; see p. 32, n. 28.

purse. Therefore, my Spalatin, to speak freely, as with my dearest friend, see to it that you people [at the court] do not undervalue Melanchthon because of his person or age. This man is worthy of every honor. I do not want us and our University to expose ourselves as country-bumpkins, from which our enemies could make such a splendid story at our expense.

I am sending you my silly trifles, in a most extemporaneous fashion composed against Sylvester[9]—truly my wood-and-field sophist[10]—which I have turned out in two days.[11] He does not seem to me worthy of vainly putting an undue amount of brainpower and effort to work against his trivialities—those "water-bubble syllogisms," as they call them. I thank both God and you that my case is in your care.

Farewell, and love [me] in Christ.

August 31, 1518 FRIAR MARTIN LUTHER
Augustinian

Doctor Andrew Karlstadt[12] is undertaking another battle

---

[9] See p. 71, n. 7; p. 72, n. 14.

[10] Cf. p. 72, n. 15.

[11] Prierias bragged that it took him only three days to write his *Dialogue* and thus refute Luther's *Ninety-five Theses;* see *EA, Var. arg.* 1, 345. Luther, in turn, claims that it took him only two days to prove Prierias a fool.

[12] Andrew Bodenstein of Karlstadt/Main (1480?-1541) was graduated as Doctor of Theology from the University of Wittenberg in 1510. He was appointed archdeacon of the All Saints' Chapter at the Castle Church in Wittenberg and taught at the University there. Stimulated by his colleague Luther, he intensively studied the works of St. Augustine in 1516/17 (see p. 54, n. 7) and became persuaded that Luther's position was right. In Leipzig in 1519 (see p. 126), both men struggled together against Eck (see note 13). During the Wittenberg disturbances of 1521/22 (see p. 386, n. 1), however, basic differences erupted between him and Luther, resulting in bitter hostility between them. Karlstadt's legalistic understanding of Scripture and spiritualistic interpretation of the Christian religion precipitated the first internal crisis in the Reformation movement. The spiritualists (Luther called them *Schwärmer*) rejected "concreteness" as a medium of divine expression and saw an infinite chasm between matter and spirit. This led Karlstadt to his iconoclasm and his denial of Christ's real presence in the Lord's Supper (see *LW* 40, 61 ff., 73 ff.). During Luther's stay at the Wartburg, Karlstadt, in co-operation with Gabriel Zwilling (see p. 39, n. 3) and the "Zwickau prophets" (see p. 364, n. 28), abolished the old forms of worship (the mass) in Wittenberg and helped destroy symbols of piety (religious pictures, statues, crucifixes, etc.; see pp. 401 f.). These were, according to him, contrary to Scripture. Through Luther's sudden return from the Wartburg in March, 1522 (see pp. 386 ff.), and his strong intervention, Karlstadt's radical reforms were curbed and some of the traditional symbols restored. Soon

against Eck's[13] *Defense.*[14] As far as I can see, Eck has accomplished nothing by his *Defense* but to point out the very spot where he can most conveniently be destroyed.

25

To George Spalatin Wittenberg, September 2, 1518

Luther expresses his fear that the name and reputation of Elector Frederick may suffer because of the indulgence controversy. He

after this Karlstadt withdrew to the parish in Orlamünde (which was a part of his benefice as archdeacon), where he established a "puritanic" church system (Bainton, pp. 256 ff.). He became antagonistic to the faculty at Wittenberg. At the same time he directed his whole attention to the laity, especially to the "poor" peasants. Thus he came dangerously close to the radical Thomas Münzer (see *O.D.C.C.*, p. 933). In the fall of 1524 he was exiled from Electoral Saxony. From that time on he and his family had to endure years of restless wandering and great hardship. In 1534 he finally was able to take up permanent residence in Basel as a preacher and a professor at the University, and eventually he died there. See *O.D.C.C.*, p. 237.

13 John Maier of Egg/Günz, hence Eck (1486-1543), was a professor of theology and the vice-chancellor of the University of Ingolstadt in Bavaria. He had been exposed to Humanism, and some of his early writings were almost anti-Scholastic in their theology. He was the only theologian who was even remotely a match for Luther's learnedness. On various occasions Eck and Luther clashed violently. During the Leipzig Disputation (June/July, 1519; see p. 126), Eck was able to draw out the statement from Luther that popes and councils of the church can err and have erred; as a result, Eck branded Luther a Hussite, and thus he was largely responsible for procuring the bull "*Exsurge, Domine*" (see p. 179, n. 1), which he propagated throughout southern and central Germany. From 1518 on, he dedicated himself to refuting the theological position of the Reformation and to organizing Roman Catholic political opposition to the Reformation. He became famous in connection with the Diet of Augsburg (1530), where he was the spearhead of the Roman Catholic attack on the Reformation, and for his part in the colloquies held between the Reformers and the Roman church from 1540 to 1543. See *O.D.C.C.*, p. 436.

14 Early in 1518 Luther had received Eck's *Obelisci*, in which Eck developed a radical criticism of Luther's *Ninety-five Theses.* Luther replied at once with his *Asterisci;* see *WA* 1, 281 ff. Later in the spring of 1518 Karlstadt issued certain theses (see *WA*, Br 1, 183, n. 2) in which he refuted Eck's *Obelisci.* Eck replied in a *Defense* published August 14, 1518; Karlstadt immediately began to work on his answer, which he published in October, 1518 (see *WA*, Br 1, 193, n. 7). Luther is referring to this answer.

discusses a tax for a war against the Turks and forwards important questions the student body and faculty have raised about the reorganization of the curriculum; he also praises Melanchthon.

On George Spalatin, see pp. 8 f.

Text in Latin: WA, Br 1, 195-196.

To my most learned and upright friend, George Spalatin, a priest of Christ, chaplain to the Elector of Saxony

Jesus

Greetings. You write, my Spalatin, that there are people who try to ruin our Most Illustrious Sovereign[1] before heaven and earth. For goodness' sake, what kind of a monstrosity is that? I hope from my heart that I am not the cause of this. As I have said, so I say again: I do not wish our most innocent Sovereign to do anything in this affair to defend my theses;[2] I am ready and willing to be exposed to all who want to act or write against me.[3] I hope the Sovereign will not get involved in my affairs, unless he could, without inconvenience, keep force from being used against me. Even if he cannot do this, I still want to carry the whole danger alone. In spite of all the opinions of the Thomists,[4] I hope I can well defend what I have undertaken to defend, so that I may glory in Christ's leadership. Even if it [then] will be necessary to yield to violence, at least truth will not be hurt.

I believe that my *Explanations* (printed quite full of mistakes) and the rebuttal of Sylvester's *Dialogue* have reached you.[5] I ask you to tell everyone you can that it is Martin who has debated this. If anyone wants to argue against [these writings] or hopes to produce something better, he will find me ready to learn, or, in turn, to teach. Therefore they should be dealing with me. Why do

---

1 Elector Frederick; see pp. 49 f.

2 *The Ninety-five Theses;* see p. 49, n. 22.

3 See p. 74, n. 7.

4 These are the followers of St. Thomas Aquinas (see *O.D.C.C.*, pp. 1352 f., 1225 f.). The arguments which Prierias (see p. 71, n. 7; p. 72, n. 14), and Cajetan (see p. 73, n. 3; p. 85, n. 11), for instance, used against Luther's statements were drawn from late medieval Thomistic teachers.

5 See p. 69, n. 21; p. 72, n. 14; p. 75.

they vainly plague the Sovereign or others in this affair? But enough of this.

Among our fine young people here a problem has arisen. I consulted with friends, and it seemed wise to report it to you, or rather through you to inform the Sovereign.[6] This is the problem: since now by God's grace the best lectures flourish and the students are astonishingly eager for Scripture and unadulterated theology, it seems hard to them to have to neglect the best courses because of other courses[7] required for graduation, or at least to have to carry a load that is far too heavy and composed of both kinds of courses. [The students] petition, therefore, that if possible the course on ethics[8] (which obviously is related to theology as the wolf is to the lamb) be made elective, that is, that it should be free to all who wish to attend it but not be required for graduation.

The other question under discussion is this: what should be the rule for those who are to be examined as bachelors and masters according to the new courses?[9] But here we shall have to attend to this matter ourselves, unless you have some better advice at hand on this problem.

We have a certain letter from the city of Rome, quite learned yet extremely violent [in tone] against the Roman cunning in the matter of the new tithe to be levied for the war against the Turks.[10] Obviously this tax was thought out by the Florentine [bankers], the most avaricious of all people under heaven. They use the pope's good nature to satisfy their bottomless greed. But I believe

---

[6] As territorial lord Elector Frederick was the secular superior of the University; the bishop of Brandenburg was the ecclesiastical superior of the University; see p. 64.

[7] See p. 41; p. 42, n. 7; pp. 38, 57 ff., 96.

[8] A course on the *Nicomachean Ethics* of Aristotle and the Scholastic commentaries on it. See p. 25, and note 10 there.

[9] See p. 41. Between 1517 and 1519 the University undertook a basic reconstruction of its curriculum; see also p. 95; Schwiebert, pp. 294 ff.

[10] One of the issues on which the Diet of Augsburg (see p. 70, n. 1) had to act was a tax for a crusade against the Turks; it was brought to the floor by the papal legate (see p. 73, n. 3). This tax was violently opposed by many people. Their feelings were expressed in a pamphlet by an opponent of the papal request, entitled *Exhortatio . . . ad principes, ne in decimae praestationem . . . consentiant* (*Admonition Directed to the Sovereigns not to Consent to the Tithe*); see Böcking 5, 168 f.; *WA*, Br 1, 197, n. 8. Luther is referring to this pamphlet. The Pope and his legate supported the tax, hence Luther's remark concerning the cardinals.

you [at Augsburg] have had a copy of this letter for some time; if not, write and I shall send one. The cardinals are certainly legates of avarice (in case you do not know it) if what the letter says is true.

Farewell in the Lord, and hold Philip[11] in the greatest possible esteem; he is an excellent Greek teacher and a most learned and kind man. His classroom is jammed with students.[12] He especially makes all theologians zealous to study Greek—the most outstanding ones, as well as the average and the weak.

Wittenberg, September 2, 1518

FRIAR MARTIN LUTHER
Augustinian

26

To George Spalatin
Augsburg, October 14, 1518

The efforts of the Imperial and Electoral Saxon governments at the Curia to have Luther's trial conducted in Germany, or at least begun there (see p. 71), were successful. As a result Luther was summoned to appear in Augsburg before the papal legate to the German diet, Cardinal Cajetan (see p. 73, n. 3); he traveled almost the entire journey from Wittenberg to Augsburg on foot; see WA, TR 5, No. 5349. This letter is a report on the hearing he was given by the Cardinal.

See Schwiebert, pp. 344 ff. On George Spalatin, see pp. 8 f. Text in Latin: WA, Br 1, 214-215.

To my most learned friend George Spalatin, a priest of Christ,
chaplain to the Elector of Saxony,
highly esteemed in Christ,

---

[11] Philip Melanchthon; see p. 77, n. 3.

[12] On December 10, 1518, Spalatin wrote to a friend in Augsburg that Melanchthon's lectures on Greek were attended by approximately four hundred students, which would have been about two-thirds of the entire student body of the University of Wittenberg; see *WA*, Br 1, 197, n. 10.

Master George Spalatin: *Personal*

Jesus

Greetings. My Spalatin, with great reluctance I write to our Most Illustrious Sovereign.[1] So, please, you who are close to him, accept this letter and take care that its content is communicated to the most merciful Sovereign. The Legate [2] is negotiating with me, or rather I should say, maneuvering against me, for the fourth day already.[3] Indeed he neatly promises to handle everything leniently and in a fatherly way for the sake of the Most Illustrious Sovereign;[4] in reality, however, he is handling everything with nothing but mere inflexible power. He did not want me to reply in a public disputation, nor did he want to debate with me in private. He continually repeated one thing: recant, acknowledge that you are wrong; that is the way the Pope [5] wants it and not otherwise, whether you like it or not—and other things like that. He pushed me extremely hard with a certain *Extravagante* of Clement VI, which begins with the words: "The only-begotten." [6] Here, he said, here you see that the pope determines that the merits of Christ form the treasury of indulgences. Do you believe this or don't you? He did not allow any explanation or counterarguments, although he himself threw around strong words and shouted. At last, barely moved by the pleading of many people,[7] he permitted

---

1 Toward the end of September, 1518, Spalatin and Elector Frederick (see pp. 49 f.) returned from the diet in Augsburg to Saxony; see p. 70, n. 1.
2 Cardinal Cajetan; see p. 73, n. 3.
3 Luther met with Cardinal Cajetan on October 10, 12, 13, and 14.
4 It is not clear under what circumstances the Legate made this promise. Yet it is understandable if one realizes that the Curia was in great need of the Elector's good will and support for its plans concerning the future election of the emperor (see pp. 96 f.) and for the tax for the war against the Turks (see p. 82, n. 10).
5 Pope Leo X; see p. 100; p. 91, n. 13.
6 *Unigenitus Dei Filius* (*God's only-begotten Son*). This bull was issued by Pope Clement VI in 1343 (see *O.D.C.C.*, pp. 297 f.). It is found in the *Corpus Iuris Canonici* among the *Extravagantes communes*, lib. v, tit. IX (*De poenitentiis et remissionibus*), cap. 2. *CIC* 2, 1304 f. See *O.D.C.C.*, pp. 346, 486; Denzinger, Nos. 550 f.; Bettenson, pp. 259 f. See also in this volume, p. 186, n. 1.
7 According to Spalatin's report, Luther was accompanied to the hearing of October 13 by Philip von Feilitzsch (see note 8) and three Imperial officials; see *St. L.* 15, 564. They must have been among the petitioners.

me to make a written defense. This I did today in the presence of Sir Philip von Feilitzsch,[8] whom I took along for that purpose; he reminded him again, in the Sovereign's name and on his behalf, of the Sovereign's request.[9] In the end the Legate disdainfully flung back my little sheet of paper[10] and yelled again for me to recant. He considered me defeated and refuted by a verbose and long speech which he drew from the stories of St. Thomas.[11] Almost ten times I started to say something and each time he thundered back and took over the conversation. Finally I started to shout too, saying, "If it can be shown that that *Extravagante*[12] teaches that Christ's merits are the treasury of indulgences, then I will recant, as you wish." O God, how much gesticulation and laughter that caused! Suddenly he grabbed the book[13] and read hastily and feverishly until he came to the passage where it is written that Christ acquired the treasury by his suffering, and so on.[14] Here I interrupted, "See, Most Reverend Father, and consider carefully the word, 'He has acquired.' If Christ has acquired the treasury *by* his merits, then the *merits* are not the treasury; rather, the treasury is that which the merits earned, namely, the keys of the church; therefore my thesis is correct."[15] Here he was

---

[8] One of the reasons for the Electoral Saxon councilor, Philip von Feilitzsch (who in 1532 became Electoral Saxon ambassador to the Council of Regency), remaining in Augsburg was to assist Luther.

[9] I.e., he repeated the Elector's request to the Cardinal that Luther be treated with lenience and fairness. The Elector had also urged the Imperial government to make a similar request; see *St. L.* 15, 550.

[10] This statement contained Luther's defense against Cajetan's arguments, which were based on the bull mentioned in note 6. For the text, see *WA* 2, 9 ff.; *LW* 31, 264 ff.

[11] See p. 81, n. 4. The Nominalistic school in which Luther had been trained (see p. 59, n. 19) had little respect for the system of St. Thomas; see also p. 96, n. 8.

[12] See note 6.

[13] The *Corpus Iuris Canonici* (see note 6).

[14] The passage reads: "Wherefore therefrom [the death of Christ] (so that the pitifulness of such an effusion be not rendered idle, useless, or superfluous) how great a treasure did the holy Father acquire for the church militant, wishing to enrich his sons with treasure, . . . and those who avail themselves thereof are made partakers of God's friendship." See Bettenson, p. 260. The "treasury" is a reserve fund of good works accumulated by Christ and the saints, upon which the pope could draw when he remitted satisfactions by indulgences; see p. 44.

[15] Theses 58 and 60 of the *Ninety-five Theses*. Thesis 58: "Nor are they [the treasures of the church out of which the pope grants indulgences] the merits of Christ and the saints, for, even without the pope, the latter always

all of a sudden confused, and since he did not want to appear confused, he pushed on to other things and shrewdly wanted to bypass this subject. I, however, was excited and interrupted (I am sure quite irreverently), "Most Reverend Father, you should not believe that we Germans are ignorant even in philology. There is a difference between 'there is' a treasury and 'to acquire' a treasury." That crushed his self-confidence, although he still shouted for revocation. When I left he told me, "Go and do not return to me again unless you want to recant."

But listen to the following. Soon after lunch [the Legate] called the Most Reverend Father Vicar, Doctor Staupitz,[16] and urged him, with much flattery, to persuade me to recant, assuring him, in my absence, that I had no better friend than he is. After [von Staupitz] answered that he had attempted (and that even today he was continuing) to convince me that I should humbly submit myself to the church, as I previously had stated in public that I would,[17] he added that he was not equal to me (in his opinion, of course) in knowledge of Scripture and in talents; further, since he [Cajetan] here represents the Pope, and in that position is the superior of all of us, he himself should convince me to recant. In the end it was decided that [the Legate] would draw up the articles I should recant and set forth the teaching I should hold.[18] This is the status of the case thus far. Yet I am not hopeful, nor do I trust him. However I am working every day on an appeal[19] so that not a single syllable will be recanted. Moreover

---

work grace for the inner man, and the cross, death, and hell for the outer man." *WA* 1, 236; *LW* 31, 30. Thesis 60: "Without want of consideration we say that the keys of the church, given by the merits of Christ, are that treasure." *WA* 1, 236; *LW* 31, 31. The "keys of the church" are the administration of the sacraments, especially the proclamation of absolution, preaching of the gospel, and excommunication of the impenitent sinner.

[16] John von Staupitz; see p. 64, n. 1.

[17] Reference to the offer made in the letter to von Staupitz of May 30, 1518; see p. 74, and note 7 there.

[18] It is not known whether the Legate ever did this. Luther, however, made it quite clear at which points and under what circumstances he would recant; see Luther's letter of October 17, 1518, to the Papal Legate; *WA*, Br 1, 221.

[19] This is the *Appellatio M. Lutheri a Caietano ad Papam* (*Appeal of M. Luther from Cajetan to the Pope*). *WA* 2, 28 ff. This appeal was notarized on October 16 and was issued to the public on October 22; see p. 90, n. 4.

I shall publish the answer I gave him,[20] that it may be spread through the whole world if he continues to use force, as he has begun.

Farewell, in haste.

Augsburg, October 14, 1518

FRIAR MARTIN LUTHER
Augustinian

27

To the Papal Legate, Cardinal Cajetan
Augsburg,[1] October 18, 1518

The Augsburg negotiations for a peaceful settlement of Luther's trial collapsed due to Cardinal Cajetan's unwillingness to deal with Luther's objections to the indulgence traffic. This letter is Luther's final message to the Cardinal. It seemed that Luther was definitely in danger of being kidnapped and taken to Rome; to avoid this, he secretly and hurriedly left the city.

See Schwiebert, pp. 353 f. On Cardinal Cajetan, see p. 73, n. 3.

Text in Latin: WA, Br 1, 222-223.

To the Most Reverend Father and Lord in Christ,
Cardinal Thomas, titular priest of Saint Sixtus [2]

Most Reverend Father in Christ: You, Most Reverend Father, have seen—and I emphasize this—and become sufficiently acquainted with my obedience. This obedience made me undertake

---

[20] Luther apparently planned at this point to publish the reply he had given to Cajetan (see note 10) separately from his appeal (see note 19). Later he changed his mind and incorporated this answer into the *Proceedings at Augsburg;* see p. 91, n. 12; p. 94, n. 6.

[1] The source of this letter does not give the place from where Luther wrote; however one can infer from the contents that it was Augsburg.

[2] Every cardinal was titular priest of one of the parish churches in Rome, such as St. Sixtus.

such a long journey and endure so many dangers—weak in body[3] and with extremely limited means—in order to appear before you and make myself available to you, Most Reverend Father, according to the orders of our Most Holy Lord, Leo X.[4] Moreover, in the little book I published, the *Explanations*,[5] I have thrown myself and all that is mine at the feet of His Holiness. I have demonstrated that I am ready to accept whatever would seem good to His Holiness, be it condemnation or be it approval.[6] I know of nothing that I have omitted which could pertain to a devoted and obedient son of the church.

Therefore I do not want to spend time here in vain, nor can I, since I lack the resources and have been and still am more than a burden to the Carmelite fathers.[7] The most important reason, however, is that you, Most Reverend Father, have ordered me, with a loud voice, not to return to your sight unless I wish to recant.[8] What and how much I can recant, I have indicated in a previous letter.[9] Consequently I am now leaving and am going somewhere else, where I shall be able to stay.[10] And although I have been advised by people[11] who are able to influence persons greater than I to appeal from you, Most Reverend Father, even from our ill-informed Most Holy Lord, Leo X, to a pope who should be better informed,[12] for I know that I will please our Most Illustrious Sovereign[13] more by appealing than by recanting—yet I would rather not have appealed, as far as I was concerned. In the first place I do not consider it necessary to appeal or commit

---

3 Luther traveled from Wittenberg on foot to within three miles of Augsburg; see *WA*, TR 5, No. 5349. His constitution had been severely impaired by his manner of life as a monk; see p. 69, n. 26.
4 Pope Leo X; see p. 100.
5 See p. 69, n. 21.
6 See p. 69, n. 24.
7 Augsburg had no Augustinian monastery; therefore Luther stayed in the monastery of the Carmelites.
8 See p. 86, and note 18 there.
9 See Luther's letter to Cardinal Cajetan: Augsburg, October 17, 1518. *WA*, Br 1, No. 103.
10 This sounds as if Luther was thinking at the time of dropping out of sight instead of returning to Wittenberg.
11 Perhaps Philip von Feilitzsch; see p. 85, n. 8.
12 On the appeal, see p. 86, n. 19; p. 90, n. 4.
13 Elector Frederick; see pp. 49 f.

the case to judges [14] since, as I have said, I would leave everything to the church's judgment and await only its verdict.[15] What else should or can I do? There is no need that I should be accused or that I should defend myself since I direct attention not to what I have said but rather to what the church will say,[16] nor do I want to fight as if I were an antagonist, but rather, listen as a disciple. In addition I am almost convinced that this case is irritating to you, Most Reverend Father, and that an appeal would be most welcome [to you]. As I have not deserved any censures, I have no reason to be afraid of any. Therefore by the grace of God I am in such a condition that I fear any punishments far less than errors and wrong opinions concerning faith, since I know that punishment does no harm but rather is beneficial, if sound faith and understanding of truth will have been mine.

As a result, I ask you, for the sake of Christ's mercy and your eminent clemency which has been shown to me, to be so gracious and deign to acknowledge this, my flawless obedience, which I have hitherto rendered, and commend it in a kind way to the Most Holy Lord, our Pope; [I also ask] that you interpret in a favorable way my departure and my appeal as being undertaken out of necessity on my part, and under the influence of friends.[17] I cannot ignore their voices and arguments when they say: What will you recant? Aren't you by your revocation establishing a law of faith for us? [18] The church must first condemn, if there is something to be condemned, and you follow its judgment; but the church may not follow your judgment. And so I give in as defeated.

Farewell, Most Reverend Father, most highly esteemed in Christ.

From the Carmelite monastery, October 18, 1518

Most Reverend Father—your dedicated son
FRIAR MARTIN LUTHER
Augustinian

[14] See Luther's request, p. 71.

[15] I.e., a dogmatic definition regarding indulgences which so far was lacking; see p. 44; p. 69, n. 24; p. 74, n. 8.

[16] See p. 69, n. 24.

[17] See notes 11, 12.

[18] Since his views on indulgences had not yet been defined as heresy by the church, the question was why Luther should recant any of them as being heresy; see p. 74, n. 8.

28

To George Spalatin
Wittenberg, October 31, 1518

After his safe return from Augsburg (see p. 87), Luther gained the full support of the University of Wittenberg. In this letter he informs Spalatin that he next plans to appeal to a General Council and to publish his side of what transpired at Augsburg. In addition he comments on University affairs.

See Schwiebert, pp. 356 f. On George Spalatin, see pp. 8 f.
Text in Latin: WA, Br 1, 224-225.

To my most learned friend in Christ, George Spalatin,
chaplain to the Elector of Saxony, etc.

Jesus

Greetings. By God's grace I have safely arrived today [1] at Wittenberg. I do not know how long I shall be able to remain here [2] because my case is such that I both fear and hope.[3] I have appealed from a pope ill-informed to a pope who should be better informed.[4] Then I departed, leaving behind a friar who together with the notary and witnesses was to inform the Cardinal of this appeal. In the meantime, since I am here, I shall prepare another appeal to a future council.[5] I will follow the example of the

[1] October 31, 1518. On this date, see *WA*, Br 1, 225, n. 1.

[2] See p. 88. Luther could expect excommunication since he had rejected the Papal Legate's demand to recant; see p. 86. If Luther were excommunicated, the secular authorities would be obligated to turn him over to his ecclesiastical superiors. Since he was not sure whether the Elector would protect him at that point, and since he wished to avoid further complications for the Electoral government, Luther seriously considered leaving Wittenberg.

[3] For similar statements, see pp. 86, 94, 263.

[4] See p. 86, n. 19. Luther had drafted his appeal to the Pope with the help of a lawyer and had it notarized on October 16. He left town during the night of October 20/21. His companion, Leonard Beier (see p. 39, n. 4), was to inform Cardinal Cajetan (see p. 73, n. 3) on October 21 of Luther's action. On October 22 the appeal was nailed to the door of the cathedral in Augsburg as a notice to the public. For the text, see *WA* 2, 28 ff.

[5] Luther did this on November 28; for the appeal to a future General Council of the church, see *WA* 2, 34 ff.

Parisians [6] in case the Pope [7] should repress the first appeal in the fulness of his power, or rather his tyranny. I am filled with such joy and peace that I wonder why my struggle seems to be important to many and great men.[8]

The good will and mildness which the Cardinal Legate [9] had promised our Most Illustrious [Sovereign][10] to show me was certainly extraordinary and was demonstrated in abundance; we, however, did not recognize it as such. He offered to handle everything in a fatherly, even in a most fatherly manner.[11] No doubt he would have done so had I only been willing to recant my statements, for the whole case was tied up in that knot. Since I did not want to do it, and he wanted only that (I do not believe that he had any orders other than to condemn me), I was forced to appeal.

I shall prepare my replies to his arguments for publication, together with the appeal.[12] I will add theological notes on the apostolic, or rather, diabolic breve [13] which you have so often men-

[6] "Parisians," i.e., the theologians of the University of Paris. The University of Paris had opposed the concordat concluded in 1516 between the king of France, Francis I, and Pope Leo X, and on March 27, 1517, had appealed to a future General Council of the church for a decision in this case; see *WA*, Br 1, 226, n. 5. Luther is therefore following a recent ecclesiastical precedent. During the fourteenth and fifteenth centuries the University of Paris had strongly advocated conciliar control over papal supremacy. See *O.D.C.C.*, p. 539; *LCC* 14, 91 ff.

[7] Pope Leo X; see p. 100.

[8] For a similar statement, see p. 147.

[9] Cardinal Cajetan; see p. 73, n. 3.

[10] Elector Frederick; see pp. 49 f.

[11] For this promise, see p. 84.

[12] See p. 87, n. 20. At this point, Luther had changed his original plan and intended to publish his replies to the Cardinal together with his appeal, mentioned on p. 86, n. 19. It is not clear, however, whether the *responsio*, the reply or the defense Luther had given in writing to Cajetan (see p. 85, n. 10; p. 87, n. 20), is identical to the *responsiones*, the replies, which Luther now mentions. Perhaps Luther was considering an edition of his written answer, enlarged by still other material, a plan which was realized in the *Proceedings at Augsburg* (see p. 94, n. 6).

[13] This is the original instruction of Leo X to his legate Cajetan concerning the way he should proceed against Luther; it envisioned no discussion with Luther, but ordered Cajetan to obtain Luther's arrest under any circumstances and by every possible means; it threatened with excommunication everyone who might help Luther or interfere with his arrest. This breve was issued on August 23, 1518; see *WA* 2, 23 ff.; *LW* 31, 286 f. In view of the situation at the Diet of Augsburg (see p. 84, n. 4), Cajetan requested the Curia to change its planned procedure against Luther. As a result a second breve was issued on September 11, permitting a hearing but no discussion between the Legate and Luther; see *LW* 31, 256.

tioned to me, and of which you have recently sent a copy; when I stopped in Nürnberg on my way back it was delivered to me, together with other letters of instruction.[14] [It must be diabolic] for it is unbelievable that such a monstrosity should have been released by a pope, especially by Leo X. Therefore whoever that worthless wretch was who, under the name of Leo X, set out to frighten me with such a decree—he will come to understand that I can recognize nonsense. If it really was issued by the Curia, then I will teach them a lesson [by showing them] their impudent temerity and unheard-of ignorance.[15]

The Cardinal Legate has settled everything marvelously in his own mind; yet I strongly suspect that the Romans[16] are beginning to be afraid and to put little trust in their own case. Consequently they are painfully searching for loopholes. I shall report other details, and I hope in person. Remember me to the Sovereign; assure him of my grateful thoughts.

In concluding, since the Sovereign's good reputation is your responsibility, inform him of the arrival of the Father Licentiate, the prior of the Carmelites at Augsburg.[17] He treated me beyond the call of duty with great generosity and kindness. In many ways he is worthy that we treat him in like manner and thus show our grateful appreciation. He left Augsburg the twenty-third of October. He came, as he says, in the hope that his graduation expenses would be paid by our Sovereign,[18] as promised. If the Sovereign

[14] It seems that Luther arrived in Nürnberg on October 23 or 24; see *WA*, Br 1, 226, n. 8. The "letters of instruction" could not be identified.

[15] In view of the complexity of the indulgence issue; see p. 44; p. 74, n. 8.

[16] I.e., the Italian churchmen. The relations between the Italian Catholics, who considered themselves to be sophisticated, and those of the northern countries were often far less than cordial. See, for instance, Luther's remark to Cardinal Cajetan that the Italians take it for granted that the Germans are ignorant of philology (see p. 86), or Luther's remarks concerning the impressions he got during his visit to Rome of the piety of the Italian clergy (see Bainton, pp. 49 f.).

[17] John Frosch was prior of the monastery where Luther stayed while in Augsburg; see p. 88. He had studied in Wittenberg, where he was graduated as a Licentiate in Theology in 1516. After a short stay in Augsburg, he returned to finish his studies for the theological doctorate, which he obtained on November 22, 1518; see *WA*, Br 1, 226, n. 10.

[18] As a patron the Elector often underwrote the administrative expenses of doctoral graduations and the expenses of the traditional banquet which followed the academic portion of the graduation exercises. He had done so in Luther's case (see S-J 1, 26); during his visit to the Diet of Augsburg

has promised this, I don't mind contacting you about it; no doubt all will be done. Please see to it that everything the Father Licentiate is expecting is done with all propriety, etc.

Farewell in Christ.

October 31. I had hoped that you and the Sovereign would be here today, but I was wrong, and hurried in vain.[19]

Wittenberg, 1518 FRIAR MARTIN LUTHER
Augustinian

29

To George Spalatin
Wittenberg, November 25, 1518

Expecting to be banned by the church and exiled from Wittenberg, Luther discusses certain documents in connection with the aftermath of his meeting with Cardinal Cajetan at Augsburg.

On George Spalatin, see pp. 8 f.

Text in Latin: WA, Br 1, 253.

To my George Spalatin, an excellent and most learned man, my dearest friend in Christ

Jesus

Greetings. I am returning the letter which is supposed to have come from the Bishop of Liege,[1] my Spalatin, together with the one from Crotus.[2] Please take care that the Most Illustrious Sover-

(see p. 70, n. 1), the Elector must have promised Frosch to underwrite his graduation expenses, and Frosch now came in the hope that this promise would be kept.

19 I.e., on the journey back from Augsburg.

1 Luther is referring to a letter supposedly written by Erard de la Marck, bishop of Liege, to Emperor Maximilian and the Diet of Augsburg in 1518, in which corruption within the church is sharply criticized; the actual author, however, is unknown. For the bibliography of this letter, see *WA*, Br 1, 253, n. 1; for the text, see *St. L.* 15, 466 ff. On Erard de la Marck, see Allen 3, 738, Introduction.

2 It is difficult to identify this letter; for possibilities, see *WA*, Br 1, 254, n. 2. On the Humanist Crotus Rubeanus, see p. 143, n. 7.

eign[3] sees the memorandum [drawn up jointly by the University administration and myself].[4] I am waiting for your criticisms of my *Answer*[5] to the Legate's letter, unless perhaps you think it should not be written at all. My *Proceedings*[6] are already being published. Besides that, I daily expect the condemnation from the city of Rome;[7] therefore I am setting things in order and arranging everything so that if it comes I am prepared and girded to go, as Abraham,[8] not knowing where, yet most sure of my way, because God is everywhere. But I will of course leave a farewell letter; see to it that you have the courage to read the letter of a man who is condemned and excommunicated.

Farewell for now, and pray for me.

November 25, 1518 MARTIN LUTHER
Augustinian

---

[3] Elector Frederick; see pp. 49 f.

[4] After the collapse of negotiations at Augsburg, the papal legate Cajetan (see p. 73, n. 3) wrote to Elector Frederick on October 24, 1518, giving his version of the unsuccessful meetings with Luther and demanding that Luther, as a heretic, be turned over to the authorities of the church or exiled from Electoral Saxony; for Cajetan's letter, see *WA*, Br 1, No. 110, Document I. The Elector forwarded a copy of Cajetan's letter to Luther and ordered him to reply; see note 5. On November 22 or 23, the University of Wittenberg sent an official petition to the Elector asking him not to yield to Cajetan's request but rather to support Luther in his demand to be shown his error on the basis of Scripture and the ancient Fathers. This petition was written for the University by Luther himself, yet it bears corrections and additions by another hand, perhaps that of the president of the University, Bartholomew Bernhardi (see p. 95, n. 1). This is the "memorandum" to which Luther refers. See *WA*, Br 1, 254, n. 3; for the text, see *EA Var. arg.* 2, 426 ff.; *S-J* 1, 131 f.

[5] After Elector Frederick had received Cajetan's letter (mentioned in note 4), he forwarded it to Luther asking for a reply. Luther's *Answer* (*WA*, Br 1, No. 110, Document II) was actually intended to be forwarded by the Elector to the Papal Legate. The Elector did attach it, together with the petition of the University of Wittenberg (also mentioned in note 4), to his reply to Cajetan; for the Elector's letter, see *WA*, Br 1, No. 110, Document III. Luther is now asking for Spalatin's reaction to this *Answer* he had written for the Elector.

[6] *Acta Augustana* (*Proceedings at Augsburg*) (Wittenberg: J. Grünenberg, 1518). *WA* 2, 6 ff.; *LW* 31, 259 ff. Luther is referring to the first printed sheets of this work, which were completed at the beginning of December.

[7] See p. 90, n. 2.

[8] Gen. 12:4; Heb. 11:8. See pp. 88, 90.

30

To George Spalatin
Wittenberg, December 9, 1518

While Luther's trial was dragging on, he worked on the reorganization of the University curriculum. In this letter he is seeking approval of a plan to drop some courses in Thomistic studies in favor of a course in Ovid.

See pp. 41, 82. On George Spalatin, see pp. 8 f.

Text in Latin: WA, Br 1, 262.

To my dearest George Spalatin, patron of studies and culture

Jesus

Greetings. The President[1] and I agreed, my George, on several things concerning the curriculum: it seems to be good not only to eliminate the course on Thomistic *Physics*[2] (which is now being dropped by Master Gunckel, who is taking over the President's reading course),[3] but also to eliminate the course on Thomistic logic,[4] which is now taught by Master Premsel from Torgau.[5] Instead the same master is to lecture on Ovid's *Metamorphoses*,[6] since he is well qualified to teach classical literature. For we

---

[1] Bartholomew Bernhardi was then president (*rector*) of the University; see p. 115, n. 21.

[2] A course on St. Thomas Aquinas' commentary on Aristotle's *Ta peri physeos* (*Eight Books on Physics*).

[3] A reading course in Aristotelian texts. The President was planning to leave the teaching of philosophy for the teaching of theology, while also dedicating himself to his duties at Kemberg; see p. 115, n. 21. John Gunckel was graduated from Wittenberg University as Master of Arts in 1507 and had taught there since 1509 on the Faculty of Liberal Arts. In 1525 he was elected to an office similar to that of a controller of a present-day university; he died in 1535. See WA, Br 1, 262, n. 1.

[4] A course on St. Thomas Aquinas' commentary on Aristotle's *Peri hermeneias* (*On Interpretation*) and *Analytika ystera* (*Posterior Analytics*).

[5] James Premsel of Torgau was graduated from Wittenberg University as Master of Arts in 1512 and had taught there on the Faculty of Liberal Arts since 1516. In later years he switched to the teaching of medicine; he died in 1543; see WA, Br 1, 263, n. 3.

[6] The *Metamorphoses* by the Roman classical poet Ovid (43? B.C.-A.D. 17?). See *O.C.D.*, pp. 630 f.

consider the course on Scotistic philosophy and logic, together with the reading course in *Physics* and logic,[7] to be enough until such time as the Chair of the Scotistic Sect[8]—that equally useless and unfruitful occupation of gifted men—is also abolished.[9] In this way the subtle hair-splitting finally may perish altogether, and genuine philosophy, theology, and all the arts may be drawn from their true sources. We would appreciate your advice in this matter.

Farewell.

December 9, 1518

FRIAR MARTIN ELEUTHERIUS[10]

31

To Elector Frederick[1]
Altenburg, in the morning of January 5 or 6, 1519

The Diet of Augsburg in 1518 had already dealt with the matter of a successor to Emperor Maximilian I. The Emperor's death on

[7] A reading course in the texts of Aristotle's *Physics* and his works on logic (see notes 2, 4).

[8] The Scotists, opponents of the Thomists, were the followers of Duns Scotus (1264?-1308). Next to St. Thomas Aquinas (see *O.D.C.C.*, pp. 1352 f.) and St. Albertus Magnus (see *O.D.C.C.*, p. 30), Scotus (see *O.D.C.C.*, pp. 426 f.) was the most famous Scholastic theologian. In the fourteenth and fifteenth centuries, however, the struggles between Thomists (see p. 81, n. 4) and Scotists decreased in importance and were replaced by the philosophical warfare between the *via antiqua*, represented by the Thomists and Scotists, and the *via moderna*, taught by the followers of William of Occam (1300?-1349?; see *O.D.C.C.*, pp. 1462 f.); see also p. 59, n. 19. Wittenberg was at first a center of the *via antiqua*. Under Luther's influence, most of the courses that were dear to the members of the *via antiqua* were gradually eliminated, giving way to Humanistic studies. See Schwiebert, pp. 275 ff., 297 ff.; *ARG* 49 (1958), 60 ff.

[9] Luther was aware that the Humanistic reforms of the curriculum could not all be achieved at once.

[10] See p. 55, n. 12.

[1] The autographs of this and letter No. 32 do not give the place from where Luther wrote, nor do they give an addressee. Addressees and place have to be inferred from the contents of the letters. The exact dating of these letters depends on whether the meetings with von Miltitz took place January 4 and 5 or 5 and 6, and this cannot be definitely established. See *WA*, Br 1, Nos. 128, 129, Introductions.

January 12, 1519, made the election of a new ruler, who would be de facto emperor, immediately necessary. The Curia had its own very definite ideas about this election (see Grimm, pp. 116 ff.), for which it needed Elector Frederick's support. This turn in events caused the Curia quite abruptly to reverse its tough policies toward Luther (see p. 91, n. 13; p. 94, n. 4) and to pursue a comparatively mild course of action against him as the protege of the Elector. To gain the good will and support of the Elector, the Curia dispatched a special envoy, Charles von Miltitz. At the same time and of his own accord, von Miltitz embarked on a campaign to settle the case of Luther. This letter is Luther's official report of his first meeting with von Miltitz at Altenburg.

See Fife, pp. 307 ff.; Schwiebert, pp. 370 ff. On Elector Frederick, see pp. 49 f.

Text in German: WA, Br 1, 289-291.

Jesus

Most Serene, Noble Sovereign, Most Gracious Lord: I am disturbed that Your Electoral Grace is drawn so deeply into my affair and trouble.[2] But since necessity and God will it so, I beseech Your Electoral Grace to deal with it in grace and favor toward me.

Sir Charles von Miltitz[3] sharply accused me yesterday of having committed offense and outrage against the Roman church. I have offered most humbly to do all in my power to atone for this. I now beseech Your Electoral Grace to consider my suggestions,[4] which I am herewith making known to your Electoral Grace, since I want to make some definite proposals to you.

1. I was willing to promise henceforth to be silent in regard to this affair[5] and to let it bleed to death by itself (if the opposing

[2] For similar statements, see pp. 69, 81.

[3] Charles von Miltitz (1490?-1529), a Saxon noble, held relatively minor positions at the Curia. Thanks to his family connections, however, he was entrusted with the delicate mission of keeping Elector Frederick from giving his electoral vote to Charles of Spain in the forthcoming Imperial election. The Curia wanted to flatter Frederick by decorating him with the Golden Rose, which von Miltitz was to present.

[4] Luther made these suggestions during the meeting with von Miltitz at Altenburg on the previous day.

[5] The controversy on indulgences as stirred up by Luther's *Ninety-five Theses*.

side would be silent too). For it seems to me that if one would have let my writing go unhindered, everything would have been quiet long ago. The song would have been sung, and everyone would have become tired of it.[6] I am worried that this affair really will blow up into the open and the skirmishing turn into fighting if this proposal for settlement is not accepted and one continues to fight with swords or words, for I still have my reserves intact. Therefore I consider it best that one should let the matter rest at this point.

2. I was willing to write[7] to His Papal Holiness[8] and submit myself with greatest humility. I wanted to confess that I had been too passionate and sharp, yet that I did not intend to disparage the holy Roman church with this tone; I wanted to show the reason why I, a faithful child of the church, had fought against the blasphemous preaching[9] which has brought the Roman church great scorn, slander, dishonor, and scandal among people.

3. I was willing to issue [a little book][10] to admonish everyone to follow the Roman church, to be obedient and respect it, and to understand my writings as having been intended to bring not dishonor but honor to the holy Roman church. [In this little book] I also wanted to confess that I had pointed out the truth too heatedly and brought it to the attention of the public at what was perhaps the wrong time. [I wanted to demonstrate] that while the issue is quite important, I have done enough, and that in this matter it is sufficient for everyone to know the proper difference between indulgences and good works.[11]

4. Master Spalatin[12] proposed, upon the recommendation of Sir Fabian von Feilitzsch,[13] that the matter be referred to the

---

[6] In later years Erasmus of Rotterdam held a similar view; see Allen 8, 2315; 9, 2443, 2445.

[7] For this letter, see p. 100.

[8] Pope Leo X; see p. 100.

[9] The preaching of the indulgence commissioners; see pp. 46 ff.

[10] Luther wrote *zcedell*, i.e., a little piece of paper. He published this little book in February, 1519; see *WA* 2, 69 ff.

[11] For a similar statement, see p. 47.

[12] George Spalatin; see pp. 8 f.

[13] Fabian von Feilitzsch (who is not to be confused with Philip von Feilitzsch, the Electoral Saxon councilor who had assisted Luther in Augsburg; see p. 85, n. 8) attended the meetings as the Elector's representative.

Reverend, etc., Archbishop of Salzburg;[14] I should accept his decision, if it be drawn up with the help of learned and unprejudiced men;[15] if I could not accept it, however, I could return to my appeal.[16] This way the case would be pending before a court, and would develop by itself. But I am afraid that the Pope will not permit any judge; consequently I shall also not acknowledge the Pope's verdict. If [this] first proposal for settlement is not accepted, then this matter will develop in such a way that the Pope will dictate the conditions, and I shall comment on them. That would not be good.

I discussed the proposals with Sir Charles [von Miltitz], who thinks they do not go far enough. On the other hand he did not demand recantation; so we parted for further deliberation. If Your Electoral Grace knows of anything else that I should do, for the sake of God let me know Your Electoral Grace's gracious will.

---

[14] Apparently the reference is to Matthew Lang of Augsburg (1468-1540), who was at that time, however, only coadjutor of Salzburg. He had studied in Ingolstadt, Tübingen, and Vienna and joined the Imperial chancellory in 1494. As a member of the chancellory he became one of the great politicians of his time and made himself indispensable. His diplomatic shrewdness, which he used most successfully in the service of Emperor Maximilian and to his own advantage, made him rise to the highest ecclesiastical positions in the Empire: from 1505 to 1523 he was bishop of Gurk/Carinthia, in 1512 he became coadjutor of Salzburg, in 1519 archbishop of Salzburg, and in 1529 primate of the Roman Catholic Church of Germany. As an ecclesiastical sovereign he successfully resisted all interference from the rising territorial state in the administrative affairs of the church. When Charles V came to power in 1519 Lang gradually disappeared from the active diplomatic service of the Empire (see p. 217) and dedicated himself almost exclusively to his administrative duties in Salzburg, though this shift should not be considered an indication that his power and prestige were declining. Lang was a typical representative of the Renaissance church. Humanistically inclined, he supported Reuchlin against the Dominicans (see p. 9). Apparently for this reason Luther suggested Lang for the position of impartial judge (see above). Later on, however, Luther's opinion of Lang changed; see p. 359. Lang worked hard for the reform of the church, especially in the fields of moral and religious education of the laity and the theological education of the clergy. He was ruthless, however, in putting down any attempt to introduce the Reformation into his archdiocese, and during the Diet of Augsburg (1530) he strongly urged the Emperor to put an end to the Reformation by means of military force. It is interesting to observe that in 1520 Erasmus suggested a plan to Elector Frederick which was almost the same as the one discussed by Luther and von Miltitz at Altenburg; see W. K. Ferguson (ed.), *Erasmi Opuscula* (The Hague: M. Nijhoff, 1933), p. 336.

[15] For this plan, see pp. 104, 109, 127 ff., 195 f., 201 f., 208.

[16] On the appeal, see p. 90, nn. 4, 5.

I shall be glad to do anything and to suffer everything if only I am no longer called upon to drag this matter out into the public. But there is positively no chance of a revocation.

Your Electoral Grace's dedicated priest,
DOCTOR MARTIN

32

To Pope Leo X
Altenburg, January 5 or 6, 1519

One of the topics discussed at the meetings between Luther and Miltitz at Altenburg on January 5 or 6, 1519 (see p. 97), was a letter of apology to the Pope from Luther. This letter is the draft of that letter, which, however, was never sent, since von Miltitz offered to write to the Pope himself.

Leo X (pope 1513-1521), a member of the famous Medici family, was, like his predecessor Julius II, a typical representative of the Renaissance. His main interest was the political, economic, and cultural growth of the papal state and the Medici family. As a result he was more a politician than a priest, and was totally incapable of understanding Luther, whose case he had to handle.

See O.D.C.C., pp. 798 f.; Bainton, pp. 74 f.

Text in Latin: WA, Br 1, 292-293.

Draft of the letter to the Lord Pope [1]

Most Holy Father: Necessity again [2] forces me, the lowest of all men and dust of the earth,[3] to address myself to Your Holiness and August Majesty. May Your Holiness therefore be most gracious and deign to lend your ears in a fatherly fashion for a short time, and willingly listen to the bleating of this, your little sheep, for you truly stand in the place of Christ.

---

[1] This sentence is written in German.

[2] Luther had sent his *Explanations of the Ninety-five Theses* to the Pope through John von Staupitz on May 30, 1518; see pp. 64 ff.

[3] Isa. 49:6 (Vulgate).

The honorable Sir Charles Miltitz, chamber secretary to Your Holiness, has been with us.[4] In the presence of the Most Illustrious Sovereign Frederick[5] he very harshly accused me in the name of Your Holiness of lacking respect for and being rash toward the Roman church and Your Holiness, and demanded satisfaction for this. Hearing this, I was deeply grieved that my most loyal service has had such an unhappy outcome and that what I had undertaken—to guard the honor of the Roman church—had resulted in disgrace and was suspected of all wickedness, even so far as the head of the church was concerned. But what am I to do, Most Holy Father? I do not know what to do further: I cannot bear the power of your wrath, and I do not know of any means to escape it. The demand is made that I recant my theses.[6] If such a revocation could accomplish what I was attempting to do with my theses, I would issue it without hesitation. Now, however, through the antagonism and pressure of enemies, my writings are spread farther than I ever had expected and are so deeply rooted in the hearts of so many people that I am not in the position to revoke them. In addition since our Germany prospers wonderfully today with men of talent, learning, and judgment, I realize that I cannot, under any circumstances, recant anything if I want to honor the Roman church—and this has to be my primary concern. Such a recanting would accomplish nothing but to defile the Roman church more and more and bring it into the mouths of the people as something that should be accused. See, Father, those whom I have opposed have inflicted this injury and virtual ignominy on the Roman church among us. With their most insipid sermons, preached in the name of Your Holiness, they have cultivated only the most shameful avarice and have substituted for sanctification

---

[4] See p. 97. Luther does not make it clear when the meeting between von Miltitz and the Elector (referred to by Luther in the following lines) took place. On December 29, 1518, Elector Frederick wrote to Duke George of Saxony (see p. 110, n. 20), "I have with me a papal ambassador, Charles von Miltitz, who is not satisfied with Doctor Luther and has great power to proceed against him. And it might well happen that he would refuse to give me the Golden Rose [see p. 97, n. 3] unless I banished the monk and said that he was a heretic." See *Akten und Briefe* 1, 51; S-J 1, 143.

[5] Elector Frederick; see pp. 49 f.

[6] *The Ninety-five Theses;* see p. 49, n. 22.

the vile and abominable Egyptian scandal.[7] And as if that had not been bad enough, they accuse me before Your Holiness—me, who opposed their tremendous monstrosities—of being the author of the temerity which is theirs.

Most Holy Father, before God and all his creation, I testify that I have never wanted, nor do I today want, to touch in any way the authority of the Roman church and of Your Holiness or demolish it by any craftiness. On the contrary I confess the authority of this church to be supreme over all, and that nothing, be it in heaven or on earth, is to be preferred to it, save the one Jesus Christ who is Lord of all—nor should Your Holiness believe the schemers who claim otherwise, plotting evil against this Martin.

Since in this case I can do only one thing, I shall most willingly promise Your Holiness that in the future I shall leave this matter of indulgences alone, and will be completely silent concerning it (if [my enemies] also stop their vain and bombastic speeches). In addition I shall publish something[8] for the common people to make them understand that they should truly honor the Roman church, and influence them to do so. [I shall tell them] not to blame the church for the rashness of [those indulgence preachers], nor to imitate my sharp words against the Roman church, which I have used—or rather misused—against those clowns,[9] and with which I have gone too far. Perhaps by the grace of God the discord which has arisen may finally be quieted by such an effort. I strive for only one thing: that the Roman church, our Mother, be not polluted by the filth of unsuitable avarice, and that the people be not led astray into error and taught to prefer indulgences to works of love.[10] All the other things I consider of less importance, since they are matters of indifference. If I can do anything else, or if I discover that there is something else I can do, I will certainly be most ready to do it.[11]

---

[7] Josh. 5:9.
[8] See p. 98, n. 10.
[9] The indulgence commissioners; see pp. 45 ff., 98.
[10] For similar statements, see pp. 47, 98.
[11] The printed editions of this letter add some sentences which have to be translated: "May Christ preserve your Holiness forever. From Altenburg [a wrong date is added here], 1519. Friar Martin Luther, D." See *WA*, Br 1, No. 129, Introduction.

33

To Elector Frederick[1]
Wittenberg, between January 13 and 19, 1519

Luther discusses a memorandum on settling his case as prepared by the papal envoy Charles von Miltitz for Elector Frederick. He outlines the circumstances under which he could recant and scrutinizes a new papal decretal concerning indulgences.

On Elector Frederick, see pp. 49 f.

Text in German: WA, Br 1, 306-308; translation based on S-J 1, 153-155.

Jesus

Most Serene, Noble Sovereign, Most Gracious Lord: To be of humble service to Your Electoral Grace, I herewith give my opinion and judgment concerning the articles and proposals for settling the weighty matter between me and the papal indulgences, which were forwarded to me by Your Electoral Grace.[2]

1. I am ready to honor the Roman church in all humility and to place nothing in heaven or on earth above it, save only God himself and his word. Therefore I am willing to recant at whatever point my error is demonstrated. However to recant everything indiscriminately is impossible.

2. I am not only willing to endure the fact that I may never again preach or teach, but I even wish never again to do so. For I derive no pleasure or enjoyment, wealth or honor from it. I also

[1] On the controversial dating of this letter, see WA, Br 1, No. 136, Introduction. Although the letter does not show an addressee, the contents makes it clear to whom Luther was writing.

[2] After the meeting with Luther at Altenburg (see p. 97), Charles von Miltitz (see p. 97, n. 3) had a conference with Elector Frederick. Von Miltitz drew up a memorandum in which he listed the following points: (1) Luther should humbly and obediently subordinate himself to the church and respectfully acknowledge its authority. (2) Should Luther refuse to do this, then the Elector should prevent him from preaching and teaching. (3) Impartial judges, whom Luther would recognize, should hear his case. (4) See note 5, below. (5) The decretal (see note 9) is the church's answer to Luther; therefore Luther can no longer complain that the church does not want to listen to him or does not want to instruct him. Rome has spoken, therefore Luther ought to be silent. Luther is now commenting on these five points. For the text of the memorandum, see *St. L.* 15, 693 f.

well know that the preaching of God's word is an intolerable task on this earth. But in this matter I always have been and I am still subordinated to God's command and will.

3. It is my greatest desire to have an impartial judge in this case,[3] and this would be of advantage to me. For this task I also nominate the Most Reverend in God, etc., Archbishop of Trier, or the one of Salzburg, or perhaps the Serene Lord, etc., Philip, bishop of Freising and Naumburg.[4]

4. For a long time I have been stirred by the thought that in the time of Pope Julius nine cardinals with all their followers were unable to accomplish anything, and that also emperors and kings were often humiliated.[5] On the other hand I have been strengthened by the firm conviction that the Roman church would not, and would have no desire to, tolerate or even permit or defend the inept and harmful sermons which are pointed out by my theses on indulgences,[6] nor would it allow Christ's poor people to be led astray by the glitter of indulgences.

One need not be too much astonished if now one or two men are suppressed in these evil latter times,[7] since we know that in

---

[3] See pp. 98 f.

[4] Luther now also nominates Richard von Greiffenklau, archbishop of Trier, and the Count Palatine Philip, who was bishop both of Naumburg and of Freising. Luther did not mention them in his official report on the meeting with von Miltitz at Altenburg (see p. 99); nevertheless the Archbishop of Trier also must have been considered, since in a later report on this Altenburg meeting Luther mentioned only the Archbishop of Trier; see p. 127.

[5] The fourth point of the memorandum was the challenging question to the Elector whether he would dare to continue to protect Luther against the pope, whose superior power had so recently been demonstrated in the case of Louis XII and Maximilian versus Julius II. Luther is referring to this. The circumstances were the following: "At the request of Emperor Maximilian and Louis XII of France, a council was held in Pisa and Milan in 1511 and 1512 with the aim of reforming the head, in this case Pope Julius II, and the members of the church. Although cited to appear before the council, Julius did not attend. Instead, Julius called his own council, the Fifth Lateran Council, whose sessions were held in Rome at various intervals from 1512 to 1517. Ultimately the papal council triumphed over its contemporary rival at Pisa and Milan so that Julius' successor, Leo X, was able to adjourn the sessions in Rome. Instead of being checked, papal prestige and authority were strengthened" (H. J. Grimm). *LW* 31, 285, n. 35.

[6] *The Ninety-five Theses;* see p. 49, n. 22.

[7] It was Luther's conviction, along with many of his contemporaries, that the age in which his generation lived was of the "last" or "latter" time. According to apocalyptic thought it was an evil time in which the Antichrist (see p. 114, n. 16) would almost triumph before his final defeat.

the time of Arius, the heretic, when the holy church was still new and pure, all bishops were driven out of their churches, and the heretics, with the support of the whole empire, persecuted even St. Athanasius throughout the whole world.[8] If God decreed such a thing for the church in those blessed times, then I am not much surprised if I am to be defeated too, poor man that I am. But the truth has remained here and will remain forever.

5. The new decretal just issued at Rome concerning the matter of indulgences[9] seems to me very peculiar. In the first place, it offers nothing new; secondly, it reproduces the old material in language which is almost more confusing and incomprehensible than that of previous decretals. Thirdly, it does not nullify the other papal laws on which I have built my case, and thus does not resolve the contradictions in the matter. Fourthly, and this is the most important point, it does not, as all other laws usually do, cite some passages of Scripture, the Fathers, or Canon Law, or give any logical argument, but offers only empty words which do not deal with my problem, nor does it reply in any way to my writings or requests.[10]

Since the church ought to give a basis for its doctrine, as St. Peter commands,[11] and is forbidden in many ways to accept anything unless it is tested, as St. Paul states,[12] I cannot acknowledge such a decretal as a firm and sufficient doctrine of the holy church. I must rather obey God's commandments and prohibitions. Although I will not reject it, yet I also will not bow down before it.

I am also afraid, Gracious Lord, since in these our present times Scripture and the ancient Fathers are being brought to the fore again and men everywhere begin now to question not *what*,

[8] In 325 the Council of Nicaea, supported by Emperor Constantine, condemned Arius for his conviction that Christ was not of the same essence as God the Father. In the years following Nicaea, the Arians were continually harassed throughout the Roman Empire. Under Constantine's successors, Athanasius and his followers, who had successfully led the battle against the Arians, were sharply persecuted. See *O.D.C.C.*, pp. 80 f., 100.

[9] This is the papal bull *Cum postquam* of November 9, 1518, which was issued after the collapse of the negotiations at Augsburg; see p. 87. It defines and affirms the theory of indulgences in terms which were opposed by Luther. For the text, see Denzinger, No. 740 a.

[10] See p. 69; p. 74, n. 7.

[11] I Pet. 3:15.

[12] I Thess. 5:21.

but *why* this or that is said,[13] if I would recant on the basis of these mere words, it would not only be unbelievable but also would be considered mockery and a public disgrace to the Roman church. What the Roman church says and does without [scriptural] foundation is not given a basis by my recanting.

On my honor, I want to tell Your Grace that regardless of [my] reputation, I am willing to recant if only I can hear the basis of my error, or of their truth. If I do not have this and am ever forced to recant, I would do it only in words, and this would mean that at the same time I believe differently in my heart. And this would be a disgrace to them.[14]

Your Electoral Grace's dedicated servant,
D. Martin Luther

34

To George Spalatin
Wittenberg, February 7, 1519

Luther again asks Spalatin for his co-operation regarding changes in the academic curriculum. In addition he reports on the latest events regarding the pending disputation between Eck and Karlstadt.

See pp. 41, 95 f. On George Spalatin, see pp. 8 f.
Text in Latin: WA, Br 1, 325.

To my excellent and dearest friend George Spalatin,
honored in the Lord

Jesus

Greetings. I hope, my Spalatin, you bear not only with a patient but also a thankful heart the fact that we are concerned with our University and weigh you down with its business. I repeat, there-

[13] Due to the influence of Christian Humanism. This passage indirectly refers to the theology taught at the University of Wittenberg; see p. 42; see also pp. 86, 101.
[14] I.e., those who would force Luther to recant.

fore, that we recently[1] acted on the elimination of those courses by which precious hours are wasted and on the substitution of better ones, especially a course on Ovid's *Metamorphoses.* We also acted on a salary increase for our Philip,[2] and we added to his salary the amount paid for the course in *Physics*[3] which we dropped. I believe I have mentioned [all this] to you.[4] Now, lest the iron cool,[5] or be discarded as scrap iron, as one says, we ask you to complete what the Lord has begun through you, so that no bad fortune intervene and bring such a praiseworthy plan to naught.

Besides this, our Eck,[6] that little glory-hungry beast, has published a small sheet of paper regarding his planned debate with Karlstadt at Leipzig after Easter. That foolish man obliquely attempts to satisfy his long-standing grudge against me; naming one person as contestant yet attacking someone else who has to handle the whole affair, he storms against me and my writings. I am fed up with that man's senseless deceit. As a result I, too, have published a refutation against him, as you will see from the enclosed printed material. This may, perhaps, be an occasion for Eck finally to treat this matter seriously, instead of as a game, as heretofore, and thus ill serve the Roman tyranny.

Farewell in the Lord.

February 7, 1519 FRIAR MARTIN LUTHER
Augustinian

---

[1] See pp. 95 f.
[2] Philip Melanchthon; see p. 77, n. 3.
[3] I.e., the course on St. Thomas Aquinas' commentary on Aristotle's *Physics;* see p. 95, n. 2.
[4] In letter No. 30, to which Luther refers, he did not mention this salary increase. See also p. 78.
[5] Cf. the English saying, "Strike while the iron is hot." See also S. Singer, *Sprichwörter des Mittelalters* (Bern: Lang and Cie, 1944 ff.), I, 95 f.
[6] Eck (see p. 80, n. 13) published twelve theses in December, 1518, which he intended to debate with Karlstadt (see p. 79, n. 12) in the upcoming disputation in Leipzig (see p. 126). Eck's theses naming Karlstadt as contestant dealt not with Karlstadt's theology but with Luther's. Luther therefore wrote a letter of protest to Karlstadt (see *WA,* Br 1, No. 142) and published it with his own countertheses (see *WA* 2, 158 f.) in February, 1519. He is now sending this material to Spalatin.

35

To John von Staupitz
Wittenberg, February 20, 1519

Luther reproaches von Staupitz for his long silence. He also reports on the tactics of von Miltitz (see pp. 103 ff.), Tetzel's disappearance, the publication of his own collected works, and the maneuvering involved in preparations for the pending Disputation at Leipzig.

On von Staupitz, see p. 64, n. 1.

Text in Latin: WA, Br 1, 344-345.

To the Reverend and excellent Father John Staupitz,
vicar of the Eremites of St. Augustine,[1] my patron and
superior, honored in Christ

Jesus

Greetings. Even though you are so far away and silent, Reverend Father, and do not write to us who are eager to hear from you,[2] I shall nevertheless break the silence. I wish—all of us wish—finally to see you in this part of the country.[3]

I believe my *Proceedings*[4] have reached you, [and that you thus know of] the Roman wrath and indignation. God is impelling me, driving me on, rather than leading me. I cannot master myself; I want to be calm, yet I am driven into the midst of uproar.[5]

Charles Miltitz has seen me at Altenburg.[6] He complained that I have pulled the whole world to my side and alienated it from the Pope.[7] He said he had explored all the inns and discovered that among five people there are hardly three or two who favored the Roman party. I later heard from the Sovereign's court[8] that he was armed with seventy apostolic breves for the

[1] See p. 6, n. 3.
[2] Literally: ". . . you do not write a highly anticipated letter to those who are waiting . . . ."
[3] Von Staupitz stayed in Salzburg all winter; see p. 72.
[4] Luther's report on the hearings before Cardinal Cajetan; see p. 94, n. 6.
[5] For similar statements, see pp. 110, 152, 162, 194.
[6] See p. 97.
[7] Pope Leo X; see p. 100.
[8] Perhaps through Spalatin; see pp. 8 f.

purpose of bringing me as a prisoner to that murderous Jerusalem, that Babylon clothed in purple.[9] Because this project proved to be hopeless, he began to push me to restore to the Roman church that of which I had deprived it, and to recant. When I requested, however, to be informed of what I should recant, we finally agreed that the case should be referred to several bishops. I nominated the archbishops of Salzburg, Trier, and Freising.[10] He entertained me in the evening, we had a good time at the dinner, he kissed me, and so we parted. I pretended not to see through this Italian act and insincerity. He also summoned Tetzel and loudly upbraided him. Finally at Leipzig he proved to [Tetzel] that he [Tetzel] had had ninety gulden income per month and in addition three horsemen and a wagon with all expenses paid.[11] Now Tetzel has disappeared and nobody knows where he has gone,[12] except perhaps the fathers of his Order.[13]

Finally my Eck, that deceitful man, is again dragging me into a new controversy, as you can see from the enclosure.[14] Thus

---

[9] I.e., Rome; this is an allusion to Rev. 17:3-6. See also pp. 127 ff.

[10] See pp. 98 f., 104, 127 ff.

[11] John Tetzel (see p. 45) by now had fallen into general disgrace, actually through no fault of his own. Not only Luther thundered against him, but also his own former "employer" in the indulgence business, the Archbishop of Mainz, turned against him. From Spalatin or other friends at court, Luther apparently had heard of this censure of Tetzel's expense account, since von Miltitz had written of it to Pfeffinger, the Electoral Saxon treasurer (see p. 32, n. 28), in a letter dated January 22, 1519; see *WA*, Br 1, 345, n. 6. Luther does not make it clear whether von Miltitz and Tetzel met once or twice. If they met once, both the "upbraiding" and the censuring of the expense account would have had to take place in Leipzig shortly before January 22; if they met twice, then the time and place of the "upbraiding" cannot be established, while the censure would have taken place in Leipzig shortly before January 22, the date von Miltitz wrote about it. A third possibility would be that von Miltitz summoned Tetzel to come to Altenburg but Tetzel did not appear and von Miltitz then "upbraided" the absent Tetzel in the presence of Luther. This is suggested by Tetzel's refusal to leave Leipzig; see note 12.

[12] Especially after the incident mentioned in note 11, Tetzel had to fear for his life. But as early as December 31, 1518, Tetzel had written to von Miltitz that his own life was in danger, and that therefore he could not leave Leipzig and come to Altenburg. In the letter of January 22 von Miltitz wrote that Tetzel planned to disappear before things got worse; see *WA*, Br 1, 345, n. 7.

[13] Tetzel was a member of the Dominican Order. On the Dominicans, see *O.D.C.C.*, pp. 413 f.

[14] John Eck; see p. 80, n. 13. The "again" refers to the clash concerning

the Lord sees to it that I am not idle. But Christ willing, this debate will end sadly for Roman laws and practices, those reeds on which Eck leans for support.[15]

I wish you could see my shorter works, published at Basel,[16] so that you could realize what educated people think of me, Eck, Sylvester,[17] and the Scholastic theologians! Those most witty fellows, [the printers], by an intentional error, call Sylvester *magirus palatii* instead of *magister palatii* (*magirus* in Greek is the same as "cook" in Latin);[18] they needle him with other remarks that are quite biting. This affair will be quite a blow to the Roman dignitaries.

I beg you, pray for me, because I am quite confident that the Lord will constrain your heart to be disturbed on my behalf. I am a person who is both exposed to and enveloped by society [with its] drunkenness, sarcasm, carelessness, and other annoyances, not counting the problems which burden me on behalf of my office.

The Faculty at Leipzig finally consented to the disputation with Eck. They accuse me of voicing an unfounded opinion because I had written that they have refused to allow this debate.[19] They sent a letter to me in which they demand a retraction. But I know from Duke George that at first they had rejected my petition.[20]

Eck's *Obelisci;* see p. 80, n. 14. Luther herewith encloses some of the material mentioned on p. 107, n. 6.

[15] Perhaps an allusion to Isa. 36:6 and Ezek. 29:6-7.

[16] John Froben of Basel printed a collection of Luther's Latin writings in October of 1518, without giving the name or location of the publishing house. He reprinted this edition in February, 1519, again anonymously. See p. 115, n. 19.

[17] Sylvester Prierias; see p. 71, n. 7; p. 72, n. 14.

[18] In his edition of Luther's works (see note 16), Froben printed Prierias' *Dialogue* along with Luther's reply (see p. 72), just as Luther had done (see p. 75). The printers changed Prierias' official position in the title of the *Dialogue* from *magister sacri palatii*, i.e., master of the sacred palace, to *magirus sacri palatii*, i.e., cook of the sacred palace. The February, 1519, edition omits this pun.

[19] It took quite some time and much writing back and forth until the Theological Faculty of Leipzig (see p. 63, n. 24) consented to the disputation (see p. 126).

[20] This letter of Duke George does not seem to be extant. Saxony was divided into two major parts: Electoral Saxony, which was then ruled by Elector Frederick (see pp. 49 f.), a member of the Ernestine family; and Ducal Saxony, which was then governed by Duke George of the Albertine family; see Schwiebert, pp. 67 ff. Following the Leipzig Disputation (see

I wrote to them twice that their dean had previously refused my request, which he actually did.[21] It is in such a miserable way that these people try to prevent a disputation of this kind. But Duke George has insisted on it.[22]

Farewell, dearest Father.

February 20, 1519 FRIAR MARTIN LUTHER
Augustinian

36

To George Spalatin
Wittenberg, March 13, 1519

Luther reports on University business, emphasizing Melanchthon's teaching load and defending the elimination of a course in Scholastic philosophy. Discussing his work, Luther mentions an explanation of the Lord's Prayer, the commentary on St. Paul's Epistle to the Galatians, a treatise on Christ's sufferings, and his study of Canon Law in preparation for the Leipzig Disputation. He complains about a tenant who is slow in paying rent and comments on various correspondence matters.

On George Spalatin, see pp. 8 f.

Text in Latin: WA, Br 1, 359-360.

To Mr. George Spalatin, an excellent man and priest of Christ, secretary to the Duke of Saxony, my friend in the Lord

Jesus

Greetings. It will be beyond the power of our Philip,[1] my Spalatin, to give so many courses, since he is already carrying too heavy

p. 126) Duke George became one of the most violent opponents of Luther, although Elector Frederick continued to protect Luther.

[21] This correspondence between Luther, the Theological Faculty of Leipzig, and Duke George does not seem to be extant. For more details, see *WA*, Br 1, 337 f. On the relationship between the universities of Wittenberg and Leipzig, see p. 63, n. 24.

[22] The University of Leipzig was within his territory and so his wishes could not easily be ignored.

[1] Philip Melanchthon; see p. 77, n. 3.

a load. Even if you think he should lecture only on alternate days, the many responsibilities would occupy his mind no less. Moreover Aristotle's *Physics*[2] is a completely useless subject for every age.[3] The whole book is a debate about nothing and, [as it were, begs the question]. It is just a rhetorical exercise, having no value, unless you want to see in it a model for oratorical practice, as if someone were exercising his talents and skills studying and playing with dung or other worthless stuff. God's wrath has condemned the human race to preoccupy itself with these follies for so many centuries, and to do it even without understanding them. I know this book inside out, since I have already explained it privately twice to my fellow friars without using the [usual] commentaries.[4] As a result, I think that the [*Physics* lectures] should be continued only until they can be abolished—and this had better be soon, since an oration of Beroald[5] would be more useful by far. In [Aristotle's *Physics*] there is no real knowledge of the world of nature. His works on *Metaphysics* and the *Soul* are of the same quality.[6] It is, therefore, unworthy of [Melanchthon's] intellect to wallow in that mire of folly. It is better that [these books] be read (merely to fulfil the requirements of the curriculum) and not understood than that they be understood.

I am forwarding a letter from Eck,[7] who boasts and triumphs as if he were already a victor in the Olympics.[8] John Froben has sent me the small collection of my works he published, and a letter.[9] If you wish to see them, I shall send them to you.

---

[2] See p. 95, n. 2; p. 41.

[3] Replying to letter No. 30 or 34, Spalatin must have suggested that Melanchthon take over the course on Aristotle's *Physics*.

[4] See p. 38, n. 9.

[5] Philip Beroald the Elder (1453-1504) was a famous Humanist who lectured on poetry, rhetorics, and classical learning in Parma, Milan, Paris, and finally in his native Bologna.

[6] Aristotle's *Metaphysics* and *Peri psyches* (*On the Soul*). Aristotle's *Prote philosophia* was generally called *Metaphysica* since the treatises collected into this work were usually placed after the *Physics*.

[7] John Eck; see p. 80, n. 13. Luther encloses Eck's invitation (see *WA*, Br 1, No. 151) to participate in the disputation between himself and Karlstadt at Leipzig in June, 1519; see p. 107, n. 6; p. 126.

[8] This was Eck's hope in regard to the upcoming Disputation at Leipzig (see p. 126).

[9] See p. 110, n. 16; for the text of the letter, see *WA*, Br 1, No. 146; S-J 1, 161. This was the covering letter of February 14, 1519, with which

I am too busy to translate my explanation of the Lord's Prayer into Latin. Each evening I expound to children and ordinary folk the Commandments and the Lord's Prayer,[10] I preach, and I am presently getting out Paul's Epistle to the Galatians;[11]

Froben forwarded to Luther a copy of the edition of Luther's works he had published.

[10] From June, 1516, to February, 1517, Luther explained the Ten Commandments to the people of Wittenberg. He published these explanations as *Decem praecepta Wittenbergensi praedicata populo* (*Ten Sermons on the Ten Commandments Preached to the People of Wittenberg*) (Wittenberg: J. Grünenberg, July, 1518). *WA* 1, 398 ff. In a letter of September 4, 1517, Luther apparently mentions a German version of these sermons, which, it seems, he himself had prepared, or at least supervised; see *WA*, Br 1, 103. These sermons on the Ten Commandments would have to be considered Luther's first writing to have been translated into the vernacular. Unfortunately this German version is not extant. In 1520 a German translation of the Latin text of 1518 was published in Basel. (Sometime during Lent, 1518, Luther published *Eine kurze Erklärung der zehn Gebote* [*A Short Explanation of the Ten Commandments*], of which only secondary editions are now available; see *WA* 1, 247 ff. This small work was to serve as a guide for self-examination in preparation for the Easter confession.) During Lent in 1517 Luther wanted to continue his efforts to help the laity understand the great themes of the Christian faith, so he undertook to expound the Lord's Prayer. These homilies on the Lord's Prayer were published in 1518 by John Agricola (see p. 220) and in 1519, in a very abbreviated form, by Nicholas von Amsdorf (see p. 218); for the texts, see *WA* 9, 123 ff., 223 ff. Unhappy with these editions, especially with the one by Agricola, Luther decided to repeat the series of addresses on the Commandments and the Lord's Prayer during the winter months of 1518/19, and he prepared his notes for publication as he went along. In April, 1519, he published the *Auslegung deutsch des Vaterunsers für die einfältigen Laien* (*German Explanation of the Lord's Prayer for Ordinary Lay People*) (Leipzig: M. Lotther, April, 1519). *WA* 2, 80 ff. Luther did not accede to Spalatin's request to translate this work into Latin. It is not known who prepared the Latin edition of the *Auslegung deutsch*, which was published in 1520 by Melchior Lotther in Leipzig. In 1519 Luther also published *Eine kurze Form, das Paternoster zu verstehen und zu beten* (*A Brief Formula to Aid in Understanding and Praying the Lord's Prayer*) (*WA* 6, 9 ff.) and *Eine kurze und gute Auslegung des Vaterunsers* (*A Brief and Sound Explanation of the Lord's Prayer*) (*WA* 6, 20 ff.). No original print of either work is available; the first one was usually incorporated into the *Kurze Form der Zehn Gebote* (see below), while the second one was added to the *Auslegung deutsch*. Both works are devotional in nature and were to help in praying the Lord's Prayer. In 1520 Luther crowned these efforts to educate the laity with his *Eine kurze Form der Zehn Gebote, des Glaubens und des Vaterunsers* (*A Short Explanation of the Ten Commandments, the Creed, and the Lord's Prayer*), which has been rightly called a forerunner of the *Small Catechism*. See *WA* 7, 204 ff.; *PE* 2, 354 ff.

[11] During the winter semester of 1516/17 Luther lectured on Galatians for the first time; see p. 30, n. 17. He reworked his notes and published them during 1519: *In epistolam Pauli ad Galatas M. Lutheri commentarius*

besides that, there are the *orationes ceremoniales*[12] and the lectures.[13] I really do not have enough time, not to speak of spare time. I am planning a treatise dealing with the meditation on Christ's passion.[14] I do not know, however, whether I shall have enough leisure to write it out. Yet I will try hard.

In addition to this, I am studying the papal decretals for my disputation.[15] And, confidentially, I do not know whether the pope is the Antichrist himself[16] or whether he is his apostle, so miserably is Christ (that is, the truth) corrupted and crucified by the pope in the decretals. I am extremely distressed that under the semblance of laws and the Christian name, the people of Christ should be so deluded. One day I shall copy my notes on the decretals[17] for you, so that you, too, may see what it is to make laws regardless of Scripture, simply from the desire to exercise tyranny. I don't even mention the other works which are so very similar to those of the Antichrist and of which the Roman Curia has an overabundance. Daily greater and greater help and support by virtue of the authority of Holy Scripture wells up in me.

Our Erasmus has edited an *Outline and Compendium* for the

(*Martin Luther's Commentary on Paul's Epistle to the Galatians*) (Leipzig: M. Lotther, 1519, completed in September). *WA* 2, 443 ff.

[12] Solemn Prayers? It is not clear what Luther meant here. Perhaps this refers to the Hourly Prayers (see p. 28, n. 9) or to the mass, i.e., to the prayers recited during the celebration of mass.

[13] Luther was then again (see p. 18, n. 3) lecturing on the Psalms and simultaneously preparing his notes for publication; see p. 121, n. 7.

[14] *Ein Sermon von der Betrachtung des heiligen Leidens Christi* (*A Treatise on the Meditation of the Holy Passion of Christ*) (Wittenberg: J. Grünenberg, April, 1519). *WA* 2, 135 ff.

[15] Luther studied the Canon Law (see p. 186, n. 1) to prepare himself for the disputation with Eck (see p. 126).

[16] The prince of Christ's enemies; see II Thessalonians 2; I John 2:18; 4:3; II John, vs. 7. In addition the Antichrist and his kingdom is symbolized at various points in the book of Revelation; see Rev. 9:13; 11:7 (the Beast); chapter 12; 13:11; 17:8. For Luther, who considered himself to be living in the "latter" days (see p. 104, n. 7), the idea of the Antichrist was a common one. At least since the days of John Huss, but probably even earlier, people concerned with the reform of the church had identified the papacy with the kingdom of the Antichrist. For more details, see H. Preuss, *Die Vorstellungen vom Antichrist im späten Mittelalter, bei Luther und in der konfessionellen Polemik* (Leipzig: C. J. Hinrichsche Buchhandlung, 1906).

[17] Luther's notes on the Canon Law are not extant.

study of Scripture.[18] Froben has sent it to me.[19] Please return the letters of Froben, Eck, and the others.[20]

The President also wishes to be freed from his teaching obligation, in order to be able to attend to his administrative duties (which are jeopardized by his absence) and his pastoral office.[21] So far Christopher Bressen, who is indebted to us, has not given a sign of himself, either in deed or in word.[22]

Farewell in the Lord.

Wittenberg, March 13, 1519 FRIAR MARTIN LUTHER
Augustinian

I enclose a letter to the Most Illustrious Sovereign[23] concerning the matter about which you wrote.[24] Please thank him on my

---

18 *Ratio seu compendium verae theologiae* (*Outline or Compendium of a True Theology*) (Basel: J. Froben, January, 1519). Clericus 5, 75 ff.; this text is based on the 1522 edition of the *Outline*. This was a separate, reworked, and enlarged edition of one of the essays Erasmus had given as an introduction to his 1516 edition of the New Testament (see p. 23). For a modern edition, see pp. xx, n. 24.

19 When John Froben sent his edition of Luther's works to Luther (see p. 112, n. 9), he also enclosed this work by Erasmus; see *WA*, Br 1, 331, n. 1.

20 See notes 7, 9.

21 Bartholomew Bernhardi of Feldkirch/Voralberg (1487-1551) studied at the University of Erfurt and the University of Wittenberg, where he also taught on the Liberal Arts Faculty. In 1512 he was dean of the Liberal Arts Faculty. Studying theology, he became one of Luther's students and was graduated as Master of the Sentences in 1516. In 1518 he was elected president of Wittenberg University. From his student days on he was a strong supporter of Luther; while president of the University he backed Luther with the full authority of the University (see p. 94, n. 4; p. 95). The University had appointed Bernhardi to be provost at Kemberg, a position from which he derived his income as a University professor without actually residing there. In 1518 Bernhardi became a member of the Theological Faculty and decided to dedicate himself more to his duties at Kemberg, and he soon settled down at Kemberg where he stayed for the rest of his life. See also p. 342, n. 20.

22 Christopher Bressen and Günther von Staupitz, a relative of the Vicar General (see p. 64, n. 1), rented a farm from the monastery; both were very slow in paying the annual rent; see *WA*, Br 1, 312, n. 10. Shortly after Luther had given this letter to the messenger, Bressen paid his debt; see Luther's letter of April 5, 1519, to Spalatin. *WA*, Br 1, 367.

23 Elector Frederick; see pp. 49 f.

24 When Luther clashed with Eck (see p. 107, n. 6), von Miltitz complained that Luther broke his promise to be silent (see pp. 97 f.). In his letter to the Elector (see *WA*, Br 1, No. 160; S-J 1, 168 f.) Luther defends himself against this accusation.

behalf for his most kind care. It is extraordinary that His Grace is constantly so concerned; I am sorry about this, for I do not wish it. I have answered Eck nothing but a few words,[25] namely, that it is his fault, not mine, that he has the reputation of a sophist throughout the world. I do not want to have any more dealings with this man; he is completely faithless and has openly destroyed the right to friendship.[26]

37

To Erasmus of Rotterdam
Wittenberg, March 28, 1519

Two movements were especially important in shaping the religious life of the first part of the sixteenth century: the Reformation and Christian Humanism, of which Erasmus of Rotterdam (1466?-1536) was the acknowledged leader. Both movements shared the desire to return to the original sources of the Bible and the early Fathers, on the basis of which conclusions could be drawn and then applied to a reform of the church, the individual's faith, and society as a whole. Luther got acquainted with Erasmus' work in 1516 when he used the Humanist's Greek text of the New Testament as the basis for his biblical studies; see p. 23. Luther had a deep respect for Erasmus' learning but quickly realized the fundamental difference between his own theological position and that of Erasmus. Although he did not hesitate to express his opinion, he did his best not to make an issue out of this divergence; see pp. 40, 53. Erasmus had known of Luther since the Ninety-five Theses were spread throughout Germany (see Allen 3, 785), and it seems that he was impressed with the Wittenberg professor; see Allen 3, 939. However Erasmus also was aware of differences existing between them, although for him they were more a matter

[25] For the text of this letter, see *WA*, Br 1, No. 149.

[26] This postscript was not written on the same paper as the rest of the letter; it was a loose sheet of paper which editors added to different letters. We follow the *WA*, Br editor, who attached it to this letter. For the basis of this, see *WA*, Br 1, 361, n. 13.

of propriety than of theology. Yet both men—and especially their friends (see p. 122; p. 150, n. 10; pp. 184 f.)—hoped that mutual respect would bind them together so that they could and would support each other's program. This hope was eventually destroyed by the development and clarification of Luther's thought and the events of the Reformation after the Leipzig Disputation (June/July, 1519; see p. 126). In 1524/25 Erasmus and Luther clashed on the question of free will. This controversy brought out the differences and clearly established the line which separated both men and made it impossible for them to be tolerant of one another's point of view. Depending on their denominational ties, different scholars have characterized Erasmus' thought either as Roman Catholic or Protestant. In either case, Erasmus is misunderstood. He was, as the Litterae obscurorum virorum stated, "homo pro se," an entity unto himself (see Böcking, Supplementum 1, 279). See O.D.C.C., pp. 459 f.; Bainton, pp. 125 f.; Fife, pp. 416 ff.; C. R. Thompson (ed.), Inquisitio de Fide: A Colloquy by Desiderius Erasmus Roterodamus, 1524 ("Yale Studies in Religion," Vol. XV [Yale University Press, 1950]).

This letter is Luther's first direct approach to Erasmus. In a typically Humanistic way, Luther discusses mutual problems and seeks Erasmus' friendship.

Text in Latin: WA, Br 1, 361-363.

Jesus [1]

Greetings. I speak so often to you and you to me, my Erasmus—our glory and hope—and yet we do not know each other personally. Is that not most peculiar? Actually this is not strange at all, but something that obviously happens every day. Where is there someone whose heart Erasmus does not occupy, whom Erasmus does not teach, over whom Erasmus does not hold sway? I speak of course of those who truly love learning. I am very glad that you displease many,[2] since this, among other things, is also

[1] The address is missing in the earliest printed editions of this letter, on which the *WA*, Br text is based. The addressee is identified in the heading and the first line of the letter.
[2] I.e., the Scholastic opponents of Humanism.

to be counted among the gifts of Christ. By this[3] I usually differentiate between the gifts of the merciful and of the wrathful God. As a result I congratulate you that while you delight all good people tremendously, you no less vex those who want to be alone on top and want to be the most popular.

Yet I am foolish that I, with unwashed hands and without a reverential and honorific introduction, address you, such a great man, in the most familiar tone, as [is usually done among common people]. But in your kindness, may you attribute this either to my affection [for you] or to my lack of skill. Although I have spent my life among sophists, yet I have not learned enough to greet a learned man by letter. Were this not so, I would have troubled you a long time ago with I don't know how many letters, and would not have endured that you should always speak to me only in my cell [through your books].

Now I have heard from the excellent Fabricius Capito that you are acquainted with my name through those trivial writings on the indulgences;[4] I also realize from your preface to the latest edition of the *Enchiridion* that you not only know but also approve of my unimportant statements.[5] Therefore I feel compelled to acknowledge (even if in a most primitive letter) your outstanding spirit, which has enriched my own and that of all others. I know that it will make little difference to you that I express my affection and gratitude in a letter. You are completely content if, known only to God, the hearts [of your readers] are glowing with gratitude and love toward you. So we too are satisfied to have you and your services reach us only through your books, without knowing you personally, exchanging letters, or talking to you directly. Yet neither good manners nor conscience permit this gratitude to remain unspoken—especially since my name, too, begins to be known—lest someone consider such a silence to be malicious and mean in nature.

---

[3] I.e., the fact that Erasmus displeases.

[4] Erasmus had known of Luther's *Ninety-five Theses* at least since March, 1518; see Allen 3, 785. In September, 1518, Capito (see p. 305, n. 2) informed Luther of Erasmus' opinion concerning Luther's attack on the indulgences; see *WA*, Br 1, 197 f.; *S-J* 1, 110 f.

[5] Luther is referring to Erasmus' letter of dedication in the 1518 edition of the *Enchiridion*. The passage where Luther could find some acceptance of his thoughts is found in Allen 3, 858.

As a result, my Erasmus, amiable man, if it seems acceptable to you, acknowledge also this little brother in Christ. He is certainly most devoted to you, and has the greatest affection for you. By the way, because of his ignorance he has earned nothing but burial in some little corner and anonymity as far as everyone under sky and sun is concerned. This I have always also ardently desired, since I am very well aware of my weaknesses.[6] I do not know by what fate this developed into just the contrary, so that now, to my great shame, I am forced to endure [the fact] that my disgrace and sad lack of knowledge are known even to the learned and are discussed by them.[7]

Philip Melanchthon is doing well,[8] except that we all can hardly keep him from ruining his health through excessive zeal for academic work. He burns with the enthusiasm of youth and wants to become and to do all things for all men at the same time.[9] You would do us a service if you would admonish that man by letter to take care of himself for our sake and for the sake of good learning.[10] For if he stays well, I do not know from whom we may expect greater things.

Andrew Karlstadt,[11] in great reverence for the Christ dwelling in you, sends greetings.

The Lord Jesus himself preserve you unto life eternal, excellent Erasmus. Amen. I was verbose; but remember that one ought not always read only learned letters. Sometimes you have to be weak with the weak.[12]

Wittenberg, March 28, 1519 [13]

---

[6] An allusion to an expression used by the Roman satirist A. Persius Flaccus (d. A.D. 62); see *WA*, Br 1, 363, n. 6; *O.C.D.*, p. 669.

[7] For similar statements, see pp. 69, 75, 103, 146, 152, 178, 232, 274.

[8] Philip Melanchthon; see p. 77, n. 3.

[9] I Cor. 9:22.

[10] *Bonae literae* is the technical term used by the Humanists for Humanistic studies. Erasmus fulfilled Luther's wish in a letter to Melanchthon dated April 22, 1519; see Allen 3, 947. On Luther's concern for Melanchthon's health and work load, see pp. 111 f., 165 f., 258, 304.

[11] See p. 79, n. 12.

[12] I Cor. 9:22.

[13] Some of the printed editions add: "F. Martin Luther." The earliest printed edition omits the signature, since Luther is identified as the writer of this letter in the heading of the letter.

38

To Elector Frederick
Wittenberg, about May 15, 1519[1]

In spite of the excitement and disturbance stirred up by the controversy on indulgences, the pace of Luther's life continued to be set by his relationship to the University and monastery. He dedicated himself to the great theological questions of the day and to the administration of the University (see pp. 41, 63, 82, 95 f., 111 f.) and monastery. In this letter he requests the Elector's help in obtaining a building permit; he also asks for a cowl that has been promised to him for some time.

On Elector Frederick, see pp. 49 f.

Text in German: WA, Br 1, 386-387.

To my Most Gracious Lord, Duke Frederick,
elector in Saxony, etc.: *Personal*

Jesus

Most Serene Sovereign, Most Gracious Lord: Necessity forces us to build a room.[2] We humbly petitioned the gentlemen of the Wittenberg city council to give us permission to build out from the wall above the town moat.[3] We have received no answer to our petition. We therefore ask Your Grace graciously to grant us the favor and permission to undertake this needed construction; we shall await Your Grace's kind answer, which, God [is our witness], we deserve.

---

[1] On the dating of this letter, see WA, Br 1, No. 173, Introduction.

[2] Luther does not make it clear what kind of a room was to be built, or where—in the University or the monastery. The statement following suggests, however, that the room was to be added to the monastery, since the monastery was built right against the city wall; see note 3. Enders (*Briefwechsel* 2, 35, n. 2) suggests that this room was intended as a toilet, for toilets were usually built on the city walls to carry the sewage outside the city. This seems wrong in view of Luther's statement (made in a letter of May 30, 1519) that the prior of the monastery was building a kitchen; see p. 125.

[3] For the location of the monastery, see the plan of the city of Wittenberg in Schwiebert, facing p. 192.

I also pray Your Grace to buy for me a white and a black cowl at this year's Leipzig Fair.[4] Your Grace owes me the black cowl; I humbly beg for the white one. For two or three years ago Your Grace promised me one which I have not yet received, in spite of Pfeffinger's fair words.[5] Maybe he was too busy, or, as people accuse him, he is slow to spend money; [in either case] he procrastinated so long that I was forced to buy one myself. Therefore I was taken care of, and did not have to make use of Your Grace's promise. In this my need I now also humbly ask that the Apostle[6] earn a white cowl if the Psalter[7] deserves a black one. I also beg that this may not be neglected again by Pfeffinger, etc.

Your Grace's willing subject
PRIEST D. MARTIN
Augustinian at Wittenberg

---

[4] The Spring Fair of Leipzig opened on Jubilate Sunday, May 15; see *WA*, Br 1, No. 173, Introduction.

[5] On December 14, 1516, Luther had thanked the Elector for a piece of cloth, obviously to be used for a cowl; see p. 33. On November 6, 1517, he reminded the Elector of his promise made a year ago and asked that it be kept; see pp. 50 f. This reminder apparently refers to the gift of December 14, 1516, for which Luther must have thanked the Elector somewhat prematurely. On November 11, 1517, he apparently received this cloth; see *WA*, Br 1, 124. Now, in May, 1519, Luther writes that "two or three years ago" the Elector promised him a black cowl. This promise, obviously made in 1516 or 1517, had not been kept due to Pfeffinger's thriftiness (Pfeffinger was the Electoral Saxon treasurer; see p. 32, n. 28), as Luther suspects. This must be a different promise from the promise mentioned in previous letters, where Luther spoke of "cloth" for a cowl (see p. 33; *WA*, Br 1, 124) or *Kleid* ("clothing"), which we translated freely as "cowl" (see pp. 33, 50, 51). Luther now reminds the Elector of this promise, two or three years old by now, and asks at the same time for a new white cowl, which was a type of undercoat worn under the black cowl.

[6] "Apostle," i.e., Luther's *Commentary on Galatians* (see p. 113, n. 11), which was then on the press.

[7] "Psalter," i.e., Luther's *Second Lectures on the Psalms* (Wittenberg: J. Grünenberg, 1519-1521). *WA* 5, 26 ff.; *LW* 14, 287 ff.; see p. 114, n. 13. On March 27, 1519, Luther dedicated this commentary to the Elector; see *WA* 5, 19 ff.; *LW* 14, 280 ff.

39

To George Spalatin
Wittenberg, May 22, 1519

On April 14, 1519, Erasmus of Rotterdam (see pp. 116 f.) wrote a letter (see Allen 3, 939; S-J 1, 177 ff.) to Elector Frederick (see pp. 49 f.) asking him to protect Humanistic learning against the dangerous attacks of the traditionalists within the church. Since Luther was also attacked by these traditionalists, Erasmus dealt with him in this letter too. He did this in such a fair way, pointing out Luther's high moral reputation, that one cannot avoid the impression that he approved of the Reformer; see Allen 3, 939. Yet Erasmus also noted that a common enemy does not necessarily make for a common cause. Nevertheless this letter was construed by Erasmus' friends and enemies as approval of Luther and his work; this interpretation may convey some idea of how close Humanism and the Reformation were considered to be in the years from 1517 to 1520.

In this letter Luther expresses his reaction to Erasmus' letter; he also discusses the appointment of a professor of Hebrew and the rising popularity of Wittenberg's university.

On George Spalatin, see pp. 8 f.

Text in Latin: WA, Br 1, 404.

To the excellent Mr. George Spalatin, a priest of Christ,
my superior and patron, venerable in Christ

Jesus

Greetings. The letter of Erasmus[1] pleases me and our friends very much.[2] I, however, would have preferred not only not to have been mentioned in it but also not to have been praised,

[1] See the Introduction; for the text, see Allen 3, 939; S-J 1, 177 ff.

[2] For Melanchthon's reaction, see C.R. 1, 80; S-J 1, 188. The people around Luther published Erasmus' letter at once. Spalatin even furnished a German translation. By the end of July, Erasmus' letter was known almost all over Germany. Thus it became powerful propaganda for the Reformation, something Erasmus certainly had not intended.

especially by such an outstanding man. I know myself too well, at least on this point.

I also ask that before leaving you sound out the Most Illustrious Sovereign's[3] opinion concerning a professor of Hebrew and let us know what he thinks.[4] John Keller from Burgkundstadt[5] has been with us; he plans to return shortly. He taught Hebrew at Heidelberg and is the author of a small grammar[6] (which I believe you have seen), in which he shows that he does know something in this field. He promised us he would do everything in his power to be a reliable teacher if he could be sure that he would be provided with a decent salary by our Most Illustrious Sovereign. At the moment he is in Leipzig, waiting for our answer. Therefore please reply promptly. At the same time please return the letter from Duke George.[7]

The number of students is growing tremendously, and they are of good quality. In fact the Licentiate of Theology from Nürnberg, a man of advanced age and a preacher at the hospital and at St. Sebald's, has come here.[8] Our town can hardly hold

---

[3] Elector Frederick; see pp. 49 f. Spalatin was supposed to accompany the Elector to Frankfurt/Main, where the Elector was to take part in the election of the new Roman king; see pp. 96 f.; Grimm, pp. 116 ff.

[4] Luther was not as successful with his plea for a professor of Hebrew as he was with his plea for a professor of Greek; see p. 63, n. 23; pp. 132 f., 160, 162; p. 154, nn. 1, 3.

[5] Luther wrote Cellarius Gnostopolitanus, Keller's Humanistic name. Keller taught Hebrew at Louvain, Mainz, Tübingen, and Heidelberg. He was a personal acquaintance of Erasmus, Melanchthon, and Reuchlin. Discussions about this call were long and drawn out; he was finally offered a yearly salary of fifty gulden, but by then he had committed himself to teach at the University of Leipzig. Later he taught for a short time in Ingolstadt, where he even defended some theses in which Luther was attacked. From 1520 on he sided with Zwingli, but he later became a strong supporter of Luther. He died in 1542 while a superintendent in Dresden. Melanchthon apparently was not as impressed with Keller's knowledge of Hebrew as Luther was; see *WA*, Br 1, 405, n. 2.

[6] *Isagicon in Hebraeas literas* (*Introduction to Hebrew*) (Hagenau: T. Anshelm, 1518).

[7] This letter, dated May 7, 1519 (see *WA*, Br 1, No. 170), was concerned with securing the necessary permissions for the pending Disputation at Leipzig. See p. 110, n. 19; p. 126.

[8] A certain John Herholt, who had matriculated on May 26; see *WA*, Br 1, 405, n. 5. Luther had met him in the fall of 1518 when he stopped over in Nürnberg on his journey to and from the meetings with Cajetan; see pp. 92, 170.

them all, due to the lack of lodging facilities.[9] Other news at another time.

Farewell.

May 22, 1519

FRIAR MARTIN LUTHER
Augustinian

40

To Martin Glaser
Wittenberg, May 30, 1519

Martin Glaser was a fellow-friar of Luther at Wittenberg; from 1517 to 1518 he was prior of the Augustinian monastery in Ramsau/ Upper Bavaria; later he broke away from the Roman church and from 1524 until his death (1553?) he was a prominent evangelical pastor in Franconia, especially in the area surrounding Nürnberg. During all this time he was a faithful friend of Luther, though they had little contact. In 1518 he had been in Augsburg while the diet was in session there (see p. 70, n. 1) and tried to mediate between Cardinal Cajetan and Luther. The chances are that Luther used Glaser's horse to escape from Augsburg (see p. 87)—without Glaser's knowledge. Luther now apologizes for having done this. Luther also reports on his academic work, comments on some actions of his enemies, and tells of the construction of a kitchen in the monastery.

Text in Latin: WA, Br *1, 408-409; translation based on* S-J *1, 191-192.*

To the Reverend Father Martin Glaser,
Bachelor of Sacred Theology, prior of the Eremites[1] in Ramsau,
my dearest friend in the Lord

[9] See pp. 125, 161 f.
[1] See p. 6, n. 3.

Jesus

Greetings. You have every right to be amazed, or even indignant, my venerable Father, that I have not written a single line to you before this. Even though I have excuses, I prefer to confess my guilt. I hope you will be indulgent with a very poor man like me in regard to your horse,[2] on account of the intercession of the Reverend Father Vicar.[3] You gave it to God, to be sure, not to me.

What a pleasure that we may see you here again! I have heard from the Reverend Father Vicar that this will be the case. I believe that you know of my coming Disputation at Leipzig,[4] and of all my other activities. I am lecturing on the Psalms [5] again; the University flourishes, and the town is full of students.

Rome is burning to destroy me, but I coolly laugh at her. I am told that in the Campo di Fiore a Martin-in-effigy has been publicly burned, cursed, and execrated.[6] I am ready for their rage.

My commentary on the Epistle to the Galatians is already being printed.[7] You will see it any day now.

Besides this, we live well and quietly and at last are less poor than we were.[8] Our Helt [9] is ruling quite well and also building, but only a kitchen.[10] For thus far he cares only for the belly; later he will also care for the head.

I have read what you wrote [11] some time ago about that

[2] See the Introduction and *WA*, TR 1, No. 1203.
[3] John von Staupitz; see p. 64, n. 1. The letter is not extant.
[4] See p. 126.
[5] Luther's *Second Lectures on the Psalms;* see p. 121, n. 7.
[6] The date of this event is controversial. For various possibilities, see *WA*, Br 1, 409, n. 6; R. F. Kerr (trans.), L. Pastor's *History of the Popes from the Close of the Middle Ages* (40 vols.; London: Kegan, Trench, and Trübner, 1891-1954), VIII, 36 f.
[7] See p. 113, n. 11.
[8] See p. 30.
[9] Conrad Helt of Nürnberg was at that time prior of the Augustinian monastery in Wittenberg. He had matriculated in Wittenberg University in 1512 and was graduated as Master of Arts in 1516. In 1518 he was elected prior of the Wittenberg monastery, a position he held until 1522 when he left Wittenberg. After short stays in Nürnberg and Nordhausen, Helt became prior of the Heidelberg monastery. He died there in 1548. See *ARG* 7 (1910), 264 f.
[10] This must be the room to which Luther referred on p. 120.
[11] Glaser's letter is not extant. The "Franciscan babbler" could not be identified exactly. Perhaps it was Bernhard Dappen, who was lector (see p. 7, n. 9) in the Franciscan monastery at Jüterbog; *WA*, Br 1, 410, n. 9. In 1518

Franciscan babbler. But I am used to such ill will. The whole world is wavering and shaking, in body as well as soul. God knows what the outcome will be. I predict massacres and wars. God have mercy upon us.

Farewell in Him, and pray for poor me.

May 30, 1519

FRIAR MARTIN LUTHER

41

To George Spalatin
Wittenberg, July 20, 1519

This letter is Luther's report on the disputation between Eck, Karlstadt, and himself, which took place in Leipzig from June 27 to July 16, 1519.

See Fife, pp. 349 ff.; Schwiebert, pp. 391 ff.; Bainton, pp. 102 ff. On George Spalatin, see pp. 8 f.

Text in Latin: WA, Br 1, 420-424. *For the text in translation by Harold J. Grimm, see LW 31, 318 ff.*

42

To George Spalatin
Liebenwerda, October 9, or Wittenberg, October 10, 1519[1]

Luther reports on a meeting with Charles von Miltitz (see p. 97, n. 3) at Liebenwerda on October 9, 1519.

On George Spalatin, see pp. 8 f.

Text in Latin: WA, Br 1, 525.

Dappen had violently criticized Luther. Luther heard about it, and he in turn complained to the monastery in Jüterbog concerning Dappen's action. The monastery, of course, sided with its lector, and the whole affair was brought before the Bishop of Brandenburg. See WA, Br 1, No. 174, Introduction.

[1] The autograph of this letter is not dated, nor does Luther give the place

Jesus

To begin with, he[2] ordered me to greet our Most Illustrious Sovereign[3] in his name. Secondly, he also ordered me to give his greetings to you, too. Thirdly, he asked whether I would stand by the agreement we had made at Altenburg, to the effect that the Archbishop of Trier should be judge.[4] I said I would. This was the last act of the drama. At the end he said that by this conversation he had fulfilled his apostolic commission[5] and would soon go back to Rome, and that he had not wanted to leave without having directly discussed the case with me.

MARTIN LUTHER

Instead of a tragedy, we had a comedy regarding the power of the pope. We agreed that the pope does not have by divine right the power which he now wields, yet that his commission is indeed different from that of the other apostles. When I asked him how this power [of the pope] differs [from that of the other apostles], he said that it was really the same, except it was given to Peter for a different part of the earth. Oh, he said, we would soon agree on the matter![6]

43

To Elector Frederick
Wittenberg, October 15, 1519

During the meetings with Charles von Miltitz (see pp. 97 ff., and above) Luther had agreed to submit his case to a neutral court.

where he wrote it. Spalatin, however, wrote on the back of the original: "D. Martin Luther's conference with Sir Charles von Miltitz at Liebenwerda. 1519"; see *WA*, Br 1, 525. From the letter of von Miltitz to the Elector, dated October 10, 1519, we know that this meeting took place on October 9; see *WA*, Br 1, No. 204, Document II. Luther must have written his letter either immediately after the meeting, while still in Liebenwerda, or on the next day after he had returned to Wittenberg.

2 Von Miltitz; see p. 97, n. 3.

3 Elector Frederick; see pp. 49 f.

4 See p. 99; p. 104, n. 4. In his report on the meeting at Altenburg, Luther did not mention the Archbishop of Trier.

5 Commission of the Apostolic See.

6 This sentence is written in macaronic German and Latin.

Luther's willingness to do so was used by von Miltitz in an attempt to get Luther out of Electoral Saxony and deprive him of the Elector's immediate protection. This, in turn, would have enabled von Miltitz to lay hold of Luther and perhaps bring him to Rome. In a letter to the Elector (see WA, Br 1, No. 204, Document II), von Miltitz pretended, therefore, that Luther had previously expressed his willingness to accompany him at once to Trier, since the Archbishop of Trier was one of the neutral judges Luther was willing to accept. In this letter Luther clarifies his position on this matter.

On Elector Frederick, see pp. 49 f.

Text in German: WA, Br 1, 535-536.

To the Most Serene, Noble Sovereign and Lord, Sir Frederick, duke in Saxony, elector and archmarshal of the Holy Roman Empire, and vicar of His Imperial Majesty in Saxonian territory, landgrave in Thuringia, margrave in Meissen, my Most Gracious Lord and Patron

Jesus

Most Serene and Noble Sovereign, Most Gracious Lord: Before all else, my humble prayer and services are always at the disposal of Your Electoral Grace.

Most Gracious Lord: I understand that my friend and master, Sir Charles von Miltitz, has written to Your Electoral Grace to the effect that I have obligated myself to accompany him to Trier.[1] It amazed me to hear this. He asked nothing else of me[2] than whether I was still willing to accept the Archbishop of Trier as judge,[3] as was agreed upon at Altenburg;[4] I said I was and that I would adhere to the agreement made between Your Electoral Grace and the Most Reverend, etc., [Archbishop][5]

[1] Von Miltitz's letter to the Elector (see *WA*, Br 1, No. 204, Document II) had been forwarded to Luther. See also pp. 108 f.

[2] During the meeting at Liebenwerda; see p. 127.

[3] Richard von Greiffenklau; see p. 104, n. 4.

[4] See pp. 97 ff., 103 f.

[5] Of Trier; see note 3.

at Frankfurt.[6] I especially mentioned Your Electoral Grace's advice and agreement, as our Prior,[7] who was present, also heard and still affirms. I never considered traveling with anyone to Trier prior to the diet,[8] nor was it ever discussed. Even Charles [von Miltitz] stated that now he had accomplished his mission and intended to travel by the most direct route to Rome.[9] Of course I am still willing and ready to come to the diet[10] upon Your Electoral Grace's advice and promise, and do what I should do. But now in such times of dangers of war, plague, and other hazards all around, I do not want to promise it, not to speak of fulfilling [such a promise].

I wanted to inform Your Electoral Grace of this in humble obedience, so that Your Electoral Grace might know the subject of our discussion at Liebenwerda from a trustworthy source.

With this, I humbly commend myself to Your Electoral Grace.

Wittenberg, October 15, 1519

Your Electoral Grace's dedicated priest
and servant,
D. [MARTIN LUTHER][11]

---

[6] From June 11 to July 4, 1519, the Elector was at Frankfurt, where according to an old custom the Electoral College met for the election of the new king; see p. 70, n. 1; p. 123, n. 3; pp. 96 f.; *WA*, Br 1, 424, n. 1. Since the Archbishop of Trier was also a member of the Electoral College, he too was in Frankfurt and both electors discussed Luther's case.

[7] Conrad Helt; see p. 125, n. 9.

[8] "Prior to the diet," i.e., before the meeting of the Electoral College of the diet at Frankfurt. Luther meant that after the meeting at Altenburg (where this idea had been discussed) he never would have traveled anywhere to appear before any neutral judges until the Elector had had a chance to sound out the Archbishop of Trier (one of the proposed judges) at the meeting in Frankfurt.

[9] See p. 127.

[10] As far as this editor can see, this passage is usually ignored. Did Luther consider appearing before a session of the diet as early as October, 1519? Then the ideas which led to Worms would have had their origin here, at least as far as Luther was concerned. Another possible way to understand this passage would be: the Electoral proclamation of the election of Charles V (see notes 6, 8; pp. 175 f.) demanded calling the Council of Regency into session (see p. 70, n. 1), and perhaps Luther was thinking that he should appear before this body of the diet, or that the meeting with the judges was to take place in the framework of a commission created either by the diet or the Electoral College or the Council of Regency.

[11] The autograph is not signed but has ". . . ." Luther wrote this letter, as the handwriting shows and as is confirmed by a note in Spalatin's handwriting which is inserted after the address.

44

To George Spalatin
Wittenberg, November 1, 1519

Luther asks Spalatin to forward the Treatise on Preparing for Death to Mark Schart in appreciation for a gift of ten gulden. He asks for Spalatin's advice about aid for some needy people. He also discusses Eck's latest publication against him and his own reply to it. He adjures Spalatin to see that Langenmantel is properly supplied with all the printed sheets of the Second Lectures on the Psalms.

On George Spalatin, see pp. 8 f.

Text in Latin: WA, Br 1, 548-549.

To my friend in the Lord, George Spalatin,
an esteemed servant of Christ

Jesus

Greetings. I ask you, my Spalatin, to thank Mark Schart[1] on my behalf for those ten gulden[2] and send him as many of these little books[3] as you see fit. To tell the truth, on that very same day that I became so rich, the need of certain people made me poorer. I had to loan them some money. It disgusts me that no love at all is left among the people of Christ, so that not even one of those who have something will help his neighbor with twenty gulden. I even think that those gulden were given to me because the Lord wanted to help those people through me; but it is not enough. Therefore if you will advise me to do so,

---

[1] Mark Schart was a noble retainer of Elector Frederick. Owning many farms and being extremely wealthy, he was a patron of the University and at different times gave gifts of money to Luther, other faculty members, and students. On Schart, see *ARG* 8 (1911), 33 f.

[2] On the gulden, see p. 11, n. 2.

[3] These evidently are copies of Luther's *Sermon von der Bereitung zum Sterben* (*Treatise on Preparing for Death*) (Wittenberg, J. Grünenberg, 1519). *WA* 2, 685 ff. An extant copy of the original printing bears the following dedication in Luther's handwriting: "Mr. Mark Schart, my dear friend"; see *WA*, Br 1, 549, n. 1.

I shall even knock at the most clement Sovereign's[4] door regarding this need. By God's grace, I ask nothing for myself.

Furious Eck has published a *Defense* against the letter I sent to you. I have already answered him with six sheets which were finished this week and are already at the press.[5] It is just amazing how the man rages; and also how he is so full of lies. This attack comes at a most convenient and opportune time for me. [Eck] carelessly uncovered his hypocrisy; at this point alone —while saying nothing about others—I laid hold of him, forcing him to expose himself and his gang from Leipzig further. I shall send you a copy soon. If Langenmantel[6] does not have the complete *Second Lectures on the Psalms,* then send him this copy.[7] But if he has some printed sheets, then return it and tell me the number [he has] so that we do not cause the printer a loss.

Farewell in the Lord.

November 1, 1519

MARTIN LUTHER

---

[4] Elector Frederick; see pp. 49 f.

[5] In August of 1519 Luther sent his *Resolutiones Lutherianae super propositionibus suis Lipsiae disputatis* (*Luther's Explanations of his Theses which had been Disputed in Leipzig*) to George Spalatin, dedicating it to him; see *WA* 2, 391 ff.; *WA*, Br 1, No. 191; for the text of the letter, see *WA* 2, 391 ff. The letter of dedication was printed at once, although not in the present form; see *WA*, Br 1, No. 191, Introduction. In it Luther sharply criticized the conduct of John Eck and the Theological Faculty of Leipzig (see p. 63, n. 24) during the Disputation at Leipzig (see p. 126). At the same time he criticized Eck's theological position. Eck answered immediately with a *Defense* (for the title, see *WA* 2, 699), to which Luther now refers. During the first week of November Luther worked on his rebuttal of this *Defense*. When this letter was written, the rebuttal had grown to six sheets. On November 7 it was completed: *Ad Iohannem Eccium M. Lutheri epistola . . .* (*Martin Luther's Letter to John Eck*) (Wittenberg: J. Grünenberg, November, 1519). *WA* 2, 700 ff. Some documents concerning the aftermath of the Disputation at Leipzig are available in *St. L.* 15, 1258 ff.

[6] Christopher Langenmantel, a canon at Freising, had attended the Diet of Augsburg in 1518 as a member of the delegation of Matthew Lang (see p. 99, n. 14) and supported Luther during the latter's interviews with Cardinal Cajetan (see p. 83). In the spring of 1519 he visited Electoral Saxony and renewed his acquaintance with Luther. See *WA*, Br 1, No. 113, Introduction.

[7] *The Second Lectures on the Psalms* (see p. 121, n. 7) was published in fascicles, each one containing several printed sheets. Each fascicle included one or two Psalm explanations. It was sold by the fascicle, but sometimes individual printed sheets could also be bought. See *WA*, Br 1, 371, n. 30; W. Maurer, *Von der Freiheit eines Christenmenschen. Zwei Untersuchungen zu Luthers Reformationsschriften* 1520/21 (Göttingen: Vandenhoeck and Ruprecht, 1949), pp. 109 ff., 159 ff.

45

To George Spalatin
Wittenberg, November 7, 1519

In connection with the reorganization of the University curriculum (see pp. 41 f., 82, 95 f.; p. 63, n. 23; p. 123, n. 4), Luther wonders about calling Matthew Adrian as professor of Hebrew to the University of Wittenberg. He comments once more on Eck's Defense (see p. 131, n. 5) and encloses his own reply to Eck. He also expresses his gratitude for a gift of venison.

On George Spalatin, see pp. 8 f.

Text in Latin: WA, Br 1, 551.

To my dearest friend in Christ, George Spalatin, a most blameless priest of God

Jesus

Greetings. Matthew Adrian,[1] a Jew from Louvain, has written to me, my Spalatin, as you will see from the [enclosed letter].[2] He was forced to leave there by their[3] tyranny and asks to teach Hebrew [at our University]. You know the fame and learnedness of this man. Therefore please bring to the attention of the Most Illustrious Sovereign[4] the gifts of God of a most distinguished opportunity to promote the study of Hebrew among us. I ask you

[1] Matthew Adrian, a Spanish Jew who was converted to Christianity, at first studied medicine, but later, upon the suggestion of John Reuchlin, he taught Hebrew in Tübingen, Basel, Heidelberg, Liege, and Louvain. Here, on March 21, 1519, he praised the three classical languages (Greek, Latin, and Hebrew) in a public lecture and demonstrated that a thorough knowledge of them was the absolute prerequisite for theological studies. This caused a fury among the traditionalists, especially with James Latomus (see p. 229, n. 3). As a result of their harassment, Adrian had to leave Louvain. In April, 1520, he was called to the University of Wittenberg as professor of Hebrew. In 1521 he was asked to resign, and he went to Leipzig, then later to Freiburg/Breisgau. His linguistic abilities were outstanding, but it seems that his personal conduct often caused him trouble (see p. 162). See WA, Br 1, 551, n. 1.

[2] This letter apparently is not extant.

[3] The traditionalists; see note 1.

[4] Elector Frederick; see pp. 49 f.

to reply as quickly as possible, so that I may give him an answer. His messenger is staying with me in the meantime. You see, he[5] thinks he heard an announcement of our Sovereign's death. May God prevent this for a long time! May that be a false omen!

I enclose Eck's nonsense, with my short reply.[6] I shall answer at greater length when he has totally betrayed himself[7] by that most impious hypocrisy of his.

Farewell, and pray for me. We thank the Most Illustrious Sovereign for the venison.

November 7, 1519 MARTIN LUTHER

46

To George Spalatin
Wittenberg, November 29, 1519

Luther describes the visit of a dignitary of the Teutonic Order. He disparages the approval given Eck by the University of Leipzig, touches briefly upon some of his publications, and extends thanks for a gift.

On George Spalatin, see pp. 8 f.

Text in Latin: WA, Br 1, 563-564.

To my friend in Christ, George Spalatin, a servant of God, a priest [and] a good and learned man

Jesus

Greetings. You have neatly handed back to me the task of marking the passages, which I had shoved at you.[1] You have won! Besides this, I thank you for the princely gift.[2]

---

[5] Adrian; because of this rumor he was eager to receive a commitment as soon as possible.

[6] See p. 131, n. 5.

[7] In his *Defense* (see note 6) Eck announced a work on the primacy of the papacy; Luther is anticipating this work. See *WA*, Br 1, 450, n. 3.

[1] It is not clear what Luther meant here; for a possible interpretation, see *WA*, Br 1, 564, n. 1; 557, n. 1.

[2] The nature of the gift cannot be established; perhaps it was some clothing or jewelry; see p. 121, n. 5.

I read a long time ago the printed nonsense the people of Leipzig had sent to Eck.[3] A most verbose treatise on the Eucharist is in the press.[4] Philip is pleased that he is urged by the Sovereign to wear his gift.[5]

The Count of Isenburg of the Teutonic Order[6] visited me for a night and a day; he had led those soldiers and conducted himself quite nobly. He requested me to greet you in his name. He had come here to see me. But listen to the "civility" of the gatekeeper of Wittenberg! He was drunk, and so he had closed the city gate at five o'clock. The Count, who arrived late, asked to be admitted to the town in the name of the Abbot of Zinna,[7] after he had asked in vain in his own name. [The gatekeeper], however—or rather the beer in him—shouted, "The Abbot of Zinna has never given me one single tip!"[8] What more do you want? The Count and two noblemen[9] were forced to dismount at the tavern outside the upper gate. I did not want to hide this story from you, so that you too can boast with us of this "courtesy"!

Farewell, and pray for me. Of course I don't care how you formulated the title of my *Tessaradecas*,[10] as long as it does not smell of arrogance; after all, the title itself is of little importance.

November 29, 1519 MARTIN LUTHER
Augustinian

---

[3] On July 25, 1519, the Theological Faculty of the University of Leipzig issued a proclamation (see *WA*, Br 1, 438 f.) in which Eck was announced as the victor of the disputation which had taken place between Eck, Karlstadt, and Luther in Leipzig (see p. 126). Spalatin must have written Luther about it.

[4] *Ein Sermon von dem hochwürdigen Sakrament des heiligen wahren Leichnams Christi und von den Bruderschaften* (*The Blessed Sacrament of the Holy and True Body of Christ, and the Brotherhoods*) (Wittenberg: J. Grünenberg, December, 1519). *WA* 2, 742 ff.; *LW* 35, 49 ff.

[5] Philip Melanchthon; see p. 77, n. 3. This may have been some jewelry or cloth given Melanchthon by Elector Frederick.

[6] William of Isenburg, or Eisenberg, had served the Teutonic Order in Prussia for many years and was the Order's grand-marshal from 1501 to 1514. At this point he was retiring from office and returning to his family estate in the Rhineland; he eventually introduced the Reformation there, and became deeply involved in the controversy with the Counter-Reformation. See *WA*, Br 1, 564, n. 5.

[7] On Benedict, the abbot of Zinna (1506-1536), see *WA*, Br 1, 564, n. 6.

[8] This quotation is written in German.

[9] Not known.

[10] In the summer of 1519 Luther wrote the *Tessaradecas consolatoria* (*The Fourteen of Consolation*). *WA* 6, 104 ff.; *PE* 1, 110 ff. This little book was intended to comfort the Elector if he should be sick or in low spirits. Spalatin

47

To John Lang
Wittenberg, December 18, 1519

Luther reports on one of the friars of the Erfurt monastery who is studying in Wittenberg. He discusses the publication of his Second Lectures on the Psalms, mentions his revision of the Sermon on Usury, and tells about an anonymous treatise from Bohemia which is circulating in Wittenberg. He comments at some length on the latest moves of his enemies (the Faculty of the University of Leipzig, Eck, Emser, and von Miltitz), and also gives some news of Wittenberg.

See Fife, pp. 368 ff.; Schwiebert, pp. 423 ff. On John Lang, see p. 14.

Text in Latin: WA, Br 1, 596-597.

To the Reverend Father John Lang, theologian, Augustinian at Erfurt,[1] district vicar,[2] my esteemed friend in the Lord

Jesus

Greetings. We shall do with the money of Friar Caesar[3] as you have written, Reverend Father. When the letter arrived, Caesar was not at home. It is up to you, however, whether he will stay here or not. You wrote previously that he would remain here until he would return to you as [Bible lecturer]. He is now attending theological lectures and studies solid books; I am only sorry that I cannot send all the friars into Philip's theological

was to translate it into German. Spalatin apparently wanted Luther's opinion on his version of the title. The book was available in German and Latin by the beginning of 1520.

1 See p. 6, n. 3.

2 See p. 61, n. 6.

3 John Caesar, or Kaiser, an Augustinian of Erfurt, had matriculated in the University of Wittenberg on May 22, 1518; see WA, Br 1, 416, n. 7. The Erfurt monastery sometimes sent friars to the University of Wittenberg; Luther, for instance, had been sent there for a year; see p. 5. On October 14, 1519, Caesar was graduated as Bachelor of Arts and began his theological studies. He was supposed to stay in Wittenberg until he could graduate as *cursor Bibliae*, or Bible lecturer (see p. 5), the first degree in a theological career; see WA, Br 1, 598, n. 2. All letters mentioned by Luther are not extant.

lectures on Matthew[4] at six o'clock in the morning. That little Greek scholar outdoes me even in theology itself.

I did not know you received the *Second Lectures on the Psalms*[5] twice, once from me and once from Philip. The other trivial publications[6] I believed would reach you without my effort. I am revising the *Sermon on Usury*[7] and will see to it that the true doctrine of Christ strikes home with a large number of people. I am sending all the other things.[8] Please provide us with the printed disputation as soon as possible.[9]

Eck threatens me,[10] Philip, Karlstadt,[11] our whole University, and even the Sovereign[12] himself with I don't know what kind of terrible things. He spat out some chaotic stuff in German against the Sovereign;[13] you would have thought Almighty God himself was speaking. It is good that such a sophist clashes with such a sovereign.

It pleases us that your people at Erfurt have abstained from

---

[4] Philip Melanchthon; see p. 77, n. 3. On this course, see *C.R.* 14, 531 ff.; O. Clemen (ed.), *Supplementa Melanchthoniana* (Leipzig: Heinsius Nachfolger, 1926 f.), 6, I, 80. "At six o'clock in the morning" and "friars" are missing in the manuscript copy (perhaps of the original) but were added in even the earliest printed editions, perhaps on the basis of the original, which is now missing.

[5] See p. 121, n. 7; p. 131, n. 7.

[6] It is not clear to what publications Luther refers.

[7] In November, 1519, Luther published *Ein [kleiner] Sermon von dem Wucher* (*A [Short] Sermon on Usury*) (Wittenberg: J. Grünenberg). *WA* 6, 3 ff. In December, 1519, he reworked this treatise and in January, 1520, he published it as *Ein [grosser] Sermon von dem Wucher* (*A [Long] Sermon on Usury*) (Wittenberg: J. Grünenberg). *WA* 6, 36 ff.; *LW* 45, 273 ff.; see also *LW* 45, 233 ff.

[8] Perhaps new fascicles of the *Second Lectures on the Psalms* (see p. 131, n. 7).

[9] Soon after the Disputation at Leipzig (see p. 126), the University of Leipzig and John Eck (see p. 80, n. 13) had asked the universities of Paris (see p. 258, n. 7) and Erfurt to decide on the victor and to establish whose teachings were dogmatically correct; see p. 134, n. 3. It is most probable that the minutes of the disputation were attached to these requests. Because of his connections with the University of Erfurt, Lang must have been able to copy these minutes, and apparently set out to publish them at once. Luther is now requesting a copy of this edition. For the bibliography and for the text of Lang's edition, see *WA* 2, 250 ff.

[10] John Eck; see p. 80, n. 13.

[11] Andrew Karlstadt; see p. 79, n. 12.

[12] Elector Frederick; see pp. 49 f.

[13] In his letter to the Elector of November 8, 1519; see *WA*, Br 1, No. 192, Document VI; *S-J* 1, 246 ff.

passing judgment.[14] Therefore the debate was in vain and the judgment of the Parisians is meaningless. As a result, by the grace of God an opportunity has opened for attacking the Roman Antichrist.[15]

A treatise is circulating here, supposedly written by a certain Bohemian; highly erudite, theological, and [written] in both languages, it is against the tyranny of the Roman Curia.[16]

I did not quite understand what you meant (when you wrote in Greek) that it was not without great effort on your part that the disputation [minutes] were sent back to Duke George,[17] and also why your theologians and lawyers were so highly disturbed.[18]

I shall not answer Emser[19] in a separate book because that great bungler not only affirms and grants everything I accuse him of, but he does not even touch the essential point of the case at all, raging only with insults. When the promised attack

---

[14] Luther was not sure, at this point, of the position the University of Erfurt would take on the Disputation at Leipzig; see note 9. He had written to Lang that the Leipzig Faculty was spreading the rumor that Erfurt had decided in favor of Eck; see *WA*, Br 1, 539. Lang, in turn, must have informed Luther that the University would not pass judgment. The University delayed announcing its decision until December 29, and then returned the case (including the minutes) to the court of Duke George (see p. 110, n. 20) in Leipzig; see *Akten und Briefe* 1, No. 149.

[15] See p. 114, n. 16.

[16] This treatise, perhaps written in German and Latin, or in Czech and Latin, cannot be identified.

[17] Lang must have urged the University of Erfurt not to pass judgment (see notes 9, 14) and obviously must have informed Luther of the result of his efforts, although the University delayed announcing this decision until December 29; see note 14. On Duke George, see p. 110, n. 20.

[18] This word is written in Greek.

[19] I.e., Emser's *A venatione Luteriana Aegocerotis assertio* (*Declaration Concerning Luther's Chasing of Goat Emser*) (Leipzig: M. Landsberg, November, 1519); this was already the fourth publication in a battle between Emser and Eck on the one side and Luther on the other. For details, see *WA* 2, 655 ff.; *PE* 3, 277 ff. Jerome Emser (1478-1527) was secretary and chaplain to Duke George of Saxony (see p. 110, n. 20). He had studied law and theology at the University of Tübingen and before he entered the service of Duke George he obtained his Master's degree from the University of Erfurt. After the Disputation at Leipzig he became one of the most violent and sarcastic opponents of Luther, and after 1520 he attacked almost all the major writings of the Reformer. Emser's coat of arms contained a he-goat; Luther clashed with this "goat of Leipzig" at various times, and his tone was equally biting. See *O.D.C.C.*, p. 450.

by Eck is published,[20] I shall answer him and Emser at the same time.

Charles Miltitz [21] is now in Torgau, now in Lochau,[22] busily trying to take me with him to Trier.[23] My enemies are strangely afraid; they try all kinds of maneuvers and act almost like madmen over the delay of my destruction. The bishops write to Rome against me.[24] What the future will bring even I myself do not know; if I receive a safe-conduct and a summons from the [Arch]bishop of Trier, perhaps I shall go to Trier.

The Reverend Father Vicar [25] is at Salzburg; he is well and honored there. He writes that Eck heedlessly courts prominent men; but his "unassuming" conduct displeases the bishop, Cardinal Lang.[26] Lotther from Leipzig is establishing a publishing house here, with type faces for printing in the three languages.[27] The University is prospering, especially the study of theology.[28] Leipzig is Leipzig, according to her custom.[29] I myself am terribly busy.

Farewell and pray for me.

Wittenberg, December 18, 1519

---

20 This was Eck's (see note 9) *Pro Hieronymo Emser contra malesanam Luteri venationem responsio* (*Reply in Behalf of Jerome Emser Against Luther's Mad Chase*) (Leipzig: M. Landsberg), signed on October 28, 1519. It was some time, however, before Luther had a copy. Apparently Luther did not give a special answer to these two writings.

21 Charles von Miltitz; see p. 97, n. 3.

22 These two cities were of major importance for the administration of Electoral Saxony. The Electoral court resided at Lochau. It seems that von Miltitz was trying to reach the Elector, whom he believed to be in either place; see *WA*, Br 1, 595, n. 1. For the discussions, see *St. L.* 15, 760 ff.

23 See pp. 108 f., 127 ff.

24 On December 8, 1519, von Miltitz wrote to the Elector that the Pope's patience with Luther was at an end, and that he (von Miltitz) was afraid that some bishops had informed the Curia how many people were being led astray by Luther's preaching and writing; see *WA*, Br 1, 598, n. 15. The correspondence with Rome could not be further identified.

25 John von Staupitz; see p. 64, n. 1; p. 72.

26 Matthew Lang; see p. 99, n. 14.

27 Melchior Lotther established his press in Wittenberg in the summer of 1519. The "three languages" were German, Latin, and Greek. The first book in Hebrew was not published in Wittenberg until 1523; see *WA*, Br 1, 383, n. 2. See also p. 19, n. 8.

28 For similar statements, see pp. 123, 125.

29 On the relationship between Leipzig and Wittenberg, see p. 63, n. 24.

May your new licentiates make good progress.[30] Amen. Greetings to Father Master Usingen.[31]

FRIAR MARTIN LUTHER
Augustinian

48

To Thomas Fuchs
Wittenberg, December 23, 1519

Because of the controversy on indulgences and his courageous opposition to clerical abuses, Luther became a champion for all who were unjustly treated by the clergy, or at least thought they were. This letter has to be seen in this light.

In this case the Bishop of Regensburg had requested one-third of all the donations and income of a certain pilgrimage chapel which had been built in 1519; to the best of our knowledge it had been constructed primarily with monies from private sources and not from the Bishop or the city. The city council, however, had doubts about the legal and moral grounds of the Bishop's request and sought the opinion of various authorities. Thomas Fuchs, representative of the Imperial government in the city of Regensburg, took it upon himself to ask Luther for advice; see WA, Br 1, 573. In his answer Luther suggests a peaceful Christian settlement.

On Luther's relation to German city officials, see H. J. Grimm, "The Relations of Luther and Melanchthon with the Townsmen," V. Vajta (ed.), Luther and Melanchthon (Philadelphia, 1961), pp. 32 ff.

Text in German: WA, Br 1, 599.

---

30 These licentiates could not be identified; on this degree, see p. 264, n. 3.
31 Bartholomew Arnoldi of Usingen, Luther's former teacher in Erfurt; see p. 30, n. 18. This last paragraph is omitted in some editions, although it appears in a manuscript copy (perhaps of the original) from which the editor of WA, Br took it.

To the courageous and honorable Sir Thomas Fuchs, knight at Schneeberg, representative of His Imperial Majesty[1] and of the Holy Roman Empire at Regensburg, etc., my special lord and patron

Jesus

Before all else, my humble prayer and wishes for the best in everything. Courageous, honorable, dear sir and friend: I have received and carefully studied your letter and question.[2] Having experienced at Augsburg your great faithfulness toward me,[3] I know that I am obliged to render every service to Your Honor and would like to answer this question correctly and clearly. I am motivated, of course, by the gospel, since in all such matters Christ gives a short statement of true counsel, saying, "If anyone would quarrel with you and sue you to take away your coat, let him have the cloak as well."[4] According to my responsibility as a theologian I can give you no other advice in this matter. No party among you will do justice to the gospel unless it permits the other to do what it wishes. Your legally appointed bishop[5] should let the city council have its way, and vice versa. His spiritual jurisdiction[6] is of no aid to the Bishop, as usage and custom do not help the city council, because the gospel stands above both. It is true, of course, that the pope has decreed that one-third of such an offering should go to the legally appointed bishop;[7] whether he has a right to do so is his own responsibility. It almost looks like selfishness; but we are obliged to suffer violence and injustice. Therefore it would be my counsel

---

[1] Charles V; see pp. 175 f.
[2] See the Introduction; for the text of the letter, see *WA*, Br 1, 573.
[3] During Luther's stay at Augsburg, 1518 (see pp. 70 f., 83 ff., 87 ff.); the circumstances are not known.
[4] Matt. 5:40 (Vulgate?).
[5] "Bishop" is written in Latin here and throughout the letter.
[6] This is the jurisdiction of the church (see also pp. 257 f.) as exercised by the priests, bishops, archbishops, and popes over other members of the hierarchy (who were subordinated to them), as well as over the laity, which was subjected to the spiritual and sometimes even worldly (i.e., territorial) rule of the church.
[7] For the papal decision, see *Decreti Secunda Pars*, causa X, ques. 1, cap. 7. *CIC* 1, 614.

and request that bishop and city council come to an agreement in a friendly way, without arguing, use of force, or help [of the law]. Maybe the Bishop can be prevailed upon to give in. But if not, they [8] have no right to refer [the case] to the Roman See.[9]

Take my considered opinion in good will and friendship, as coming from a theologian for whom it is not proper to advise strife and lawsuit but rather peace and patience. I am, of course, always ready to serve Your Honor.

Written at Wittenberg, December 23, 1519

FRIAR MARTIN LUTHER
Augustinian at Wittenberg

49

To George Spalatin
Wittenberg, December 31, 1519

In this letter Luther forwards a petition from the city council of Kemberg (one of the many letters of supplication he continually received) to Spalatin, who is to intervene with the Electoral government for any possible help. Luther also discusses the matter of a certain widow.

For similar letters, see Luther: Letters. LCC 18, 171 ff. On George Spalatin, see pp. 8 f.

Text in Latin: WA, Br 1, 604.

To the learned and honorable man, George Spalatin, chaplain to the Sovereign at Lochau,[1] my superior in Christ

---

[8] Both parties: the Bishop and the city council.

[9] Another way to translate this sentence would be: "But if they [the city councilors] cannot accomplish this, they have no legal basis for claiming [such offering] before the Roman See."

[1] On Lochau, see p. 138, n. 22.

Jesus

Greetings. My Spalatin, I am enclosing a petition from the city council of Kemberg[2] to the Sovereign,[3] in which they complain of being oppressed by taxes that are far too high. I ask your help in this matter, since you can do it without endangering yourself. Perhaps the Most Illustrious Sovereign will not wish to intervene in this whole affair and change the situation with an abrupt order (which is not necessary). In that case just help those people to understand that in this matter they have the Sovereign's good will and sympathy. For the people there are absolutely sucked dry by this extreme usury, and the situation gets worse every day because of the most evil example of sinning: both the priesthood and the services of the church, and also certain religious fraternities, are supported by these sacrilegious taxes and ungodly plunderings, which should not take place at all. You may be sure that you serve God and his will with the finest service if in this case you can accomplish something yourself and also accomplish anything at all with the Sovereign.

The widow is returning;[4] I myself have inspected her house, and I have seen that the canons are not disturbed without reason. It is something that can be expected in this case.

---

[2] Kemberg was a small town a few miles south of Wittenberg, with which Luther had many connections. His former student and colleague, Bartholomew Bernhardi, was provost there (see p. 115, n. 21); while returning from Augsburg on October 31, 1518, Luther celebrated mass in Kemberg (see pp. 87, 93; Schwiebert, p. 355); and he also preached there on various occasions (see p. 148). During the Christmas season of 1519 he preached a sermon there which later became part of his [*Long*] *Sermon on Usury* (see p. 136, n. 7); see Schwiebert, p. 443.

[3] Elector Frederick; see pp. 49 f.

[4] A certain Walpurga Landmann, who caused Luther quite a few headaches; see pp. 148, 162, 172. She had willed her house to the All Saints' Chapter of the Castle Church in Wittenberg, but suddenly wanted to change her will and retain the house for herself or her widowed sister. The canons of the chapter claimed the house, arguing that a will is identical with a gift. They were willing, however, to pay the yearly sum of fourteen gulden to the widow until her death (on the gulden, see p. 11, n. 2). She had approached Luther for help, and he, in turn, had asked Spalatin for help; see *WA*, Br 1, 555, n. 1. Luther is now reporting on his own investigation.

Our Hess[5] would have sent the *Method of Investigating Heretics*[6] to Crotus[7] in Italy if you had returned it.

Farewell for now. I am terribly busy right now and at the same time completely overwhelmed by trials.[8]

Wittenberg, December 31, 1519

MARTIN LUTHER
Augustinian

50

To George Spalatin Wittenberg, January 14, 1520

Soon after Luther had attacked the Roman Curia, he was linked with the Bohemian reformer John Huss (1369?-1415; see O.D.C.C., pp. 667 f.), who had been burned as a heretic. The Hussites insisted that contrary to the practice of the church in the West, the Lord's Supper must be celebrated "sub utraque speciei," or with "both kinds," that is, both elements of the Lord's Supper must be given to the communicant. In December, 1519, Luther published

[5] John Hess (1490-1547), known as the Reformer of Breslau, studied theology in Wittenberg from 1510 to 1513 and became friends with Luther and Lang. He was deeply interested in Humanism and for a while studied in Italy, where he struck up a friendship with Crotus Rubeanus (see note 7). On his return in 1519 he stayed in Wittenberg again. In 1523 he was called as a pastor to Breslau, where he introduced the Reformation. Although Hess was basically a Humanist, he was able, like Melanchthon, to understand Luther and co-operate with him. In later years in Silesia he curbed the enthusiasts, especially Schwenckfeld.

[6] A satire on the treatment of people accused of heresy; for the complicated bibliography of this pamphlet, see *WA*, Br 1, 604, n. 1.

[7] Crotus Rubeanus (the Humanistic name of John Jäger) (1480?-1539) was a famous Humanist of Erfurt who had supported Reuchlin (see p. 9) and was one of the major contributors to the *Epistolae obscurorum virorum* (*Letters of Obscure Men*); see *O.D.C.C.*, p. 459. From 1517 to 1519 he was in Italy, where he met Hess. Returning to Erfurt he was elected president of the University in 1520 and openly expressed his sympathy for Luther, whom he officially welcomed to Erfurt during the latter's trip to Worms. After 1521, however, he retreated from Luther and finally accepted a canonry in Halle in 1531 from the Archbishop of Mainz. The Reformers denounced him for this action. He died in Halle shortly after 1539.

[8] See p. 28, n. 10.

a treatise on the Eucharist (see p. 134, n. 4) in which he suggested following the practice of the early church in distributing both elements to the communicant. He was charged at once with being a Bohemian and an heir of Huss's thought. Reporting in this letter on his own life and family background, Luther establishes the fact that he had no connection with the Bohemian people.

On George Spalatin, see pp. 8 f.

Text in Latin: WA, Br 1, 610-612.

To Mr. George Spalatin [1]

Jesus

Greetings. My Spalatin, I am very happy and thank God that my case has progressed to the point that, other charges having been dismissed, they accuse me now because of my stand on "both kinds" [in the sacrament] and because of my ancestry.[2] For the sake of the great mercy of Christ which has been shown to me, a worthless creature, I hope that I shall not [now] perish on account of some great and weighty view, for example, [concerning] free will, grace, and the keys of the church.[3] For it seems that my enemies have given up hope of trapping me in these important points, since they now search out such ridiculous things. Just as

[1] This heading is missing in the manuscript copy of this letter but can be found in some of the oldest printed editions.

[2] Even before Luther had published the treatise on the Eucharist in December, 1519 (see the Introduction), he was accused of following Hussite teachings. This treatise (written in German), however, caused this charge to be widespread among the people, since its front page was decorated with a woodcut depicting two monstrances. Popular propaganda seized this at once to spread the statement that Luther maintained the doctrine of the Lord's Supper held by the Bohemian party known as Utraquists. In addition Luther's birth was questioned; his mother, it was rumored, conceived him under peculiar circumstances, etc. See *WA*, Br 1, 608, n. 2. Thus Luther was linked with those Bohemians involved in the Hussite wars. These slanderous rumors became rather dangerous when, on December 27, 1519, Duke George of Saxony (see p. 110, n. 20) wrote an official letter to Elector Frederick, accusing Luther of being a Bohemian. The Duke sent a similar letter to the Council of Regency, demanding that it put an end to Luther's Hussite agitation. For the letters, see *Akten und Briefe* 1, No. 146.

[3] On free will and grace, see pp. 25 f., 40, 53 f., 156 ff.; on the keys of the church, see p. 85, n. 15.

Christ was crucified because of the title "King of the Jews,"[4] so I too [am crucified] because of [my stand on] "both kinds" [in the sacrament], which I have never commanded to be received [thus] or prohibited, just as the schoolmen themselves also have taught.

Concerning my family background, no one can give more trustworthy information than the counts of Mansfeld.[5] I believe that these nobles have enough of a name and authority in the Empire to deserve to be believed on this subject. I suspect that this story about my family background was cooked up by the Leipzig theologian Ochsenfurt;[6] in order to spy on us, he also had pretended that Eck had been killed.[7] He is a man who cannot stand peace, either for himself or for others, is always ready to inflict harm—most wretched and yet feeble. I was born, by the way, at Eisleben,[8] and baptized there in St. Peter's Church.[9] I do not remember this, but I believe my parents and the folks at home. My parents moved there from [a place] near Eisenach. Nearly all my kinfolk are at Eisenach, and I am known there and recognized by them even today, since I went to school there for four years,[10] and there is no other town in which I am better known. I hope the people there would not have been so stupid that any one of them would call the son of Luther "nephew," another "uncle," another "cousin' (I have many of them there), had they known that my father and my mother were Bohemians or other such people, rather than those born in their midst. The rest of my life I spent in school[11] and in the monastery at Erfurt[12] until I came

---

4 Matt. 27:37.

5 One of them was Count Albrecht to whom Luther dedicated the *Wartburg Postil;* see p. 337, n. 1.

6 All during 1519 and 1520 Luther and Jerome Dungersheim of Ochsenfurt were battling each other. Dungersheim (1465-1540) had studied theology at the University of Leipzig and had received his Master of Arts degree there in 1489. After some advanced theological work at Cologne, he began teaching in Leipzig shortly after 1496. His controversy with Luther was stirred up by the Leipzig Disputation (see p. 126).

7 John Eck; see p. 80, n. 13. The circumstances are not known.

8 November 10, 1483.

9 November 11, 1483, St. Martin's Day (in memory of Martin, bishop of Tours; see *O.D.C.C.*, p. 864).

10 The years 1498-1501. See Fife, pp. 24 ff.

11 The years 1501-1505.

12 From July, 1505, on; see p. 3.

to Wittenberg.[13] I was also in Magdeburg for one year at the age of fourteen.[14]

Now you know my life and family. I would prefer, however, to be silent about [my background], just as Christ was silent when accused before Herod and Annas,[15] so that these furious people believe something which is worthy of them, until they finally blush. This is a generation which isn't moved by either song or mourning,[16]—in which it is vain to look for a man to help them.

This very hour I have received your letter about Charles Miltitz; you write that he swore he has not seen me.[17] Why then did he say to the barber Andrew, who was his traveling companion as far as Pretisch[18] (as Andrew currently boasts around here), that he had seen me and had raised up against me I don't know what terrible things? But let them lie, invent things, and be as clever as they please. Everything is against me, and I only wish something would quickly happen to free me from the obligation to lecture and teach,[19] for I desire nothing as much as this, as far as it is up to me. But if I have to continue teaching, my Spalatin, I do not understand your advice[20] and that of your friends (whom you mentioned) that sacred theology could be taught without offending the prelates. Scripture most powerfully attacks the abuse of holy things, which the prelates cannot bear to hear.

I have surrendered and made myself available [to them] in the name of the Lord;[21] his will be done. Who asked him to make

---

13 Winter semester, 1508/09, for the first time; spring, 1511, permanently.

14 In 1497/98 Luther attended school in Magdeburg; see Fife, pp. 20 f.

15 Luke 23:6-12; John 19:9.

16 See Matt. 11:16-17.

17 On one of his trips (see p. 138) von Miltitz (see p. 97, n. 3) must have passed through Wittenberg and tried to see Luther. He must have been unsuccessful; probably to gain prestige, however, he boasted to the contrary. Another possibility is that he actually saw Luther but accomplished nothing; then, to make up for it, he told a different story to the barber. This second interpretation is suggested by Luther's question: Why did von Miltitz boast? Either he lied to Spalatin or to the barber, or the barber lied.

18 Andrew Engelhard, a barber, physician, farmer, "hardware" store owner, and one of the wealthiest citizens of Wittenberg (see *WA*, Br 1, 612, n. 9), must have accompanied von Miltitz to Pretisch, a small village on the Elbe not far from Wittenberg.

19 For similar statements, see pp. 232, 274.

20 When Spalatin gave this advice is not known. For Luther's reply, see pp. 103 f.

21 Luther does not make it clear to whom he has surrendered (*tradere*) and

me a doctor [of theology]?[22] If he has made me one, then he must have his reasons; if he is sorry that he has made [me a doctor], then let him destroy his work again. This tribulation does not frighten me at all, but it blows up the sails of my heart with an incredible wind, so that I experience within myself the reason demons are compared to winds in Scripture.[23] While they wear themselves out by their raging, they but strengthen others with suffering. My only concern is that the Lord be merciful to me in those matters which are between me and him. Please help me in this as you can [with your prayers].

Let us, therefore, commit the affairs of men to God in faithful prayer, and be calm. What can they do? Will they kill [me]? Will they revive [me] again in order to kill [me] again?[24] Will they brand [me] a heretic? Christ was condemned with the wicked, with the seducers and cursed men.[25] Whenever I meditate on the Lord's Passion, I really burn to think that my tribulation is not only considered to be "something" by such prominent people, and so many, but even a most important "something," when in reality it is just nothing.[26] We are completely unaccustomed to suffering and evil, that is, to the Christian life. Therefore let it be; the more powerfully they[27] rise up, the more securely I laugh at them. I am determined to fear nothing in this and defy every-

---

made himself available (*offere*). He could mean a surrender to God's will or making himself available to his enemies. The latter possibility is suggested by Luther's use of *offere,* which at that time he generally used to mean making himself available or presenting himself to his enemies; see p. 74, n. 7.

[22] On Luther's understanding of his office as a doctor of theology, see p. 49, n. 23.

[23] Perhaps Luther was thinking of Eph. 2:2.

[24] Luther means that men can kill a person only once and that their power is hence very limited. Or perhaps he was thinking of the following: the Council of Constance (1414-1418; see *O.D.C.C.*, pp. 333 f.), which had sentenced John Huss to be burned at the stake, condemned John Wycliffe (1329?-1384; see *O.D.C.C.*, pp. 1480 f.) and ordered his bones to be dug up and burned. When Luther wrote "revive again," he may have been thinking of this event, asserting that if he too were killed, it would be of course impossible to revive him and kill him a second time, even though his corpse could be desecrated.

[25] Mark 15:28.

[26] For similar statements, see pp. 75, 91.

[27] Luther does not make it clear to whom or to what this refers: his enemies, or the suffering and evil?

thing. If I were not afraid of involving the Sovereign,[28] I would publish a courageous defense to provoke those furies even more and to ridicule their silly rage against me.

Regarding the widow,[29] I shall talk to you personally.

I have told Philip[30] and also read to him what you wrote.

You are not correct in blaming the Provost of Kemberg;[31] the fault is Master Spalatin's. I asked you the previous day whether or not the Sovereign would stay over Sunday. You answered that you didn't know. After that, no one told me anything about the sermon.[32] On the other hand I had already promised the Provost long before to visit him on that day and preach to his people. It seemed to me that this promise should be kept, since no other obligation prevented me from doing so. In any case I think there is no danger involved because of the distance between the two places.[33]

Farewell and pray for me.

January 14, 1520

MARTIN LUTHER
Augustinian

51

To John Lang
Wittenberg, January 26, 1520

In sending Lang the explanation of his December, 1519, treatise on the Eucharist, Luther discusses the slanderous remarks made by his enemies about his family background. He comments briefly

[28] Elector Frederick; see pp. 49 f.

[29] Most likely this is a reference to Walpurga Landmann; see p. 142, n. 4.

[30] Philip Melanchthon; see p. 77, n. 3; the circumstances are not known, since Spalatin's letter is not extant.

[31] Bartholomew Bernhardi; see p. 115, n. 21.

[32] Spalatin had accompanied the Elector to a meeting in Zerbst which began on January 8; see *WA*, Br 1, 608, n. 1. On the way they passed through Wittenberg, and Luther was to preach in their presence on a Sunday; the editor of the *WA*, Br suggests that this was January 8 and that the question was whether or not the Elector would still be in Wittenberg then. On the other hand Luther had promised to preach in Kemberg on that Sunday. On Luther's preaching in Kemberg, see p. 142, n. 2.

[33] This statement is not clear; perhaps Luther is referring to some remarks he made in his sermon in Kemberg.

on various documents dealing with his case, especially a letter of Erasmus to the Archbishop of Mainz. He also reports on a new way of publishing and selling his works on the Psalms and mentions a banquet for the Spanish ambassador which he and Melanchthon had attended.

On John Lang, see p. 14.

Text in Latin: WA, Br 1, 619.

To the Reverend Father John Lang, Master of Sacred Theology, vicar of the Eremites of St. Augustine at Erfurt,[1] my superior in the Lord

Jesus

Greetings. We have nothing new, my Reverend Father, for you have seen *The Unlearned Canons.*[2] We shall publish the German *Defense* from Nürnberg[3] if we can, in view of the lack of time. I am sending the explanation of my treatise on the Eucharist;[4] it is directed against the wickedness of the people of Leipzig; they are spreading the rumor that I was born in Bohemia with such assurance that they even persuaded the courts of sovereigns. They have won Duke George, taken him in tow, and make him extremely hostile toward me.[5] In fact it is said he has threatened [the Augustinians at] Dresden with expulsion because of me.[6]

---

[1] See p. 6, n. 3.

[2] *Canonici indocti* (*The Unlearned Canons*), a polemical pamphlet published by John Oecolampadius (see p. 230, n. 14) in 1519, in which he refuted Eck's (see p. 80, n. 13) accusation that only the unlearned members of the less important cathedral chapters sided with Luther; for more details, see *WA*, Br 1, 609, n. 5.

[3] *Schutzrede und Christliche Antwort* (*Defense and Christian Answer*) (Wittenberg: M. Lotther, 1520). The author was Lazarus Spengler (see p. 184) of Nürnberg, who defended Luther's 1519 treatise on the Eucharist (see p. 134, n. 4) and Luther himself against charges of Bohemianism; see p. 144, n. 2.

[4] *Verklärung etlicher Artikel* (*Explanation of Some Articles*) (Wittenberg: J. Grünenberg, 1520). *WA* 6, 78 ff. This is Luther's defense of his 1519 treatise on the Eucharist; see p. 134, n. 4.

[5] Luther means that the Faculty of Leipzig (see p. 63, n. 24), and Eck, gained the upper hand over Duke George (see p. 110, n. 20) and duped him. And in this he was right; see p. 144, n. 2.

[6] This statement—or rumor—was based on the following: Duke George (see note 5) wrote to his chancellor Doctor John Kochel that he had found out that the Augustinians of Dresden (which was within his territory) were

The *Second Lectures on the Psalms*[7] will be published in a new way, since the printer has suffered a loss because of the many printed sheets he still has left.[8] In addition it eventually will be published in a more distinguished type face by Lotther's press.[9]

Some people have in hand a magnificent letter of Erasmus to the Cardinal of Mainz. [Erasmus] is quite concerned about me [in this letter] (perhaps it will be published sometime) and protects me quite nobly, yet in his usual skilful way, which is to defend me strongly while seeming not to defend me at all.[10]

The Ambassador of the Spaniards is staying with our Sovereign.[11] I and Philip[12] dined[13] with him yesterday; it was a

---

reading Wycliffe's and Huss's books; if they dared to follow the Augustinians of Wittenberg, then he would replace them with other friars; see *Akten und Briefe* 1, Nos. 264 f.

[7] Luther's *Second Lectures on the Psalms;* see p. 131, n. 7.

[8] From this time on Luther published this work in a way that can be compared to the modern subscription system: the buying of a first fascicle meant the purchase of the whole work; therefore the sale of the first fascicle could serve as a basis for estimating how many of the following fascicles should be printed. To the best of our knowledge, Luther's *Second Lectures on the Psalms* and Karlstadt's edition of Augustine's *On the Spirit and the Letter* (see p. 54, n. 7) were the first books ever published this way.

[9] The *Second Lectures on the Psalms* were being published by John Grünenberg, who had only old and undistinguished type faces; see p. 19, n. 8. It seems, however, that Lotther never published the edition Luther envisions.

[10] Erasmus to Cardinal Albrecht of Mainz: October 19, 1519. Allen 4, 1033; S-*J* 1, 238 ff. Erasmus stated in this letter that although he was not familiar with Luther's writings, he thought that Luther was being treated unfairly. He demanded a fair trial for the Reformer and made the corruption within the Roman church responsible for Luther's attacks on Rome. Then he stated that this corruption was the reason that both Humanistic studies and Luther were suffering. In a "skilful way" he disassociated himself from Luther, directing attention to the importance of Humanistic studies and the ignorance and ill will of those who attacked all good men. Luther realized only too well that this letter was not particularly concerned with him. Ulrich von Hutten (see p. 163, n. 1), the carrier of this letter to the addressee, published it at once; he wanted to demonstrate Erasmus' positive attitude toward Luther. During the summer of 1520 many editions of this letter appeared all over Germany (Cologne, Wittenberg, Nürnberg) in an attempt to stamp Erasmus either as a member of the Reformation camp (by the idealistic adherents of the Reformation) or as a heretic (the goal of members of the Roman opposition).

[11] The Imperial ambassador Jerome Brunner visited Elector Frederick (see pp. 49 f.) in Zerbst (see p. 148, n. 32) and returned with him to Lochau via Wittenberg; on January 25 the Electoral party stayed in Wittenberg.

[12] Philip Melanchthon; see p. 77, n. 3.

[13] The earliest printed editions offer *certavimus,* "we struggled," which makes little sense. The manuscript copy reads *coenavimus,* "we dined."

splendid party! You will soon see in print the address [14] Philip delivered yesterday.

Farewell and pray for me.

January 26, 1520

Greet the Reverend Father, Master Bartholomew Usingen,[15] and Nathin,[16] and all the others.

FRIAR MARTIN LUTHER

52

To George Spalatin
Wittenberg, about February 14, 1520[1]

Luther soon realized that one of the major shortcomings in the church of his time was the comparative lack of a thorough knowledge of Scripture, on the part of both clergy and laity. Therefore beginning in the winter of 1519 he worked on a series of sermons which were to explain the Gospels and Epistles for each Sunday of the church year. In this letter he encloses a sample of this work. Realizing the uproar the Bohemian charge against him had caused, Luther emphasizes his good conscience and the confidence in which he entrusts everything to God. He is very surprised to find that many of his thoughts are the same as Huss's.

On Luther's concern for bringing the message of the church to the people, see p. 113, n. 10. On George Spalatin, see pp. 8 f.

Text in Latin: WA, Br 2, 41-42.

To my dearest friend George Spalatin, beloved in Christ

---

[14] O. Clemen (ed.), *Supplementa Melanchthoniana,* 6, I, 87 ff. According to Spalatin's information, Melanchthon's address dealt with the differentiation between true and Scholastic theology; see WA, Br 1, 620, n. 9.
[15] Bartholomew Arnoldi of Usingen; see p. 30, n. 18.
[16] John Nathin; see p. 6, n. 2.
[1] On the dating of this letter, see WA, Br 2, No. 254, Introduction.

Jesus

Greetings. I am sending a sample of the Gospels and Epistles.[2] It may show that I have been extremely busy—yet the work has not fulfilled my expectations. This matter demands a man's complete attention (as I see); therefore I am almost sorry that I began it.

I have consulted friends in regard to writing our Sovereign [3] for advice. I realize that [this time] it is impossible for me to offer peace or have it offered in my name without endangering respect.[4] Up to now I have offered enough,[5] and I stand alone. I have always been dragged into this affair, and now it is not right to withdraw as long as Eck [6] keeps shouting. I [7] have to entrust this affair to God and let myself be led, yielding the ship to the winds and waves. I can do only one thing, that is, to ask God for mercy.[8]

I have heard that there will be some tremendous uproar in the future if God will not restrain Satan.[9] I am aware of Satan's fiendish plans for my ruin and the ruin of many others. What do you want? God's word [10] can never be handled without causing

---

[2] Sermons on portions of the Epistles and Gospels read at mass on Sundays in accordance with the prescribed order of the church year. On February 8, 1520, Luther reported to Spalatin that he was working on a series of sermons to cover the period from Advent to Easter; see *WA*, Br 2, 36. Spalatin must then have asked for a sample, which Luther is now sending. See also pp. 237 ff.

[3] Elector Frederick; see pp. 49 f. The manuscript copy of this letter added "our" to "friends," but then shows it crossed out.

[4] Luther wrote *pietatis*, which can also mean piety or godliness. Spalatin must have suggested that Luther ask for the Elector's mediation in some dispute; it could not be established, however, between whom the Elector was to mediate. Luther and Eck? Luther and Duke George?

[5] For Luther's offers, see p. 74, n. 7; pp. 97 ff., 127 ff., 246. In letters of February 4, 1520, to the Bishop of Merseburg and Cardinal Albrecht of Mainz, Luther had again expressed his willingness to listen to the judgment of the church and had asked to be shown where he erred. For the letters, see *WA*, Br 2, 24 ff.; *S-J* 1, 281 f.

[6] John Eck; see p. 80, n. 13.

[7] At this point the printed editions read *enim*, i.e., "for" or "namely," which is missing in the manuscript copy.

[8] For similar statements, see pp. 162, 183, 194.

[9] Luther may be referring to some rumors about further hostile actions—perhaps on the part of Duke George; see p. 149, n. 6.

[10] Literally: "word of godliness."

storm, tumult, and danger.[11] The word is of an infinite majesty, accomplishes great things, is wonderful in high and lofty matters;[12] as the prophet says, "It kills the fat ones in Israel and checks her chosen men." [13] Therefore in this affair one has either to abandon the desire for peace and quietness, or one has to deny the word [of God]. The war is the Lord's, who did not come to bring peace.[14] Therefore give up the hope of advancing Christ's cause on earth in peace and pleasantness, since you can see that Christ has fought with his own blood, and all the martyrs after him.

I have taught and held all the teachings of John Huss, but thus far did not know it.[15] John Staupitz [16] has taught it in the same unintentional way. In short we all are Hussites and did not know it. Even Paul and Augustine are in reality Hussites. See the monstrous things into which we fall, I ask you, even without the Bohemian leader and teacher. I am so shocked that I do not know what to think when I see such terrible judgments of God over mankind, namely, that the most evident evangelical truth was burned in public and [17] was already considered condemned more than one hundred years ago. Yet one is not allowed to avow this.[18] Woe to this earth.

Farewell. MARTIN LUTHER

---

[11] For similar statements, see pp. 104, 146.
[12] Ps. 93:4 (Vulgate).
[13] Ps. 78:31 (Vulgate).
[14] Matt. 10:34.
[15] During the Disputation at Leipzig (see p. 126), Luther was visited by a member of the Hussite church in Bohemia. Having told his visitor he wanted to read something by Huss, Luther received a copy of Huss's *De ecclesia* (*On the Church*) on October 3, 1519 (see *O.D.C.C.*, pp. 667 ff.). The result of Luther's study of this book by Huss is the statement: "We all are Hussites and did not know it." See p. 155, n. 7.
[16] John von Staupitz; see p. 64, n. 1.
[17] The manuscript copy of this letter reads *et* ("and") which was later changed to *pro*, i.e., "for."
[18] The fact that John Huss, whom Luther now had discovered to be a teacher of evangelical truth, was condemned by the Council of Constance and burned at the stake on July 6, 1415.

53

To George Spalatin
Wittenberg, March 19, 1520

Luther discusses the calling of a professor of Hebrew. He also comments on the publication of a work by Huss, and on "signs" in the sky.

On George Spalatin, see pp. 8 f.

Text in Latin: WA, Br 2, 72.

To the venerable Mr. George Spalatin, servant of Christ, court chaplain, etc., my dearest friend in Christ

Jesus

Greetings. I thought you had written Doctor Kopp,[1] my Spalatin, about the Most Illustrious Sovereign's[2] decision concerning Werner.[3] Therefore I admonished Kopp in a letter[4] to speed the man's arrival here. You will see what he answers.

---

[1] Gregory Kopp of Kalbe (one of the house physicians of Cardinal Albrecht of Mainz; see pp. 44 f.) studied in Wittenberg and Frankfurt/Oder. Kopp had recommended to Spalatin Werner Einhorn of Bacharach as instructor of Hebrew for the University of Wittenberg; see *WA*, Br 2, 50, n. 6. On February 24, 1520, the University was to decide on Einhorn's call (see *WA*, Br 2, 48). The University must have invited him to come for an interview since Luther mentions a letter in which he urged Kopp to speed Einhorn's arrival in Wittenberg. Einhorn was third on a list of candidates (Keller, see p. 123, n. 5; Adrian, see p. 132, n. 1). At this point the University was stalling with regard to Adrian to take a look at Einhorn; see p. 160. It is not known whether Einhorn ever followed this invitation to come to Wittenberg.

[2] Elector Frederick; see pp. 49 f.

[3] Werner Einhorn of Bacharach, a convert from Judaism to Christianity, was an instructor of Hebrew. Little is known of his life. He had matriculated in Erfurt in 1518, in Tübingen in February, 1523, and in Ingolstadt in April, 1523, and there he apparently was employed to teach for three years. In the fall of 1523 he reported a fellow faculty member to the Inquisition. It seems that in various heresy trials he served as a crown witness for the Inquisition; see *WA*, Br 2, 50, n. 6. Perhaps these strong leanings toward the traditional forces within the church prevented Einhorn from accepting the invitation to Wittenberg.

[4] This letter is not extant.

I am sending [the work] of the asses of Louvain and Cologne,[5] which I am now answering in print.[6] Read John Huss's [book],[7] too, if you wish, and return it when you have read it. Not only does the work please all people, but its spirit and learnedness are wonderful. Two thousand copies have been printed by Thomas Anshelm.

It is said that you have new books, like the one about the flames and fires that were seen in the sky over Vienna.[8] I would like to take a look at those books. Perhaps my tragedy too is contained in them, as it was in former [signs].[9]

Farewell and pray for me.

Wittenberg, March 19, 1520 MARTIN LUTHER
Augustinian

---

[5] After Luther's Latin works had been reprinted in February, 1519 (see p. 110, n. 16), the theologians of the University of Louvain collected certain of Luther's statements which they branded as heresy and sent to the University of Cologne. On August 30, 1519, the University of Cologne condemned Luther, and on November 7, 1519, Louvain did the same. Both universities sent their verdicts to the Inquisitor for Aragon and Navarre, Cardinal Adrian, bishop of Tortosa (who in 1522 became Pope Adrian VI; see *O.D.C.C.*, p. 601). In February, 1520, this material was published by Dirk Martens in Louvain. Luther is now sending it to Spalatin; it is not clear, however, whether he is sending a manuscript copy which he obtained in a way unknown to us, or a copy of the Martens edition.

[6] *Responsio Lutheriana ad condemnationem doctrinalem per magistros nostros Lovanienses et Colonienses factam* (*Martin Luther's Reply to the Doctrinal Condemnation Issued by the Faculties of Louvain and Cologne*) (Wittenberg: M. Lotther, 1520). *WA* 6, 181 ff.

[7] John Huss, *De ecclesia* (*On the Church*) (Hagenau: T. Anshelm, 1520). See p. 153, n. 15. For the text and bibliography, see S. H. Thomson (ed.), *Magistri Johannis Huss, Tractatus De Ecclesia* (University of Colorado Press, 1956).

[8] For these meteorological "signs" and a bibliography of books dealing with them, see *WA*, Br 2, 73, n. 6.

[9] Perhaps Luther is thinking of the lightning near Stotternheim which terrified him and was partially responsible for his vow to enter a monastery if St. Anne would protect him from the storm. See Bainton, pp. 21 f.

54

To George Spalatin
Wittenberg, April 13, 1520[1]

In response to a request by Spalatin, Luther explains John 15:5, and distinguishes between his understanding of it and that found in Scholastic theology.

On George Spalatin, see pp. 8 f.

Text in Latin: WA, Br 2, 80-82.

Mr. George Spalatin

Jesus

Greetings. I have received the question, my Spalatin, which you have asked about the meaning of Christ's word in John 15 [:5], "Without me you can do nothing."

To begin with, I think you know the two discerptions (I meant to say *distinctions*)[2] of our teachers[3] which were taught about this passage. The first one of these is: God's "influence" is of two kinds, general and specific. They understand this as follows: through the "general influence" we are able to do those things which nature is able to do without grace. They consider such things to be neither meritorious nor sinful but rather neutral, or morally good works, such as walking, standing, working, praying,

[1] The autograph is undated; on the date, see note 17 and *WA*, Br 2, No. 277, Introduction.

[2] *Distinctio*, i.e., a subdivision in the arguments of the schoolmen about a certain statement, or thought, differentiating between certain opinions concerning it.

[3] Luther, of course, generalized here. For the Scholastic opinions on this subject, which one may assume Luther had studied, see, e.g., Peter Lombard, *Sentences*, II, dist. XXIV, cap. 1; XXV, 5; XXVI, 1; XXVII, 4; William of Occam, *Commentary on the Sentences of Peter Lombard*, IV, ques. 8, 9; II, ques. 19 A; I, ques. 17, 2 E; Gabriel Biel, *Commentary on the Sentences of Peter Lombard*, II, dist. XXVI, cap. 9. The classical formulation of this thought was given by Thomas Aquinas, *Summa Theologica*, I, ques. 1; ques. 2, art. 2; II, 1, ques. 109-114. See also A. M. Fairweather (ed.), *Aquinas on Nature and Grace. LCC* 11, 35 ff., 137 ff. For general information, see *O.D.C.C.*, pp. 576 f.; E. Gilson, *Reason and Revelation in the Middle Ages* (New York, 1954).

eating, and whatever else we see done externally by people which is not plainly wrong. Through the "specific influence" we are enabled to do those things which are [done in the realm] of grace, and are beyond [the capability of] nature; that is to say, only by this influence can we do meritorious works, and avoid sin. Consequently the "general influence" pertains to being and activity [in the realm] of nature,[4] while the "specific influence" pertains to being and activity [in the realm] of grace.[5]

Now follows the second *distinction*: there is a difference between an action which begins something[6] and an action which is completed.[7] The action which begins something pertains to the realm of the "general influence," the action which is completed pertains to the realm of the "specific influence."[8]

When it is said, "You can do nothing without me,"[9] it means in this context that without the "specific influence" we can do nothing perfectly. Of course on the basis of the "general influence" we can indeed do something which as a "beginning action" is good.[10] This means that on the basis of the "general influence" we can prepare ourselves by our own strength for receiving grace (or the "specific influence") so that we may do something meritorious; we cannot, however, do something meritorious in itself by this "[general] influence" and by our own strength. This is the way this passage has been understood and explained so far.

Christ totally rejects, however, the "general influence," or the natural existence, because nature cannot but seek that which is its own and [thus] abuse the gifts of God. Christ declares simply and without *distinction* that without the "specific" (as [the schoolmen] call it) "influence"—or the grace of God—nothing can be done that in the eyes of God is not worthy [only] of fire. And

---

[4] *Esse et operari naturae,* i.e., natural existence, or existence not exposed to the infusion of the grace of God.

[5] *Esse et operari gratiae,* i.e., existence exposed to the infusion of the grace of God, the specific influence.

[6] *Inchoative . . . facere.*

[7] *Perfective facere.*

[8] Compare Luther's report on the Scholastic argumentation with Thomas Aquinas' *Summa Theologica,* I, ques. 1, arts. 1-6; II, 1, ques. 109-111, 113, arts. 2-5, 7-8. *LCC* 11, 35 ff.; 137 ff., 169 ff., 185 ff., 193 ff.

[9] John 15:5.

[10] See note 6.

so [Christ] goes on to say, "Whoever does not abide in me will be thrown away like a branch and will wither and people will gather it up and throw it into the fire and it will burn."[11] Now see, the branch which is not in Christ not only does not grow and bring fruit, but it also withers (that is, weakens and perishes); not only does it weaken and wither, but it is also taken and cut off from the vine and thrown into the fire, etc. In this way he who is only supported by the "general influence" and the strength of nature continuously gets worse and farther away from Christ; he is being prepared for the fire, no matter how much he outwardly appears to be moral and to do good.

Here we should realize that we cannot do anything without Christ, either through a "general" or a "specific influence." [We should see that] whatever is done only on the basis of the "general influence," however outstanding it may be, is rather against Christ than for Christ; this becomes obvious enough in the case of hypocrites, who do great and many things but do them with the worst motivation.

As a result, Christ reminds [us] with such earnestness that the branches should remain in him as in a vine. It is impossible for them not to become continuously worse if they do not remain in him, just as it is impossible for those who stray not to err constantly more and more unless they return to the way. Here absolutely no *distinction* is necessary (as though, for instance, the "general influence" were not [itself] the way of error) since already this ["general influence"] is a gift of God, given to those who are unworthy and who constantly abuse it, as wine and gold are daily abused by godless people.

At this point you could say that the gift bestowed by God is good, but that its use cannot be good unless those who use it have been healed by grace. The "general influence" (this dangerous term), which is being and activity [in the realm] of nature,[12] if used by anyone who does not remain as a branch in Christ, is misused and of no avail. Just as to the pure all things are pure, so to the unclean nothing is clean; Titus 1 [:15]. And as for the

---

[11] John 15:6.
[12] See note 4.

saints everything works together for good,[13] so for the ungodly everything works for evil. Who can deny that a fornicator, adulterer, murderer, or blasphemer does his deed with the help of the "general influence"? How can he do these things unless he possesses being and activity [in the realm] of nature? [14] Yet who would dare to say that his deeds are actions which begin the good [15] and prepare him for grace? Therefore a deed done without grace, however good it may appear to be, can be nothing but bad and contrary to grace, since without grace there is no good desire in the heart of man; it can by no means be an action which begins [16] conditioning man for the receiving of grace.

All these points, of course, touch that most important and time-consuming topic of grace and free will very briefly indeed. For this reason one cannot solve all problems in so few words.

Farewell and pray for me.

The hour in which you left. [*April 13, 1520*][17]

Martin Luther
Augustinian

55

To George Spalatin
Wittenberg, April 16, 1520

Luther comments on the calling of Matthew Adrian or Werner Einhorn of Bacharach as professor of Hebrew. He also tells of a rumor concerning his own possible assassination.

On George Spalatin, see pp. 8 f.

Text in Latin: WA, Br 2, 82-83.

To my dearest friend in the Lord, Mr. George Spalatin, a servant of Christ in the castle at Lochau [1]

[13] Rom. 8:28.
[14] See note 4.
[15] See note 6.
[16] For a similar statement, see p. 25.
[17] The date was added by Spalatin.
[1] Residence of the Elector of Saxony.

Jesus

Greetings. We have agreed with Adrian,[2] my Spalatin, that he should wait a little. He promised to remain for eight days in Berlin, and await a letter from us. Now our task is to get an answer from Werner of Bacharach as soon as possible.[3] Adrian, of course, demands a salary of one hundred gulden in all. In this whole affair we have to be extremely careful that, as the saying goes, in trying to sit on two chairs, we don't fall between them! This would be the case if we should turn down this one and the other should by chance go somewhere else, either of his own accord or because he was called by Mainz. Many of our friends have strongly urged me to see that Matthew be hired, at least for a year.[4] [We should do this], they believe, if only to avoid any notoriety, because that Eclipse,[5] rumor has it, might call him just out of spite for us. However, if you cannot reply in such a short time what is to be done, then one should at least write this to him in Berlin, so that he does not become annoyed at a further delay in this affair. I suspect he has made up his mind to accept a Hebrew professorship either at Frankfurt[6] or Leipzig if we do not call him. Do answer quickly.

Concerning my case, it is said that the most severe of all punishments is ready for me. As to this, the Provost of the Neuwerk [Chapter] in Halle[7] had me "warned and advised," as they call it. Even certain of my enemies who were sorry for me sent me a warning through friends from Halberstadt that there is a certain doctor of medicine[8] who, with the help of magic, can make himself invisible at will and then kill someone; he [supposedly]

---

[2] Matthew Adrian; see p. 132, n. 1.
[3] Werner of Bacharach; see p. 154, n. 3.
[4] This matter was soon settled. Luther wrote on April 30 (see *WA*, Br 2, 94) that Adrian had been called for a salary of one hundred gulden.
[5] *Eclipsis* (a Latin word meaning absent) is a pun for *Lipsim* or Leipzig and seems to have been used occasionally during Luther's time; see *WA*, Br 2, 83, n. 5.
[6] The University of Frankfurt/Oder was founded in 1506.
[7] This was Nicholas Demuth, provost of the Neuwerk Chapter of Augustinian Regular Canons (see *O.D.C.C.*, p. 109) in Halle, who was held in high regard for his Humanistic learning. After 1523 he sided with Luther. See *WA*, Br 2, 83, n. 7. The circumstances of the warning are not known.
[8] Not known.

has the order to kill Luther and is to arrive here next Sunday[9] when the relics[10] are being shown. This is a persistent rumor.

Farewell.

April 16, 1520 MARTIN LUTHER

56

To George Spalatin
Wittenberg, May 1, 1520

In spite of a violent campaign on the part of Rome against the University of Wittenberg and its "heretical" faculty, increasing numbers of students went there to study. In this letter Luther reports on the lack of housing for these students and the faculty. He also mentions some of the everyday matters that reach his desk.

On George Spalatin, see pp. 8 f.

Text in Latin: WA, Br 2, 96.

To my friend George Spalatin, venerable and dear in the Lord, chaplain to the Elector of Saxony, a servant of Christ

Jesus

Greetings. I am returning the letter of your Dean[1] and adding to it what I received from Nürnberg.[2] Matthew Adrian[3] suggests that we should write to Doctor Pascha[4] at Magdeburg for Hebrew books. As soon as you have done so, I shall do it too, and in a hurry. See to it that it is done. I shall do my part.

The number of students increases every day, but the small city cannot hold them all and many are forced to go away again.[5]

---

[9] Misericordias Domini, which fell on April 22.

[10] See pp. 33 f.; p. 338, n. 8.

[1] Konrad Gerhard, the dean of the chapter at Altenburg, of which Spalatin was a member; see *WA*, Br 2, 96, n. 1. The letter is not extant.

[2] Perhaps Luther included the letter from von Staupitz and the one from Link, which he mentions below.

[3] Matthew Adrian was finally called to Wittenberg as professor of Hebrew.

[4] Apparently Busse de Alvesleben, a canon and provost in Magdeburg who was in the diplomatic service of Archbishop Albrecht of Mainz (on Albrecht, see pp. 44 f.); for more details, see *WA*, Br 2, 96, n. 2.

[5] Between 1516 and 1520 an average of five or six hundred students a year

We cannot provide lodging for Adrian to suit this man. We do not wish to push others out because of him, even though he is now starting to work on us to do so. Should he write anything about this or discuss it with you (for he wanted to present his case personally there),[6] you know my opinion and Philip's.[7] We shall not have a part in or consent to having anyone pushed out of the city treasurer's house or anyone else's, if they are unwilling to move; if they wish to leave out of kindness, we shall be pleased and grateful.

If you can obtain a reply for our widow Landmann,[8] whether negative or positive, for goodness' sake do so quickly. I have discovered something in this case which is trivial but which almost makes me sorry that I became mixed up in this business. Now everything is entangled and confused. Consequently I have tried to persuade her that if everything should not come out according to her wishes, she should be satisfied with what can be brought about, and drop the rest;[9] peace is better than war. I do not know whether I accomplished anything.

Farewell in the Lord.

I have received a letter from Staupitz in Nürnberg.[10] He finally praises my cause and has a firmer hope for it, which is certainly different from what I am used to hearing from him. Wenceslas[11] writes, "We have received the *Doctrinal Asses*,"[12] and he is of good hope. Thus my ship is tossed about: now hope, now fear rules; but this does not concern me.

Wittenberg, May 1, 1520 MARTIN LUTHER
Augustinian[13]

---

attended the University of Wittenberg; yet Wittenberg had only approximately twenty-three hundred inhabitants. See *WA*, Br 2, 97, n. 3.

[6] At the court of the Elector.

[7] Philip Melanchthon; see p. 77, n. 3.

[8] See p. 142, n. 4.

[9] Literally: ". . . her wishes, she should permit to go that which can go, fall, that which falls; peace. . . ."

[10] This letter of John von Staupitz (see p. 64, n. 1) is not extant.

[11] Wenceslas Link; see pp. 169 f.

[12] This is the condemnation of Luther's thought and work which was issued by the faculties of the universities of Louvain and Cologne; see p. 155, nn. 5, 6.

[13] The postscript to this letter is omitted here.

57

To George Spalatin
Wittenberg, May 31, 1520

Luther is asking Spalatin to forward some letters for him. He reports on rumors concerning the University of Leipzig and complains about the inefficiency of the Wittenberg city government.

On George Spalatin, see pp. 8 f.

Text in Latin: WA, Br 2, 111.

To my dearest friend in the Lord, Master George Spalatin, court chaplain and secretary, a most honest friend

Jesus

Greetings. I am enclosing letters to Hutten,[1] Sickingen,[2] and our Taubenheim,[3] my Spalatin. Please take on the job of forwarding

[1] Ulrich von Hutten (1488-1523), a Franconian noble, was the most colorful and important representative of a Humanism that combined strong nationalistic feeling with opposition to Rome. In 1505 he ran away from the famous school of the Benedictine monastery of Fulda and began the life of a wandering student, poet, and knight. He sided with Reuchlin and was a major contributor to the *Letters of Obscure Men* (see p. 9, n. 2). In 1517 he was made poet laureate by Emperor Maximilian and was appointed court poet by the Archbishop of Mainz. After the Leipzig Disputation von Hutten saw in Luther the most powerful element for bringing about his major concern: the freeing of the Empire from the influence of the Roman hierarchy and restoring the glory of the Empire. Praising Luther and at the same time attacking the corruption within the Roman church, von Hutten set out on a powerful anti-Roman drive (see p. 193, n. 13; p. 231, n. 16), without, however, actually professing the faith of the Reformation. As an admirer of both Erasmus and Luther, he tried hard to create unity between Humanism and the Reformation; see p. 150, n. 10. When Erasmus rejected these efforts, Hutten turned against him and quarreled violently with the great Humanist. Later, when Rome began to act against von Hutten, he took up refuge at the castle of Francis von Sickingen. Prevented by sickness from participating in von Sickingen's war against the Archbishop of Trier, von Hutten escaped von Sickingen's disastrous defeat and found refuge in Switzerland with Ulrich Zwingli. He died a lonely, sick, and disillusioned man. See *O.D.C.C.*, p. 668 f.

[2] Francis von Sickingen; see pp. 244 f.

[3] John von Taubenheim, a member of a long established Saxon noble family, apparently came to the Electoral court in his early youth. In 1504/05 he was reported as studying in Leipzig, and in 1513 he was appointed by Elector Frederick as administrator of the Electoral household, a position

them; try especially to see that Taubenheim gets his at once, since I have delayed longer in answering him than he perhaps has expected.

Lonicer will finish his work tomorrow.[4] The people of Leipzig, anxious to retain students, boast that Erasmus[5] is coming to them. How busy, and yet how miserable, envy is! When they derided us a year ago as being "extinct," they did not foresee that this very cross would hang over them too.[6] The Lord rules so we can feel it.

It is said that Ochsenfurt[7] arms himself against Feldkirch's little book, in which he was ridiculed.[8] I have completed something in German against the ass Alveld; it is already being printed.[9]

---

he continued to hold even after the death of the Elector in 1525. As administrator of the Electoral household von Taubenheim was deeply involved in the financial, political, and administrative affairs of Electoral Saxony. As a result Luther was very interested in having von Taubenheim join the teams of visitors, who in 1527/28 set out to inspect and organize the parishes of Electoral Saxony. In 1532/33 von Taubenheim took over the office of *Landrentmeister* of Electoral Saxony, a position comparable to a present-day controller general. Von Taubenheim died in 1541 or 1542. See *ARG* 8 (1911), 37 ff. None of the letters mentioned by Luther is extant.

[4] John Lonicer, an Augustinian from Eisleben who was then studying in Wittenberg for his Master's degree, was Luther's *famulus*, or private assistant; the *famulus* assisted the professor in return for tutoring. Under Luther's guidance, he wrote a sharp pamphlet against Alveld (see note 9), who had attacked Luther's view on the primacy of the pope. Luther is referring to this work. For the bibliography, see *WA* 6, 279; On Lonicer, who later became a professor in Marburg, see *WA*, Br 2, 99, n. 10.

[5] Erasmus of Rotterdam; see pp. 116 f.

[6] After the disputation in 1519 (see p. 126), the University of Leipzig boasted (see p. 134, n. 3) that Wittenberg, that "nest of Hussite heresy," then suffering from the plague, would soon cease to draw any students. Now it was Leipzig's turn to suffer.

[7] Jerome Dungersheim of Ochsenfurt; see p. 145, n. 6.

[8] John Bernhardi of Feldkirch (not to be confused with his brother Bartholomew Bernhardi; see p. 115, n. 21) wrote a pamphlet against Alveld (see note 9) in which he also attacked Dungersheim. John Bernhardi was a student of Melanchthon and in a short time became professor of philosophy at the University of Wittenberg. In 1531 he was president of the University. See *C.R.* 1, No. 75; O. Clemen (ed.), *Supplementa Melanchthoniana*, 6, I, 103 f.

[9] *Von dem Papstum zu Rom, wider den hochberühmten Romanisten zu Leipzig* (*The Papacy at Rome: An Answer to the Celebrated Romanist at Leipzig*) (Wittenberg: M. Lotther, June, 1520). *WA* 6, 285 ff.; *PE* 1, 337 ff. Asked by the Bishop of Merseburg to defend the primacy of the pope, Augustine Alveld, a Franciscan of Leipzig, published an attack in 1520

Advise me whether I should write to the Sovereign[10] for his help in our city affairs. Everything is very expensive, the supplies brought in are insufficient, nor is anything administered properly in this most confused and careless city. Something could be accomplished at Wittenberg, were there any order in the city government. Here there is need for the counsel and authority of the Sovereign. Please answer.

Farewell.

Wittenberg, May 31, 1520 MARTIN LUTHER
Augustinian

58

To George Spalatin
Wittenberg, June 25, 1520

Luther is commenting on Melanchthon's academic responsibilities and personal life.

On George Spalatin, see pp. 8 f.

Text in Latin: WA, Br 2, 130; translation based on S-J 1, 332.

To the learned and good man, George Spalatin, a servant and a priest of Christ, my friend in the Lord

Jesus

Greetings. It seems both to me and to many others, my Spalatin, that Philip[1] should not be burdened with the course on Pliny,[2]

against Luther; for the bibliography, see *WA* 6, 277. Lonicer and John Bernhardi assumed the task of answering Alveld. While they were working on their rebuttals, Alveld published a second attack against Luther, this time in German; for the bibliography, see *WA* 6, 280. Luther felt compelled to answer, which he did with the work mentioned; it was completed on June 26.

10 Elector Frederick; see pp. 49 f.

1 Philip Melanchthon; see p. 77, n. 3. On Luther's worry that Melanchthon worked too much, see p. 119, n. 10.

2 One of Luther's major aims was to break the dominance of Scholasticism at the University of Wittenberg and replace it with Humanistic studies. On March 11, 1518, he sent Spalatin a program for the reorganization of the

on account of his lectures on the Apostle Paul, which are so fruitful. The students should not be deprived [of this blessing] since what they would get out of Pliny could in no way compensate for it. We should fear that it may be the Spirit (whom we should not rashly resist) who moved Philip to lecture [on Paul] and that it may perhaps be Satan's plot by which, under this cover,[3] the cultivation of such great fruit should be hindered. We think that if Pliny is to be taught at all, it should be turned over to Master John Hess.[4]

I don't know what [Melanchthon] will do about marrying, especially as far as the girl you mentioned is concerned.[5] I wish the man a wife; but on the other hand I do not want to be held responsible for nor advise him in his selection. I also do not see that the man is eager to marry.

Although I hope Philip is not leaning toward the Bavarians,[6] yet it is true that I have always wished that he be honored with a more respectable salary, so that he might nullify the hopes

---

Liberal Arts School; see *WA*, Br 1, No. 63. Apparently the Elector approved this program. On March 21, 1518, Luther wrote Lang as if he had some definite reason to hope that his suggestions would be adopted; see *WA*, Br 1, 155. In the summer semester of 1518, the University curriculum underwent its first major change, and further steps were to be taken. See pp. 38, 41 f., 63, 82, 95 f., 106 f., 111 f., 123 f., 125, 132 f., 160. In 1520 it was Melanchthon's turn to take over the course on Pliny, in addition to lecturing on Paul's Epistle to the Romans. The Pliny course was to cover some books of the *Naturalis Historia* (*History of Nature*) by Pliny the Elder (see *O.C.D.*, p. 704).

[3] I.e., that Melanchthon has to lecture on Pliny.

[4] This John Hess was Master John Eissermann (not to be confused with the John Hess mentioned on p. 143, n. 5). At Wittenberg in the years following 1518 he alternated between giving courses on Aristotle's *Peri ta zoa istoria* (one of Aristotle's works on natural science, generally known as *Historia Animalium*) and on Quintilian's *Institutio Oratoria* (*The Education of an Orator*). According to the plans for reorganizing the curriculum, he was to drop the course on Aristotle (see *WA*, Br 1, No. 222); for Luther's criticism of Aristotle's work on natural science, see p. 112. Having finished his course on Quintilian, he was to begin lecturing on Pliny's *De animalibus* (*On Zoology*, a portion of Pliny's *Naturalis Historia*), so that Melanchthon would not have to spend time on it. Hess became president of Wittenberg University in 1527, and then he went to the University of Marburg where he later became chancellor; he died there in 1558.

[5] Melanchthon married Catharine Crapp on November 27, 1520; she was the daughter of the mayor of Wittenberg.

[6] The University of Ingolstadt in Bavaria was at that time discussing an appointment for Melanchthon; see *C.R.* 1, 262.

they have conceived because they know that he is here on a smaller salary than he would be there.[7] If there should be an occasion to further this cause, be alert to it. For no one should neglect caring for himself when an opportunity arises, that is, when God calls.

I shall, in its proper place, mention the tragedy of Strassburg in a satisfactory way.[8] Tomorrow Sylvester will be concluded,[9] and also the Romanist in German.[10]

Farewell.

June 25, 1520 MARTIN LUTHER
Augustinian

59

To George Spalatin
Wittenberg, July 14, 1520

In a clash between town and gown, Luther took the side of the town. In this letter he requests the Electoral government to censure the President of the University, who had done nothing to prevent the disorderly conduct of the students.

On George Spalatin, see pp. 8 f.

Text in Latin: WA, Br 2, 142-143.

To the learned and good man, Master George Spalatin, court chaplain, my superior in the Lord

---

[7] For similar statements, see pp. 78, 107, 269.

[8] The Bishop of Strassburg tried to do away with the corruption of his clergy and to reorganize the ecclesiastical system in his diocese. However he was hindered by papal interference. Luther dealt with this event in greater detail in his little book *To the Christian Nobility of the German Nation* (see p. 171, n. 5); see *WA* 6, 422; *PE* 2, 90.

[9] In the fall of 1519 Sylvester Prierias (see p. 71, n. 7; p. 72, n. 14) had published a comprehensive work against Luther in which he claimed to demonstrate that the dogmatic resolutions issued by the pope were to be considered as decisions from heaven. The Reformer did not consider it necessary to write a reply; he only reprinted it, adding some rather sarcastic notes; his reference is to this edition. See *WA* 6, 328 ff.

[10] For the answer to the Romanist, see p. 164, n. 9.

Jesus

Greetings. I beseech you earnestly, my Spalatin, if you have any influence with the Most Illustrious Sovereign,[1] persuade him to write an extremely harsh and severe letter to our President.[2] Yesterday in his great folly, the President almost involved us in murder and bloodshed.[3] That senseless man stirred up a riot on the part of a student mob against the city council and innocent people, which he should have curbed instead. I was present at the senate meeting where they[4] raged as though they were totally drunk. Nothing was said except what would incite the fierceness of the young people even more. This disorder in our University infuriates me; it will finally bring us real disgrace. Doctor Peter Lupin[5] spoke excellently against the riot, but he was answered by Mr. Thomas Eschaus[6] in such a way that I rose at once and left, since I saw Satan presiding at this meeting. I even hear that the youths have been allowed to carry arms, contrary to the Sovereign's order.[7] It would be better if only a small number of students studied here than that we be exposed to such riots. All sensible people condemn this nonsense. In the sermon tomorrow I shall also try to curb this if I can, with God's grace. The

---

[1] Elector Frederick; see pp. 49 f.

[2] Peter Burchard, a professor of medicine, was then president of the University. Soon after this incident he accepted a call to Ingolstadt and became a bitter opponent of Luther.

[3] The rivalry between the students and members of the local painters' guild led to violent clashes between the two groups in February of 1520 and again on July 13. For details, see Friedensburg, *G.U.W.*, pp. 150 ff.; *S-J* 1, 291.

[4] "They" could refer to the students or to the members of the senate.

[5] Peter Lupin, or Wolf, a Doctor of Theology since 1508, was a professor of philosophy and theology, as well as treasurer of the University of Wittenberg at one time. Luther dedicated his *Commentary on Galatians* (1519; see p. 113, n. 11) to him and to Karlstadt (see p. 79, n. 12). Although Lupin was a Thomist, he was deeply interested in Luther's thoughts and became a faithful friend of the Reformer. Lupin died in 1521; see p. 230.

[6] Thomas Eschaus, or Eschhausen, Doctor of Medicine since 1518 and a professor of medicine and pharmacology (who had also studied some Canon Law and was once registrar), apparently wanted to support his fellow faculty member who was then the president; see note 2. Luther's anger with Eschaus was of short duration. Perhaps as early as 1520, Luther made him his personal physician. Eschaus died in 1535. See *WA*, Br 2, 143, n. 5.

[7] Following a riot in February Elector Frederick issued orders that neither students nor guild members were to carry arms; on the riot in February, see *WA*, Br 2, 51, n. 16.

orders the Sovereign just issued were not kept at all. The old men were wilder than the young. I know that Satan has his hand in this. Since he cannot in anyway harm the word of God which is returning to us, he seeks at least to bring it into disgrace by this maneuver. We must oppose this, however, with every possible effort, so that he does not win with these bloodthirsty people.[8]

I believe, by the way, that you have received all the letters that I sent, together with the one from Sylvester von Schaumberg;[9] please return them so that friends may read them too.

Farewell and pray for me.

July 14, 1520 MARTIN LUTHER
Augustinian

60

To Wenceslas Link[1]
Wittenberg, August 19, 1520

In this letter Luther is defending the harsh tone of his polemical writings, especially of his To the Christian Nobility of the German Nation, which he had recently published.

Wenceslas Link (1483-1547), an Augustinian, entered Wittenberg University in 1503 and was graduated from there as a Doctor of Theology in 1511. He was dean of the Theological Faculty when Luther was graduated as a Doctor in 1512, and became prior of the Wittenberg monastery in 1512 or 1513. In 1516 he left Wittenberg for Munich (see p. 31), and soon afterward he became a preacher in Nürnberg. In 1520 he was elected

---

8 Law and order in Wittenberg were not restored until the Electoral Saxon marshal Hans von Dolzig occupied the town with a company of soldiers and pressured the University into curbing the students.

9 In June of 1520, Sylvester von Schaumberg, a noble of Franconia, had offered military protection to Luther; see *WA*, Br 2, No. 298; *S-J* 1, 330 f. Like von Sickingen (see pp. 244 f.) and von Hutten (see p. 163, n. 1), he too was a member of the German nationalistic opposition to Rome and saw in Luther his champion. The other letter could not be identified.

1 The addressee is missing in the manuscript copy of this letter but appears in the earliest printed editions.

vicar general, succeeding John von Staupitz (see p. 64, n. 1). Under his leadership the general convention of the Saxon (or German) Congregation of Reformed Augustinians (see p. 6, n. 3), which was held in Wittenberg in February, 1522, allowed all monks to leave the Order if they wished. In 1523 Link resigned from his office and became a pastor in Altenburg. From 1525 to the end of his life he was a pastor in Nürnberg. Link was one of Luther's oldest friends. He met Luther in the Wittenberg monastery in 1508, and, incidentally, he accompanied him from Nürnberg to Augsburg in the fall of 1518, after presenting him with a new cowl; see WA, TR 5, No. 5349.

Text in Latin: WA, Br 2, 168.

Jesus

Greetings. I do not try to seek praise and fame, my Father, with my writings and little books. Almost all condemn my stinging tone. Yet I share your opinion that perhaps in this way God reveals the figments of man's imagination. For I realize that those things which in our age are treated quietly will soon be forgotten, and nobody will care about them. But the womb of Rebecca also [had] to bear children who were contentious and kicked each other.[2] The present age passes an unfavorable judgment; the judgment of future generations will be better. Even Paul calls his enemies now "dogs," now "mutilation," now "babblers," "false workmen," "servants of Satan," and names of that kind and strikes the face of the whitewashed wall.[3] Who does not see that the prophets attack [the sin of the people] with the greatest violence? But we have become accustomed to these things, and therefore they no longer disturb us.

The Reverend Father Vicar[4] wrote to me yesterday from Erfurt and asked me not to publish the little book on the reform

[2] Gen. 25:22.

[3] Phil. 3:2; Titus 1:10; II Cor. 11:13, 15; Acts 23:3.

[4] The manuscript copy is illegible at this point; but apparently the word rendered as "vicar" begins with "L." This suggests that Luther is referring to the district vicar John Lang (see p. 61, n. 6). Lang's letter (in which he must have asked or ordered Luther not to publish the little book mentioned in note 5) is not extant; see WA, Br 2, 167, 168, n. 5.

of the state of Christendom.[5] I do not know on what point[6] [this little book] should have been censured. But his letter came too late; the little book was already published. Try to pacify him when you meet him.[7] Who knows whether the Spirit himself is not driving me on with his force, since it is certain that I am not carried away by zeal for fame, money, or pleasure.[8] I say nothing of vengeance—may the Lord forgive here. This also is not undertaken by me to stir up a revolt, but to affirm the freedom for a General Council [to meet and decide].

Farewell in the Lord.

August 19, 1520 Yours,

FRIAR MARTIN LUTHER

61

To George Spalatin
Wittenberg, August 23, 1520

Luther is complaining that he did not receive a satisfactory answer for the widow, Walpurga Landmann; see p. 142, n. 4. He reports on a letter to Cardinal Carvajal and encloses a draft of his Protest and Offer and some other material.

On George Spalatin, see pp. 8 f.

Text in Latin: WA, Br 2, 169-170.

[5] *An den Christlichen Adel deutscher Nation, von des Christlichen Standes Besserung* (*To the Christian Nobility of the German Nation, Concerning the Reform of the Christian Estate*) (Wittenberg: M. Lotther, August, 1520). *WA* 6, 404 ff.; *PE* 2, 61 ff.

[6] Other possibilities of translating and interpreting this passage would be: ". . . know why (on what pretense) this little book should have been . . ."; or, ". . . know on what authority this little book. . . ."

[7] Link was to meet Lang at a forthcoming chapter meeting of the Augustinians in Eisleben; see *WA*, Br 2, 101, n. 2. The last triennial chapter meeting had taken place in April, 1518; see p. 60. The next one was to have taken place in April, 1521. The vicar general von Staupitz, however, called it for the end of August, 1520, in Eisleben. Von Staupitz, weary of the development of the Reformation and its impact on the Augustinians, resigned at this meeting. Link was elected his successor.

[8] For similar statements, see pp. 103, 196.

To that friendly man, Mr. George Spalatin, a servant of Christ, my friend in the Lord

Jesus

Greetings. First of all, my Spalatin, no answer has been given to the widow Landmann,[1] except (as I hear) harsh reproaches; consequently that supplication accomplished nothing. If you can, please write what is to be done now.

I have taken care of your letter and forwarded it to Nürnberg.[2]

Additions will be made to the little book[3] in the second edition, which Lotther is preparing; they will also expand it. Please note that I am enclosing the *Elogion*[4] and the letter[s][5] for correction.

The subject of the letter to the Cardinal of the Holy Cross is as follows:[6] since he is unusually famous in the world, I wanted to ask him to be the arbiter in the case and settle it by every means possible.[7] I would also offer every condition necessary for peace, except recanting, suffering the stigma of a heretic, or being deprived of the liberty of teaching the Word. I am not afraid of censures and force, however, since in the midst of Germany I can now be safe. At the same time they should be careful having crushed one not to arouse many others. With

---

[1] See p. 142, n. 4.

[2] This letter could not be identified.

[3] The second edition of *To the Christian Nobility of the German Nation* (see p. 171, n. 5), released sometime in October or November, 1520. Originally Lotther printed four thousand copies; they must have sold rapidly, because now, on August 23, Luther is already considering a second edition.

[4] *Elogion.* This is apparently Luther's draft of his *Protest and Offer* to the Emperor; see *WA* 6, 476 ff. Here the Reformer points out that he has taught nothing but the Word of God, that he is a faithful son of the church and willing to be better instructed. See also p. 174, nn. 5, 6.

[5] *Literae,* the Latin word used by Luther, can mean both letter and letters. We are certain that Luther enclosed a draft of his letter to Emperor Charles V (see p. 175); for another possible enclosure, see p. 174, n. 6.

[6] This is either a suggestion for a letter of Elector Frederick (see pp. 49 f.) or a report on a letter planned by Luther. Bernardino Carvajal, bishop of Cartagena and Ostia, cardinal and titular priest of the Church of the Holy Cross in Rome since 1495, was known for his opposition to Pope Julius II (during the Council of Pisa; see p. 104, n. 5) and his support of the enemies of Reuchlin (see p. 9).

[7] Literally: ". . . that he would make himself, with all possible zeal, the agent for the settling of the case. . . ." On this plan, see pp. 98 f.

God's help I shall be a match for my enemies both in talent and knowledge.

Farewell and pray for me.

Wittenberg, August 23, 1520 MARTIN LUTHER
Augustinian

I commend Master Francis Günther to you.[8] Take care to give this letter to the Sovereign.[9]

62

To George Spalatin
Wittenberg, August 24, 1520

Luther recommends Francis Günther, and once more he asks Spalatin to polish the draft of his appeal to the Emperor and the other material.

On George Spalatin, see pp. 8 f.

Text in Latin: WA, Br 2, 170-171.

To my dearest friend in Christ, Mr. George Spalatin at Lochau,[1] a servant of Christ

---

[8] Francis Günther of Nordhausen was graduated as Bachelor of Arts from the University of Erfurt in 1512 and as Master of Arts from the University of Wittenberg in 1516. While teaching on Wittenberg's Liberal Arts Faculty he studied theology and became one of Luther's students. In 1517 he was graduated as Bachelor in Biblical Studies (see *LW* 31, 6) and in October, 1521, as Licentiate of Theology (see p. 264, n. 3). In 1519 he was called as a preacher to Jüterbog, where he got involved in a controversy with the Franciscans. Due to his outspoken support of Luther he had to leave Jüterbog and, recommended by Luther (see *WA*, Br 2, 166; *S-J* 1, 345), was appointed to the parish in Lochau, which was the Electoral Saxon residence (see above). He died in Lochau in 1528. See also *ARG* 8 (1911), 5 f.

[9] Elector Frederick; see pp. 49 f. The letter Spalatin was to turn over to the Elector could be either this letter itself (because of the references to the widow Walpurga Landmann and the letter to Cardinal Carvajal) or the drafts mentioned in notes 4 and 5.

[1] Lochau was at that time the seat of the Electoral Saxon government.

Jesus

Greetings. I am sending Master Francis Günther[2] to you, my Spalatin, and he is ready to do what you write.[3] You, however, must provide him with more detailed instructions and information; as you know, he is unfamiliar with life at court. Yet he is eager to learn, as far as I know his disposition.

I believe that my letter,[4] together with the *Elogion*[5] and the other [letter(s)],[6] has reached you. Please take pains to polish everything with a sharp file. When I wrote these things I was pressured by I don't know what burdens of the soul. I shall also show them to other friends before they are given to the public.

Farewell.

August 24, 1520 MARTIN LUTHER
Augustinian

---

[2] Francis Günther; see p. 173, n. 8.

[3] Apparently this refers to the duties Günther was to take over.

[4] *WA*, Br 2, No. 330, Introduction, identifies this (first) letter as Luther's letter to Spalatin, dated August 23 (see pp. 171 ff.).

[5] *Elogion;* see p. 172, n. 4. Spalatin did polish Luther's draft of the *Offer and Protest* and return it. It was printed by J. Grünenberg in the last days of August and is reproduced in *WA* 6, 480 f. (see edition A on p. 478). On August 31 Luther sent a copy of this printed edition to Spalatin (see *WA*, Br 2, 179; *S-J* 1, 349), along with the final draft of his personal letter to the Emperor (see p. 175). The *Offer and Protest* was later nailed to the doors of various churches throughout Germany and thus made known to the public; see *WA*, Br 2, 208; *S-J* 1, 384 f. In January, 1521, Luther sent a copy of this edition to Elector Frederick, who was already in Worms; see p. 195. The Elector had it translated into Latin and printed along with Luther's letter to the Emperor (see p. 175), which the Elector must have received from Spalatin. Then the Elector turned both documents over to Emperor Charles V who, however, did not read them but tore them up. For this reconstruction of the events, see *WA*, Br 2, 174 f.; *WA* 6, 474 ff.

[6] *WA*, Br 2, No. 330, Introduction, says this "other [letter]" is the draft of Luther's letter to the Emperor (see p. 175), sent to Spalatin on August 23; see p. 172. According to the *WA*, Br editor, the circumstances were probably as follows: on August 23 Luther sent Spalatin the drafts of his *Offer and Protest* and of his letter to the Emperor; see p. 172. On August 24 he expressed his hope that Spalatin had received his August 23 letter (the first letter mentioned by Luther, see note 4), in which he had included the drafts of the *Offer and Protest* and of the letter to the Emperor (the "other [letter]" mentioned by Luther); see above. This interpretation seems to come to mind first, but it need not be the only one suggested by the text. Luther could have enclosed "letters" on August 23 (see p. 172) since the Latin word *literae* can connote either the singular or plural. This would raise the question of what "other [letter(s)]." A study of the various documents ex-

63

To Emperor Charles V
Wittenberg, August 30, 1520

This letter is an official communication to Charles V. Luther gives a short report on the development of his case and calls upon the Emperor for protection and for a fair hearing to decide whether his position or his enemies' is correct. He also states his willingness to forego any Imperial protection if found guilty of doctrinal errors.

Charles V (1500-1558) was the grandson of Emperor Maximilian I and heir to the territories of the Hapsburg dynasty.

---

changed between Luther and Spalatin brings forth a somewhat different picture of the events than the *WA*, Br editor developed. On August 31 Luther sent Spalatin the printed edition of his *Offer and Protest* (see note 5), the final draft of his letter to the Emperor (see pp. 175 ff.), and the final draft of a letter no longer extant to the Imperial knight Francis von Sickingen (see *WA*, Br 2, 208; *S-J* 1, 384). The content of this letter is not known, but one may assume that Luther tried to recommend his case to the Knight and perhaps asked him for moral support. The suggestion made by Enders (*Briefwechsel* 2, 470, n. 1) that Luther asked von Sickingen to turn the letter (see pp. 175 ff.) and the *Offer and Protest* over to the Emperor seems doubtful (see *WA*, Br 2, 174), although it is a possibility which should not be as totally disregarded as the *WA*, Br editor did (see *WA*, Br 2, 174). In any case the von Sickingen letter must be viewed against the background of Luther's appeal to the Emperor. It is very possible that Luther also included a draft of this von Sickingen letter as early as August 23, when he sent Spalatin the drafts of his *Offer and Protest* and his letter to the Emperor; on p. 172 one would, therefore, have to read "letters" (as is suggested), which is grammatically possible. Spalatin was to polish the three documents and return them to Luther for the final copying of the two letters and the typesetting of the *Offer and Protest*. The "other [letter(s)]" mentioned by Luther on August 24 (see p. 174) would then refer to both the von Sickingen letter and the one to the Emperor, while the first letter Luther mentioned would be the August 23 letter to Spalatin (see pp. 171 ff.). This differs somewhat from the commentary in *WA*, Br 2, No. 330, and in *WA* 6, 474, where it is assumed that Luther did *not* need Spalatin's polishing hand for his letter to von Sickingen, but only for the letter to the Emperor; consequently the "other [letter]" could only be the one to the Emperor. However, why should Luther not have sent the drafts of all three documents connected with this important step (namely, the appeal to the Imperial government) to Spalatin for correction? On June 29 he had already mentioned to Spalatin that he would write to von Sickingen "tomorrow" (see *WA*, Br 2, 131). It is hardly believable that he did not keep Spalatin informed of the status of the work on this letter, and that he did not also take advantage of Spalatin's able aid for this important document.

Educated in the Spanish Netherlands (which he inherited from his father, Philip the Fair of Austria-Burgundy, and his mother, Joanna the Mad of Aragon-Castile), he always remained a stranger to German life and thought. In 1516/17 he became Charles I, king of Spain. When his grandfather Maximilian died in 1519 (see p. 123, n. 3; p. 129, n. 6; pp. 96 f.), he inherited the German portions of the Hapsburg territories and was elected Roman king (a position which made him de facto emperor), although Pope Leo X and King Francis I of France tried to prevent this. The accumulation of such territorial power and political strength in the hands of one person involved the German Empire in a bitter, century-long struggle with France, in which the Papal See repeatedly shifted its support on the basis of political opportunism. The beginning of the rule of Charles V coincided with the rather rapid development of the Reformation and the dragging out of Luther's trial for heresy. In this situation Luther appealed to the young Emperor for help. In November, 1520, Elector Frederick (see pp. 49 f.) urged Charles to take the case of Luther into his hands; see S-J 1, 397 ff. The Emperor's situation was infinitely more complicated than it might seem at first glance. To avoid interference from secular governments, the papal court finally, on June 15, 1520, issued the bull Exsurge, Domine (Arise, O Lord), which condemned Luther's teachings as heresy and threatened him with excommunication unless he recanted; see Denzinger, Nos. 741 ff. According to the close relationship which then existed between church and state, such excommunication would necessarily be accompanied by a ban under which Luther would be considered an outlaw. In spite of the pressure which the papal legate, Jerome Aleander (see O.D.C.C., p. 32), put on the Emperor not to interfere in Luther's trial and to turn Luther over to the authorities of the church (see Kidd, pp. 80 ff.; see also Aleander's letters written from Worms, a selection of which may be found in S-J 1), the Emperor yielded to the urging of Elector Frederick and summoned Luther to appear before the diet scheduled to be in session in Worms in the spring of 1521; see S-J 1, Nos. 342, 361, 412 f. See also R. Tyler, The Emperor Charles V (London: Allen, 1956); Bainton, pp. 151 ff.; Fife, pp. 507 ff., 587 ff.; Schwiebert, pp. 466 ff.

This letter is available in two versions: one is a sixteenth century manuscript kept in the British Museum in London, on which, it seems, all later editions are based. The other is a printed version published by J. Grünenberg in Wittenberg late in 1520. Both versions are identical in content; however they have important stylistic variations. To the best of our knowledge the manuscript is an incorrectly dated copy of the draft Luther sent to Spalatin for correction (see pp. 172, 174); see WA, Br 2, 175. It would therefore be closer to Luther's original thought than the printed copy; the translation is based on it.

Text in Latin: WA, Br 2, 175-178, col. 1.

Jesus

Grace and peace from our Lord Jesus Christ

Everyone will be astonished, and rightly so, that I dare to address a letter to Your Most Serene Imperial Majesty, excellent Emperor and Caesar Charles. For what can be more disrespectful than that the king of kings and lord of lords be addressed by an absolutely unworthy and lowly man? However he will be less astonished who has contemplated the magnitude of this case and realized that it concerns evangelical truth. The truth of the gospel is worthy of approaching even the throne of the heavenly Majesty; therefore it should not seem unworthy of calling upon an earthly sovereign. In addition to this, as earthly sovereigns are images of the heavenly Sovereign, they ought to imitate him, and while sitting in high places, they should still have regard for the lowly things on earth, raise the helpless from the ground, and lift up the poor from the dung heap.[1] Therefore I come, helpless and poor; as the most worthless of men, I am prostrate before the feet of Your Most Serene Majesty, yet I bring forward a most worthy cause.

I have published certain little books by which I have aroused for myself the envy and indignation of many and important men, although I should have been safe for two reasons.

First, I came out into the public eye against my will. What-

[1] See Ps. 113:5 ff.

ever I have written, I have written after being provoked by the violence and plots of others. I desired nothing more ardently than that I could stay hidden in my corner.[2]

Second, I strove for nothing other than spreading the truth of the gospel against superstitious opinions stemming from human tradition. My own conscience as well as the judgment of excellent men bear witness to this.

For this, then, I am now for the third year enduring limitless provocations, insults, perils, and whatever evil the wicked can devise. In the meantime I vainly offer silence,[3] I vainly suggest conditions for peace,[4] I vainly request to be informed of teachings more correct than mine.[5] There is only one thing prepared for me: to be annihilated, together with the whole gospel.

I have vainly tried everything. Therefore it has finally seemed wise to appeal to [Your] Imperial Majesty, according to the example of St. Athanasius,[6] in case the Lord deigns to help his cause through [Your Imperial Majesty]. Humbly and on my knees, therefore, I beseech Your Most Serene Majesty, Charles, foremost of kings on earth, to deign to take under the shadow of your wings not me but this very cause of truth, since it is only by this truth that authority is given you to carry the sword for the punishment of the evil and for the praise of the good.[7] [I beseech the shield of your protection] neither farther nor longer than I need to defend this case and either have won it or lost it. I do not want to be protected if I am found ungodly or a heretic. I ask for only one thing, that neither truth nor falsehood

[2] Luther made similar statements as far back as 1517/18, in the early stages of his case; see pp. 69, 75, 103; p. 119, and note 7 there.

[3] See pp. 97 f.

[4] See pp. 88, 97 ff., 181, 195 ff., 246; p. 74, n. 7; p. 152, n. 5.

[5] See p. 74, n. 7.

[6] Luther is thinking of the role the Emperor Constantine (see *O.D.C.C.*, pp. 334 f.) assumed shortly before and during the Council of Nicaea (see *O.D.C.C.*, pp. 951 f.). Called upon by Arians and by the orthodox party, whose theological leader was the Alexandrian deacon Athanasius (see *O.D.C.C.*, pp. 334 f.), the Emperor summoned the council and presided over its opening session. The decisions of the council, which were finally passed with the Emperor's approval, condemned Arius and his followers. In the bitter controversies which followed that council, Athanasius sought the help of the Imperial government on various occasions, though not always successfully. See *Patrology*, pp. 309 ff.

[7] Rom. 13:1 ff.

be condemned without being heard and defeated. Your Most Serene Majesty owes this to Christ, who has power over so many kingdoms. He demands in his grace that Your Most Serene Majesty protect this truth. [To comply with this demand] would be the greatest mark of distinction for your Empire. It will be the remembered glory of your age if Your Most Sacred Majesty will not allow the unjust to crush and swallow him who is more just, [and will not allow] men, when . . .[8] and affliction[9] become increasingly powerful, to resemble the fish of the sea and the reptiles who have no leader, as the prophet says.[10]

Thus I commend myself to Your Most Sacred Majesty in trust and hope. May our Lord Jesus preserve Your Majesty to us and exalt Your Majesty to the eternal glory of his gospel. Amen.

Written at Wittenberg, August 30, the year of our Lord 1520

Your Most Serene Imperial and
Royal Majesty's dedicated [though]
insignificant subject,[11]
FRIAR MARTIN LUTHER
Augustinian

64

To George Spalatin
Lichtenberg, October 12,[1] 1520

At their first meeting Luther and Charles von Miltitz (see p. 98) discussed the possibility of Luther apologizing to the Pope, but

[8] The manuscript is illegible at this point; the printed edition reads *iudicium*, which can mean judgment, judicial investigation, or trial.

[9] Luther wrote *contradictio*, i.e., reply, answer, counterargument; a *contradictor* is an opponent. If one combines this with *iudicium*, the reading supplied by the printed edition for the illegible word of the manuscript, then Luther could have meant, ". . . when trial and affliction [or opposition] become stronger . . ."; or, ". . . when judicial investigation and counterargument become more powerful."

[10] Hab. 1:14.

[11] Luther wrote *clientulus*, "little client," suggesting that he entrusted himself and his case to the Emperor, as a client entrusts his case to a lawyer.

[1] Missing in the autograph; on the dating, see *WA*, Br 2, 193 f. On October 10, or shortly before that date, the bull *Exsurge, Domine* (see p. 176)

they abandoned this idea; see p. 100. Completely underestimating the issues involved, von Miltitz hoped that a personal apology on Luther's part could settle the affair. Von Miltitz continued to think about this possibility and at one of his later meetings with Luther he took it up again. This letter is Luther's report on this meeting, which took place October 12 in the house of the Hospital Brothers of St. Anthony in Lichtenberg (or Lichtenburg), north of Torgau, near Prettin.

See LW 31, 329 f. On George Spalatin, see pp. 8 f.

Text in Latin: WA, Br 2, 197.

To the devout and learned man, Mr. George Spalatin, Saxon court chaplain, my friend in the Lord

Jesus

Greetings. My Spalatin, Sir Charles Miltitz and I have met at Lichtenberg. We agreed—and as I understand from him, this has great possibilities—that I should publish a letter in German and in Latin, addressed to the Pope, as a preface to some brief writing.[2] In this letter I am to relate my whole story and show

arrived in Wittenberg; see *WA*, Br 2, 194 f. John Eck (see p. 80, n. 13) had sent it to the University and asked that the University put it into effect. The senate refused to do this without having first received the advice and orders of the Electoral court. The bull was never handed over to Luther directly. This papal declaration condemned as heretical forty-one propositions attributed to Luther and threatened him with excommunication unless he recanted within sixty days. For the text, see Denzinger, Nos. 741 ff. The excommunication was proclaimed on January 3, 1521, in the bull *Decet Romanum pontificem* (*It Is Right that the Roman Pontiff*).

[2] Luther fulfilled this promise with his *Open Letter to Pope Leo X*. The original of this letter, composed by Luther immediately after his return from Lichtenberg, was in Latin. Luther translated it at once into German and had it printed at the same time as the German version of his (then apparently completed but as yet unpublished) *Freedom of a Christian*. The Latin text of this letter, published shortly after the German text, is the preface to Luther's Latin version of *The Freedom of a Christian* (of which the German version is only an extract): *Ein Sendbrief an den Papst Leo X* (*An Open Letter to Pope Leo X*) (Wittenberg: J. Grünenberg, the beginning of November, 1520). *WA* 7, 3 ff.: *Von der Freiheit eines Christenmenschen* (*On the Freedom of a Christian*) (Wittenberg: J. Grünenberg, beginning of November, 1520). *WA* 7, 20 ff. This version was dedicated to Hermann Mühlpfordt, mayor of Zwickau; *LW* 31, 333. *Epistola Lutheriana ad Leonem Decimum . . . Tractatus de libertate Christiana* (*Luther's Letter to Leo X . . . Treatise on Christian Freedom*) (Wittenberg:

that I never wanted to attack the Pope personally, and throw the whole blame on Eck.[3]

As all this is true, I can easily do it, and I will offer, as humbly as I can, to keep silent, provided that others keep silent too, so that I may not seem to omit anything in my power to make peace. This is my desire, and, as you know, I have always been ready to do it. I shall prepare this, therefore, at the earliest possible moment. If it turns out the way we hope, it is well; if it turns out differently, it will also be well, because this is then the will of the Lord.

Farewell.

Lichtenberg, [in the house of the] Antonians,[4] *1520*

MARTIN LUTHER

65

To Duke John Frederick[1]
Wittenberg, October 30, 1520

Luther thanks the Duke for supporting his case and tells of his determination to continue his public activities in spite of the bull Exsurge, Domine (see p. 179, n. 1).

Duke John Frederick (1503-1554) was the son of Duke John, the brother and successor (1525-1532) of Elector Frederick (see pp. 49 f.). Educated by George Spalatin (see pp. 8 f.), he was deeply attracted by Luther and by the Reformer's thought and work. In 1532 he became Elector of Saxony; he was the last member of the Ernestine family to hold this office. During the tragic battle between the Protestant Smalcald League and the Imperial army at Mühlberg on April 24, 1547, he was cap-

J. Grünenberg, second half of November, 1520). *WA* 7, 42 ff.; *LW* 31, 334 ff.

[3] John Eck; see p. 80, n. 13. Occasionally Luther put the blame for the indulgence controversy on Tetzel. See pp. 46, 339 f.

[4] See p. 327, n. 10.

[1] Missing in the autograph; the addressee, however, can be supplied from an old manuscript copy of this letter; see *WA*, Br 2, No. 347, Introduction.

tured by the Emperor and sentenced to death for rebellion and high treason. Later his death sentence was commuted to life imprisonment and the forfeiture of his Electoral dignity. Shortly afterward, however, his imprisonment was ended. In comparison with the shrewdness of Elector Frederick, John Frederick's political abilities were limited, especially in dealing with the Emperor. Yet his character was strong; this was especially evident in the days of his imprisonment. Throughout his entire life he had been convinced of the correctness of the Reformation; as a result he was not willing to yield a single point to the political and religious demands of the Roman Imperial party, and, although defeated by the Emperor, he refused to acknowledge any decisions concerning religious issues which might be reached by any council in which the Reformation party was not granted equal representation. From his earliest youth he had dedicated his whole energy to the development of the Reformation; together with his father he instituted the visitations of the congregations in Saxony and Thuringia. Especially after 1530 he tried to strengthen the political position of the Protestant Estates against the Emperor and his policy of supporting the Roman church.

Text in German: WA, Br 2, 205-206.

Jesus

Serene, Noble Sovereign, Gracious Lord: Before all else, my humble prayer and all my services are always at Your Grace's disposal. Gracious Lord, I have received Your Grace's letter, and read it with great joy.[2] From it I have learned of Your Grace's special good will and favor toward me, unworthy though I be, and also of your great steadfastness and enthusiasm for the holy and divine truth. Although I am too lowly to have brought this about in Your Grace even in a small way, yet at all times I want to be diligent in thanking and praising God for it, according to my humble ability; may he strengthen and preserve Your

---

[2] Correspondence between Duke John Frederick and Elector Frederick regarding the bull; see p. 179, n. 1; for details, see *WA*, Br 2, No. 347, Introduction.

Grace's heart and mind in such a Christian attitude. Your Grace's constant concern in this cause, so as to write so assiduously to my Most Gracious Lord, Duke Frederick, elector, etc., stirs up great hope in me that God will help his gospel through Your Grace.

As the bull[3] has in no way frightened me, I intend to preach, lecture, and write in spite of it. I suspect, however, that the people of Leipzig,[4] if they could, would drive me out of Wittenberg, with the help of Duke George and the Bishop of Merseburg,[5] who have developed toward me a hatred defying description. But I have commended all this to the divine will. I well realize that they try to destroy not me but rather Your Grace's small university at Wittenberg. They have played with this thought for some time, and now they rejoice that they have found a "just" reason.[6] May they do whatever God has destined them to do. I shall await the next throw of the dice.

With this, I want humbly to commend myself—but before all else, the cause of the Christian truth—to Your Grace. May God bless, strengthen, and govern you for us, according to his divine will. To him be praise and honor. Amen.

Wittenberg, October 30, 1520

Your Grace's dedicated priest,
D. Martin Luther
Augustinian

---

3 On the bull, see p. 176; p. 179, n. 1.
4 On the hostilities between the University of Wittenberg and the University of Leipzig, see p. 63, n. 24.
5 On Duke George, Luther's bitter opponent since the Leipzig Disputation, see p. 110, n. 20; p. 149, n. 6. Adolf of Anhalt, bishop of Merseburg from 1514 to 1526 (a brother of William of Anhalt, the begging prince who made such a strong impression on young Martin during his school days in Magdeburg; see p. 146; *WA* 38, 105), was responsible for Alveld's attacks on Luther; see p. 164, n. 9.
6 Namely, the bull.

66

To Lazarus Spengler
Wittenberg, November 17, 1520

Lazarus Spengler was the city clerk of Nürnberg, that is, the legally trained counselor and liaison man between council and mayor; in this position he was able to influence events in the city to a great extent. He became one of the most prominent figures of the Reformation movement in Nürnberg and the Brandenburg-Ansbach-Franconia territory. Disturbed by rumors of a possible split in the Wittenberg Faculty, as well as between Luther and Erasmus, he turned to Luther for information. Luther is assuring him that everything is fine. Luther also comments on a second edition of his appeal to a General Council (see p. 90, n. 5) and on the bull Exsurge, Domine (see p. 179, n. 1).

Text in German: WA, Br 2, 217-218.

To the prudent and wise Lazarus Spengler, city clerk of the City of Nürnberg, etc., my special lord and friend

Jesus

My service, etc., [is always available to you]

Honorable and wise sir, my dear lord and friend: I have read your letter[1] with special joy and seen your great courage in the matter of Christian truth. God strengthen you and all of us with his grace. I also appreciate very much the great and kind concern that you show in behalf of me and all the people of Wittenberg. You certainly should believe, however, that Doctor Karlstadt[2] and Philip[3] agree entirely. Occasionally, of course, in the University one person says something differently than another; this fact, perhaps, gave rise to this rumor. But Master Philip is, by God's grace, so gifted that he will not have any controversy with Karlstadt. Likewise, it never occurred to me to bear a grudge

[1] This letter is not extant.
[2] Andrew Karlstadt; see p. 79, n. 12.
[3] Philip Melanchthon; see p. 77, n. 3.

against Erasmus[4] or to dislike him. It is all right with me that he does not want me to make any references to him. I also answered him and promised not to mention him in this way any more, nor any other good friends, since it is dangerous for them.[5] People imagine and write many such things about me; therefore don't be disturbed by their gossip. God willing, Erasmus and I will of course remain one. It is true, however, that once in a while I debate privately with Philip on how close Erasmus is to the [right] way or how far he is from it. He and everyone else may also do that about me with impunity and in friendship. I will not attack anyone first. It is sufficient for me to defend myself if attacked.

I have now arranged for a second printing of my *Appeal* in Latin and in German,[6] although I thought there was no real need for it, since the bull[7] was so open and shameless in condemning me in a totally anti-Christian manner. We do not know whether the bishops will put the bull into effect.[8] I do not regard myself as having legally received the bull.[9]

With this I commend myself to you before God. Amen.

Wittenberg, November 17, 1520

D. MARTIN LUTHER
Augustinian

---

4 Erasmus of Rotterdam; see pp. 116 f.; p. 150, n. 10.

5 In his reply to the "asses of Louvain and Cologne" (see p. 155), published in March of 1520, Luther charged both universities with arrogance and stupidity, and demonstrated that in the past they occasionally had made fools of themselves in condemning certain scholars. Luther referred to individual cases and concluded that he did not want to discuss the universities' conduct toward John Ruchrath of Wesel (see *O.D.C.C.*, p. 741), Faber Stapulensis (see p. 26, n. 15), and Erasmus. See *WA* 6, 184. In a letter dated August 1, 1520, Erasmus (although he was impressed with the courage shown by Luther in this reply; see Allen 4, 1113; see also Allen 9, 2445) complained to Luther that he did not want to be involved in the Reformer's business, since he had enough trouble of his own. See *WA*, Br 2, 157. Luther's answer is not extant.

6 The second edition of Luther's appeal to a General Council, which he had issued for the first time in November, 1518. See p. 90; *WA* 7, 75 f. It was supposed to be a powerful countermeasure to the bull (see p. 179, n. 1).

7 On the bull, see p. 176; p. 179, n. 1.

8 Certain bishops, like the one at Bamberg, refused or for various reasons hesitated to publish and execute the bull in their dioceses; see *WA*, Br 2, 212, n. 19.

9 The bull was never delivered to Luther personally but only to the University. Right after Luther saw the bull he decided to act as if it had not

67

To George Spalatin
Wittenberg, December 10, 1520

Luther reports on the burning of certain papal books. He also comments on a request for a leave of absence made by the preacher of Eilenburg.

See LW 31, 381 ff.; Schwiebert, pp. 486 ff. On George Spalatin, see pp. 8 f.

Text in Latin: WA, Br 2, 234.

To the learned and devout man, George Spalatin, court chaplain and my friend in the Lord

Jesus

Greetings. On December 10, 1520, at nine o'clock in the morning, all the following papal books were burned in Wittenberg at the eastern gate near the Church of the Holy Cross: the *Decretum*, the *Decretals*, the [*Liber*] *Sextus*, the *Clementines*, the *Extravagantes*,[1] and the most recent bull of Leo X;[2] likewise the *Summa*

been legally turned over to him, or as if the bull had been forged by Eck. See *WA*, Br 2, No. 341, Introduction; *S-J* 1, 365 ff.

[1] Luther is referring to parts of the Canon Law. They are collections of decretals, or official proclamations of the Papal See, in which issues of faith and morals or of the administration of the church were decided, or in which suggestions were made for such decisions. (a) Gratian's *Decretum* of approximately 1150 was the first major collection of decretals. (b) The *Decretals* or the *Liber extra* was a collection issued by Pope Gregory IX in 1234. It contained the decretals which were missing in (a) and those which were issued between 1150 and 1234. (c) In 1298 Pope Boniface VIII issued the *Liber Sextus;* it contained the decretals which were promulgated between 1234 and 1298. (d) The *Clementinae* are a collection of decretals issued mostly by Clement V (pope: 1305-1314), published by John XXII in 1317. (e) The *Extravagantes*, published in 1325, are a collection of the decretals of Pope John XXII. (f) The *Extravagantes communes* are decretals issued between 1281-1484, but not included in other collections. The Council of Basel (1437) collected (a) to (d) into one *corpus* of legal material, to which (e) and (f) were later added. In burning the Canon Law, Luther rejected the legal and administrative authority of the Roman See, which had condemned his teachings. See *CIC; O.D.C.C.*, p. 346.

[2] *Exsurge, Domine* (*Arise, O Lord*); see p. 176; p. 179, n. 1.

Angelica,[3] Eck's *Chrysopassus*[4] and other books by this author, writings of Emser,[5] and certain other books that were added by different people. This was done so that the incendiary papists may see that it doesn't take much to burn books they cannot refute.[6] This is the news here.

Besides this, what you have asked me to do for the preacher of Eilenburg[7]—look, I am doing right now. For he asks that with your help I get the Most Illustrious Sovereign[8] to obtain permission from his [the preacher's] superiors which would allow him to stay for eight years wherever he wants to, perhaps in concentrated study. Since he was moved around at their command for many years, it seems fair that for once he spend some time in peace to his own profit. This I have now done and am doing, asking you to do your part. Now you have what you wanted.

Farewell.

Wittenberg, December 10, 1520 MARTIN LUTHER

---

[3] I.e., *Summa de casibus conscientiae*. This was a handbook to guide priests in hearing confession; it was issued by Angelo Carletti di Chivasso (1411-1495). See also *WA* 6, 553; *LW* 36, 96, n. 166.

[4] A work by John Eck (see p. 80, n. 13) on predestination. For some information on this work, see *WA*, Br 2, 235, n. 3.

[5] Jerome Emser; see p. 137, n. 19.

[6] As a result of the bull, Luther's books were burned in various cities of Germany. Luther's decision to burn the decretals was brought about by the burning of his books (or at least rumors about it) by the faculty and students of the University of Leipzig; see *WA*, Br 2, 235, n. 1. Perhaps it is significant, as Schwiebert (p. 482) has pointed out, that the burning of the bull took place exactly at the end of the period of grace allowed to Luther for recanting.

[7] George Kunzelt was then preacher at Eilenburg, a town close to Merseburg. Nothing could be found out about him except that Luther wrote to him on June 15, 1520, concerning some homiletical problem; see *WA*, Br 2, 124; *S-J* 1, 331 f.

[8] Elector Frederick; see pp. 49 f.

68

To George Spalatin
Wittenberg, December 29, 1520

Luther expresses his willingness to appear before the Diet of Worms if summoned, regardless of any danger which might be involved. In addition he mentions some matters relating to his correspondence and his rebuttal of the bull (see p. 179, n. 1).

On George Spalatin, see pp. 8 f.

Text in Latin: WA, Br 2, 242-243.

To the learned and devout man, Mr. George Spalatin, Saxon court chaplain, my friend in the Lord

Greetings. Today I received the copies of the letters from Allstedt as well as your letter from Kindelbrück.[1] In it you ask me what I would do if called by Emperor Charles and if [I could do anything] without endangering the gospel and the public welfare, since you see that [my] enemies do everything to bring this affair to a head.[2]

Of course I would by all means come, if called, in so far as it would be up to me, even if I could not come by my own power and instead would have to be driven there as a sick man.[3] For it would not be right to doubt that I am called by the Lord if the Emperor summons. Further, if they should employ force in this matter, which is most probable (for they do not want me called

[1] Spalatin accompanied Elector Frederick (see pp. 49 f.) to Worms for the diet. The Electoral party stayed in Allstedt (near Weimar) from December 14 to 20 (see WA, Br 2, 237, n. 1), and was in Kindelbrück (near Erfurt) on December 21 (see WA, Br 2, No. 365, Introduction). The "letters" were copies of those letters exchanged between the Elector and the Emperor concerning Luther's appearance before the diet; for more details, see p. 193, n. 9. Spalatin's letter is not extant; its contents however can be deduced from Luther's answer here.

[2] Having a close acquaintance with the correspondence between the Elector and the Imperial government (see note 1 and WA, Br 2, No. 365, Introduction) and therefore familiar with the strong antipathy toward Luther on the part of the Emperor's advisers, Spalatin must have told Luther he was worried about this antipathy (in the Kindelbrück letter which is not extant, see note 1).

[3] On Luther's health, see p. 69, n. 26; p. 217, n. 15.

there because they want to learn something), then this matter can only be commended to the Lord. For He who saved the three men in the furnace of the Babylonian king[4] still lives and rules. If He does not want to preserve me, then my head is of slight importance compared with Christ, who was put to death in greatest ignominy—a stumbling block to all, and the ruin of many. No one's danger, no one's safety can be considered here. We must rather take care that we do not expose the gospel (which we have finally begun to promote) to the derision of the godless and thus give our enemies a reason for boasting over us because we do not dare confess what we have taught and are afraid to shed our blood for it. May the merciful Christ prevent such cowardice on our part and such boasting on their part. Amen.

Of course it has to come about that the kings and rulers of the earth would gather and rage with the nations and peoples against God and his Christ.[5] Yet the Spirit teaches in that same Psalm that those who trust in God will be blessed; and not only this, but also that the Lord will laugh and deride those who don't.[6] Certainly it is not up to us to decide whether my life, or for that matter my death, will bring greater or less danger for the gospel and the public welfare. You know that God's truth is a rock of stumbling set for the fall and rising again of many in Israel.[7]

The only concern remaining to us is to pray to the Lord that Charles's reign would not stain its first actions[8] with my blood—or anyone else's—to protect ungodliness. I would rather perish (as I have often said) by the hands of the Romanists[9] alone, than that he and his administration should be involved in this affair. You know what misery followed Emperor Sigismund after the death of Huss.[10] After that nothing prospered for him any more. He

[4] Daniel 3.
[5] Ps. 2:1-2.
[6] Ps. 2:4, 10-11.
[7] Isa. 8:14; Luke 2:34.
[8] Charles was crowned Roman king in Aachen on October 23, 1520, and shortly afterward the Pope agreed to Charles's assuming the title "chosen Roman Emperor." The Diet of Worms, scheduled to open on January 27, 1521, was the first diet over which the young king presided.
[9] On the term "Romanists," see p. 92, n. 16.
[10] During the Council of Constance (1414-1418) John Huss (1369?-1415), the Bohemian Reformer, was executed as a heretic; Emperor Sigismund (1410-1437) thus violated the safe-conduct he had granted to Huss. The

died without a [male] offspring, and later on even Ladislas, the son of his daughter, died. In one generation his name became extinct. His wife Barbara even turned out to be a disgrace for all queens, and many other things happened that you know, I believe. However, if it has to come to pass that I am not only handed over to the hierarchy but also to the nations,[11] then the will of the Lord be done. Amen.

Now you have my judgment and opinion on this matter. You may expect everything of me except flight and recanting. I do not want to escape, much less recant; may the Lord Jesus strengthen me in this. I could do neither without endangering piety and the salvation of many.

I return the copies of the letters;[12] in due time I shall send a letter to the Sovereign, as you have outlined in the draft.[13] Until now I thought that all my [writings] reached this court at the earliest moment via other people.[14] So now take whatever is off the press, for the German edition, based on the Latin, is now being printed.[15]

Hussite War, which started soon after the Council of Constance, devastated Bohemia and parts of Germany. Sigismund had one daughter who was married to Emperor Albrecht II (1438-1439) of the Hapsburg family. Albrecht died during a war against the Turks; his posthumous son Ladislas died in 1457 without children. Sigismund's second wife Barbara, countess of Cilly, became known for her immoral life.

[11] I.e., government of nations, as contrasted with the government of the church.

[12] See note 1.

[13] This is probably letter No. 70, for which Spalatin must have sent a rough draft.

[14] It is not quite clear what Luther meant here. Perhaps Spalatin complained in his lost letter (see note 1) that he had not received all the printed sheets of the *Assertio* (see note 15), of which he had seen only the first in late November or early December (see *WA*, Br 2, 230, n. 4). This might explain why Luther is including whatever was thus far published of the German and Latin texts of the *Assertio*.

[15] Soon after Luther had read the bull (see p. 179, n. 1), and having been urged by Elector Frederick to do so, he replied to it with the *Assertio omnium articulorum M. Lutheri per bullam Leonis X novissiman damnatorum* (*Assertion of All the Articles of M. Luther which were Condemned by the Latest Bull of Leo X*) (Wittenberg: M. Lotther, January, 1521). *WA* 7, 94 ff. In order to make his position known to the lay people Luther reworked this little book and treated the same issue in German as well: *Grund und Ursach aller Artikel, so durch die römische Bulle unrechtlich verdammt worden sind* (*Defense and Explanation of All the Articles . . .*) (Wittenberg: M. Lotther, March, 1521). *WA* 7, 308 ff.; *LW* 32, 7 ff.

Farewell and be strong in the Lord.

Wittenberg, the day of St. Thomas the Martyr (as many believe),[16] *1520*

MARTIN LUTHER

69

To John von Staupitz
Wittenberg, January 14, 1521

Using the very words with which von Staupitz had once encouraged him, Luther challenges his former superior to have confidence in the cause of the gospel and assures him of his own courage. He reports on the burning of some papal books and tells about the actions of some of his enemies (Emser, Duke George, Thomas Murner) as well as of the burning of his books. He comments briefly on von Hutten's paraphrase of the bull (see p. 179, n. 1).

On John von Staupitz, see p. 64, n. 1.

Text in Latin: WA, Br 2, 245-246; translation based on S-J 1, 440-441.

Jesus

Greetings. When we were at Augsburg[1] and discussed my case, Most Reverend Father, you said to me among other things, "Remember, Friar, you began this in the name of our Lord Jesus Christ." I have accepted this word not as coming from you but as spoken to me through you, and I have kept it firmly in mind ever since.

Therefore I now challenge you with your own statement: remember that you said this to me.[2] Up to now one has only

[16] A reference to the martyrdom of St. Thomas a Becket on December 29, 1170 (see *O.D.C.C.*, pp. 146 f.).

[1] October, 1518; see p. 86.

[2] Having resigned from the office of vicar general in the summer of 1520 (see p. 171, n. 7), von Staupitz went to Salzburg seeking tranquillity. But he did not find it. On January 4, 1521, he wrote to Link (see pp. 169 f.)

played around in this case; now something serious is at hand.[3] As you have said, unless God executes it, it cannot be executed at all. All these things are now completely in the hand of Almighty God. No one can deny this. Who can advise here? What can man plan? There is such a tremendous turmoil that I think it cannot be quieted except by the arrival of the Last Day, so great is the animosity on both sides.

The papacy is not now what it was yesterday and the day before. Even if it excommunicates me and burns my books, and even kills me, doubtless something portentious is at the door. How happy the Pope would have been if he had begun this affair with good mediators for establishing peace rather than with force and storms for the destruction of Luther. I have burned the books of the pope and the bull,[4] at first with trembling and praying; but now I am more pleased with this than with any other action of my life, for [these books] are worse than I had thought.

Emser is writing against me in German from Leipzig.[5] He is

---

that Cardinal Lang, the archbishop of Salzburg, had been instructed to make him (Staupitz) "assert that Martin's opinions are respectively heretical, erroneous, . . . and to reject them in the presence of a notary and witnesses." See *WA*, Br 2, 246, n. 2; *S-J* 1, 437. The *WA*, Br editor suggests that Link informed Luther of Staupitz's letter and that Luther's encouraging statement should be seen against this background. How great the pressure von Staupitz was exposed to after the bull (see p. 179, n. 1) was published can be seen from the fact that even Erasmus, who lived in Louvain, knew of it; see Allen 4, 1166.

[3] This must refer to the pending Diet of Worms and the fact that the Emperor would deal with the case of the heretic, who was now excommunicated. Since Luther did not recant (as was stipulated in the bull *Exsurge, Domine*), the Pope issued the bull *Decet Romanum* on January 3, 1521, in which Luther was excommunicated. Thus the Papal See tried to prevent further interference by the secular authorities. The only thing the Emperor could do if he wanted to be a faithful son of the church was to turn Luther over to the papal authorities.

[4] See pp. 186 f.

[5] Jerome Emser; see p. 137, n. 19. He published the first part of a sharp rebuttal of Luther's little book *To the Christian Nobility of the German Nation* (see p. 171, n. 5) in December, 1520, which he completed in January, 1521; for bibliographical details, see *WA* 7, 260. As soon as Luther had seen this first fascicle of Emser's work, he wrote a preliminary reply: *An den Bock zu Leipzig* (*To the Leipzig Goat*) (Wittenberg: M. Lotther, January ?, 1521). *WA* 7, 262 f.; *PE* 3, 282 f. Emser answered at once with his *An den Stier von Wittenberg* (*To the Wittenberg Bull*) (for a bibliography, see *WA* 7, 266), dated January 20, 1521, which Luther countered with his *Auf des Bocks zu Leipzig Antwort* (*Reply to the Answer of the Leipzig Goat*) (Wittenberg: J. Grünenberg, February ?,

strongly influenced by Duke George,[6] who is furious at me. While breathing threats and murder,[7] the Duke has proposed in the court[8] the most ungodly actions against me.

I have been summoned by the Emperor in a letter delivered to the Sovereign; but the Sovereign objected to it, and soon the Emperor revoked the summons in another letter.[9] God knows what will happen.

Our Vicar Wenceslas[10] has gone to Nürnberg. Zeschau is in Grimma.[11] One says he has left [the Order]. May God keep him. Everything is flourishing here, as previously.

Hutten[12] has written a commentary upon the bull[13] with the sharpest remarks against the pope; he is planning other steps in regard to this affair.

1521). *WA* 7, 271 f.; *PE* 3, 289 f. On January 20, 1521, the rest of the fascicles of Emser's work against Luther's *To the Christian Nobility of the German Nation* (see above) were completed (see *WA* 7, 260); they reached Wittenberg at the beginning of February. Luther began to work on his reply at once. It developed into a basic rebuttal of Emser's attacks on the position Luther had taken in *To the Christian Nobility of the German Nation.* Luther's answer is entitled: *Auf das überchristlich, übergeistlich und überkünstlich Buch Bocks Emsers zu Leipzig Antwort* (*Dr. Martin Luther's Answer to the Superchristian, Superspiritual, and Superlearned Book of Goat Emser of Leipzig*) (Wittenberg: J. Grünenberg, 1521); it was completed March 29, 1521; see *WA* 7, 621 ff.; *PE* 3, 310 ff.

6 On Duke George, see p. 110, n. 20; p. 144, n. 2; p. 149, n. 6.

7 Acts 9:1.

8 It is not clear to which court Luther refers, the Duke's, the Elector's, or the Emperor's.

9 Luther refers to the letters of which Spalatin had sent copies with letter No. 68: Emperor Charles V (see pp. 175 f.) to Elector Frederick (see pp. 49 f.): November 28, 1520. *DRTA. JR* 2, No. 61; *S-J* 1, 398. This was an invitation to bring Luther along to the diet. Elector Frederick to Emperor Charles V: December 20, 1520. *DRTA. JR* 2, No. 63; *S-J* 1, 429 f. In this letter the Elector refused to bring Luther to the diet; apparently he did not want to risk Luther's safety but rather wanted to force the Emperor to grant a safe-conduct. However, on December 17, 1520, the Emperor revoked the invitation, since in the meantime he had been informed of the bull *Exsurge, Domine* (see note 3); he wanted to discuss the affair with the Elector in person before deciding on further action; see *DRTA. JR* 2, No. 62; *S-J* 1, 424 f.

10 Wenceslas Link; see pp. 169 f.; he was then on a visitation trip as vicar general.

11 Wolfgang Zeschau, former prior of the monastery in Grimma; see *WA*, Br 1, 227, n. 1.

12 Ulrich von Hutten; see p. 163, n. 1.

13 See p. 179, n. 1. This was an attack by von Hutten against the bull; for biographical details, see *WA*, Br 2, 233, n. 12; for the text, see Böcking 5, 301 ff.

They[14] have burned me three times [in effigy]: at Louvain, at Cologne, and at Mainz. At Mainz, however, it was done with great scorn, even with danger for those who did the burning.[15]

Thomas Murner has also written furiously against me.[16] I will wait to see about that barefooted ass of Leipzig.[17]

Farewell, my Father; pray for the Word of God and for me. I am carried away and tossed about by the waves.

Wittenberg, January 14, 1521

MARTIN LUTHER
Augustinian

70

To Elector Frederick
Wittenberg, January 25, 1521

Luther thanks the Elector for sending information on the Emperor's stand on his case; he renews his offer to come to the diet, if provided with sufficient guarantees, and asks the Elector to intercede with the Emperor on his behalf.

On Elector Frederick, see pp. 49 f.

Text in German: WA, Br 2, 253-255.

---

[14] Luther's enemies.

[15] When the bull *Exsurge, Domine* (see p. 179, n. 1) became known, Luther's books and Luther-in-effigy were burned in many places; see also *WA*, Br 2, 225, n. 15.

[16] Thomas Murner of Oberehnheim/Alsace, O.F.M. (1475-1537), made poet laureate by Emperor Maximilian in 1505, was graduated as Doctor of Theology by the University of Freiburg/Breisgau in 1506 and as Doctor of Canon and Secular Law by the University of Basel in 1519. After some time spent in the service of Henry VIII of England and in the service of the Bishop of Strassburg he returned to his native town to be a preacher there. Murner was famous for the biting humor to which he exposed his contemporaries in his many satires. He was perhaps the most popular enemy of Luther, whom he attacked primarily in German. In 1520 Murner published a little book against Luther's *To the Christian Nobility of the German Nation* (see p. 171, n. 5); for biographical information on this attack, see *WA* 7, 615. Luther replied to him in a separate chapter of his *Answer to the Superchristian . . . Book of Goat Emser;* see note 5.

[17] Augustine Alveld; see p. 164, n. 9.

To the Most Serene and Noble Sovereign and Lord, Sir Frederick, duke in Saxony, elector and viceroy of the Holy Roman Empire, landgrave in Thuringia, margrave in Meissen, my Most Gracious Lord and Patron

Jesus

Most Serene, Noble Sovereign, Most Gracious Lord: Before all else, my poor prayers and my humble services are always obediently at Your Electoral Grace's disposal.

Most Gracious Lord: I have received Your Electoral Grace's gracious information with regard to the deliberation and opinion of His Roman Imperial and Spanish Royal Majesty,[1] my Most Gracious Lord, concerning my case.[2] I most humbly thank His Imperial Majesty and Your Electoral Grace for this favor. I heartily rejoice that His Imperial Majesty wants to take upon himself this case; God willing, it is a case of God, of universal Christendom, and of the whole German nation—and not of a single man, much less my own.

I repeat: I am humbly willing to do or to omit doing all that I can before God and with Christian dignity, or to do or to omit doing all that I am told, on an honorable, Christian, and satisfactory basis of holy divine Scripture. That I have always been willing to do this may be seen by my manifold offers [3] and especially by that offer which was printed recently, of which I am enclosing a copy for Your Electoral Grace.[4]

Therefore I beseech Your Electoral Grace in all humility to intercede most humbly on my behalf with His Roman Imperial Majesty, in order that he may graciously provide me with sufficient security and a safe-conduct against all violence, about which I

---

1 Charles V; see pp. 175 f.

2 Luther is referring to a (not extant) letter from Elector Frederick in which the Elector apparently informed him of his meeting with the Emperor. This meeting seems to have changed the attitude the Emperor had expressed in his December 17 letter to the Elector. See p. 193, n. 9; *DRTA. JR* 2, 476, n. 2.

3 See p. 74, n. 7.

4 Luther is enclosing a printed copy of his *Offer and Protest;* see p. 172, n. 4; p. 174, nn. 5, 6.

have to be especially careful.[5] May [His Imperial Majesty] also [graciously] arrange that this case be turned over to devout, learned, understanding, trustworthy, and Christian men, both clergymen and laymen, who are well versed in the Bible and who understand and differentiate between divine and human laws and commands, in order to discuss the case carefully with me. May [His Imperial Majesty], for the sake of God, not allow the use of force against me until I have been shown to be un-Christian and wrong. [May His Imperial Majesty], as secular head of holy Christendom, be concerned that in the meantime my opponents, the papists, cease their storming and un-Christian actions against me, their burning of my books, and their raging plots against my body, honor, welfare, life, and salvation (undertaken although I have not been investigated or convicted). [Please intercede on my behalf with His Imperial Majesty] that I may be graciously excused for whatever I may have done (or may in the future be forced and provoked to do) in necessary defense against these things—more in order to save the divine evangelical truth than my own insignificant and unworthy self—and that [His Majesty] may hold me in gracious protection, in order that the divine Word may be saved, and that he may be to me a most gracious lord. For this and all the other virtues and favors worthy of a Christian emperor and sovereign, I confidently look to His renowned Imperial Majesty and Your Electoral Grace, as to my [most gracious lords].

For in humble obedience, I am prepared to come to the pending Diet of Worms if I receive sufficient guarantee and a safe-conduct for the journey there and back. I am willing to appear before said devout, learned, and neutral judges. With the help of the Almighty I am ready to present myself and give account so that each one may truly learn that I have until now done or said nothing out of a blasphemous, rash, or inordinate desire, or for temporal and worldly glory and profit.[6] [Then one may truly learn that] all that I have written or taught was for the sake of my conscience and my oath and obligation as a humble teacher of

---

[5] The summons and the safe-conduct were issued on March 6, 1521; see *WA*, Br 2, No. 383; *S-J* 1, 482 ff.

[6] For similar statements, see pp. 69, 103, 171.

Holy Scripture,[7] to the praise of God, for the welfare and salvation of all Christendom, and for the good of the whole German nation. [Then one may truly learn that] I have worked for the eradication of dangerous abuses and superstitions and the liberation of holy Christendom in its entirety from so many endless, innumerable, un-Christian, and damnable tyrannical diminutions [of the gospel], burdens, and blasphemies.

May Your Electoral Grace and His Roman Imperial Majesty harbor a Christian attitude[8] and understanding for the deeply troubled situation of all Christendom. Knowing that divine mercy and grace is with you, still, for the sake of His Imperial Majesty and Your Electoral Grace, I, a poor and humble priest, am both bound and willing in all humility always to pray for this[9] to God with my poor supplication.

Written at Wittenberg, January 25, 1521

Your Electoral Grace's obedient,
dedicated priest,
MARTIN LUTHER

71

To George Spalatin
Frankfurt/Main, April 14,[1] 1521

Luther is on his way to Worms; he expresses his determination to appear before the diet in spite of all adversities.

On Luther's journey to Worms, see Schwiebert, pp. 496 f. On George Spalatin, see pp. 8 f.

Text in Latin: WA, Br 2, 298.

---

7 For Luther's understanding of his obligations as a doctor of the church, see p. 49, n. 23.

8 Luther wrote *Auge,* i.e., "eye."

9 The antecedent of "this" is unclear; it could be the "troubled situation," or the fact that both sovereigns should have or develop a Christian understanding of the situation.

1 Missing in the autograph; for the dating, see *WA,* Br 2, 298, n. 1. Accompanied by the Imperial herald Caspar Sturm, Luther and his party left Wittenberg on April 2 and arrived in Frankfurt/Main on April 14.

To my friend in the Lord, Master George Spalatin, Saxon court chaplain, honored in Christ

Jesus

Greetings. I am coming, my Spalatin, although Satan has done everything to hinder me with more than one disease. All the way from Eisenach to here I have been sick; I am still sick in a way which previously has been unknown to me.[2] Of course I realize that the mandate of Charles has also been published to frighten me.[3] But Christ lives, and we shall enter Worms in spite of all the gates of hell and the powers in the air.[4] I enclose copies of the Emperor's letters.[5] It is not wise to write further letters until I first see in person what has to be done, so that we may not encourage Satan, whom I have made up my mind to frighten and despise. So, prepare the lodging.

Farewell.

Frankfurt, 1521 MART[IN] LUTHER

---

[2] What troubled Luther's health (never the best anyway; see p. 69, n. 26; p. 217, n. 15) is not known; nevertheless it must have been quite serious. During the stopover in Eisenach Luther's friends even feared for his life. After being "bled" and taking some medicine, Luther was able to get a good night's sleep, enabling him to continue his journey; see *WA*, Br 2, 298, n. 2.

[3] This was a mandate issued by Charles V on March 10 to confiscate Luther's books, which were declared heretical; see *DRTA. JR* 2, No. 75. Luther was informed of this hostile step as soon as he reached Weimar. Friends suggested that he not continue his journey. However he replied, ". . . regardless of the fact that I have been placed under the ban and that it has been publicized in all the towns, I shall proceed and trust in the Kaiser's [Emperor's] safe-conduct"; see *WA*, TR 5, No. 5342; 3, No. 3357.

[4] Matt. 16:18; Eph. 2:2. *WA*, TR 5, No. 5342; 3, No. 3357. "I would enter Worms even if as many devils were in that city as tiles on the roofs." Luther had written a similar statement in 1518 when he went to Augsburg (see p. 83); see *WA*, Br 1, No. 96. See also in this volume, p. 390.

[5] Probably copies of the summons and safe-conduct; for the text, see *WA*, Br 2, No. 383; *S-J* 1, 482 ff.

72

To John Cuspinian
Worms, April 17, 1521[1]

Within a few hours after his first hearing before the Diet of Worms, Luther gives this report of what took place.

John Cuspinian (the Humanistic name of John Spieszhaimer) was a prominent figure at the Hapsburg court in Vienna, president of the University of Vienna in 1500, curator of the library, keeper of the archives, famous poet, diplomat, and physician. One of his relatives was in Worms and urged Luther to write to Cuspinian. In the beginning Cuspinian had been favorably inclined toward Luther and the Reformation and had even worked toward reorganizing the church in the Hapsburg territories. Later however, after the Reformation was accompanied by the Wittenberg disturbances (see p. 386, n. 1) and the Peasants' War, he retreated. Apparently he then became antagonistic to the cause of the Reformation. He died in 1529. Hans A. v. Kleehoven, Der Wiener Humanist Johannes Cuspinian, Gelehrter und Diplomat zur Zeit Kaiser Maximilians I (Köln-Graz: Böhlau, 1959).

See pp. 201 f., 204 ff.; LW 32, 101 ff.; Schwiebert, pp. 501 ff.

Text in Latin: WA, Br 2, 300.

To the most distinguished and learned Mr. Cuspinian, librarian of His Imperial Majesty at Vienna, my friend, honored in the Lord

Jesus

Greetings. Your brother,[2] most distinguished Cuspinian, has easily convinced me to dare to write to you from the midst of this turmoil, since even prior to this I wanted to be acquainted with you because of the fame of your name. Please add me to the list of your friends, that I may attest the truth of what your brother has

[1] Luther arrived in Worms on April 16 before noon.

[2] Luther wrote *Frater carnis tuae,* literally, "the brother of your flesh." It is not clear whom Luther means; for several possibilities established by the WA, Br editor, see *WA,* Br 2, 300, n. 1.

reported to me with such great enthusiasm concerning you [and your kindness].

I appeared at this hour before the Emperor and the Imperial diet.[3] I was questioned as to whether I would want to renounce my books. I answered then that these were certainly my books and that I would tell them my opinion concerning any renunciation the following day, since more opportunity and time for deliberation on this issue has been neither asked nor granted.[4] With Christ's help, however, I shall not in all eternity recant the least particle.

Farewell, my dearest Cuspinian.

Worms, April 17, 1521[5]

73

To Lucas Cranach
Frankfurt/Main, the morning of April 28, 1521[1]

On his way back from Worms Luther reports to Cranach on the final outcome of the diet and informs him that he will go into hiding for a while. He asks Cranach to express his appreciation to the city council for the transportation they had provided him. He

---

[3] April 17, 4:00 P.M. Luther wrote *Senatu Romano,* "Roman senate." On the diet, see p. 70, n. 1. Luther was accompanied by Doctor Jerome Schurf (see p. 219, n. 2), who acted as his legal counsel and insisted that the titles of the books be read before Luther acknowledged them. The interrogation was conducted by John von Eck, a member of the staff of the Archbishop of Trier; he is not to be confused with the John Eck who had opposed Luther in the Leipzig Debate (see p. 80, n. 13).

[4] Luther means that not having been informed in advance that he would be asked only these two questions, he had not petitioned for time to deliberate in private or to elaborate on his stand before the diet, and consequently this time was not available to him. Therefore he could not give an answer but had to delay until the following day. After a short consultation of the three colleges of the diet (see p. 70, n. 1), Luther was dismissed on the condition that he would give his answer the following afternoon. For a detailed report on the events from a papal point of view, see S-J 1, 525 ff.

[5] The autograph apparently is unsigned, since *WA,* Br does not reproduce any signature.

[1] Luther had left Worms on April 26 about 10 A.M.

also suggests someone for the post of preacher which had become vacant by his absence.

Lucas Cranach the Elder (1472-1553), one of the most famous artists of the Reformation, had a very close relationship with Luther. Cranach and his school produced many of the outstanding altar pieces of the sixteenth century, portrayed many of the theological and politically important figures of the Reformation, and furnished countless numbers of woodcuts for satirical pamphlets, as well as illustrations for the German edition of the Bible. See O.D.C.C., p. 352; G. and K. Noehles, "Cranach, Lucas, the Elder," Encyclopedia of World Art (New York), IV (1959), 64 f.

Text in German: WA, Br 2, 305.

To the subtle master craftsman, Lucas Cranach, painter in Wittenberg, my dear fellow-godfather [2] and friend

Jesus

My services [are yours]. Dear fellow-godfather Lucas: I bless you and commend you to God.

I shall submit to being "imprisoned" and hidden away, though as yet I do not know where.[3] I would have preferred to suffer death at the hands of the tyrants, especially those of the furious Duke George of Saxony,[4] but I must not disregard the counsel of good men; [I must await] his appointed time.[5]

My arrival at Worms was not expected. You can all see from the mandate with which I was suddenly confronted on my way, just how the safe-conduct was kept.[6] I thought His Imperial

---

[2] Luther wrote *Gevatter*, "fellow-godfather." This can have two meanings: a literal one (in this case, the godchild is unknown to us) or a figurative one, in which it connotes closeness, friendship, or kinship. In Luther's time this latter meaning was frequently used, so one could also translate "my dear friend."

[3] When the negotiations collapsed on April 25 Elector Frederick (see pp. 49 f.) discussed with his staff his plan to hide Luther for some time, and someone informed Luther accordingly; see WA, Br 2, 306, n. 3.

[4] Duke George of Saxony; see p. 110, n. 20.

[5] "His," i.e., Duke George's.

[6] See p. 196, n. 5; p. 198, n. 3.

Majesty [7] would have assembled one or fifty scholars and overcome this monk in a straightforward manner. But nothing else was done there than this: Are these your books? Yes. Do you want to renounce them or not? No. Then go away! O we blind Germans, how childishly we act and allow the Romanists [8] to mock and fool us in such a pitiful way!

Give my greeting to my fellow-godparent, your dear wife,[9] and tell her to take it easy in the meantime.

The Jews once in a while have to chant: *"Jo, Jo, Jo."* [10] But Easter Sunday will also come for us, and then we will chant "Alleluia." For a little while one has to be silent and suffer. For a little while you will not see me, and again in a little while you will see me—so said Christ.[11] I hope it will now be the same way [with me]. But God's will, the very best possible, be done in this—as in heaven, so also on earth. Amen.

Greet master craftsman Christian and his wife.[12] Please express my deep appreciation to the city council for my ride.[13] If you do not find Licentiate Feldkirch [14] satisfactory, then you may ask Mr. Amsdorf [15] to be your preacher; he will gladly do it.

Goodbye. With this I commend you all to God. May he pro-

---

[7] Charles V; see pp. 175 f.

[8] On the term "Romanists," see p. 92, n. 16.

[9] On the term "fellow-godparent," see note 2. Cranach's wife was Barbara nee Brengbier, a daughter of the Mayor of Gotha; see *WA*, Br 2, 306, n. 6.

[10] On the basis of the context it is clear that this is a reference to the "Crucify" of Good Friday.

[11] John 16:16.

[12] Christian Düring, the goldsmith; see p. 42, n. 8. Düring's wife was a certain Barbara nee Blankenfeld, who died in 1564; see *WA*, Br 2, 306, n. 10.

[13] Düring had made available to the city council the wagon and the horses Luther used for his trip to Worms. In addition to this ride the city council provided Luther and his party with twenty gulden (on the gulden, see p. 11, n. 2).

[14] I.e., John Dölsch of Feldkirch/Voralberg (1485?-1523). He matriculated in Heidelberg University in 1502 and Wittenberg University in 1504. In 1510 he was appointed a canon of the All Saints' Chapter in Wittenberg, in 1518 he was graduated as Licentiate of Theology (on this degree, see p. 264, n. 3) and as Doctor of Theology in 1521. Although he was an early supporter of Luther, he turned against the Reformation when Luther directed his attention to the reform of the All Saints' Chapter (see p. 338, nn. 8, 11).

[15] Nicholas von Amsdorf; see p. 218.

tect in Christ the minds and faith of all of you from the Roman[16] wolves and dragons and all their followers. Amen.

Frankfurt/Main, April 28, 1521[17]

D. MARTIN LUTHER

74

To Emperor Charles V
Friedberg, April 28, 1521

In this letter, written on his way back from Worms, Luther gives a resume of his conduct before the Diet. He expresses his gratitude for the safe-conduct and asks for the Emperor's continued protection, repeating his willingness to submit his case to neutral judges.

According to Spalatin's notation, inserted on the autograph after the address, this letter never was given to the Emperor; see WA, Br 2, 307. This raises the question of how Spalatin came into possession of the autograph. Perhaps this problem can be solved by considering the autograph on which the WA, Br text is based as Luther's first draft; Luther copied from it the final draft which he sent to the Emperor. On the same day Luther wrote an almost identical letter in German to the Imperial Estates so that his version of the events of the past days could become general knowledge; see WA, Br 2, No. 402. Both letters were published almost at once and served Luther's cause well. On Emperor Charles V, see pp. 175 f.

Text in Latin: WA, Br 2, 307-310; translation based on S-J 1, 547-551.

To the Most Serene and invincible Lord Charles V, chosen emperor of the Romans, Caesar Augustus,[1] king of the Spaniards,

[16] See note 8.

[17] Luther wrote "Cantate Sunday, 1521," i.e., April 28. He arrived in Frankfurt/Main on April 27 and left on the 28th, about 10 A.M.; see WA, Br 2, 306, n. 1.

[1] On the title "chosen emperor," see p. 129, n. 6; p. 189, n. 8; pp. 96 f. It was not before February 24, 1530, that Charles was crowned emperor. The title "Caesar Augustus" was one of the many titles of the Roman

of both Sicily and Jerusalem, etc., archduke of Austria, duke of Burgundy,[2] etc., my most clement Lord

Jesus

Grace and peace with all my submission in Christ Jesus our Lord.

Most Serene and invincible Emperor, most clement Lord: Your Sacred Majesty had summoned me to Worms with a public guarantee and a safe-conduct[3] in order to investigate my opinion concerning the little books that were published under my name. Complying with this summons, I appeared in all humility before Your Sacred Majesty and the whole Imperial diet,[4] thus being obedient in every way. Your Sacred Majesty ordered that I be asked first whether I would acknowledge said little books as mine, and second whether or not I would be ready to revoke them, or would uphold them.

When I had acknowledged that [these little books] were mine (in so far as no opponents or wiseacres have smuggled anything into them or changed them), I pointed out with great reverence and submission that the following was my opinion: since I had fortified my little books with clear and intelligible Scripture passages, it does not seem to me right or just to deny the Word of God and revoke my little books in this way, nor could I do it in any way. I humbly begged that Your Sacred Majesty under no circumstances allow me to be forced into such a recanting. [I further begged] that [Your Sacred Majesty] instead be so concerned and either examine my little books yourself or provide for others of any estate, even the lowest, whoever can, to examine them—and that [Your Sacred Majesty] deign worthy of refutation on the basis of divine, that is, evangelical and

---

emperor. In German documents it is sometimes translated with the equivalent of "Always promoter (or augmenter) of the Empire."

[2] This list of titles represents the offices Charles held and the territories he governed. The title "king of Jerusalem" had been used by the Roman emperor since 1229, when Jerusalem had been peacefully surrendered to Frederick of Hohenstaufen (see *O.D.C.C.*, pp. 525 f.), who then had himself crowned king of Jerusalem. At Charles's time this title had little political meaning; it symbolized only the emperor's claim to the Holy Land and his responsibility toward the sacred places of Christianity.

[3] On the safe-conduct, see p. 196, n. 5; p. 198, n. 3; p. 201.

[4] On the diet, see p. 70, n. 1.

prophetical Scripture, such errors as are charged against these books. With Christian willingness, I offered, if refuted and convicted of error, to recant everything and be the first to throw my books in the fire and trample them underfoot.

In addition to all this, it was requested and demanded of me that I answer simply and plainly whether or not I was ready to recant. Again I answered as humbly as I could: since my conscience is bound by the Scripture passages which I have quoted in my little books, I could under no circumstances recant anything, unless I would be better informed.

After this [interrogation],[5] some electors, sovereigns, and [members of] other Estates of the Empire urged me to submit my little books to the investigation and judgment of Your Sacred Majesty and other Imperial Estates.[6] The Chancellor of Baden[7] and Doctor Peutinger[8] tried hard to persuade me to do this. I offered myself again in the same way as before [willing to recant], provided only that I be instructed by divine Scripture or plain reason. The possibility was finally discussed that I should make a concession, and entrust some articles selected [from my books] to the judgment of an Ecumenical Council.

I, however, who was always humbly and zealously ready to do and suffer everything possible for me, could not obtain [the fulfilment] of this one obviously completely Christian wish: that the Word of God should remain free and unbound for me; that presupposing this, I should submit my little books to Your Sacred Majesty and the Estates of the Empire or even entrust them to

---

[5] After the public negotiations were thus deadlocked, Luther was further urged to recant through "behind-the-scenes" diplomacy. This situation was quite dangerous. The Emperor's mind was made up: Luther is a heretic and will be treated as such. On the other hand a strong pro-Luther sentiment had developed, and men like von Sickingen (see pp. 244 f.) were ready to take up arms for Luther. See Schwiebert, p. 506.

[6] The archbishops of Mainz (see pp. 44 f.) and Trier, the electors of Saxony and Brandenburg, and others (Vehus and Peutinger, see notes 7, 8) met with Luther for an informal discussion on April 24.

[7] This was Jerome Vehus, who had studied law in Freiburg and had been a pupil of the then highly renowned Ulrich Zasius (a close friend of Erasmus). Luther praised him for the fairness he demonstrated during these meetings; see *WA*, Br 2, 322; *S-J* 1, 557.

[8] Famous Imperial councilor and representative of the city of Augsburg. Both officials met with Luther on April 25 early in the morning; see *DRTA. JR* 2, No. 86.

the judgment of a council; and that nothing against God's gospel should be submitted by me or decreed by them.[9] This was the crux of the whole controversy.

God, who searches the heart, will be my witness that I am definitely ready to comply with and obey Your Sacred Majesty, whether it bring me life or death, glory or shame, gain or loss. For I have often offered myself in this way,[10] and now do so again. I make no exceptions save the Word of God,[11] by which not only man lives, as Christ teaches in Matthew 4 [:4], but which also the angels long to see, according to I Peter 1 [:12]. Since [the Word of God] is above everything, it has to be held absolutely free and unbound in all things, as Paul teaches.[12] [The Word of God] is never subject to any man's whim to lower its importance or challenge it, no matter how great, how numerous, how learned, and how holy the men are. This is true to such an extent that St. Paul in Galatians 1 [:8] dares to exclaim and reiterate, "If we or an angel from heaven should preach to you a gospel [contrary to that which we preached to you] let him be accursed." And David says, "Put not your trust in princes, in children of men, in whom there is no help."[13] Nor is anyone able to depend on himself, as Solomon says, "He who trusts in his own mind is a fool."[14] And Jeremiah says, 17 [:5], "Cursed is he who trusts in man."

Now in earthly things, which have nothing in common with the Word of God and with eternal values, we ought to trust each other. For to surrender these earthly things, to jeopardize and lose them, does no harm to salvation, since we shall finally have to give them up, even though we have guarded them. Concerning the Word of God and the eternal values, however, God does not allow this risk, that is, that man should surrender [the Word of God] to man. For he has ordered that all men and all things should be submitted only to him, as he alone has the glory of the

[9] It is not clear whom Luther means, the members of a council, or of the Imperial Estates, or the representatives of the Emperor, or perhaps all of them together.
[10] See p. 74, n. 7.
[11] See p. 74, n. 7; p. 178, n. 4.
[12] II Tim. 2:9.
[13] Ps. 146:3-4.
[14] Prov. 28:26.

truth and is truth himself, while "every man" is "false" and vain, as St. Paul excellently points out in Romans 3 [:4]. This is not wrong; for this faith and submission is actually the true service and worship of God, which should not be offered to any creature, as St. Augustine teaches in the *Enchiridion* 1.[15] Therefore St. Paul considers neither the angels nor himself nor, without doubt, any of the saints either in heaven or on earth, to be worthy of this faith; on the contrary, he curses it.[16] They[17] would not tolerate this either, much less expect it. For to put one's confidence in man in matters concerning eternal salvation would mean to give to the creature that glory which is due only to the Creator. I most humbly beg Your Sacred Majesty, therefore, not to consider this decision[18] concerning the Word of God as stemming from an evil motive, nor to interpret it harshly. My decision has arisen from the said Scripture passages to which every creature rightly yields. The authority of this Scripture is greater than the comprehension of the whole of man's reason, as St. Augustine says.[19]

I have sincerely demonstrated my esteem and loyalty for Your Sacred Majesty. Your Sacred Majesty may easily see this from the fact that I presented myself under Your Sacred Majesty's safe-conduct as a most obedient subject, fearing nothing, even though I knew that my little books were burned by my enemies. [I also knew] that in the meantime an edict was issued against me and my little books in the name of Your Sacred Majesty, and publicly posted in many places.[20] These things could have frightened and held back this poor little monk, and with good reason, had I not expected from the good Lord, Your Sacred Majesty, and the Imperial Estates whatever is best, which I still do.

I could in no way obtain a refutation of my little books on the basis of Scripture, and I was forced to leave without having

---

15 Luther apparently confused this passage with *De civitate Dei* (*The City of God*) (see *Patrology,* pp. 503 f.), X, 1, 2 (*MPL* 41, 277 f.); see also *Enchiridion,* cap. 3. *MPL* 40, 232.

16 Gal. 1:8.

17 Either angels or saints, or both.

18 Luther wrote *praeiudicium,* which can mean a (judicial) examination prior to a trial, or a judgment (decision) during or after a trial.

19 See note 15.

20 See p. 198, n. 3.

been refuted. The whole controversy, as I have mentioned, rests upon the fact that no one was willing to refute on the basis of Holy Scripture any erroneous articles [of faith] which are supposed to be in my little books. No one gave me any hope or promise that an examination or investigation of my little books would be conducted in the light of God's Word at some time in the future. Nevertheless I thank Your Sacred Majesty most humbly for having so carefully observed the safe-conduct to Worms and for having pledged to uphold it until I arrived again at my safe quarters.[21] I beg Your Sacred Majesty once more for Christ's sake not to allow me to be crushed by [my] enemies, to suffer violence and be condemned, since I have so often made myself available, as is becoming to a Christian and an obedient man. For I am still absolutely ready to stand, under Your Sacred Majesty's protection, before trustworthy, learned, free, secular as well as ecclesiastical judges, and to be instructed by Your Sacred Majesty, by the Imperial Estates, by councils, doctors, or anyone else who can and is willing to do it. [I am ready] to submit my little books and my teachings most willingly to all and to endure and accept their examination and judgment, excepting nothing, provided only that the Word of God remain unobstructed, clear and free; certainly [the Word of God] ought to remain above everything, and be the judge of all men.

For this reason, I now make my humble petition, not on my behalf (since I am of no importance) but on behalf of the whole church; it was my concern for the church that

[21] On April 25, during an afternoon meeting with the Archbishop of Trier which had been arranged by Vehus (see notes 7, 8), Luther, whose patience was nearly exhausted, asked the Archbishop to obtain the Emperor's permission for him to leave the diet. Asked by the Archbishop to suggest ways of mediating, Luther, quoting Gamaliel (Acts 5:38-39), replied, "If . . . this work be of men, it will come to naught. But if it be of God, you cannot overthrow it" (see *WA* 7, 854). The gracious dismissal requested by Luther was delivered to him between 5 and 6 P.M. the same day, along with the promise that the safe-conduct would be observed (giving him twenty-one days for a safe return) and an order not to preach, write, or make a commotion among the people in any other way while traveling home. On April 26, about 10 A.M., Luther and his party left Worms; he was again accompanied by the Imperial herald Caspar Sturm, who had escorted Luther from Wittenberg to Worms; see *WA* 7, 866 f.

motivated me to send this letter after having left town.[22] With my whole heart I desire, of course, that Your Sacred Majesty, the whole Empire, and the most noble German nation may be served in the best possible way, and all be preserved in God's grace as happy people. Hitherto I have sought nothing but God's glory and the welfare[23] of all men. Even now I have not considered my own advantage, whether my opponents will condemn me or not. For if Christ my Lord prayed for his enemies while on the cross,[24] how much more should I, with joy and trust in Christ, be concerned about and pray and plead for Your Sacred Majesty, for your Empire, for my most beloved superiors, and all native Germany. I expect nothing but the best from them, relying on my afore-mentioned offer.

With this I commend myself to the shelter of Your Sacred Majesty's wings. May the Lord God guide and keep you for our well-being and happiness. Amen.

Written at Friedberg, April 28, 1521

Your Most Serene Majesty's
most dedicated supplicant,[25]
MARTIN LUTHER

---

22 On the basis of this statement, Schwiebert's (p. 509; cf. Schwiebert, p. 513) assumption that Luther wrote this letter and the letter to the Imperial Estates (see p. 203) on April 25 in the evening has to be modified. Luther, knowing of the Elector's plan to hide him for some time (see p. 201, n. 3), wrote both letters in Friedberg (a small town north of Frankfurt/Main), perhaps upon Spalatin's suggestion (see Schwiebert, p. 513). Thus Luther had a good reason for dismissing the Imperial herald, whom he ordered to return to Worms to deliver the letters. The herald had to guarantee with his life Luther's safety; he would only have been in the way when Luther was kidnapped.

23 Luther wrote *salutem*, which can also mean "salvation."

24 Luke 23:34.

25 Luther wrote *orator*, which can mean orator, speaker, ambassador, or one who entreats, connoting someone who prays for something or someone, or speaks in behalf of someone.

75

To Philip Melanchthon[1]
Wartburg,[2] about May 8, 1521

Discussing the outcome of the Diet of Worms, Luther expresses some thoughts about the silence temporarily imposed on him.

Luther's "stiff-necked reply" (so Charles V, see Kidd, p. 86), the Emperor's inability to understand Luther's concern, and the pressure of the Curia resulted in the Edict of Worms (see Kidd, No. 45). This edict was accepted by a pro-papal minority of the diet in a rump session after the official closing of the diet and issued on May 26, 1521. It stated that after the expiration of the safe-conduct, Luther was to be treated as an excommunicated heretic and as one who was banned. No one was to house or feed him, and his books were to be burned. Anyone who saw Luther was required to turn him over to the Imperial authorities; if he did not do so, then he himself was guilty of treason, which was punishable by confiscation of property and all privileges and even the death sentence.

Two major factors made the immediate execution of this edict impossible: (1) While the Diet of Worms was still meeting, Charles V became deeply involved with preparations for the first war against France. He did not successfully end this war until 1526, and this prevented him from giving his full attention to German internal affairs; (2) Elector Frederick was convinced that the way in which Luther had been treated was unfair and that the edict was unconstitutional; therefore he made "arrangements" for Luther to disappear for a while.

Until March of 1522, Luther was hidden in the Wartburg. These months were a breathing spell for the Reformer. The legal side of his case, though not settled, no longer disturbed him; he was banned, yet for the time being he was safe from the consequences of the ban. The church had excommunicated

[1] On the identity of the person to whom this letter is written (who is controversial) and the date of this fragment, see WA, Br 2, No. 405, Introduction; 8, 661.

[2] Obviously, none of the Wartburg letters gives the place from where Luther wrote; the place can be inferred, however, from the contents.

him and thus substantiated for him the fact that it did not want to listen to the Word of God, to which Luther had tried to direct it. The ruling powers in the church had made it obvious that they did not intend to co-operate in any reform of the church. In the solitude of the Wartburg confinement, Luther's thoughts developed, and he became increasingly concerned with reshaping the life of the church on the basis of his insight into Scripture.

In spite of the Edict of Worms the Reformation movement grew steadily in the decade from 1520 to 1530. Many monks and nuns left the monasteries and convents, and many individuals, congregations, and secular governments clamored for the preaching of the true Word of God. Luther's insight into the Word of God, his rediscovery of the gospel, became the foundation for a new concept of church and society. Thus a church system different from the Roman one came into being and spread rapidly over all of Germany.

New problems arose.[3] *The situation became quite complicated when during Luther's absence, some men in Wittenberg tried to force the issues to a radical solution; the complexities*

[3] To name but a few problems: How should this new church understand and practice the sacrament of penance, which had stirred up Luther's controversy with Rome? (See pp. 244 ff.) How should one deal with monasticism and the many questions which arose due to deserted monasteries (see pp. 277 ff., 283 ff., 297 ff., 310, 329 ff.) and the monks and nuns who were abandoning their monastic lives? How could Luther's concern for the gospel be expressed in liturgy? (See pp. 324 f.) How should the administration of parishes and discipline of congregations and their pastors be regulated and supervised? See *WA*, Br 4, No. 1091. How should one understand the authority of secular government? (See pp. 258 ff.) How should usury be handled and how should crimes be punished? See *WA*, Br 3, Nos. 673, 780. How should the legal authority of the Roman hierarchy be replaced in the administration of the church at large, or in specific questions such as divorce cases? See *WA*, Br 3, No. 780. The church visitations conducted in Electoral Saxony in the second part of the decade of 1520 to 1530 clearly showed how complex the situation was. Nevertheless the Protestant territorial church which developed between 1521 and 1530 was, under the circumstances, the best possible answer to these questions, although it was by no means the ideal solution.

Problems connected with the internal structure of the church of the Reformation were complicated by another issue. Sovereigns supporting the Reformation had to deal with political questions: What should their relation be to one another? to the Imperial government? How should they counter the political maneuvers of the Roman Catholic party? The policy of political federations on a religious basis offered the only way out of this dilemma, dangerous though it was.

increased when the work Luther had begun was confronted with theological and social ideas which jeopardized the essence of the Reformer's thought. This crisis of the Reformation can be seen in the Wittenberg disturbances of 1521/22 (see p. 386, n. 1), the movement of the religious enthusiasts and the social radicals, and in the understanding of the Lord's Supper held by those who rallied around Zwingli. From 1522 to 1529, Luther separated his cause from his former friends and followers who misinterpreted his basic concepts.

Letters No. 75 through 116 are all of Luther's extant letters from the Wartburg (with the exception of three letters which are prefaces to some of his writings). These letters show Luther's tremendous working capacity (see pp. 319 f.), which can be sufficiently appreciated only if one remembers that he was barred from using any library and from participating in any discussion and receiving stimulation from such an encounter. The letters document his deep concern for the Word of God as the basis of the newly developing ecclesiastical system and for its application to the situation, especially in Wittenberg. They record the progress of the Reformation, and show how it eventually became necessary for Luther to return to Wittenberg. Finally they give insight into the feelings of this man who had been the center of a circle of cordial friends and of a university, and who suddenly had to live in solitary seclusion—exactly like a hermit. As a substitute for the fellowship he lacked, Luther seized every opportunity to exchange letters; every letter carrier who went back and forth between Wittenberg and the Wartburg brought letters and personal greetings to and from various friends.

On Philip Melanchthon, see p. 77, n. 3.

Text in Latin: WA, Br 2, 330-331.

I have had much ado to get this letter off, so great is the fear that my whereabouts may somehow be revealed.[4] Therefore you people, too, be careful. If you think it is to the glory of Christ that the question of my disappearance (that is, whether friends or enemies hold me) remains or becomes dubious, then be

[4] Address, greeting, and signature are missing, since this letter and the next one are only fragments. See p. 218, n. 1.

silent.[5] With the exception of you and Amsdorf,[6] it is not necessary that other people know anything else than that I am still alive.

Who knows what God plans to work with these mighty men[7] by this counsel of silence? The priests and monks who raged against me while I was free now dread me as a captive, so that they start to soften their campaign against me. They cannot bear the weight of the common people's threats, but also they do not know how to escape them. Behold, the hand of the Mighty One of Jacob,[8] what it accomplishes while we are silent, suffer, and pray. Is not the word of Moses true: "You will be silent and the Lord will fight for you"?[9]

A certain Romanist wrote the Cardinal of Mainz:[10] We got rid of Luther as we wanted; but the people are so stirred up that I suspect we hardly shall save our lives unless we light candles and search for him everywhere and invite him to return. He was joking. But what will happen if the joke leads to serious business? Meditate on it privately and be silent, etc.[11]

76

To Philip Melanchthon[1]
Wartburg, about May 8, 1521

Luther expresses his distaste for student riots against the clergy of Erfurt, and his concern over the effects such events will have on the Reformation.

---

5 Literally: "Therefore you people too be careful and silent, if you think it can be done to the glory of Christ that it remain or will become dubious whether they are friends or enemies who hold me."
6 Nicholas von Amsdorf; see p. 218.
7 His enemies; perhaps an allusion to Isa. 5:14-15.
8 Gen. 49:24.
9 Exod. 14:14 (Vulgate).
10 On "Romanist," see p. 92, n. 16; on Cardinal Albrecht, see pp. 44 f.
11 Literally: "Speak on your beds, and be silent," etc. Smith (S-J 2, 22) translates, "Speak upon your couch, and be still," and considers this a quotation of Ps. 4:4.
1 For the addressee and date of this fragment, see *WA*, Br 2, No. 406, Introduction; 8, 661.

On Philip Melanchthon, see p. 77, n. 3.
Text in Latin: WA, Br 2, 331-332.

I hear that there has been violence in Erfurt against the houses of priests.[2] I am amazed that this is tolerated and bypassed by the city council and that our Lang is also silent on this.[3] Although it is good that those lazy, ungodly priests are harassed, yet this method creates disgrace and just repulsion for our gospel.[4] I would have written to Lang [about this], but I still can't.[5] This kind of service toward us on the part of these people shocks me tremendously. We clearly see from it that we are not yet worthy before God to be servants of his Word, and that Satan mocks and ridicules our efforts. How afraid I am that our work may be the fig tree of the parable, of which it is predicted in Matthew 21 [:19] that it will grow only [leaves] before the Judgment Day and not come to fruit.[6] The truth is indeed that it is only foliage and words as long as we do not act in accordance with our teaching.

---

[2] Address, greeting, and signature are missing; see p. 218, n. 1.
[3] Luther must have received news from Erfurt about these riots (for details, see p. 224, n. 8) and also must have heard that Lang did not oppose them. For a different interpretation of this passage, see *WA*, Br 2, 322, n. 1. On John Lang, see p. 14.
[4] Luther was afraid that such riots would be blamed on the Reformation, in spite of the fact that the rioters often had little or nothing to do with Luther's ideas.
[5] See also p. 212. Hans von Berlepsch, the castellan of the Wartburg, tried to keep Luther incommunicado as much as possible. Since Erfurt was under the jurisdiction of the Archbishop of Mainz, it could have been quite dangerous if a letter from Luther to Lang, who was then in Erfurt, had fallen into the wrong hands.
[6] See also Luke 13:6-9.

77

To Philip Melanchthon
Wartburg, May 12, 1521

Luther reports on the aftermath of the Diet at Worms and expresses his concern for the sad condition of the church. Worried about any consequences his sudden disappearance could have for the church, he admonishes Melanchthon to be steadfast and to continue the good fight for the gospel.

On Philip Melanchthon, see p. 77, n. 3.

Text in Latin: WA, Br 2, 332-333.

To Philip Melanchthon, evangelist of the congregation at Wittenberg, my dearest brother in Christ

Jesus

Greetings. What are you doing these days, my Philip? Are you not praying for me that this retreat to which I unwillingly consented may result in something great for God's glory? I am quite eager to know your reaction [to my disappearance]. I was afraid it would look as if I had deserted the battle array; and yet there was no way to resist those who wanted and advised this. I desire nothing more than to meet the fury of my enemies head on.

Sitting here all day, I picture to myself the state of the church and I see fulfilled the word of Psalm 89 [:47]: [1] "Hast thou made all sons of men in vain?" God, what a horrible picture of God's wrath is that detestable kingdom of the Roman Antichrist! I abhor the hardness [of my heart], that I am not completely melted to tears, so that I too might shed fountains of tears for the slain sons of my people.[2] But there is no one who arises and lays hold on God, or places himself as a wall for the house of Israel[3] on this last day of God's wrath. O kingdom of the pope, worthy of the end and dregs of the ages![4] God have mercy upon us!

[1] Vulgate, but RSV numbering.
[2] As Jeremiah did; 9:1.
[3] Isa. 64:7; Ezek. 22:30; 13:5.
[4] See p. 104, n. 7.

You, therefore, as minister of the Word, be steadfast in the meantime and fortify the walls and towers of Jerusalem until [the enemy] also attack you. You know your call and your gifts. I pray for you as for no one else, if my prayer can accomplish something—which I do not doubt. Return, therefore, this service so that we carry this burden together.[5] So far I stand alone in the battle; after me they will seek you.

Spalatin writes[6] that an extremely harsh edict[7] is in preparation; challenging the conscience, they will now search the whole world for my little books and in so doing swiftly prepare destruction for themselves. The Rehoboam of Dresden[8] rejoices and is very eager to execute such an edict. The Emperor[9] has also been urged to write to the King of Denmark not to shelter the leftovers of the Lutheran heresy. They chant this song, "When will he die and his name perish?"[10]

Hartmuth Cronberg has renounced the Emperor's stipend of two hundred gulden, being unwilling to serve one who listens to those ungodly people.[11] I believe that the edict[12] will do no

---

[5] Gal. 6:2.

[6] George Spalatin; see pp. 8 f. Luther had received Spalatin's (no longer extant) letter from Worms on May 12 (see p. 222) and forwarded it on the same day to Melanchthon (see below). For some of the content of Spalatin's letter, see Luther's following statements and pp. 222 ff.

[7] Reference to the first draft of the Edict of Worms. After the collapse of the negotiations, Charles V and his cabinet on May 1 commissioned Jerome Aleander, the papal legate to Germany, to draw up the final resolution concerning Luther. Aleander presented a first draft to the Emperor on May 2; the Emperor, in turn, forwarded it to the German Privy Council for judgment, much against the will of Aleander. Discussions and revisions of this first draft took some time and it was not before May 12 that Aleander could present the final draft to the Emperor. See *DRTA. JR* 2, Nos. 89 ff.

[8] I Kings 12:12-14. Luther occasionally used this name for Duke George of Saxony (see p. 110, n. 20) to stigmatize the Duke's arrogance.

[9] Charles V; see pp. 175 f.

[10] Ps. 41:5, in reference to Luther.

[11] Luther must have received this information through Spalatin's letter (see note 6). Von Cronberg (1488-1549) was one of the Imperial knights whose family estates were located in the Rhineland. He was involved in von Sickingen's defeat (see pp. 244 f.), in which he lost all his property. Yet his relationship with Luther was more sober than that of the hotheaded von Sickingen and von Hutten. Between 1520 and 1525 he published various smaller works which show a genuine understanding of the Reformer's cause. In later years, however, he became disillusioned with the Reformation, because the Reformers were unable and unwilling to become the champions of nationalism and Imperial reform. On Cronberg, see S-*J* 2, 23, n. 4.

[12] See note 7.

damage anywhere, except under that Rehoboam [13] and your other neighbor,[14] both of whom are plagued by vanity. God lives and reigns in time and eternity. Amen.

The Lord has afflicted me with painful constipation.[15] The elimination is so hard that I am forced to press with all my strength, even to the point of perspiration, and the longer I delay the worse it gets. Yesterday on the fourth day I could go once, but I did not sleep all night and still have no peace. Please pray for me. This affliction will be intolerable if it continues as it has begun.

The Cardinal of Salzburg [16] accompanied Ferdinand [17] to meet his bride at Innsbruck on April 30, that is, four days after our departure [from Worms]. It is said that Ferdinand was not pleased with his traveling companion, nor was the Emperor,[18] as Spalatin writes.[19] But you read his letter yourself.[20] Be sure to write everything that happens at your place and how everything is.

Farewell to you and your wife.[21]

May 12, 1521, in the land of the birds

Yours,

MARTIN LUTHER

---

13 Duke George; see note 8.

14 Elector Joachim I of Brandenburg, whom Luther occasionally compared with Ben-hadad of Damascus (I Kings 20:3 ff.); see p. 56, n. 3; p. 220.

15 This was a chronic ailment which especially bothered Luther while he was at the Wartburg; see pp. 219, 255, 257, 268 f., 276, 291, 316.

16 Matthew Lang, whom Luther had considered as a possible neutral judge of his case; see p. 99, n. 14.

17 Ferdinand I (1503-1564) was the brother of Charles V (see pp. 175 f.). In 1521 Charles turned the governing of the German portions of the Hapsburg territories, primarily Austria, over to Ferdinand. During the long absences of the Emperor he was also viceroy. In 1556 Ferdinand succeeded Charles as Emperor. Luther is referring to Ferdinand's marriage to Anne of Hungary, which took place in the spring of 1521. Luther confused Innsbruck with Linz, where the marriage festivities took place; see *WA*, Br 2, 334, n. 16.

18 Charles V (see pp. 175 f.) was unhappy with Lang, since the Archbishop was a strong representative of the German territorial sovereigns who intended to preserve their independence against the Imperial policy.

19 See note 6.

20 At this point Luther apparently decided to include Spalatin's letter.

21 Luther wrote "your flesh," which obviously is a reference to Gen. 2:23 and Eph. 5:28-29. On Melanchthon's wife, see p. 166, n. 5.

78

To Nicholas von Amsdorf
Wartburg, May 12, 1521

In this letter Luther informs von Amsdorf of some correspondence matters and tells briefly of his capture and ride to the Wartburg. He asks von Amsdorf, his traveling companion to and from Worms, to report on the last leg of that journey, which von Amsdorf had had to make alone. Luther also comments briefly on the Edict of Worms and on his health; he encourages his friend to be steadfast in the cause of the gospel.

Nicholas von Amsdorf (1483-1565) was already teaching theology and philosophy at the University of Wittenberg when Luther joined the faculty. Luther soon gained in him a very able theological supporter and co-worker, as well as personal friend. Von Amsdorf accompanied Luther to the Leipzig Disputation (see p. 126) and to the Diet of Worms. In 1524 von Amsdorf went to Magdeburg to lead the Protestant opposition against the Roman Catholic clergy and to reform the congregations. In later years he introduced the Reformation into many central German towns and smaller territorial states. In 1542 Luther installed him as evangelical bishop of the diocese of Naumburg, a position to which he had been appointed by the Elector of Saxony. After the Smalcaldic War, he had to resign this office due to the general political situation. He went as superintendent to Eisenach, and later to Magdeburg. In the doctrinal controversies which harassed the church of the Reformation after Luther's death, he stubbornly maintained Luther's position, sometimes unfortunately interpreting Luther's ideas in a one-sided fashion. See O.D.C.C., p. 45.

Text in Latin: WA, *Br* 2, 334-335.

Jesus

Greetings. I recently wrote to all of you, my Amsdorf, but I listened to better advice and tore up everything, since it was not yet safe to send out any letters.[1] Now I have written to Doctor

[1] Perhaps Nos. 75 and 76 are some fragments.

Jerome [2] concerning the books and printed sheets,[3] and with this letter I am also writing to the Prior [4] about it. All of you please take care of those things which have to be done.

My constipation has become bad.[5] The Lord afflicts me. But pray for me, because I always pray for you, that God may strengthen your heart. Be faithful, therefore, and when [you are given] an occasion to speak the Word of God, speak it with boldness. Also write how everything went with all of you on the journey,[6] and what you heard or saw at Erfurt.[7] You will find with Philip [8] the letter Spalatin has written me.[9]

The day I was snatched away from you, I arrived about eleven o'clock in the dark of night at my quarters, tired out—as a brand-new rider—from the long trip.[10] Here I am now a man of leisure, like a free man among captives. Beware of the

[2] Jerome Schurf of St. Gall (1481-1554) studied medicine in Basel and later jurisprudence in Tübingen. In 1506/07? he settled down in Wittenberg to practice law; he also taught law at the University and became an Electoral Saxon councilor. He stayed in Wittenberg until 1546, when he was driven by the events of the Smalcaldic War to Frankfurt/Oder. While he was in Wittenberg he became very close to Luther; their friendship was based on mutual respect for each other's knowledge. He served Luther as legal counsel during the first hearing before the Diet of Worms on April 17 (see p. 200, n. 3), and we may assume that he was with Luther in the critical hours from the early evening of April 17 to the late afternoon of April 18, when the Reformer's famous answer to the diet was taking form. Luther's letter to Schurf is not extant.

[3] This is a reference to the books Luther needed for the work he planned to do at the Wartburg; see p. 225. "Printed sheets" refers to the first printed pages of the *Magnificat;* see p. 225, n. 17.

[4] Conrad Helt; see p. 125, n. 9. Luther's letter is not extant.

[5] Written in German, this sentence is omitted in all the early printed editions of this letter and also in many translations; it can be found, however, in a manuscript copy of the letter. If one realizes that Luther used a rather strong word for "constipation," one will understand that some editors omitted this sentence to avoid giving offense to some "tender" ears. In Luther's day, however, such language was not considered vulgar. On Luther's constipation, see p. 217, n. 15.

[6] Von Amsdorf accompanied Luther on the journey to and from Worms. When Luther was captured on May 4, von Amsdorf continued the journey alone. Luther now asks about the rest of von Amsdorf's trip. For details, see pp. 227 f.

[7] See pp. 214, 223 f.

[8] Philip Melanchthon; see p. 77, n. 3.

[9] See p. 216, n. 6.

[10] The armed horsemen who captured Luther in the late afternoon crisscrossed the Thuringian Forest to avoid any possible pursuers and also to avoid leaving any trace of their path. For details, see pp. 227 f.

Rehoboam of Dresden, and your neighbor, the Ben-hadad of Damascus.[11] A sharp edict has been issued against me.[12] But the Lord will laugh at them.[13]

In Him farewell, and greet all to whom greetings are due.

May 12, 1521, in the land of the open skies

Yours,
MARTIN LUTHER

79

To John Agricola
Wartburg, May 12, 1521

Trying to maintain his ties with his friends, Luther sends best wishes for the expected birth of Agricola's child. He also expresses his concern about the preaching situation at Wittenberg.

John Agricola of Eisleben (1494?-1566) was one of Luther's students who became a faithful and intimate friend. In 1518 he was graduated from the University of Wittenberg as Master of Arts; in the same year he published (from his own notes) Luther's homilies on the Lord's Prayer; see p. 113, n. 10. In 1519 he accompanied Luther to the Leipzig Disputation (see p. 126). He married in 1520 and after 1525 worked as a reformer in Eisleben. He became well known as a preacher and was temporary Electoral Saxon court chaplain. Having difficulty with his territorial lords, the counts of Mansfeld, Agricola returned to Wittenberg and began to teach at the University in 1536. His close friendship with Luther continued until sometime in 1537 or 1538, when the second Antinomian controversy brought it to an abrupt end. In 1540 Agricola went as court chaplain to the Brandenburg court in Berlin. He died in 1566 while general superintendent of the church of Brandenburg. See O.D.C.C., p. 27.

Text in Latin: WA, Br 2, 335-336.

---

[11] I Kings 20:3 ff.; this is a reference to Duke George of Saxony and Elector Joachim of Brandenburg; see p. 217.

[12] See p. 216, n. 7. On May 2 Aleander forwarded the first draft of the edict to the Emperor; see *DRTA. JR* 2, No. 90. Luther assumed that this draft had been adopted. By May 12, however, the Emperor still had not signed the revised copy of this first draft.

[13] Ps. 2:4; 37:13.

To my friend John Agricola, a married theologian[1] and a free man of Christ, living in Wittenberg

Jesus

Greetings. Of course I consider that all my letters written to Philip and the others[2] are also addressed to you, my John (unless with my disappearance fellowship among friends has likewise disappeared, which God prevent). Yet I considered it good to greet you with a personal letter, too.[3] Greetings therefore and remember this word: "A servant is not greater than his master."[4] Greet your flesh and rib.[5] May the Lord grant that she has a happy delivery. Amen.

I am a strange prisoner, since I sit here both willingly and unwillingly: willingly, since the Lord wants it this way; unwillingly, since I would want to stand up in public for the Word of God, but I have not yet been worthy of this. Wittenberg is hated by its neighbors,[6] but the Lord [will see to it] that his time will come; then he will laugh at them,[7] if only we have trusted in him. Write what the situation is with the preaching and who was entrusted with it[8] so that I may strengthen either my hope or my fear for the Word. Since you too are called in part to the office of teaching the Word to the children, fulfil your ministry and bear what the Lord lays upon you.[9] Look, I have written this only to write something.[10]

---

[1] Since in the West theologians traditionally were priests and priests had for some time been required to live in celibacy, a married theologian was unusual. See also note 5.

[2] See pp. 215 ff., 218 ff.; p. 219, nn. 2, 4.

[3] Literally: ". . . to greet you also with my hand," which is a technical term for a letter (or any piece of writing) in one's own handwriting.

[4] John 13:16.

[5] I.e., his wife (see Gen. 2:21-23; Eph. 5:28-29). Agricola had married Else (or Elizabeth) Moshauer on September 10, 1520; see *WA*, Br 2, 148, n. 7.

[6] See p. 220, n. 11.

[7] Ps. 2:4; 37:13-14.

[8] I.e., in Luther's stead; see p. 202. Luther was preacher at the *Stadtpfarrkirche*, i.e., the parish church of the city (see p. 28), and was very much concerned that his pulpit be properly filled during his absence.

[9] In the spring of 1521 Agricola was appointed catechist of the city parish. As such he was responsible for the religious instruction of the young; he also helped with the preaching.

[10] This sentence is missing in one manuscript copy of this letter.

Farewell to you and your whole family.
In the land of the birds, May 12, 1521

MARTIN LUTHER

Please [11] give one gulden [12] to the newborn, another to the mother in childbirth confinement so that she can have wine and have enough milk [for nursing]; for were I present, I would of course be godfather.[13]

80

To George Spalatin
Wartburg, May 14, 1521

Luther comments on the Edict of Worms, on the student riots against some clergy of Erfurt, and on a similar incident which took place in Gotha. He also reports on his return from the diet, his life in "captivity," and his plans.

On Spalatin, see pp. 8 f.

Text in Latin: WA, Br 2, 337-338.

To my dearest friend in Christ, George Spalatin, a most faithful servant of Christ at Altenburg

Jesus

Greetings. I received your letter,[1] my Spalatin, and that of Gerbel and the one from Sapidus,[2] on Exaudi Sunday. I have purposely not written to you previously so that the recent rumor of my

[11] This postscript is missing in one manuscript copy of this letter.
[12] On the gulden, see p. 11, n. 2.
[13] And thus give the mother and child a present from the child's godfather.
[1] This is the letter to which Luther referred in the letter to Melanchthon dated May 12 (see p. 216, n. 6). He received it on May 12, which was Exaudi Sunday, or the Sunday after Ascension.
[2] Two (not extant) letters which were sent to Luther at Worms; since Luther had already left, Spalatin forwarded them to the Wartburg. On Nicholas Gerbel, see pp. 317 f. Sapidus, or John Witz (1490-1561), of Schlettstadt/-Alsace, studied under the Humanist Lefevre (see p. 26, n. 15). From 1510 to 1525 he was president of the famous college-type Latin school

capture would not cause anyone to intercept the mail. Various stories about me are told in this area. The opinion becomes stronger, however, that I was captured by friends who were sent from Franconia.[3] The Imperial safe-conduct expires tomorrow.[4] I am grieved to hear from what you write that they will rage with such a stiff edict, attempting to search even the consciences.[5] I am not so much concerned about myself as about those rash people who thus call down evil upon their heads and continue to burden themselves with such great hatred. What tremendous hostility such shameless violence will arouse! But very well; maybe the time of their visitation is at hand.[6]

So far I have had no word from our friends at Wittenberg or anywhere else. The young people at Erfurt damaged some houses of priests during the night (at the time we were coming to Eisenach). They were annoyed because the Dean of St. Severin, a great papist, grabbed Master Draco (a man of sound opinion)[7] by his robe and dragged him publicly out of the chancel, alleging

---

at Schlettstadt, which was a center of Humanism. He became a stout adherent of the Reformation and was therefore pushed out of office. In 1526 he went to Strassburg, where he stayed for the rest of his life; as at Schlettstadt, so here too he was able to make the Latin school famous. See Allen 2, 323, Introduction.

[3] This rumor could easily have started, since Sylvester von Schaumberg, a leading Franconian nobleman (see p. 169, n. 9), had offered Luther military protection as early as June, 1520. On May 11, 1521, it was reported to Aleander, the papal legate, that Luther had been kidnapped near Eisenach and taken to Franconia; see *WA*, Br 2, 338, n. 5.

[4] See p. 208, n. 21. Luther's safe-conduct, issued on April 25 late in the afternoon, guaranteed him twenty-one days for his return journey and thus expired on May 15.

[5] On the edict, see p. 216, n. 7; for a similar statement, see p. 216.

[6] Perhaps an allusion to Jer. 46:21.

[7] The dean of St. Severin's Chapter was then a certain James Schröder (also known as Doleatoris). John Draco (or Draconites) (1494?-1566) of Karlstadt/Main matriculated in Erfurt in 1509, and later became a canon of St. Severin in Erfurt. In 1521 he was forced to resign his canonry; soon afterward he went to Wittenberg to study. After being graduated as Doctor of Theology from Wittenberg University in 1523, he was a pastor for a short time in Miltenberg, and Eisenach. From 1534 to 1547 he was a professor of theology at Marburg University, and from 1551 to 1560 he held the same position at the University of Rostock. In 1560 he was made bishop of the Protestant church of Pomerania, a position he held for the remainder of his life. He concentrated on compiling a polyglot Bible; between 1563 and 1565 some parts of this polyglot were published. See Allen 3, 371, Introduction.

that [Draco] was under excommunication because he, together with others, had come to meet me when I arrived at Erfurt.[8] Meanwhile they fear worse; the city council ignores these things, and the priests there have a bad reputation. It is said that the young artisans conspire with the students. It is possible that they may put into actuality the prophetic proverb, "Erfurt, a second Prague." [9]

Yesterday I was told that a certain priest at Gotha was roughed up. The priests there procured some things—I don't know what—in order to enlarge the revenues of the church. Claiming the ecclesiastical tax-exemption, they refused to pay the burdens, as they call it, or taxes.[10] We see that the people are neither able nor willing (as Erasmus also writes in his *Advice*)[11] to put up with

---

[8] According to *WA*, Br 2, 339, n. 9, the events Luther refers to have to be reconstructed in the following way: On his way to Worms Luther stayed in Erfurt and was welcomed by Master Draco and other members of the Chapter of St. Severin. Since Luther had been officially excommunicated since January (see p. 179, n. 1; p. 192, n. 3), Draco was by his action automatically excommunicated too. The day after Luther had left for Worms, on April 9, the Dean of St. Severin decided to discipline the clergy who had participated in the reception for Luther. Draco did not comply with the Dean's orders and as a result was disciplined in public; he was removed from the chancel during a service and declared excommunicated. This infuriated the people of the city, especially the students and apprentices. On May 1 and 2, returning from Worms, Luther stopped in Eisenach. During that night the situation in Erfurt exploded. The rioting students and apprentices reinforced the University's demand that Draco be reinstated in his former position. The Dean of St. Severin finally gave in, and Draco's excommunication was nullified. Soon afterward Draco resigned his canonry and went to Wittenberg. Luther heard rumors of these events (see p. 214) and on May 12 asked von Amsdorf for a report (see p. 219). Since he complains that he has received nothing thus far, his information must have come from people at the Wartburg.

[9] In 1409 the ideas of John Huss caused a split in the then famous University of Prague. This resulted in great disadvantages for the German professors and students, many of whom left; some went to Erfurt, others founded the University in Leipzig. Accompanied by rioting, this exodus gave rise to a sharp decline of the University at Prague. By quoting this saying, Luther wants to suggest that riots within a University may be a foreboding of its decline; see *WA*, Br 2, 340, n. 11.

[10] This incident could not be verified.

[11] Apparently Erasmus' *Consilium cujusdam* . . . (*Someone's Advice* . . .). W. K. Ferguson (ed.), *Erasmi Opuscula* (The Hague: Martinus Nijhoff, 1933), pp. 352 ff.; the passage Luther refers to is found on p. 358: "We hear daily of serious accusations made by many people, who assert that they could no longer endure the yoke of the Roman See." On the authorship and significance of this work, see *WA*, Br 2, 340, n. 13. Luther could also possibly be referring to the *Axiomata* of Erasmus (see Ferguson, *op. cit.*, p. 336; *S-J* 2, 27, n. 4); yet Luther's words seem to fit the *Consilium* better.

the yoke of the pope and the papists[12] any longer. And yet even now [the papists] do not stop pushing and burdening the people. Since the light reveals everything, they have lost their good name and reputation; therefore their display of piety can no longer be of any value and cannot dominate, as it has up to now. Thus far they have increased hatred through violence and forcibly crushed [their opponents]; but they will see whether such oppression can continue.

I am sitting here all day, drunk with leisure.[13] I am reading the Bible in Greek and Hebrew. I shall write a German tract on the freedom of auricular confession.[14] I shall also continue working on the Psalms[15] and the *Postil*[16] as soon as I have received the necessary things from Wittenberg—among which I also expect the unfinished *Magnificat*.[17]

You would not believe in what a friendly fashion the Abbot of Hersfeld[18] received us! He sent the chancellor and the treasurer

---

[12] *S-J* 2, 27, gives the following translation of the passage from note 12 to the end of the paragraph: ". . . of the Pope and the papists; therefore let us not cease to press upon it and to pull it down [the yoke of the Pope], especially as we have already lost name and fame by so doing. Now the light reveals all things and their [papists] show of piety is no longer valuable and cannot rule as hitherto. We have grown by violence and driven them back by violence; we must see if they can be driven back any more." This paraphrased translation can be supported by the original text. Nevertheless this translator did not consider this support strong enough to adopt Smith's rendering. In the last sentence this translator used the text taken from the manuscript copy of this letter, which differs from the printed editions.

[13] For a similar statement, see p. 221.

[14] See p. 246, n. 10.

[15] See p. 121, n. 7.

[16] See pp. 237 ff. Luther used the word *Postilla*. This is a technical term of medieval exegesis; it is derived from *post illa verba*, i.e., "after those words of [Scripture]," and designates the exegesis which follows the quoted text. The most famous *Postilla* was by Nicholas of Lyra (see p. 26, n. 14). The word can be used in the singular, designating a *postil*, i.e., an explanation of a biblical text, and in the plural, designating many *postils*, many explanations of many biblical texts, or a book that provides a running commentary on biblical texts. It can be assumed that Luther used the term in the latter meaning.

[17] "Unfinished" is missing in the manuscript copy of this letter but can be found in the earliest printed editions. "*Magnificat*," that is, the first printed sheets of the *Magnificat* (Wittenberg: M. Lotther, 1521). *WA* 7, 544 ff.; *PE* 3, 123 ff. The printing of this work probably was begun at the end of 1520. Luther finished the manuscript at the Wartburg; see p. 254, n. 4. The printing was not completed before September, 1521.

[18] "Hersfeld" was a famous Benedictine monastery north of Fulda, founded

a good mile out to meet us; then he himself, together with many riders, met us at his castle and accompanied us into town. The city council welcomed us inside the gate. He fed us sumptuously in his monastery and made his private chamber available for my use. On the fifth morning[19] they compelled me to preach. I pleaded in vain that the monastery might lose the royal privileges if the Emperor's officials should interpret this as a breach of the safe-conduct, since they had forbidden me to preach while on my way. Nevertheless I said that I had not consented that the Word of God should be bound; and this is true.[20] I also preached at Eisenach;[21] the fearful parish priest, however, protested before me in the presence of a notary and witnesses. Yet he humbly apologized for the necessity of doing so, pleading fear of his tyrants.[22] Perhaps you may hear at Worms, therefore, that I broke the safe-conduct by this, but it was not broken. The condition that the Word of God should be bound was not within my power [to uphold], nor did I agree to it;[23] and even if I had agreed to it, it would not have been binding since it would have been against God's will.

---

in 742, or shortly thereafter. From 1516 to 1556, Kraft Myle of Hungen was abbot there; see *WA*, Br 2, 340, n. 20; *S-J* 2, 28, n. 3. After this meeting with Luther he was favorably inclined toward the Reformation, allowing his monks to abandon monastic life and leave the monastery. Through Myle's careful diplomacy, Hersfeld was freed from the jurisdiction of the diocese of Fulda and became a part of the territory of the Landgrave of Hesse. In 1606 the monastery was dissolved, and a member of the ruling family of Hesse became administrator of the monastery's territory and funds. In 1648 it became a secular state and was incorporated into Hesse-Kassel.

[19] I.e., on the fifth day after leaving Worms: May 1; see also p. 208, n. 21.

[20] On the safe-conduct, see p. 208, n. 21. Luther is correct here. Replying to the two officials who delivered the gracious dismissal, the safe-conduct, and the order not to preach, he stated in the presence of a notary: ". . . he wanted to comply obediently with His Majesty's order and instruction and do all things . . . excepting nothing here on earth, than the very Word of God, which he wanted to consider to be free and unbound, to confess and profess it." See *WA* 7, 856.

[21] May 3; see note 26.

[22] Luther had been excommunicated since January, 1521; see p. 179, n. 1; p. 192, n. 3. For a parish priest voluntarily to allow an excommunicated person even to enter the sanctuary, not to speak of one who was a priest, was dangerous and invited excommunication for the priest and even the interdict for the parish.

[23] Luther made a similar statement in his April 28 letter to Emperor Charles V; see pp. 205 ff.

[The Abbot] at last accompanied us on the next day[24] as far as the forest; he sent the chancellor with us, and had us all dine again at Berka.[25] Finally we were met by the people of Eisenach who came out of the town on foot, and we entered Eisenach in the evening.[26] The next morning all the traveling companions left, together with Jerome.[27] I went on through the forest to my relatives (who occupy almost all that region).[28] We[29] left them when we turned toward Waltershausen. After a short while, close to the Altenstein Castle,[30] I was captured.[31] Amsdorf knew of course that I was to be captured by someone but does not know where I am in custody. My fellow-friar,[32] seeing the horsemen in time, jumped off the wagon and is said to have arrived in Waltershausen in the evening, unseen and on foot.

---

24 May 2.

25 A small village at the Werra River, about halfway between Hersfeld and Eisenach.

26 May 2; Luther then preached on May 3.

27 On May 3 Luther's party split up. Luther and his companions (see notes 29, 32) went from Eisenach straight south for about twelve miles to Möhra to visit relatives, with whom they stayed overnight. Peter Swawe, a student (see p. 236), and Justus Jonas (see p. 275, n. 3) traveled with Jerome Schurf (see p. 219, n. 2) along the direct route from Eisenach to Wittenberg. This split was obviously premeditated to make the kidnapping easier.

28 See p. 145; *WA*, Br 2, 340, n. 28.

29 Luther, von Amsdorf (see p. 218), and John Petzensteiner (see note 32).

30 Möhra is located about twelve miles south of Eisenach. Turning sharply to the east and slightly to the north, the road to Waltershausen passes by the Altenstein Castle, which is located on the southwestern slopes of the Thuringian Forest, southwest of Erfurt or Gotha, and almost straight southeast of Eisenach. It had been the residence of the Saxon family Hund von Wenckheim since Elector Frederick (see pp. 49 f.) had given it to his faithful servant Burckhard Hund von Wenckheim (who had accompanied the Elector on a pilgrimage to the Holy Land in 1493).

31 The capture took place in the late afternoon. Elector Frederick (see pp. 49 f.) entrusted this difficult task (see p. 201, n. 3; p. 209, n. 22) to two of his most faithful servants, Hans von Berlepsch (a member of a noble family residing in Saxony and Hesse since 1233), the castellan of the Wartburg, and Burckhard Hund von Wenckheim of Altenstein Castle (see note 30); see *WA*, Br 2, 340, n. 29. Heading north for about fifteen miles in the general direction of Eisenach, they took Luther on a crisscross ride through the Thuringian Forest and finally reached the Wartburg near Eisenach late at night; see p. 219.

32 According to the Rule of the Augustinians (see p. 20, n. 3), each traveling friar had to be accompanied by at least one fellow-friar. John Petzensteiner of Nürnberg went with Luther to Worms. He had matriculated in Wittenberg in 1507 and was graduated as Master of Arts in 1515. See *WA*, Br 2, 297, n. 9.

Here I was stripped of my own clothes and dressed in a knight's cloak. I am letting my hair and beard grow, so that you would hardly know me; I can't even recognize myself any longer.[33] Now I am living in Christian liberty and am free of all the laws of that tyrant.[34] I would have preferred of course that that Hog of Dresden [35] had been considered worthy of killing me while I preached in public, had it pleased God that I should suffer for his Word. The will of the Lord be done.

Farewell and pray for me. Greet your whole court.[36]

Written on the mountain,[37] *May 14, 1521*

MARTIN LUTHER

81

To Philip Melanchthon
Wartburg, May 26, 1521

Luther comments on his literary work (Against Latomus, the Postil, On Confession, Exposition of Psalm 68), as well as on Oecolampadius' book on confession, and praises the Passion, an illustrated book about Christ's life and sufferings which was published in Wittenberg. He requests information about Francis Faber and about the preaching situation in Wittenberg. After discussing some news and rumors concerning both friends and enemies, he tries to strengthen the faith of his friends in Wittenberg and encourages them in their stand for the cause of the gospel. He also assures them of his well-being. He closes with greetings to many friends.

[33] Lucas Cranach the Elder (see p. 201) portrayed Luther as a knight (see p. 352, n. 13) and, indeed, the Reformer can hardly be recognized in this picture. For the picture, see Schwiebert, Plate LV.
[34] The context gives no clue to the identity of "that tyrant." Perhaps one can assume that Luther thought of the "yoke" of the pope (see above).
[35] Duke George; see p. 110, n. 20; pp. 201, 216, 221.
[36] Elector Frederick's court. This sentence is written in Greek.
[37] The Wartburg was located on a high mountain since it was supposed to serve as a lookout post for the protection of Thurginia (a district within Electoral Saxony) against any possible invasion by an enemy from the east or northeast.

On Philip Melanchthon, see p. 77, n. 3.
Text in Latin: WA, Br 2, 347-349.

To Philip Melanchthon, theologian, teacher of the congregation at Wittenberg, my dearest brother in Christ

Jesus

Greetings. What I may have written in this letter which has already long been sealed,[1] I have forgotten, my Philip, but I wanted to answer your letter[2] for a second time. I am replying to James Latomus[3] unwillingly, since I have already set my soul on quiet studies, but I see it is necessary that I answer him myself. In addition there is the disgust of having to read his verbose and badly written stuff. I had decided to put the expositions of the Epistles and Gospels into German, but you have not yet sent me a copy of the *Postil.*[4] I am sending the Psalm that was sung on these days.[5] If you wish, and the presses are idle, you may have it printed, and dedicated to whomever you wish. I have worked on this in my leisure, since I have no books here. However, if you

[1] An enclosure which is not extant.
[2] This letter is not extant; one may draw conclusions about its content from Luther's answer on pp. 232 ff.
[3] James Masson of Cambron/Hainaut, also known by his Humanistic name as James Latomus (1475?-1544), was Luther's bitter opponent at Louvain. He studied in Paris and Louvain and was graduated as Doctor of Theology from the University of Louvain in 1519. Latomus had just published a sharp defense of the condemnation of Luther's teachings which was issued by the University of Louvain (see p. 155, nn. 5, 6); for the bibliography, see *WA* 8, 37 f. Luther completed his reply on June 20, 1521 (see *WA* 8, 128); it came off the press in late September and was entitled: *Rationis Latomianae . . . Lutheriana Confutatio* (*Luther's Refutation of Latomus' Argument* or *Against Latomus*) (Wittenberg: M. Lotther, 1521). *WA* 8, 43 ff.; *LW* 32, 137 ff.
[4] Luther is waiting for a desk copy of his Latin *Advent Postil*, the *Enarrationes epistolarum et evangeliorum, quas postillas vocant*, which had been published in Wittenberg by J. Grünenberg in March of 1521; see *WA* 7, 458 ff.; p. 152, n. 2. This *Postil* contained eight homilies on the pericopes appointed for the four Advent Sundays: one for each Epistle text and one for each Gospel text. For more details, see pp. 237 ff.
[5] The Versicle of Ascension Day (May 9) and the Introit of Pentecost (May 19) were both Ps. 68:18 (or, according to the Vulgate, 67:18). Luther enclosed the manuscript of *Deutsche Auslegung des 67 Psalms* (*German Exposition of Psalm 67*) (Wittenberg: J. Grünenberg, August, 1521). *WA* 8, 1 ff.; *LW* 13, 3 ff.

prefer not to do this, then show this manuscript to friends and let Christian Aurifaber [6] read it, or you may give it to Amsdorf.[7]

I hope that Doctor Lupin had a blessed departure from this life.[8] Would God grant that we ourselves did not have to live in it! God's wrath is so great—I contemplate it daily more and more, since I have nothing else to do—that I doubt whether God will save, besides the little ones, any adults from that kingdom of Satan: so terribly has our God forsaken us! Yet [Lupin's] death moved me tremendously, since it reminded me of that word of Isaiah: "The righteous man perishes, and there is no one who ponders on it; and devout men are taken away, and no one reflects upon it." [9]

I would like to know who that Francis Faber of Silesia [10] is —that great hero. The play against the goat Emser gives enough indication as to its chief authors.[11] I am delighted with the illustrated Passion;[12] I see that John Schwertfeger [13] helped you compile this work. Our Oecolampadius has anticipated the treatise on confession by publishing quite an outspoken book on the ease of confession;[14] he will, of course, be a new vexation for the Anti-

[6] Christian Düring, called Goldschmidt or Aurifaber (see p. 42, n. 8), who among other things took an active part in Wittenberg's publishing business.

[7] Nicholas von Amsdorf; see p. 218.

[8] Peter Lupin; see p. 168, n. 5. He died on May 1; see *WA*, Br 2, 350, n. 6.

[9] Isa. 57:1.

[10] Francis Faber of Neisse (1407-1565) was one of the most important literary representatives of the Renaissance in Silesia. In 1520 he matriculated in the University of Leipzig; while there he wrote a poem in defense of Luther; for its bibliography, see *WA*, Br 2, 350, n. 10. Luther's attention was called to it and he is now requesting detailed information.

[11] A satire against Jerome Emser (see p. 137, n. 19), one of Luther's enemies; for its bibliography and a possible author, see *WA*, Br 2, 350, n. 11.

[12] *Passional Christi et Antichristi* (*The Passion of Christ and Antichrist*) (Wittenberg: J. Grünenberg, 1521). *WA* 9, 701 f. Luther was not the author of this picture story of the life and works of Christ and the Antichrist (see p. 114, n. 16), but he was very interested in it and was often consulted by its authors. Melanchthon probably wrote the text with the help of John Schwertfeger (see note 13); Lucas Cranach (see p. 201) contributed the pictures.

[13] John Schwertfeger of Meissen, a member of the Law Faculty of Wittenberg University.

[14] For Luther's projected book on confession, see p. 225. Oecolampadius wrote *Quod non sit onerosa Christianis confessio paradoxon* (*That Confession Is No Burden for Christians*) (Augsburg: Grimm and Wirsung, April, 1521). Luther received this little book through Spalatin; see pp. 253 f. John Oecolampadius (the Humanistic name of John Hussgen or Hausschein) of Weins-

christ[15] and his soldiers. If I did not hope that this little book was or will be sent to you by Spalatin, I myself would send it, together with the letter Hutten[16] has written against those skull-capped and hooded jay-birds[17] at Worms. If I can, I myself shall add something in German on this subject.[18]

I admire the newly-married man of Kemberg;[19] he is afraid of nothing and was in quite a hurry in these troubled times. May the Lord guide him, and blend delights into his bitter herbs;[20] this will be done even without my prayer.

---

berg/Palatinate (1482-1531) studied theology in Heidelberg, where he was graduated as Master of Arts in 1503. As a student he came under the influence of the Humanistic reform movement. After having traveled in Italy and having been a tutor in Mainz, he was ordained and had a parish in Weinsberg. From 1513 to 1515 he continued his studies at Tübingen and Stuttgart, and became a member of the Melanchthon-Reuchlin circle. In 1515/16 he was in Basel assisting Erasmus in the work on the Greek text of the New Testament. Upon Capito's (see p. 305, n. 2) recommendation, Oecolampadius was called to Augsburg as cathedral preacher in 1518; there he became acquainted with Luther during the latter's visit to Augsburg in the fall of 1518 (see p. 83). In order to have quiet for establishing a stand on Luther's ideas, Oecolampadius withdrew from Augsburg and went to St. Brigit's monastery in Altomünster. Here he wrote his work on confession (mentioned above), in which he endorsed the Reformation. As a result he was forced to leave Altomünster. After a short stay at von Sickingen's castle (see pp. 244 f.), he went to Basel in 1522 and found work there in the publishing house of Cratander (which was then engaged in a large project of editing patristic texts). He began to conduct biblical lectures and soon gained the support of the Basel city council and was appointed professor at the University. In 1525 he was appointed *Hauptleutpriester* (main preacher) at St. Martin's Church. In that position he successfully established the Reformation in Basel. Oecolampadius' theological thinking was deeply influenced by Erasmus; on the way in which the new ideas ought to be put into action, however, he differed from the great Humanist, and they clashed on various occasions. Although Oecolampadius admired Luther, he sided with Zwingli and became one of the fathers of the "Reformed" branch of the Reformation. See *O.D.C.C.*, p. 976.

15 See p. 114, n. 16.

16 Ulrich von Hutten; see p. 163, n. 1. Luther is referring to von Hutten's open letter to the cardinals and bishops assembled in Worms to fight Luther; see Böcking 2, 21 ff. Spalatin must have sent a copy of this letter to the Wartburg.

17 The cardinals; literally: "hoopoes," i.e., Old World birds with fanlike crests on their heads.

18 I.e., on confession; see p. 225; p. 246, n. 10.

19 Bartholomew Bernhardi of Feldkirch, once president of the University of Wittenberg (see p. 115, n. 21), had resigned his University position and taken up residence in Kemberg (see p. 142, n. 2). He had just recently married; see *WA*, Br 2, 350, n. 16.

20 Exod. 12:8.

I am annoyed that not a single copy of your *Loci* [21]—so far as it is printed—has arrived here.

I would like to know who fills my pulpit.[22] Is Amsdorf still snoring and lazy? Also, what is Doctor Karlstadt doing?[23] May the Lord guard and strengthen you in what you write concerning the prosperity of the University. Amen.

I definitely do not want you all to worry about me in any way. As far as I am concerned, all is well, except that the troubles of my soul have not yet ceased, and the former weakness of the spirit and faith persists.[24] My life in seclusion [25] means nothing. Since I never was engaged in the exposition of the Word by my own volition,[26] I am now excluded from it with great peace of heart. That is the state of affairs as far as I personally am concerned. However, for the glory of the Word and for the strengthening of others and in turn for my own strengthening, I would rather burn among glowing coals than rot here alone half alive—may God grant, not dead. But who knows whether Christ does not wish to accomplish more by this plan, not only in my case but also in all others?[27] We spoke so many times of faith and hope for the things not seen! [28] Come on, let's test at least once a small part of [Christ's] teaching, since things have come to pass this way at the call of God and not through our doing. Even though I should perish, the gospel will not lose anything. You surpass me now [in teaching the gospel] and succeed me as Elisha followed Elijah [29] with a double portion of Spirit—which may the Lord Jesus graciously bestow upon you. Amen.

---

[21] Melanchthon's *Loci communes rerum theologicarum* (Wittenberg: M. Lotther, 1521; the printing began in April and was completed in December). *C. R.* 21, 81 ff.; *Melanchthon,* Studienausgabe, 2, I, 3 ff.; C. L. Hill, *The Loci Communes of Philip Melanchthon* (Boston, 1944). This work was the first systematic presentation of Reformation doctrine; see *O.D.C.C.*, p. 882.

[22] Luther wrote *suggestum,* which can mean either the academic chair or the pulpit; see p. 221, n. 8.

[23] Andrew Karlstadt; see p. 79, n. 12. This sentence is missing in one of the manuscript copies and in some of the printed editions.

[24] For similar statements, see p. 28, n. 10. For ". . . of my soul" the manuscript copies have *ani,* i.e., [troubles with my] constipation; see p. 217, n. 15.

[25] This part of the sentence is in Greek.

[26] See p. 6, n. 5.

[27] For a similar statement, see p. 213.

[28] Heb. 11:1.

[29] II Kings 2:9.

Therefore, all of you, do not be downcast but sing the Lord's hymn which is appointed for the night.[30] I will sing too; and so let us be anxious only for the Word. Who is ignorant, let him be ignorant; who perishes may perish, only as long as they cannot complain that we have not done our duty toward them. Let the Leipzig people boast, for this is their hour.[31] We must go out of our country, away from our kindred and from our father's house, and must be separated from each other for a while, and go into a land that we do not know.[32] Meanwhile let them worship their idol [33] and brag about it.

It is enough for the little James of Flanders [34] to visit you; just take care that he does not become too cocky if he gets all he wants.[35]

I have not abandoned the hope of returning to you, only God must do what is good in his eyes.[36] If the Pope will take steps against all who think as I do, then Germany will not be without uproar. The faster he undertakes this, the faster he and his followers will perish and I shall return. God is arousing the spirits of many, especially the hearts of the common people. It does not seem to me likely that this affair can be checked with force; if [the Pope] begins to put it down, it will become ten times bigger. Germany has very many *Karsthansen*.[37]

---

30 Ps. 42:8.

31 Luke 22:53. The Faculty of the University of Leipzig had been bitterly opposed to Luther since the days of the disputation; see p. 63, n. 24; p. 134, n. 3.

32 Gen. 12:1; Heb. 11:8.

33 The manuscript copies of the letter have "*N.N.*," which stands for *non nominatus*, or "not named." Either Luther did not write the proper name in the original, or the copyist purposely omitted it. Luther was perhaps thinking of Duke George (see p. 110, n. 20) or John Eck, the "victor" of the Leipzig Disputation (see p. 134, n. 3).

34 James Propst of Ypres, Flemish Augustinian and prior of the monastery at Antwerp, was an early follower of Luther and sometime in 1519 or 1520 went to Wittenberg to study. He was graduated as Bachelor in Biblical Studies from Wittenberg University in May, 1521, and as Licentiate of Theology in July, 1521. Having returned to the Netherlands, he was active in spreading the Reformation, for which he was arrested and forced to recant. After escaping from the Netherlands, he again professed the Reformation, and in 1524 became a pastor at Bremen, a position he held until his death on June 30, 1562. S-*J* 1, 351, n. 3; 2, 36, n. 5.

35 What Luther meant here is not clear.

36 I Sam. 3:18.

37 Some of the older printed editions omit "very," which can be found in

Murner is silent.[38] What the Goat[39] will do I do not know; perhaps he will be a second Ortwin.[40]

I cannot believe what you write, that you are going astray without a shepherd.[41] This would be the saddest and bitterest of news. As long as you, Amsdorf, and the others are there, you are not without a shepherd. Don't talk that way, lest God be angered, and we be found guilty of ingratitude. Would that all the churches, at least the collegiate churches,[42] had one-fourth of your share of the Word and its ministers! Thank the Lord who has enlightened you. Look how verbose I have been!

One says the Cardinal of Mainz has eighteen hundred sworn enemies,[43] and that Lord Chievres[44] suffers from heavy fever; others say he died. A certain bishop, especially hostile to Luther, has fallen—that is, he has died at Worms.[45] I have no more news, since I am a hermit, an anchorite, and truly a monk, though neither shaved nor cowled. You would see a knight and hardly recognize me.[46]

---

the manuscript copies of this letter. *Karsthans* was the common name for the German peasant who opposed the pressure of the clergy, especially their tax demands. It was also the title of a little book against Murner (see note 38), published in Strassburg by J. Prüss in 1521, which set forth the grievances of the peasants. For detailed information on this little book, see *WA*, Br 2, 351, n. 35.

38 Thomas Murner; see p. 194, n. 16. Since his attack on Luther's *To the Christian Nobility of the German Nation* and Luther's reply, Murner had been silent.

39 Jerome Emser; see p. 137, n. 19.

40 Ortwin Gratius; see p. 9, n. 2.

41 Matt. 9:36.

42 Churches with more than one clergyman in residence, which were not, however, bishops' churches.

43 Cardinal Albrecht, archbishop of Mainz; see pp. 44 f. During the night of April 19/20, 1521, a proclamation was nailed to the door of the city hall in Worms; in this proclamation four hundred nobles, "who had sworn not to abandon the just Luther," declared their enmity toward all sovereigns and Romanists who persecuted Luther, especially the Archbishop of Mainz; see *WA*, Br 2, 351, n. 42.

44 William de Croy, lord of Chievres, was governor of the Netherlands and one of the guardians of Charles V during the Emperor's minority. He was one of the most influential persons surrounding the Emperor. He died May 27; see p. 255.

45 Aloisius Marlianus, bishop of Tuy, who had published an oration against Luther early in 1521, died during the night of May 10/11; see *WA*, Br 2, 351, n. 44; S-J 1, 421, n. 1; 2, 37, n. 2. The source for this news could not be established; perhaps it was Spalatin, or someone at the Wartburg.

46 See p. 228.

Tell Amsdorf that the pastor of Hersfeld,[47] an excellent man, has also taken a wife, as the rumor goes, so that you are not the only ones to have a newly-wed provost.[48] Also tell him to bear patiently the fact that this man has been preferred to him as the replacement for Peter Lupin.[49] Oh, children of man! But it is good that his[50] upright and bold spirit caused him such great loss, while the different spirit of the other caused the latter such great gain![51] Our merits are hidden but divided; yet the rewards make manifest the thoughts of the heart. I fear that the Provost of Kemberg[52] might be expelled, and that then two stomachs would suffer want, and all who may come from them.[53] But if he has faith [he need not worry]; the Lord lives and he is the shepherd of all, and he does not allow even the birds to starve.[54] Please greet him and encourage him. I want you and all to rejoice and glory [in the Lord]. I cannot tell you how much you would all gratify me by doing this, and how you would also please God and scorch Satan and his armor. Your sadness is my greatest misfortune, while your gladness is also mine. And so farewell in the Lord, to whom you will commend me, I am sure; as much as I am able, I shall also remember you [in my prayers]. Keep watch over the church of the Lord, in which the Holy Spirit has appointed you as bishops[55] and not mere imitations of bishops.

---

47 Luther must have heard of this while he was in Hersfeld; see pp. 225 f. The pastor in question was a certain Henry Fuchs; see *WA*, Br 2, 351, n. 45; *S-J* 2, 37, n. 3.

48 It is not clear who this provost was. The reference newly-wed suggests, however, that Luther is thinking of Bartholomew Bernhardi; see note 19 and Luther's statements below.

49 See note 8.

50 Amsdorf's.

51 The background of this statement could not be clarified; for possibilities, see *WA*, Br 2, 351, n. 47. It is clear, however, that the "provost" was supposed to replace Lupin, who had died on May 1; perhaps one can also assume that the "provost" was preferred to von Amsdorf as the replacement for Lupin's office. But which office? It must have been either at the University or the All Saints' Chapter.

52 See notes 19, 48.

53 I.e., the Provost himself, his wife, and any children they might have. The expulsion was to be expected because a priest who married was defying the existing laws. Luther's fear soon became a reality; see p. 342.

54 Matt. 6:26.

55 Or overseers, guardians; Acts 20:28.

Please greet all in my name (except the Master of Eisleben[56] and that fat little [Flemish] flame[57]—to these I write directly),[58] for there are many of you: John Schwertfeger,[59] Peter Swawe,[60] and the whole "church in your house,"[61] Henry of Zütphen,[62] and all the friars (I have written to the Prior),[63] Master Lucas, the painter,[64] Christian Goldschmidt,[65] Doctor Esch,[66] and all who come to your mind. You must as a matter of necessity take care of these greetings.[67]

Again, farewell.

In the land of the birds that sing sweetly in the branches and praise God with all their power night and day, Sunday, May 26, 1521

Yours,
MARTIN[68]

---

[56] John Agricola; see p. 220.
[57] James Propst; see note 34.
[58] The letters are apparently not extant.
[59] See note 13.
[60] Peter Swawe (1496-1552), a noble of Pomerania, had studied at the universities of Louvain and Leipzig and in 1519 or 1520 went to Wittenberg to continue his studies. He accompanied Luther to Worms (see p. 227, n. 27). In the fall of 1521 he returned to Pomerania and from 1526 until his death was in the diplomatic service of Denmark; see *WA*, Br 2, 352, n. 54.
[61] I Cor. 16:19. This is a reference to the students, professors, and townspeople who assembled in Melanchthon's home every Sunday to listen to him lecture. It seems that Melanchthon lectured on Genesis in 1521/22; see *WA*, Br 8, 661.
[62] See p. 31, n. 21. He had left Wittenberg in 1514 and became sub-prior in the Augustinian monastery at Cologne (see p. 31). In 1516 he was made prior of the Dordrecht monastery. Persecuted for his open support of the Reformation, he left Dordrecht and went again to Wittenberg. He was graduated from Wittenberg University in 1521 as Bachelor in Biblical Studies, and he then returned to Antwerp. He was imprisoned there, but he was freed due to an uprising of the people. Then he went to Bremen, where he preached the gospel and promoted the Reformation until November, 1524, when he went on to Meldorf. On December 9 he was seized by a mob inspired by priests faithful to Rome, and on December 10, 1524, he was put to death. See also *LW* 32, 263 ff.
[63] Conrad Helt; see p. 125, n. 9. The letter is not extant.
[64] Lucas Cranach; see p. 201.
[65] See note 6.
[66] Thomas Eschaus; see p. 168, n. 6.
[67] One of the manuscript copies of this letter and some of the printed editions have a text which S-J 2, 38, translates: "See what shameful paper I have had to use for you."
[68] The signature is written in Greek.

Excursus

As soon as Luther was settled in the Wartburg, he decided to complete his original intention (see p. 152, n. 2) to continue writing homilies on the Epistles and Gospels appointed for the Sundays and festival days of the church year; see p. 225. To begin his work, he asked his friends in Wittenberg, on May 14, to send to him a copy of the Latin *Advent Postil,* along with other materials; see p. 225 (perhaps also pp. 218 f. [May 12]); he waited in vain however; see pp. 229, 254. In the interim Luther continued to work on the Psalms; see p. 225; p. 229, n. 5; p. 252, n. 11; p. 121, n. 7; he also wrote the treatise *On Confession;* see p. 246, n. 10. Luther also must have re-evaluated his work on the *Postil* and decided on a major change, for on May 26 he announced to Melanchthon that he would publish a German *Postil.* It must have been his intention to begin by translating the Latin *Advent Postil,* when the copy finally came; see p. 229. His friends in Wittenberg could not find his personal copy, however, which he apparently had entrusted to someone who misplaced it. By June 10 he still had not received it; see p. 254.

Perhaps tired of waiting, Luther made a second change in his plans. At the end of May or the beginning of June he began working on the homilies (in German) for the pericopes of the Christmas season. Apparently he first wanted to finish the hard work of writing new homilies, and thus make good use of the time while awaiting the Latin *Advent Postil.* By June 10 he had already completed the sermon on the Epistle for Christmas Eve (Titus 2:11-14); see pp. 254 f.; *WA* $10^{I, 2}$, XLII f. Luther must have worked hard on this first of the new series of German homilies; he realized that in this German Christmas series the homilies would be more detailed than in the (still untranslated) Latin *Advent Postil.* To speed his work, he asked Spalatin on June 10 for a certain *Shorter Postil,* among other things (see p. 254) which cannot be further identified. It can be assumed, however, that it was a manuscript in Luther's handwriting, which probably contained notes and outlines for sermons he had preached or had intended to preach; see p. 321, n. 31; *WA* $10^{I, 2}$, LXII f.; *WA,* Br 2, 355, n. 7.

At the beginning of July, Luther's working capacity was greatly hindered by his illness; see pp. 255, 257, 270. Spalatin sent a strong medication, which gave Luther some relief (see p. 268), and between July 10 and 15 Luther's health improved; about July 13 he was able to resume his work; see pp. 257 f., 270. Soon after July 15 he sent some "other things" to Spalatin (see p. 271), and on July 31 he sent the "rest" of his *Postil* manuscript to Spalatin, asking that the publisher give it special attention (see p. 276). Since we do not hear of any previous shipment of *Postil* manuscripts which would justify Luther's statement that he was sending the "rest" of it, it is safe to assume (with the *WA,* Br editor) that the "other things" (which Luther forwarded to Spalatin soon after July 15) were manuscripts of the newly written German homilies on the pericopes of the Christmas season. Among these might have been the one on Titus 2:11-14, mentioned by Luther in his June 10 letter to Spalatin (see above).

In the July 31 letter to Spalatin (accompanying the "rest" of the *Postil* manuscript), Luther expressed some ideas concerning the final form of the *Postil* which show that he had changed his mind a third time. The homilies on the pericopes of the Advent and Christmas seasons were to have come out in one volume. He must have realized that it would be awkward if the homilies for the Advent Sundays followed those for the Christmas season, which obviously would have been the case had he continued to finish the homilies for the Christmas season before concentrating on those for the Advent season. Therefore he decided to move the homilies for the four Advent Sundays to the beginning of the book, where they should have been anyway, according to his original plan (see p. 229; p. 152, n. 2); this plan could not have been put to work, since his friends in Wittenberg did not send a copy of the Latin *Advent Postil.* On July 31 Luther envisioned publishing one volume of German homilies on the pericopes of the Advent and Christmas seasons. In this book he intended to give the people something from which they could learn about Christ "in the meantime," i.e., until a *Postil* covering the entire church year could be completed; see p. 276; *WA* 10[I, 2], XLVIII.

Spalatin must have immediately made the necessary arrangements with the publishing house of J. Grünenberg in Wittenberg. He also must have complained to Luther about the slowness of the printers in general. As a result, on August 3 Luther admonished Melanchthon to hurry the printers, but also to take great care that the *Postil* be well printed; see p. 288. On August 15 Luther was of the opinion that the printing of the *Postil* had begun; whether Grünenberg had already started the typesetting could not be established. Since Luther was unhappy with Grünenberg's work on another of his books, he wanted to stop the printing on August 15. Yet in spite of this he gave permission for the work to continue; see pp. 292 f., 296.

Luther made, however, a final change in the arrangement of the homilies. The *Postil,* he decided, was to be divided into four major parts, one for each quarter of the church year. In the following months Luther completed the *Postil* manuscript. On November 19 he signed the letter which prefaced the *Christmas Postil* and dedicated it to Count Albrecht of Mansfeld. Luther also urged Spalatin to keep this letter in his care until he completed the *Postil,* a task on which he was then working; see p. 337. This is obviously a reference to the Advent portion of the *Postil;* see *WA* 10[I, 2], 1 ff. The last homily was completed during the latter part of February, 1522; see *WA* 10[I, 2], LVIII. In March, 1522 (see *WA* 10[I, 2], LXII), J. Grünenberg released a (*Wartburg*) *Postil* (*WA* 10[I, 1], 1 ff.), the so-called *Christmas Postil;*

it made available German homilies on the pericopes of the Sundays and festival days of the Christmas season. In April, 1522, another (*Wartburg*) *Postil* was released (*WA* $10^{I, 2}$, 1 ff.), which was the so-called *Advent Postil;* it made available German homilies on the pericopes of the Advent Sundays.

Luther's statements concerning the *Postil* in his letters of 1521 cause problems which need further investigation if the text of the letters is to be clear. How can one explain the fact that Luther abandoned his May 26 idea of presenting a German *Postil* covering the pericopes of the Advent and Christmas seasons, yet took it up again on July 31? Why, when the work was finally completed, did the *Advent Postil* follow the *Christmas Postil?* When did Luther abandon the idea of translating the Advent homilies? These are but a few of the questions raised by Luther's statements. To these must be added the ambiguities in the statements themselves.

W. Köhler, the chief editor of the *Wartburg Postil* in the *WA*, has given a careful analysis of the development of this work; see *WA* $10^{I, 2}$, XLI ff. The first change in Luther's plans—that which he announced to Melanchthon on May 26 (see p. 229)—needs no further explanation, if one considers Luther's great concern for the laity; see, e.g., p. 113, n. 10. The second change in Luther's plans, which took place before June 10, is understandable when one realizes that Luther did not have the Latin *Advent Postil* available. The development of Luther's work up to July 13 is therefore clear. On this day, however, having just resumed his work, he intended to send a *Postil* manuscript to Melanchthon as soon as he had finished "ten"; see p. 258. Contrary to the opinion of the *WA*, Br editor (see *WA*, Br 2, 360, n. 10), this editor assumes with Köhler (see *WA* $10^{I, 2}$, XLVII) that these "ten" refer to the ten Sundays and festival days between the first Advent Sunday and Epiphany: four Advent Sundays, Christmas Day, the days of St. Stephen and St. John, the Sunday after Christmas, New Year's Day, and Epiphany. Counting all the Epistles and Gospels, this would have been twenty-four homilies: six on the (three) Epistle and (three) Gospel pericopes appointed for the different services on Christmas; nine on the Epistles; and nine on the Gospels appointed as texts for the other Sundays and festival days. Luther wanted to send a complete manuscript as soon as it was finished. He envisioned a German *Advent-Christmas Postil,* which would fulfil his intention of May 26 (see p. 229). The second change was, therefore, only a technical one due to Luther's lack of an *Advent Postil.* While waiting for it, Luther began working on the new homilies for the Christmas season, perhaps hoping that he could finish the homilies for the Advent season once he received the *Advent Postil.* Did he still intend to translate the Advent homilies? This question has to remain unanswered for the time being.

On July 31 Luther forwarded to Spalatin the "rest" of the *Postil* manuscript and promised to hurry the work on "ten of the Gospels"; see p. 276. Köhler assumed that Luther here referred once more to all the sermons for the ten Sundays and festival days of the Advent and Christmas seasons; see *WA* $10^{I, 2}$, xlvii f. But why did Luther point out especially that he would hurry the work on "ten of the *Gospels*"? Köhler overlooked this fact. In addition if Luther had maintained his intention of July 13 of not sending anything to the press until the manuscript was entirely finished, i.e., until all twenty-four sermons for the ten Sundays and festival days were completed, then the manuscript would necessarily have been completed with the shipment of July 31. No further hurry would have been necessary. Köhler circumvents this difficulty by suggesting that Luther forwarded the rest of the finished manuscript, i.e., whatever Luther had finished. The shipment of July 15 (see p. 271) can be discounted, since it could hardly have been the fulfilment of the promise made on July 13 (see p. 258), for Luther had then just resumed work after a long involuntary pause (see p. 257). It cannot definitely be shown why Luther sent anything on July 15, nor what he sent; see above. The "ten of the Gospels" which, on July 31, Luther promised to write in a hurry have to refer to something other than the "ten" mentioned by Luther on July 13; see pp. 258, 276. To what, then, do they refer? This editor suggests that they refer to ten homilies on the Gospel pericopes (hence "ten of the Gospels") of the Advent and Christmas seasons. As on July 13, so on July 31 Luther envisioned one *Postil* covering the Advent and Christmas seasons, and promised to hurry ten Gospel sermons for this *Postil*.

This assumption is supported by the following analysis: On July 31 Luther wanted to move the homilies for the four Advent Sundays to the beginning of the whole work and add the rest; see p. 276. On July 31 he also anticipated hurriedly finishing "ten of the Gospels." The texts for the Sundays and festival days from Christmas to Epiphany included only eight Gospel pericopes. Even if one assumes that on July 31 Luther had not yet begun any of the homilies on the Gospel pericopes of the Christmas season, it is obvious that he had then already included two of the four Advent Gospels in his working plans. (If he had already finished two of the homilies on the Gospel pericopes of the Christmas season—which may be assumed if one considers that Luther had been working on the Christmas series since before June 10 [see pp. 254 f.] and had already sent some manuscripts to Spalatin [see p. 271] and thus could easily have completed some of the homilies on the Gospel pericopes of the Christmas season—then, on July 31, he would have included the work on all four Advent Gospel pericopes in his plans.)

The problem thus is now: Did Luther, on July 31, still intend to *translate* the homilies for the Advent season from the Latin *Advent Postil*? Or had he at this point already decided to write new homilies for the Advent season, as he did for the Christmas season? Köhler stated that the date on which Luther decided to give up his intention of translating cannot definitely be established; he believed that this took place sometime after November 22 when Luther had completed the work on the homilies for the Christmas season and had begun to work on the *Advent Postil;* see p. 337; *WA* $10^{I, 2}$, LIV. This seems open to question. If on July 31 Luther still had the idea of translating the Advent homilies, why did he not say so? See p. 276. It seems to this editor that Luther considered the "ten of the Gospels" to be one task to be undertaken and not two, namely, *translating* (from the *Advent Postil*) and *writing new* homilies (for the Christmas season). If the Advent sermons had only to be translated, Luther would not have had to make a major change in the organization of the *Postil* on August 15 (that is, to divide the *Postil* into four parts which were supposed to be published separately; see p. 297). This change was obviously due to the fact that all the Advent homilies were not yet available. It seems to this editor that Luther had decided to abandon the idea of translating the Advent homilies at least as early as July 31. And some material of the Advent homilies must have been available on August 15, at least on the Gospel pericopes, according to Luther's promise made on July 31 (an assumption which is contrary to Köhler, whose argumentation is not convincing; see *WA* $10^{I, 2}$, LIV ff.). This is obvious if one looks more closely at Luther's statements in his July 31 letter to Spalatin; see p. 276. Luther speaks there of moving the homilies for the four (Advent) Sundays to the front of the book. Of course this could still have been only a thought and should be understood as meaning he would do it once he got around to translating the homilies. However it is certain that on July 31 Luther had already included in his work plans the writing of at least two new Advent homilies on the Gospel pericopes, and perhaps had actually begun work on them, and that he sent some of them to Wittenberg, either between July 31 and August 14 (perhaps on August 6; see p. 290), or was about to send them on August 15 (see pp. 292 f.). This statement can be supported if one considers that Luther, in his August 15 letter, requested that the *manuscripts* be *kept safely,* or even *returned* to him, yet in the same letter gave the green light for the continuation of the printing of the *Postil* manuscripts he had sent, and the printing of the ten big sheets he included; see pp. 293 f., 296. Which manuscripts were to be printed? Which were to be kept safely? The only possible answer is that the manuscripts of the *Christmas Postil* could be printed, while those of the Advent homilies were to be kept. That these manuscripts of the Advent section contained the new Advent homilies can be seen from the fact that Luther would not have had to omit the Advent homilies if they were only to be translated; this he certainly could have done in a short time. But to write new homilies for all the Advent pericopes was a task Luther realized could not be done—at least not as quickly as Luther thought it should be. Since he had had longer to work on the homilies for the Christmas season, they were to be printed first, while those for the Advent season were to be temporarily postponed. This would explain the final major change: Luther's decision on August 15 to publish the *Postil* in four parts, beginning with the *Christmas Postil.*

In considering the arrangement of the *Postil* between June 10 and July 31, Luther must have decided not to translate the Advent homilies. The date on which he gave up the idea of translating the Advent homilies must have been around July 15, the time when perhaps he finally received a copy of the Latin *Advent Postil.* Following Luther's June 10 complaint to Spalatin (see p. 254) that friends in Wittenberg had not yet sent it, and the request in the same letter for the *Shorter Postil,* Spalatin must have written to Melanchthon, for on July 6 Melanchthon sent, "as requested," the *Shorter Postil* to Spalatin for forwarding to Luther; see *C.R.* 1, 417. On July 15 Luther announced to Spalatin that he had finally received "everything"; see p. 268. Perhaps it can be assumed that "everything" included the *Shorter Postil* and perhaps also the *Advent Postil,* since Luther from that day on no longer complained of not having them; see *WA,* Br 2, 365, n. 1. Resuming his work on the *Postil* by July 13 (see pp. 257 f.), Luther must have soon examined the material that had arrived from Wittenberg and realized that the Latin Advent homilies would be no match for the already completed German Christmas homilies (see pp. 254 f.) and as a result must then have decided to write new Advent homilies. He had made up his mind to write such Advent homilies (at least for the Gospels) by July 31. Perhaps he actually had begun working on them; if not, he at least included them in his plans on July 31 (see above). It was on July 31 that he hoped "soon" to send ten Gospel homilies—that is, either all Gospel homilies for the Christmas season and a first instalment of two Advent Gospel homilies, or whichever Gospel homilies for the Christmas season were still missing and, depending on this number, more Advent Gospel homilies. Soon Luther was of the opinion that Grünenberg had begun printing the material he had sent to him on July 15 and 31. Although Luther had written ten big manuscript pages between July 31 and August 15 (see p. 293), he realized that the press would be too much delayed should it have to wait until all the new Advent homilies for his *Advent-Christmas Postil* were available. Since all of the new Advent sermons were not available, nor was Luther anywhere close to having them completed, he decided to eliminate them for the time being and divide the *Postil* into four parts, beginning with the homilies for the Christmas season, a part of which he believed to be already set in type. The publication of the Advent homilies (of which Spalatin was supposed to keep or return to the Wartburg whatever Luther had forwarded to Wittenberg; see p. 297) was to conclude the *Postil*, which eventually was to cover the entire year from Christmas to Christmas.

In the following months Luther began to meditate on some of the Gospel pericopes of the Trinity season. This resulted in the exposition of the Gospel of the ten lepers; see p. 314, n. 9. The first task Luther took up, however, after finishing the Christmas part of the *Postil*, was the writing of the rest of the Advent homilies. For him the *Wartburg Postil* was at all times one unit. Therefore on November 22, when he sent Spalatin the letter of dedication of the *Postil*, Luther urged him to keep this letter in his care until he completed the whole work; see p. 337. All changes in the arrangement of the *Postil* and in Luther's working procedure were due to technical difficulties or shortage of time. In the last homily of the Christmas series (which was finished in November) Luther again spoke of the twenty-four sermons (see *WA* 10$^{I, 1}$, 728) which were to cover the pericopes appointed for the Sundays and festival days of Advent and Christmas. Perhaps he thought that the Advent portion could precede the Christmas series when bound, or that the release of the Christmas portion could be delayed until the Advent homilies had been completed; see pp. 237 f. Yet the work on the Advent homilies must have taken up more of Luther's time than he anticipated, while the printers must have completed the Christmas portion more quickly than he had expected. Therefore the printing of the Advent series was completed about six weeks after the Christmas series had appeared on the market.

To sum up, Luther's work on the *Wartburg Postil*, as reflected in his correspondence of 1521, must be reconstructed as follows: On May 26 Luther announced to Melanchthon that he would bring out a German *Postil*, which was to begin with the Advent homilies translated from the Latin *Advent Postil*. Due to the lack of his Latin *Advent Postil* he changed his mind by June 10. He began work on the homilies for the Christmas season, postponing the translating. By July 31 he again took up his first plan to begin the *Postil* with the Advent homilies. By now, however, he had also decided to write new Advent homilies, at least for the Gospel texts; he hoped he could soon send ten Gospel homilies, among which there must have been at least two for the Advent season. Since on August 15 Luther was of the opinion that the printing had already begun, and since he was pressured for time, he finally eliminated the Advent portion, at least temporarily. He was never able to catch up, however, and the Advent homilies eventually had to come out after those of the Christmas season.

82

To Francis von Sickingen
Wartburg, June 1, 1521

In the days before the Diet of Worms, Luther had approached von Sickingen, perhaps in connection with his appeal to the Emperor (see p. 174, n. 6). In this letter which prefaces the treatise On Confession, Luther dedicates this treatise to von Sickingen.

Francis von Sickingen (1481-1523) was a powerful member of the Estate of Knights. This Estate, once the most important of the Empire, gradually lost its political, military, and cultural position during the fourteenth, fifteenth, and sixteenth centuries and was replaced by the mercenary armies and the ecclesiastical and secular territorial sovereigns. The Reformation, with its theological opposition to Rome, seemed to the knights to be a last anchor. They considered the Reformation a chance to reorganize the social structure of the Empire by cutting down the importance and influence of the territorial sovereigns, especially the ecclesiastical ones. In addition they hoped that a general intellectual uprising of the German nation might free the Empire from the thumb of the papacy. Before and after the Diet of Worms, von Sickingen offered asylum to Luther, an offer the Reformer never accepted.

After the Diet of Worms the knights became increasingly restless (see, e.g., p. 231, n. 16), and led by von Sickingen, they finally staged an uprising against the Archbishop of Trier in 1522/23. The campaign ended in a catastrophe for the knights. While defending his Castle Landstuhl against the troops of the Archbishop of Trier, which outnumbered his own by far, von Sickingen was mortally wounded and capitulated shortly before his death. With him died the romantic hopes of the whole Estate of Knights for the re-establishment of their former status. Von Sickingen's uprising has to be seen against the background of his political and economic ambition to secularize the wealth of the church, an honest enthusiasm for Luther and his work (chiefly because of Luther's anti-papal tendencies), a desire to elevate the

Estate of Knights to a position equal to the territorial sovereigns, and a nationalism which opposed the interference of Rome and its willing servants in the Empire, the ecclesiastical sovereigns.

Text in German: WA 8, 138-140, which is based on a printed version (thus there is no signature); translation based on S-J 2, 39-41.

To the brave and honorable Francis von Sickingen,
my special lord and patron—from Martin Luther
God's grace and peace in Christ our Lord

Brave Sir: We read in the Book of Joshua that when God led the people of Israel into the promised land of Canaan and smote all the people of that land, namely, thirty-one kings and all their cities, there was no city humble enough to ask for peace except Gibeon, though Israel had a command from God to offer and accept terms of peace. In their presumption they were all hardened, and fought against Israel, so that it is written in the 11th chapter [:19-20] of said book:[1] "There was no city that surrendered itself peacefully to the people of Israel except Gibeon; but they were all conquered in battle. For it was determined by the Lord that they should obstinately and boldly fight against Israel, and thereby be destroyed and find no grace."

It seems to me that this history is meant to set an example for our popes, bishops, scholars, and other spiritual tyrants, who clearly see and understand that people know their affairs and are tired of them, and that the bright light is in many ways and many places uncovering their deceitful and seducing ways, so that every cover is becoming too short and too narrow for them. Yet they neither humble themselves nor sue for peace; indeed, when peace is offered them they refuse it; they screw up their courage and undertake to quench the light by force, and remain what they are, thinking they are so securely in the saddle that no one can unhorse them. I am afraid that here also[2] it is God's doing that they are hardened in their hearts, give no thought to humility, and do not consider peace, so that at last they, too, must perish without any mercy.

[1] Luther wrote 10th chapter by mistake.
[2] As was the case with the Canaanites.

They blame me for it all, yet they know very well how proudly they have hitherto despised the poor man. I have often offered peace, even cried out for it and run to meet it.[3] I have declared my readiness to answer charges, have held disputations,[4] and have now appeared at two diets.[5] This has not helped me at all. I have not met with justice but with open wickedness and force; I have been commanded simply to recant and threatened with all sorts of misfortune. Ah, well, if the hour comes when they, too, shall vainly cry for peace, I hope they will remember what they are now earning! I can do nothing more; I have been pushed off the field; they now have time to change what people neither can, nor ought to, nor will endure from them. If they do not change it, someone else will change it without their consent; he will not teach them with letters and words, as Luther has, but with deeds. Thanks and praise be to God, there is now less fear and dread of the bugaboo at Rome, and the chapter *Si quis suadente*[6] will no longer bewitch the people; the world can now break the spell.[7]

In order to demonstrate that I am not idle in this wilderness and in my Patmos,[8] I, too, have written a Revelation for myself and will share it with all who desire it. I am herewith sending it to Your Honor to show my good will and gratitude for the many encouragements and offers[9] you have given to me, an unworthy person. It is a sermon *On Confession*,[10] which I wrote for the following reason: this last Lent I issued a mild instruction

---

[3] See p. 83; p. 178, n. 4.
[4] See, e.g., p. 126.
[5] Augsburg, 1518 (see pp. 83 ff.), and Worms, 1521 (see pp. 197 ff.).
[6] This is a reference to a decretal issued by Pope Clement V during the Council of Vienne (1311/12) concerning the punishment of crimes against members of the hierarchy. See *Clementinae* V, tit. VIII, cap. 1. *CIC* 2, 1187 f.; see also *Decreti* II, causa XVII, ques. 4, cap. 29. *CIC* 1, 822.
[7] Literally: ". . . say the benediction" (which makes the Evil One powerless).
[8] Luther considered the Wartburg his Patmos. During one of the early persecutions of the young Christian church, John, the writer of the Apocalypse, was exiled to a small island called Patmos, where he had the visions set forth in the Book of Revelation; see Rev. 1:9.
[9] See the Introduction and *WA*, Br 2, No. 349; *S-J* 1, 384 ff.
[10] *Von der Beicht, ob der Papst Macht habe sie zu gebieten* (*On Confession, Whether the Pope Has the Power to Require It*) (Wittenberg: J. Grünenberg, September, 1521). *WA* 8, 140 ff.

to penitents,[11] along with a petition to our ecclesiastical lords and tyrants asking them not to disturb simple consciences about my books, and showing, in addition, how their tyranny over the confessional was without sufficient ground. But they are so headstrong that they will neither listen to nor consider anything. Ah, well, I have seen more bubbles on the water before this, and once I saw an ambitious smoke-cloud set out to quench the sun; but the smoke is gone and the sun still shines. I will keep on polishing the truth and putting it forth, and will fear my ungracious lords as little as they greatly despise me. Neither of us is over the mountain, but I have an advantage: I walk unencumbered. God grant victory to the truth.

With this, farewell in God. I commend Sir Ulrich von Hutten[12] and Martin Bucer[13] to Your Grace.

Written on my Patmos, June 1, 1521

---

[11] *Ein Unterricht der Beichtkinder über die verbotenen Bücher* (*A Word to Penitents about the Forbidden Books*) (Wittenberg: M. Lotther, February, 1521). *WA* 7, 290 f.; B. L. Woolf, *Reformation Writings of Martin Luther* (New York, 1956), II, 92 ff. In this tract Luther set forth that confession is a privilege for the Christian who is longing for the consolation of absolution, but that it is not a right of the clergy to investigate the individual's conscience.

[12] Ulrich von Hutten; see p. 163, n. 1.

[13] Martin Bucer of Schlettstadt/Alsace (1491-1551) had attended the famous college-type Latin school there and, at the age of fifteen, was persuaded by the Dominicans to join their Order. While studying theology at Heidelberg he became acquainted with Luther during the Heidelberg Disputation in 1518 (see pp. 60 ff.). From the beginning Bucer was an enthusiastic follower of Luther, yet he was too deeply influenced by Erasmus of Rotterdam to be able to completely understand the Reformer or to agree entirely with him. Receiving a papal dispensation which released him from his monastic vows, he left the Order in 1521 and became chaplain at the Ebernburg, a castle of Francis von Sickingen (see pp. 244 f.). After a short stay in Weissenburg/Bavaria, Bucer went to Strassburg. There he won the recognition of the leading citizens and in 1524 was elected pastor of a parish. In this position he pushed the Reformation to the fore and soon became the theological advisor and spokesman of the Strassburg city council. Although deeply influenced by Luther, Bucer's Eucharistic doctrine was closer to Zwingli's than Luther's, even though he tirelessly tried to mediate between the two men. His efforts to present to the Emperor at the 1530 Diet of Augsburg a Protestant front which was united in theology and politics were unsuccessful, due to the Eucharistic controversy. Consequently the upper German cities Strassburg, Memmingen, Constance, and Lindau could not join the confessors of the *Augsburg Confession* but had to turn over to the Emperor a special confession, the *Tetrapolitana*, which had been drawn up almost singlehandedly by Bucer. After Zwingli's death in 1531, Bucer for a short time was the leader of Protestantism in southwestern Germany and in the German-

83

To the People of Wittenberg
Wartburg, June, 1521[1]

Like the last letter, this letter is a preface to one of Luther's writings. In it he dedicates his Exposition of Psalm 37 to his people in Wittenberg.

Text in German: WA 8, 210-214.

To the poor little flock of Christ in Wittenberg,
from Doctor Martin Luther
Grace and peace from God the Father and
Jesus Christ our Lord. Amen

Having preached in many places, St. Paul did not, during his imprisonment in Rome, cease to be concerned for those whom he had converted. [He expressed this] by prayers to God [in their behalf] and by writings which offered them comfort and strength, as his epistles show. Following his example, I, too, ought not and cannot be free of the worry that wolves may enter the sheep-fold now that I am away. For I do not doubt that by God's grace we have heard and come to know the true and pure gospel, which it has pleased God to open to you in part through poor me. Although by God's grace you have many others in my stead, so

---

speaking portions of Switzerland. By bringing about the *Wittenberg Concord* in 1536 Bucer hoped to unite German and Swiss Protestantism and thus eliminate the sharp differences on the Eucharist which had developed—a vain hope, however. After 1536 Bucer helped organize Protestantism in Hesse and was one of the representatives of the Reformation who participated in the conferences between Rome and the Reformation which took place in Hagenau (1540), Worms (1540), and Regensburg (1541). Called to Bonn in 1542 by Hermann of Wied, the archbishop of Cologne, Bucer wrote the *Cologne Reformation*, a document famous for its middle-of-the-road character concerning the great issues of the Reformation. Due to pressure by the Imperial government, Bucer had to leave the German Empire. He went to England in 1549 and was appointed to the Regius Professorship of Divinity at Cambridge University, which he held for the remainder of his life. In that position he was highly influential in shaping Anglican theology and liturgy, especially the *Anglican Order* of 1550. See *O.D.C.C.* p. 204.

[1] On the dating of this letter, see *WA* 8, 205 ff.

that such anxiety on my part should be unnecessary, yet the grace of the gospel requires us, of course, to bear worries which may not actually be necessary.

We are not yet worthy, unfortunately especially I myself, to suffer anything for the sake of truth except unkindness, hatred, envy, slander, shame, and disgrace from the papists. Yet had God not resisted them up to now, and had it been left up to these bloodthirsty murderers of souls, we would have been torn apart by their teeth long ago, as David says in Psalm 124 [:1-3]. Thus our greatest suffering is that they decry us in the most shameless way as "Wycliffites,"[2] "Hussites,"[3] and "heretics." Since they are unable to accomplish anything else against us, they satisfy their malice by slandering our name and Christian honor.

But, dear friends,[4] give in, give in! He is up there who will judge it. By God's grace we can glory in the fact that we have never shied away from the light as they have thus far done and for which they must feel ashamed in their hearts. They have feared this light as the evil spirit fears Judgment Day. Whether they are willing or not, they have to admit and hear with great pain and grief that I have now made myself available three times —not to my friends, but to them, my enemies—and offered to give reason and basis for our belief: First I appeared at Augsburg before the Cardinal,[5] [and thus] immediately before the most prominent of my worst enemies, who would rather have fled than hear the basis of my teaching and would have preferred that I had not come. Then, as you know, I appeared at Leipzig before those people who really did not want to see us.[6] But all their malice and guile did not help them. The third time I now appeared at Worms, where I even offered to set aside the

---

[2] Followers of the English theologian John Wycliffe (1320?-1384), who was condemned as a heretic by the Council of Constance in 1415. See p. 147, n. 24; *O.D.C.C.*, pp. 1480 f.

[3] Followers of the Bohemian reformer John Huss (1369?-1415), who was condemned as a heretic by the Council of Constance in 1415. See p. 143; *O.D.C.C.*, pp. 667 f.

[4] Luther wrote *lieber Mensch;* perhaps this can be paraphrased "for goodness' sake."

[5] Cardinal Cajetan (see p. 73, n. 3): Augsburg, 1518; see pp. 83 ff.

[6] Disputation at Leipzig, 1519; see p. 126.

Imperial safe-conduct and place myself completely in their hands.[7] O what mockery they put on then! I expected that bishops and doctors would fully investigate me there; but everyone's attention was focused only on my recanting. God gave grace that not all sovereigns and Estates approved of this plan. Otherwise I would have been mortally ashamed of Germany, that it could have been so openly fooled and tricked by the papal tyrants.[8] As everyone knows, all this was only maneuvering on the part of my enemies.

Now see, I boast in these three offers and appearances not as if they were done of my own accord but that we may recognize God's grace, praise it, and seek comfort and become bold in him who makes our enemies so stupid and timid that all together they have not enough courage to listen to or oppose a poor beggar who is present among them and is, on top of that, in their power; instead they avoid the light like bats, and like night owls they howl in the dark "Hoo! Hoo!" and think that they can frighten us with this! If they were only so daring that they, or any one of them, would come to us in Wittenberg and offer what we had offered and consent to an investigation! This would be well becoming to them, since they boast so tremendously how smart they are in comparison to us. Then for once one could see that their ability does not consist in shouting from the throat but rather that it is stored in the head and brain. Since they set themselves up as judges and shepherds and judge us so willingly, they are duty bound to debate with us, to come to us and fight like men for their faith. But what do they do? They are the biggest crowd, we are the smallest. They have power over us, we are subjects. They are the most learned people, we the most unlearned. They are the superchristians, we are the arch-heretics. Furthermore, if they are afraid, we offer them safe-conduct, free board and room. Above all this, we ask them for the sake of God to demonstrate to us that they are right. But this is of no use. They stick by themselves in their own corner. There they make decisions, there they judge, there they condemn without giving

[7] Reference to the Diet of Worms; see pp. 188 ff., 195 ff., 199 ff. What Luther meant by "set aside the Imperial safe-conduct" is not clear.
[8] For a similar statement, see p. 202.

the defendant a hearing. Once they have done this, then they say and shout that they are honest Christian people who act in a Christian way; and no one blushes.

Oh, how our ears would ring if they were able to accomplish one iota against our glory—and then how we poor people would have to bear the disgrace which is theirs! Yet when they bear their disgrace, we have to consider it an honor and praise for them. O the poor sad and forsaken Christian faith which has as its guards such cowardly bats who hate the light and run from battle. They only put on a big show with shouting and boasting while they are by themselves in the sandbox; if one single man appears on the battleground, then like mice they crawl into a hole.

Since all this is not helping them, they resort to calling out some braggarts who attack us with vicious writings and wicked books. They hope they can thus cover up their disgrace from the common man and dress it up, although they know that their authors are as talented for the task as the ass is talented [for playing] the harp!

Once we had pushed them around with our writings, they realized they were unable to deal with writings in the open. Therefore one cannot blame these poor people for comforting themselves in their disgrace with much writing—without scriptural basis—and with cursing, slandering, and condemning. For this reason I let them bleed themselves [to death] and slander to [the point of] exhaustion. It is enough that we have Scripture and they don't, and that we act in public while they hide in the corner, an honor which we will gladly let them have, since they want it this way.

Now that I appear again in public, and since you poor people have to bear with me the pains to which our name is exposed by those highly famed, learned, and cowardly[9] men, and since not all of you are of equally stout heart, I have decided to write a little letter of comfort so that you will not be terrified by these poltroons, even though I am not with you. Since I am not a man like St. Paul, who could write and comfort out of the riches of

[9] Luther wrote *hassen*, which can mean both "rabbits" and "hate"; therefore one can translate "rabbit-men," men who run like rabbits, i.e., cowards, or "men of hate."

his own spirit, I have taken up the Scripture, which is full of comfort, as St. Paul says in Romans 15 [:4]. [I have decided to] translate Psalm 36 [10] into German and send it to you, together with short notes.[11] In my opinion this Psalm almost precisely fits our needs, for in an especially loving and motherly way it quiets the rising anger against the slanderers and the arrogant. Of course it hurts that the evildoers not only slander [us] according to all their malice, but also that they even should be considered right and should be respected; in addition they will be puffed up for some time—until the day [they are deflated].

No one should doubt that our adversaries are the type of people censured in this Psalm, and that we are the people being comforted in it. For by God's grace we stand on Scripture and have an understanding of it, which they fear and from which they shy away and flee; and yet they stubbornly blaspheme against truth. Let them continue! Had they been men worthy of truth, they would have been converted a long time ago through my many writings. I teach them, but they slander me. I plead with them, but they mock me. I scold them, but they rage against me. I pray for them, but they reject it. I forgive them their malice, but they do not want it. I am willing to give myself for them, but they curse this. What more should I do than Christ did, who says in Psalm 109 [:17],[12] "He did not want to be blessed; therefore the blessing should be far removed from him. He wanted to be cursed, so let him be clothed with it." No one can move anything into heaven that does not belong there, not even if he tear it up [and try to smuggle it in]. On the other hand whatever should go into heaven must go in, even if all the devils should hang on to it and tear each other apart over it. St. Paul says, "Avoid such a stubborn man after he has been admonished twice, since he certainly is perverted and the judgment over him is already settled." [13] But we should not cease praying for the

[10] According to the Vulgate; Psalm 37 according to the RSV, which is based on the Hebrew text.

[11] *Exposition of Psalm 37* (Wittenberg: J. Grünenberg, August, 1521). *WA* 8, 214 ff.

[12] Vulgate, but RSV numbering. Luther followed the tradition of the church, which interpreted the Psalms christologically, i.e., understood Christ and his church to be the subject or object of a Psalm. See also pp. 13, 189.

[13] Titus 3:10-11.

poor multitude who are ignorant and still being led astray by them, and we should do whatever we can for them, to snatch them from the grasp of the Roman murderer of souls and his apostles.

With this, farewell in God; may he mercifully guard your faith and mind in Christ. Amen.

1521[14]

84

To George Spalatin
Wartburg, June 10, 1521

Forwarding manuscripts now ready for printing (Magnificat, On Confession), Luther discusses his literary work (Exposition of Psalms 21? and 119, Postil) and his life at the Wartburg. He comments briefly on Oecolampadius' book On Confession (see p. 230, n. 14), on the Edict of Worms (see p. 216, n. 7; p. 220, n. 12), on the printed edition of his letter to the Imperial Estates (see p. 203), and on the death of Lord Chievres. To avoid betraying his whereabouts, Luther mentions that he will not write to Duke John Frederick.

On George Spalatin, see pp. 8 f.

Text in Latin: WA, Br 2, 354-355; translation based on S-J 2, 42-43.

To an outstandingly learned and devout man, Mr. George Spalatin, Saxon court chaplain, my dearest friend in Christ

Jesus

Greetings. My Spalatin, sometime ago I received your last letter[1]

---

[14] The signature is missing since the text is based on the printed edition of the work mentioned in note 11, to which this letter is the preface.

[1] This letter is not extant. It could have been the letter that accompanied Oecolampadius' book *On Confession* (see p. 230, n. 14). Luther must have received it around May 20, since he mentioned this book for the first time in letter No. 81 of May 26. The letter must have contained more information on the Edict of Worms; see p. 220, n. 12.

and Oecolampadius' little book,[2] together with all the other things.[3] Since one may assume that you can best take care of it, I am sending to you, as you see, the completed *Magnificat*,[4] and the treatise *On Confession*, which has grown out of my [short tract] and is dedicated to Francis Sickingen.[5] If it is all right with you, then have this material[6] printed as soon as possible, for I have already sent the completed exposition of Psalm 21[7] to the printers. So see to it that these things are also taken to them, unless you think that something ought to be changed. I have not yet decided whether I prefer to have Psalm 119 combined with the rest, or to publish it as a separate little book. I shall send the remaining part [of the manuscript] when I hear what you all advise. I am working on it now, but it isn't finished yet, and so the messenger had to leave it here.[8] I have not yet received the *Postil*;[9] it has been mislaid by him to whom I entrusted it. Meanwhile I have written to Wittenberg that if they cannot find it you will see that I get a copy of the *Shorter Postil*[10] (if you have it), together with an index of the Epistles and Gospels [for the church year]. In the meantime I have finished a more detailed exposition in

---

[2] See p. 230, n. 14.

[3] Not known. Perhaps some of the material Luther had requested earlier; see pp. 218 f., 225. The Latin *Advent Postil*, however, was apparently not in this shipment; see p. 242.

[4] While at the Wartburg Luther completed his work on the *Magnificat*; see p. 225, n. 17. He is now sending the last manuscript pages along with fascicles previously printed so that the whole work can be completed.

[5] See p. 244. Previously Luther had planned to write just a short sermon on this topic (see p. 225). It had grown, however, into a small book.

[6] It is not clear whether this refers to the *Magnificat* or to *On Confession* or to both.

[7] Luther is confused here; he had sent Psalm 68 to Melanchthon for printing; see p. 229, n. 5. Or perhaps he confused it with Psalm 37; see pp. 252, nn. 10, 11.

[8] Luther had begun the exposition of Psalm 119 on the last sheets of the manuscript of *On Confession* (see p. 246, n. 10); see *WA* 8, 132. He had used this Psalm as a basis for the introductory thoughts in his work *On Confession*. The messenger took this material along, and Luther finished the exposition of the Psalm on different paper. He sent this portion later. See p. 290. He is now wondering whether or not this exposition of Psalm 119 should be published by itself. It was finally published as an appendix to the work *On Confession*; see *WA* 8, 186 ff.

[9] The Latin *Advent Postil*; see pp. 229, 237, 242.

[10] See p. 237.

German of the Epistle for Christmas Eve.[11] I must also answer Latomus,[12] who glories in the lord—namely, the pope.

I marvel at the spirit of Oecolampadius,[13] not because he has hit upon the same line of argument as I have, but because he is so outspoken, so confident, so Christian. May the Lord preserve him and make him great. Amen.

I am both very idle and very busy here; I am studying Hebrew and Greek,[14] and am writing without interruption. The man in charge of this place[15] treats me far beyond what I deserve. The trouble from which I was suffering at Worms has not left me but rather has increased.[16] I am more constipated than ever in my life, and despair of remedy. The Lord thus afflicts me, that I may not be without a relic of the cross.[17] May he be blessed. Amen.

I wonder what is delaying the Imperial Edict.[18] On my way from Worms I read a printed copy of my letter to the Estates of the Empire; but it is full of mistakes.[19] It is said here that Lord Chievres[20] has died and left a million gulden to Charles.[21] What a brave Christian, not to be afraid of these mountains of gold! If only they would finally learn that the Lord is our God! I have not yet answered the young Prince's latest letter,[22] for the place from which it was written was not given. I also do

---

11 Luther had begun working on the Christmas portion of the German *Wartburg Postil* (see pp. 237 ff.). According to the careful investigation of the editor of the *Wartburg Postil*, Luther refers to the sermon on the Epistle for Christmas Eve (Titus 2:11-14), which he had finished by June 10; see *WA* 10I, 2, XLII f.

12 See p. 229, n. 3.

13 See p. 230, n. 14.

14 See p. 225.

15 Hans von Berlepsch, the castellan of the Wartburg.

16 See p. 217, n. 15.

17 For a similar statement, see p. 387.

18 The Edict of Worms; see p. 216, n. 7; p. 220, n. 12; p. 210. Spalatin must have informed Luther that the Emperor did not sign Aleander's corrected draft of the edict on May 8. It was finally signed on May 26 and issued by a pro-Roman rump diet.

19 See p. 203; for the bibliography, see *WA*, Br 2, 311 f.

20 William de Croy; see p. 234, n. 44; he had died on May 27.

21 Emperor Charles V; see pp. 175 f.

22 This letter of Duke John Frederick is not extant. On Duke John Frederick, see pp. 181 f.

not think it necessary to answer lest by multiplying letters the location of this place[23] somehow become known.

Be sure to pray for me. This is the one thing I need, all things else I have in plenty. I do not care what they do about me in public. I, after all, sit here in peace. Farewell in the Lord, and greet all whom it is safe to greet.

From the Isle of Patmos,[24] *June 10, 1521*

HENRY NESICUS[25]

85

To Philip Melanchthon
Wartburg, July 13, 1521

Luther chides Melanchthon for various reasons. Reporting on his life and work at the Wartburg, he tells briefly of his health, discusses a rebuttal against Emser, and reports on the progress of the Postil. Commenting on the situation in Wittenberg, he encourages his friends and urges them to be steadfast in promoting the cause of the gospel. He stiffens their backbones against Electoral interference in affairs pertaining to the gospel. Replying to Melanchthon, Luther details his understanding of secular government and authority.

On Philip Melanchthon, see p. 77, n. 3.

Text in Latin: WA, Br 2, 356-359.

To Philip Melanchthon, faithful servant of Christ, evangelist of the congregation at Wittenberg[1]

---

23 Of Luther's hideout.

24 See p. 246, n. 8.

25 Luther did not know where Spalatin was and whether this letter might be read by someone else. He hoped that Spalatin had returned from the Diet of Worms; otherwise he would not have asked him to take care of the manuscripts (see above). Nevertheless to be on the safe side he used a pseudonym. That Luther wrote this letter is evident from the handwriting as well as the content. For further explanation of this name, see WA, Br 2, 356, n. 22.

1 This address is missing in one of the manuscript copies of this letter but is supplied by another manuscript copy. In the first manuscript copy, just before the fifth paragraph (beginning with "On the law of the sword"), there is a special address to Melanchthon.

Your letter[2] displeased me for two reasons: First, I realize that you carry the cross too impatiently; you give in too much to your emotions and as is your way you are just too gentle. Second, you extol me so much. You err tremendously in ascribing such great importance to me, as if I were so much concerned for God's case. Your high opinion of me shames and tortures me, since—unfortunately—I sit here like a fool and hardened in leisure, pray little, do not sigh for the church of God, yet burn in a big fire of my untamed body. In short I should be ardent in spirit, but I am ardent in the flesh, in lust, laziness, leisure, and sleepiness. I do not know whether God has turned away from me since you all do not pray for me. You are already replacing me; because of the gifts you have from God, you have attained greater authority and popularity than I had.

Already eight days have passed in which I have written nothing, in which I have not prayed or studied; this is partly because of temptations of the flesh, partly because I am tortured by other burdens.[3] If this thing does not improve, I shall go directly to Erfurt and not incognito. There you will see me, or I you, for I shall consult doctors or surgeons. It is impossible that I endure this evil any longer; it is easier to endure ten big wounds than this small sign of a lesion.[4] Maybe the Lord burdens me so in order to push me out of this hermitage into the public.

I shall not answer Emser.[5] Anyone who seems fitting to you may answer—perhaps Amsdorf,[6] if he is not too good for dealing with this dung. I have decided to translate your *Defense* against

---

[2] This letter is not extant; a glimpse of its contents may be obtained, however, from Luther's answer on pp. 257, 258 ff., 264 f.

[3] Such as constipation; see p. 217, n. 15.

[4] The constipation must have caused a lesion of the anus.

[5] Jerome Emser (see p. 137, n. 19) had just published his *Quadruplica* (for biographical information, see *WA* 8, 241), a rebuttal of Luther's *Answer to the Superchristian . . . Book of Goat Emser* (see p. 192, n. 5). Luther must have been anticipating Emser's move when he stated that he did not know what Emser would do; see p. 234.

[6] Nicholas von Amsdorf; see p. 218. Luther's friends at Wittenberg apparently wanted to spare Luther from having to reply to Emser; Melanchthon suggested that von Amsdorf could do it; see p. 246. Luther preferred a lesser, younger person to be commissioned with this task. Yet he must have realized that an inexperienced person would not do after all, since in his next letter (No. 86) he makes suggestions to von Amsdorf on how one could best reply to Emser. In the end, however, Luther himself replied; see *WA* 8, 247 f.

the Parisian asses, together with their nonsense, and add notes to it.[7] I greatly wish that Oecolampadius' book *On Confession* would be translated at Wittenberg in the same way, so that the papists would be blown apart.[8] I am working on the German *Postil*[9] to the Gospels and shall send [it] to the press at once, as soon as I have finished ten.[10]

Since things are going so well at Wittenberg, you certainly don't need me. I am unhappy with you personally, however, because you burden yourself with so much work and do not listen and spare yourself. Here you are being led by your own stubbornness. I shout this at you so often, but each time it is as if I were telling a story to someone who is deaf.[11]

On the law of the sword, I think as I did previously.[12] It seems to me that you demand[13] some commandment or some counsel of the gospel on this subject. Here I definitely agree with you that no such law is found in the gospel, either as commandment or as counsel; nor would it be at all appropriate, since the gospel is a law for those who are willing and free, those who have nothing to do with the sword or the law of the sword. But

---

[7] Eck and Luther had agreed to entrust the decision concerning the victor at the Leipzig Disputation (see p. 126) to the universities of Erfurt (see p. 136, n. 9; p. 137, nn. 14, 17) and Paris. It was not before April 15, 1521, that the University of Paris acted. As was expected, Luther was condemned. See *WA* 8, 255 ff. In July, 1521, Melanchthon published the *Condemnation* issued by the Sorbonne, together with a *Defense;* for the bibliography, see *WA* 8, 261; for the text, see *C.R.* 1, 366 ff.; for an English translation, see *Melanchthon:* S.W., pp. 69 ff. Luther's edition of the *Condemnation*, the *Defense*, and his notes was published in October, 1521, by J. Grünenberg; see *WA* 8, 262 ff.

[8] See p. 230, n. 14.

[9] I.e., on the Advent and Christmas portions of the *Postil;* see p. 229.

[10] See pp. 239 f.

[11] An allusion to a proverb recorded by Erasmus in his *Adagia;* see Clericus 2, 178 C. On Luther's criticism, see also p. 119, n. 10.

[12] Luther apparently is referring to discussions between Melanchthon and himself which had taken place before Luther went to Worms.

[13] Probably in the not extant letter of note 2. Melanchthon had discussed governmental authority in his *Loci communes* (see p. 232, n. 21), in the parts on *De humanis legibus* and *De magistratibus*. He defines the "sword" of Rom. 13:1 ff. as civil laws and ordinances as well as institutions set up to punish malefactors. The problem (now confronting him, which he must have discussed in his letter to Luther) was whether Christians were allowed to practice the "law of the sword," i.e., participate in secular offices and help maintain law and order. On Melanchthon's stand on worldly government, see also *Melanchthon:* S.W., pp. 89 ff.

in the gospel the law of the sword also is not forbidden. It is rather affirmed and commended to us.[14] We certainly do not read this about things that are only permitted; [15] fasting and external ceremonies—or any care for temporal things—are neither enjoined nor counseled in the gospel. It would not have been right for the gospel to regulate these matters in which the Spirit alone operates in his freedom. But is it therefore a law that one should not make use [of the sword]? Indeed, does not the necessity of this life even require such a law and practice?

Your argument would do quite well if all people obeyed the gospel. If the sword were abolished, however, how long would the church of God exist in this world, since, of necessity, the wicked are in the majority? Due to the licentiousness of the wicked, no one could be safe from bodily harm or the destruction of his property. But you do not want to be pushed with considerations and incongruities but rather with Scripture.

I have said above that the use of the sword is neither enjoined nor counseled in the gospel, as is the case with many other things; yet it is commended to us and affirmed, as is the law of matrimony, which also is not directly connected with the gospel. For you have John the Baptist, who in Luke 3 [:14] instructs the soldiers, saying, "Rob no one by violence or by false accusation, but be content with your wages." Had they not the right to use the sword, he certainly would have had to prohibit them from using it, since they actually asked him your question when they said, "What do we have to do?" Here you find military service not instituted, yet affirmed. Don't you think it would be much harder for you to reply to anyone who quotes this passage to you than for someone to answer your position? Paul, in I Timothy 2 [:1-2], commands prayer for those in high governmental positions, according to the example of Jeremiah, who commanded prayer for the king of the Babylonians; [16] Paul does not order praying *against* the governing authorities, as if they were something prohibited or as if they existed without right.

[14] Luther attempts to prove this in the following paragraphs.

[15] "Permitted things" for Luther are things neither commanded nor prohibited by God's Word; they are neutral in themselves and have no direct relationship to man's salvation. See also pp. 156 f., 278.

[16] Jer. 29:7.

You may object here that those were Gentiles. Yet they[17] did not pray that [those Gentiles] might come to faith but rather that they would be and remain in peace. You will not convince me that prayer could have been commanded by the apostles or prophets for things which were only permitted and were to be endured so that they could continue to exist and enjoy peace. If this were the case, we should pray for robbers and (as you explain it) unjust tyrants, that they might continue to be unjust!

I cannot allow you to reject the statements of the Apostles Paul in Romans 13 [:1-2] and Peter in I Peter 2 [:13-14] as if they were not applicable here, or as if they were only instructing the citizens. You will not accomplish this, my Philip! These are words of God—of great importance—when Paul says: [governmental] authority is from God, and whosoever resists [governmental] authority resists God's ordinance, and [governmental authority] is the servant of God.[18] You will not find this to be stated concerning things which are merely permitted. He who does wrong or imposes intolerable measures is not God's servant but God's enemy; a concession, or something permitted, cannot have the function of a servant of God. In Scripture it is written several times that God stirred up one people against another, as for instance the king of Babylon (whom God in Ezekiel calls "servant")[19] against Tyrus. According to Jeremiah,[20] God stirred up the courage of the kings of the Medes against the Babylonians. This is absolutely different from the statements in Romans 13 [:4] and I Timothy 2 [:2], where it is said that the [governmental] authorities are instituted for [the sake of maintaining] peace. For [according to the New Testament passages the governmental authorities were instituted] to frighten workers of evil and not doers of good, while [according to the Old Testament passages] they were appointed for vengeance to balance evil deeds that had already been committed.

What will you say when you read that Abraham, David, and the ancient saints have used the sword with great bravery? They

[17] The Christians whom Paul ordered to pray.
[18] Rom. 13:1-2.
[19] Ezek. 26:7?; Jer. 25:9 (Vulgate).
[20] Jer. 51:11.

certainly were evangelical men. Of course they used the sword only occasionally. It certainly is not God-fearing if the use of something that was praised when used by these men is rejected by the men of the gospel. For Abraham had no commandment or counsel concerning the use of the sword, and, what is even more important, in the gospel it is not revoked or prohibited but (as I have said) affirmed—at least for those who were Christians or believers, as were those soldiers who questioned John the Baptist.

In the gospel Christ had to provide for divine and heavenly things; what wonder, therefore, that he did not regulate the use of the sword, which can easily be regulated by human beings. Yet he treated the use of the sword in the following way: were it not contrary to the [essence of] the gospel that he provide for the use of the sword, then he wished to provide for this use. At the same time he commended it to us and affirmed it as instituted, or rather he clearly asserted that it is divinely ordained.

Likewise, how Peter and Jude[21] complain that [governmental] authorities are being mocked and slandered by the Antichrist![22] But may one not mock and slander licentious and evil things that are permitted to exist? [The Apostles],[23] however, want [governmental authorities] to be held in honor and reverence. Do [they] want the same for things [merely] allowed, or [even] unjust?

I am caught in these Scripture passages, and I have nothing with which I might challenge my position; Philip, at this point you satisfy me much less than I am successful in meeting your arguments. You have no Scripture passage which condemns or prohibits [the use of the sword], or teaches in any way that one should avoid it. I, however, find the [governmental] authority of this world affirmed, recommended, and as something to be honored and remembered in our prayers to God, and that in many ways.

---

21 II Pet. 2:10; Jude vs. 8.

22 On the Antichrist, see p. 114, n. 16.

23 The subject of this paragraph is not clear. In the third and fourth sentences Luther used singular verbs, which might suggest that God is the subject. On the other hand he begins the paragraph with Peter and Jude as subjects, to which he adds a verb in the plural. He might have continued his trend of thought, thinking only of one of the apostles, which could explain the singular verb form in the following sentences. The subject has to be either the apostles, or one of them, or perhaps God.

Only this one thing is missing [in Scripture: governmental authority] is neither commanded nor counseled in the gospel, in the same way that marriage, the family, the discipline of the home and the community, or any administration and care of earthly things [are not ordered]. If you have something else that is revealed to you,[24] show it. Produce your statements, however, so that you demonstrate [earthly authority] to be something prohibited, to be avoided, or only permitted. Christ said to Pilate that authority was given from above.[25] But I think this means that God does not give it to be used for evil purposes. But enough of this.

I congratulate Amsdorf on his increase in wealth,[26] but even more that he lectures so successfully on the Apostle [Paul].[27] You are now well supplied and you manage without me. I do not see why you miss me so much or why my work should be necessary for you. You seem to be able to think for yourself since the affairs at Wittenberg progress more favorably in my absence than in my presence. You lecture,[28] Amsdorf lectures, Jonas will lecture.[29] For goodness' sake, do you want the kingdom of God to be proclaimed only in your town? Don't others also need the gospel? Will your Antioch not release a Silas or a Paul or a Barnabas for some other work of the Spirit? [30]

I tell you: although I would be very happy to be with you all, yet I would not be disturbed if the Lord deigned to open to me a door for the Word either at Erfurt or Cologne or anywhere else, since you already have a surplus [of preachers and teachers]. Look how big a harvest there is everywhere—and how few are the harvesters! [31] You all are harvesters. Certainly we have to consider not ourselves but our brethren who are spread out all over the country, lest we live for ourselves, that is, for the devil and not for Christ. Therefore be concerned that we are not drawn to one

[24] Allusion to I Cor. 14:30.
[25] John 19:11.
[26] See p. 264, n. 2.
[27] See p. 267, n. 26.
[28] See p. 267, n. 26.
[29] Justus Jonas; see p. 275, n. 3.
[30] Acts 13:1 ff.; 15:22.
[31] Matt. 9:37.

another too strongly and seek the presence of the flesh more than the Spirit. I am ready to go where God wants me to go, either to Wittenberg or somewhere else. Concerning my return, I know absolutely nothing. You know in whose hands that is.

Spalatin writes that by order of the Sovereign[32] there was no disputation on that part of the theses which deals with confession.[33] I don't like this at all. I ask you all from now on to anticipate the court's suggestions instead of following them, just as I have done up to now. Not one-half would have been accomplished had I obeyed the court's counsel. Even at the court they are human, just as we. But I shall argue this with Spalatin.[34] These things increase the courage of our enemies and show our fear.

Farewell. Someone had promised to take along this letter which I had written some days ago, but he has not kept his word.[35] I ask all of you to pray for me, since in this seclusion I am drowning in sins.

From my wilderness,[36] *July 13, 1521*

MARTIN LUTHER
the Hermit

---

[32] Elector Frederick; see pp. 49 f. On George Spalatin, see pp. 8 f.; the letter is not extant.

[33] According to the *WA*, Br editor, this refers to two academic disputations for which Karlstadt (see p. 79, n. 12) prepared the theses. The first disputation took place on June 21 and dealt with the vows of monastic and clerical celibacy (see p. 277, n. 3); the second took place on June 28 and apparently dealt with the question of auricular confession. The Elector intervened and a part of the theses for June 28 must have been eliminated.

[34] See p. 269.

[35] The letter must have been written some days prior to July 13 but signed and sent on July 13.

[36] Luther wrote *eremo*, i.e., in the desert, in the wasteland, in the wilderness, at an isolated place. In a letter written in German, Luther wrote *Wüstung*, i.e., "wilderness"; see p. 343; *WA*, Br 2, 408. Thus it seems justified to interpret *eremo* as wilderness. This interpretation is, however, not the only one suggested by this word and by Luther's usage of it. Luther wanted to pretend that he was hiding in an Augustinian monastery (see p. 272) and called himself a hermit (see pp. 234, 270, 323). Thus one could also translate *eremo* as "from the hermitage," i.e., from a secluded place in the wilderness where he lived the life of a hermit.

86

To Nicholas von Amsdorf[1] Wartburg, July 15?, 1521

Luther congratulates Amsdorf on his appointment to a benefice and mentions his intention to go to Erfurt for medical attention. He also makes detailed suggestions about rebuffing Emser.

On Nicholas von Amsdorf, see p. 218.

Text in Latin: WA, Br 2, 361-363.

Jesus

I congratulate you on the increase of your income through the Schmölln benefice,[2] my Licentiate,[3] and I hope it may benefit you all. Forget about the rumor that I am at the Wartburg, which that secretary spread.[4] Even the sovereigns[5] themselves don't know where I am, much less that secretary. By the way, I shall soon be at Erfurt,[6] maybe even before this letter reaches you, because of my ailment. There I shall appear in public, at least if they will tolerate me for a short time.

Philip wrote[7] that you intend to answer Emser[8] if it seems

---

[1] The address and date are missing in the manuscript copy of this letter. That von Amsdorf was recipient of this letter can be established from its content. Luther must have received von Amsdorf's (not extant) letter and answered it shortly before writing to Spalatin about it on July 15. See p. 269; *WA*, Br 2, No. 419, Introduction.

[2] Von Amsdorf was to receive the benefice attached to a chapel in Schmölln, south of Leipzig, near Altenburg. However he did not have to reside there or fulfil his pastoral duties in connection with it. For details on this type of financial arrangement, see Schwiebert, pp. 257 ff.

[3] A *Licentiatus* is one whom a university has granted the *venia legendi*, i.e., the privilege to lecture officially. It is a degree between the master's and the doctor's degree.

[4] According to Luther (p. 269), a certain secretary of Duke John had written this to the Electoral Saxon court at Torgau.

[5] Elector Frederick (see pp. 49 f.) and his co-ruler Duke John (see p. 269, n. 8). Although after the collapse of the negotiations in Worms Elector Frederick planned that Luther would disappear for a while (see p. 201, n. 3), the Elector left the execution of this plan to his confidants (see p. 227, n. 31) to be able to claim that he did not know Luther's whereabouts. Nevertheless Luther's statement should be questioned.

[6] On Luther's plan to go to Erfurt to seek medical attention, see pp. 257, 270.

[7] Philip Melanchthon; see p. 257, n. 2.

[8] Jerome Emser; see p. 257, nn. 5, 6.

wise to me. But I am afraid that he is not worthy of having you as a respondent. On the other hand he may laugh and mock if one of the young people should answer him, since he is full of Satan. The spirit that rages in him seizes on words only to make a mockery of them; but he neglects the issue at stake. Whatever happens, if you people answer him then know that you are dealing with a most wicked spirit and be well aware that you don't talk to a man. For [Emser] himself does not understand what he is saying; the spirit which pushes him through a creeping illness of envy toward fury says everything for only one purpose: to exasperate and mock. Therefore one must write [against Emser] in the simplest way and must strongly fortify everything well in advance so that he cannot seize on any words or opportunities.

Let me give an example. He has to be answered in such a way that if not he himself (we might as well give up this hope), still everyone else, no matter how unlearned he may be, can understand that Emser said absolutely nothing to the point—while demonstrating from the statements of the Fathers that there is a priesthood—although I had produced Scripture passages and demanded them.[9] One must show that he blubbered in vain with his "Come out, St. So-and-so."[10] For I have asserted in my little book[11] that the Fathers called the [Christians] the [real] priests; he vainly tries to show [that this was not the case]. One has to [counter him][12] with the words of Peter[13] and of Revelation 5 [:9-10] and 20 [:6] in context with the preceding statements and the circumstances. One has to antagonize and insult the devil to make him produce one Scripture passage through which it can be proven that [the ordained clergy alone] are called priests [in Scripture], just as I previously scoffed in my book. Then one has to ridicule the fact that he wants to prove the [ordained] priest-

---

[9] In Luther's *Answer to the Superchristian . . . Book of Goat Emser;* see p. 192, n. 5. The phrase "and demanded them" is missing in some of the printed editions; it can be found, however, in the manuscript copy.

[10] This quotation from Emser's *Quadruplica* (see p. 257, n. 5) is written in German. Emser quoted saints by calling them out on a stage, so to speak.

[11] See note 9. For the specific passage Luther seems to be referring to, see *WA* 7, 633; *PE* 3, 326 f.

[12] The text has a lacuna here.

[13] I Pet. 2:5-10.

hood from that statement, "You are the salt of the earth."[14] He argues in such a way as if to prove salt and priests were identical. Children in school know the difference, since after all they use the small [Latin dictionary].[15] Finally one has to show that the authority of the Fathers is clearly ridiculed by the Apostle [Paul] when he says, "Test everything,"[16] by Augustine (dist. IX, cap. *Noli.*),[17] and by the statements of St. Jerome on Matthew 23 [:35]: "What has no biblical authority is as easily condemned as approved."[18] One should not believe the Fathers more than they themselves intended, that is, only when they quote Scripture passages. One must therefore show that this stupid man does not even understand the point of his own book because he does not discuss *what* the Fathers say, but *why* they say it in this particular way. Thus the reader may understand that there is a difference between saying and believing, and that we do not debate *what* the Fathers said, but whether one should *believe* what they said. One must show that thus far this blasphemous mouth has not centered upon his real topic.

You will see other points; only do not doubt that an evil spirit speaks in Emser as from his very own shell. He pursues only one course: to depart from the subject and multiply his blasphemies in many books. It is certainly an evil spirit. But his wickedness lacks one thing: he possesses and occupies a dumb, stupid, and unlearned shell. Yet he himself, no matter how wicked he may be, declares sufficiently by his furious attacks just how hemmed in he is by Scripture, and how he can't produce anything worthwhile in support of his kingdom among the papists. And that hurts this Satan.

I say this so that you[19] may write against him with a scornful and quiet attitude, and that you won't let yourself become incensed, as you would at a human being. For by contempt (provoking him

---

14 Matt. 5:13.
15 For this dictionary, see *WA*, Br 2, 363, n. 10.
16 I Thess. 5:21.
17 Luther quotes Augustine according to the *Decretum Magistri Gratiani*, I, dist. IX, cap. 9. *CIC* 1, 18.
18 *Commentary on St. Matthew* by St. Jerome (see *Patrology*, pp. 462 ff., especially p. 470), IV, cap. 23:35 f. *MPL* 26, 180.
19 "You" plural, i.e., the men of the Wittenberg Faculty.

by ridicule and convicting him of stupidity), you will exasperate and torture the pride of this extremely proud spirit so tremendously that he will vomit out many more blasphemies, and thus unmask himself.

Had I realized sooner that Emser was possessed by a demon, I would have harassed the demon quite violently. But even though unaware of this, I have kicked him around vigorously anyway.[20] As soon as he has written something in Latin, as he has promised,[21] I shall do what I have not yet done. Peter Swawe[22] seemed to me to be the right man for answering Emser. Yet since Swawe was recently buffeted by the Leipzig people, it seems one should not give the devil a second opportunity to display his old fury against him. This devil, the jeerer,[23] would certainly repeat the past example of his rage against him.

Praise be to God, who has not only given us this struggle against the spirits of evil but has also revealed to us that it is not flesh and blood[24] by which we are assailed in this case. Therefore be of good courage and rejoice. He who has cast out the ruler of this world[25] is not afraid of this outcast, whom he already despised before he was cast out. [Christ] rules and wants to rule in us sinners and in those who are fools for him, while Satan rages in the wise and righteous men belonging to him.

I would like to be your student in the course on Hebrews, and also Philip's in his course on Colossians.[26] Thanks be to Christ, who by the unspeakable gift of his Word makes us so rich. I rejoice so much in your abundance that I can endure my separation from you most easily. For I see that it is not you who need me, but I who need you.

---

20 In the work mentioned in note 9.

21 In his *Quadruplica* (see p. 257, n. 5), Emser stated that from then on he would write in Latin to show the world that not all Germans had been seduced by the monk and abandoned the true faith; see *WA*, Br 2, 363, n. 14.

22 Peter Swawe; see p. 236, n. 60. At Leipzig he had a sharp clash with John Keller (see p. 123, n. 5) in the aftermath of the Leipzig Disputation.

23 Emser.

24 Eph. 6:12.

25 John 12:31.

26 Von Amsdorf was then lecturing on Hebrews, while Melanchthon was lecturing on the Epistles to the Corinthians, not Colossians as Luther mistakenly wrote. See *WA*, Br 2, 364, n. 18.

Farewell, and pray for me.

Not pleasant but sad news has arrived here about Günther Staupitz. I hope it is not true. May the Lord keep this evil away from such a fine family.[27] Amen.

From my wilderness,[28] *1521* MARTIN LUTHER

87

To George Spalatin
Wartburg, July 15, 1521

Luther confirms receipt of a shipment from Spalatin and informs him that his health is somewhat improved. He expresses his pleasure about certain news of Wittenberg. Yet he urges Spalatin to care for Melanchthon. He discusses the fact that the knowledge of his hideout has leaked out. In conclusion Luther comments briefly on the political situation in the Empire, Melanchthon's Defense (see p. 258, n. 7), and his own book Against Latomus (see p. 229, n. 3).

On George Spalatin, see pp. 8 f.

Text in Latin: WA, Br 2, 364-365.

To my friend in Christ, Mr. George Spalatin, Saxon court chaplain, my friend and lord

Jesus

Greetings. I finally received everything,[1] my Spalatin. I tried the pills[2] according to the prescription. Soon I had some relief and elimination without blood or force, but the wound of the previous

[27] What Luther meant is not known. Günther von Staupitz (a relative both of von Amsdorf and of the former Vicar General; see p. 64, n. 1) and the monastery in Wittenberg had a long quarrel over the payment of interest on a loan; see *WA*, Br 1, 371, n. 20. The unpleasant news may have had some connection with this. See also p. 115, n. 22.

[28] See p. 263, n. 36.

[1] The *Shorter Postil* and perhaps also the Latin *Advent Postil* must have finally arrived; see p. 242.

[2] Medication to relieve Luther's serious constipation; see p. 217, n. 15; p. 257.

rupture isn't healed yet, and I even had to suffer a good deal because some flesh extruded, either due to the power of the pills, or I don't know what. So, I shall once more wait and see.

All your news about Wittenberg is pleasant.[3] Thanks be to Christ, who has sent others to replace me. As a result I see that they do not need me any more, except Philip;[4] he gives in too easily to his moods, and bears the cross more impatiently than is fitting for a disciple, especially for such a great teacher of teachers. Please see to it that the Most Illustrious Sovereign[5] does not let him suffer want in his living needs.[6] I am annoyed that the debate on confession was prevented.[7] This would have been a useful example against the fury of the papists, so that they would know in what "great fear" the Wittenberg people were because of my absence, since they dared to undertake such a thing even without me.

Amsdorf has written that a certain secretary of Duke John[8] wrote to a woman in Torgau that I am in the Wartburg; for this reason a rumor has started and of course it has spread all over. This rumor will be convincing since it originated in court circles, whether the secretary definitely knew or only suspected something. We have hidden this affair with such great luck until now. Satan, who had long waited in ambush for us, is betraying the matter. From my host[9] I understand that this rumor is persistently maintained all over the country, so that this affair can no longer be veiled in silence. Up to now, however, we are still bravely keeping it

[3] Spalatin must have informed Luther of major developments at the University (new appointments, new construction, etc.) which were initiated through Elector Frederick (see pp. 49 f.). See pp. 232, 258; p. 275, n. 4; *Urkundenbuch* 1, 111 ff.

[4] Philip Melanchthon; see p. 77, n. 3.

[5] Elector Frederick; see pp. 49 f.

[6] See p. 167, n. 7.

[7] See p. 263, n. 33.

[8] Duke John of Saxony (1468-1532), brother of Elector Frederick and co-ruler with him, became elector of Saxony in 1525. Like his brother, he was a faithful ruler and administrator who supported Luther openly from the very beginning. Together with his son John Frederick (see pp. 181 f.), he was responsible for the administrative organization of the church of the reformation in Electoral Saxony. In his political ability he cannot be compared with the shrewd Frederick. Through his diplomatic activity, however, the Smalcald League of Protestant Estates took shape as a defensive alliance of those territories that joined the Reformation.

[9] Hans von Berlepsch; see p. 255, n. 15.

a secret; but we are also quite indignant that our faithful and successful undertakings should be so easily made fruitless.

Besides this, I am physically healthy and in quite good spirits, so that Philip worries about me in vain. If my ailment [10] doesn't improve, I shall go to Erfurt to make use of the doctors there.[11]

It is no wonder that Charles [12] is afflicted by wars.[13] He will never have anything that prospers; this unlucky young man is forced to pay the punishment for other people's ungodliness, since at Worms, where he had wicked counselors, he repudiated truth outright. He will also involve Germany in his calamities because he has consented to ungodliness. But the Lord will recognize those who belong to him.[14]

I have seen the decree of the Parisian sophists, together with Philip's *Defense*,[15] and I wholeheartedly rejoice. Christ would not have made them so blind had he not decided to use these affairs to bring about the end of their tyranny. I have already sent the book against Latomus [16] to the press. I have nothing else to report. Now I am finally a true hermit. Therefore, farewell.

July 15, 1521 MARTIN LUTHER

88

To George Spalatin
Wartburg, soon after July 15, 1521[1]

In this brief note Luther explains that he is enclosing a letter (see No. 89) for the purpose of fooling his enemies regarding the location of his hideout.

On George Spalatin, see pp. 8 f.

Text in Latin: WA, Br 2, 366; translation based on S-J 2, 46.

[10] Constipation; see p. 217, n. 15.
[11] See p. 264, n. 6.
[12] Emperor Charles V; see pp. 175 f.
[13] Luther is perhaps thinking of the first war of Charles against France (1521-1526) and the uprisings in Spain; see Schwiebert, pp. 46 ff.; Grimm, pp. 197 ff.
[14] II Tim. 2:19.
[15] See p. 258, n. 7.
[16] James Latomus; see p. 229, n. 3.
[1] Letters No. 88 and 89 are undated. In placing them soon after July 15,

TO GEORGE SPALATIN, SOON AFTER JULY 15, 1521

Mr. George Spalatin, a servant of Christ, court chaplain to the Elector of Saxony, my friend in the Lord

Jesus

Greetings. I think my letter has reached you,[2] my Spalatin; now I am sending another and some other things.[3] Listen to my ruse. When the rumor of my whereabouts becomes so strong that people cannot be persuaded that it is not true,[4] even though they may not dare to assert it, I want you to "lose" the enclosed letter I have written to you. This should be done with studied carelessness, either by you or by your friends, and in such a stealthy way that the letter falls into the hands of our enemies and seems to be concealing some great secret. I wish that this letter in my handwriting would come into the hands of the Hog of Dresden; [5] no doubt he would gladly make it public. You take care of the arrangements that seem wise to you. The letter carrier will tell you that I am well. Yet I am hoping for better things.

Farewell in the Lord.

From the wilderness,[6] *1520* [7] MARTIN LUTHER

1521, this editor follows the *WA*, Br editor, who unfortunately does not give the reasons for the assumed dates. Dating both letters soon after July 15 is based on the following considerations: (1) Obviously the letters belong together. (2) Both letters apparently were written as a result of the news spread by a secretary of Duke John that Luther was at the Wartburg, a fact to which Luther referred for the first time in his July 15 letter to Spalatin (see p. 269). With letter No. 89 Luther wanted to counteract this rumor. (3) Luther thought that perhaps the books he was publishing might betray his hideout (see p. 272). This suggests that Luther wrote in the second half of 1521, when he could anticipate the publication of some of his works in the near future. (DeWette in *Dr. Martin Luthers Briefe, Sendschreiben und Bedenken* [Berlin: G. Reimer, 1826], II, 31, n. 1, has pointed this out already.) At first glance it seems that one should date letter No. 89 in May because of the reference to the riots in Erfurt (see p. 214). However the second consideration mentioned above seems strong enough to substantiate the *WA*, Br editor's dating.

[2] Perhaps No. 87.

[3] Perhaps a portion of the *Postil* manuscript (see p. 237) and the rest of the exposition of Psalm 119 (see p. 254, n. 8; p. 290). The "other" letter is No. 89.

[4] See pp. 264, 269 f.

[5] I.e., Duke George; see p. 110, n. 20; p. 216, n. 8; p. 228.

[6] See p. 263, n. 36.

[7] This is an error in the autograph; whether or not it was intentional cannot be established.

89

To George Spalatin
Wartburg, soon after July 15, 1521

This is the letter Luther enclosed in letter No. 88. It was intended to mislead his enemies.

On George Spalatin, see pp. 8 f.

Text in Latin: WA, Br 2, 367; translation based on S-J 2, 46-47.

To the excellent man, Master George Spalatin, court chaplain to the Saxon Elector, [my special friend]

Jesus

Greetings. I hear a rumor is being spread, my Spalatin, that Luther is living in the Wartburg near Eisenach. And this makes the people suspicious since I was captured in the forest there. While they are thinking this, I am hidden here in safety, provided that the friars around me keep the secret. If the books I am publishing betray me, I shall move my quarters. Strange that nobody now thinks of Bohemia.[1]

St. George, the duke of Saxony,[2] is still extremely furious, I hear. I hope it will be good for him; may he continue furious as long as he remains a papist. I have the same answer for him as the Landgravine of Hesse had, who is now the wife of the Count of Solm. She knew the right reply for this great man: she ordered her legates to remind Duke George of his grandfather Podiebrad and his mother, Podiebrad's daughter.[3] Don't you know what that

[1] Since Luther had been accused of being a Bohemian heretic (see pp. 143 f.), he is now wondering why no one thinks that he might have escaped to his "friends" in Bohemia. Yet some apparently thought of this, since the Papal Legate Aleander had written to the Curia on April 29, 1521, after the collapse of the negotiations in Worms, that Luther was expected to retreat to Bohemia; see *WA*, Br 2, 367, n. 2. On the other hand Luther wanted to give the impression that he was hiding in a monastery.

[2] Duke George of Saxony; see p. 110, n. 20.

[3] Anne of Hesse, the mother of Landgrave Philip (see *O.D.C.C.*, p. 1063), married Count Otto of Solms-Laubach in 1519, after having been a widow for ten

clever woman told the legates [of the Duke] at the Diet of Worms?[4]

At Erfurt Satan has been plotting against us to give our friends a bad reputation, but he will accomplish nothing. They are not our friends who do these things.[5] Since Satan is unable to halt the truth, he seeks to bring it into ill repute by inflaming the ridiculous zeal of fools against us. I am amazed that the city council puts up with this.[6]

I am well, thank God, and enjoy a vacation from the papists. Pray for me, and farewell. Our Illustrious Sovereign[7] does not yet wish that my whereabouts become known,[8] and so I am not writing to him. Again farewell.

From my quarters, 1521 Yours,

MARTIN LUTHER

---

years. Duke George reproached her for this below-rank marriage. She replied that George's father Albrecht had married the daughter of the Hussite King Podiebrad—what could be worse? See *WA*, Br 2, 367, n. 4. In identifying himself with Anne's position, Luther wanted to counter the Duke's attacks in a fashion summed up in the saying: "People who live in glass houses shouldn't throw stones." At this point it is somewhat difficult to definitely establish the text. The earliest printed editions do not contain the name Podiebrad, but only "P," from which later editors and translators have conjectured "Podiebrad," on the basis of Duke George's family relations. An old manuscript copy of this letter offers the following text: "*ut avi sui pellivicis et matris filiae pellificis recordaretur*," i.e., "that he be reminded of his grandfather *pellifex* and his mother, the daughter of *pellifex*. *Pellifex* can be derived from *pellis*, leather, hide, shoe, parchment, drum, and *facere*, to make, which suggests "shoemaker" as the translation. This may have been a popular abusive name for Podiebrad.

[4] The circumstances implied by this statement could not be verified.

[5] See p. 214; p. 224, n. 8.

[6] Luther wanted to divorce himself from any connection with the riots in Erfurt and at the same time express his displeasure with the position taken by the Erfurt city council.

[7] Elector Frederick; see pp. 49 f.

[8] This sentence seems to mean that the Elector did not want to know Luther's whereabouts so that if questioned he could honestly say he did not know where Luther was. Respecting this wish, Luther did not write to the Elector directly. Luther would thus have helped to protect the Elector's position with this letter.

90

To George Spalatin
Wartburg, July 31, 1521

Luther tells his thoughts about changing his quarters. Commenting on the appointment of Justus Jonas to the professorship of Canon Law at Wittenberg, he gives his opinion of Canon Law. He adds news about his health. Enclosing a Postil manuscript for publication, he mentions some ideas on the organization of this work as he envisions it.

On George Spalatin, see pp. 8 f.

Text in Latin: WA, Br 2, 368-369.

Mr. George Spalatin, a disciple of Christ, my dearest friend in the Lord

Jesus

Greetings. The plague has now intervened so that I cannot move to Erfurt, my Spalatin. I do not see why it would be dangerous for me to stay there for a while, had I the opportunity. Of course this would not mean a desertion of Wittenberg. Even if I were to teach somewhere else, it would be the same as if I taught at Wittenberg, since Christ is everywhere. However I do not seek an academic chair or a pulpit, nor would I go anywhere for that reason unless I were strongly urged to come.[1] I know that any teacher who pushes himself into teaching is not called by God. So far I have always shied away from the office of teaching;[2] no one need expect anything different from me on this point. I shall always flee it. Had I been eager [to teach in public], I never would have consented to go into this solitude.

---

[1] In the fall of 1521 the plague harassed Wittenberg; see *Urkundenbuch* 1, 119 ff. Luther apparently considered going to Erfurt not only to consult physicians (see p. 264), but also to live there for a while (see p. 262) and teach, if called. Spalatin must have expressed the fear that this might mean that Luther would desert the University of Wittenberg.

[2] See p. 6, n. 5; p. 119, n. 7.

Jonas [3] writes that he has high hopes concerning the [matter of the] Canon Law; you take care that the Spirit may fulfil [Jonas' hopes] through your efforts.

It is beyond my strength to fulfil your request that I alone draw up an organizational plan for a Christian university.[4] This matter requires the suggestions and judgments of many people. In Wittenberg you have an abundance of men who can do this.

It would be best if the whole Canon Law were completely removed [from the curriculum] [5] and that the sovereigns [6] for once showed courage and completely abolished the ecclesiastical jurisdiction and punishments [7] in their territories. One has to venture something when one undertakes a task that is important and beneficial! If this sacrilegious jurisdiction is not abolished and

---

[3] This letter is not extant. Justus Jonas of Nordhausen (1493-1555) studied law and theology in Wittenberg and Erfurt. He was an admirer of Erasmus of Rotterdam, whom he visited in 1519 by order of Elector Frederick for consultation on Luther's case. In 1518 he was appointed professor of Canon Law (see p. 186, n. 1) at the University of Erfurt, where he was elected president in 1519; while holding this office he introduced Greek and Hebrew into the curriculum. He was called as provost to the All Saints' Chapter in Wittenberg in 1521, and as professor of Canon Law to the University there; see p. 262. Jonas refused to accept the professorship, arguing that he could no longer teach Canon Law, which, under Luther's influence, he had come to regard as contrary to the gospel. Luther now expresses the hope that the Elector may consent to the appointment of Jonas to a theological chair instead. Jonas soon did become a member of the Theological Faculty and Luther's faithful co-worker. With Luther he attended the Diet of Worms in 1521 and the Marburg Colloquy in 1529. His legal knowledge was a great help in the visitations and for the Electoral Saxon delegation to the Diet of Augsburg in 1530. Jonas soon was responsible for introducing the Reformation into various territories of central Germany (Zerbst, Ducal Saxony, Halle). In 1541 he became superintendent in Halle. When Luther was dying in February, 1546, Jonas was at his bedside, and he preached the funeral sermon in Eisleben. The Smalcaldic War (1546-1547) uprooted Jonas from Halle. After a period of restless wandering, he finally was able to settle down as superintendent in Eisfeld, where he remained for the last years of his life. Jonas is famous for his attempts to mediate between Luther and Bucer (see p. 247, n. 13), for his contributions to the *Augsburg Confession* and the constitutions of the territorial churches, and for his translations of some works by Luther and Melanchthon into German.

[4] In connection with the events mentioned on p. 269, n. 3, Spalatin wanted suggestions for a reorganization of the University. See also p. 289.

[5] This is written in support of Jonas.

[6] Of Electoral Saxony: Elector Frederick (see pp. 49 f.) and his co-ruler Duke John (see p. 269, n. 8).

[7] On the jurisdiction of the church, see p. 70, n. 1; p. 140, n. 6; p. 186, n. 1.

thrown out, who will destroy the venomous Canon Law? My host here has made an excellent beginning by hindering the [ecclesiastical] punishments.[8] If the sovereigns do not want to do this on their own authority, then they should at least ignore it if it is done by their administrative directors and judges. This would gradually make it known to the world that nobody could be molested by Canon Law, but that everything should be settled according to regional customs and territorial law.

Concerning my health,[9] I have easier elimination now, due to the strong and powerful medications,[10] but the way my digestion functions has not changed at all. The soreness continues, and I am afraid it may develop into a worse evil with which the Lord afflicts me, according to his wisdom.

Please take care that the rest of the *Postil,* which I enclose, is added to the previous material and published in Wittenberg before everything else. I shall hurry to finish ten of the Gospels, so that we can publish them in one book. I shall move the sermons for four Sundays to another place, and add the rest.[11] I am doing this so that not too big a book frightens readers and buyers, and so that in the meantime they have something from which they can learn about Christ.

Farewell and pray for me.

From the wilderness,[12] *July 31, 1521*

MARTIN LUTHER

---

[8] Hans von Berlepsch, the castellan of the Wartburg (see p. 255, n. 15), prevented the execution of the ban (see p. 192, n. 3; p. 210) by hiding and protecting Luther.

[9] On Luther's health, see p. 217, n. 15.

[10] Sent by Spalatin; see p. 268.

[11] See pp. 238 ff.

[12] See p. 263, n. 36.

91

To Philip Melanchthon[1]
Wartburg, August 1, 1521

Commenting on Karlstadt's theses of June 21 and July 19, Luther develops his ideas on clerical and monastic celibacy, on communion "in both kinds," on the private mass, and on the dynamics of faith.

Text in Latin: WA, Br 2, 370-372.

You people do not yet convince me[2] that the vows of priests and monks are to be considered in the same category.[3] For it is of special importance to me that the order of priests was established by God to be a free order; with the monks this is not the case. They have chosen their estate and made it an offering to God of their own accord. To be sure, I am almost ready to decide that those who entered this abyss before or during the age of puberty can leave it with a clear conscience; but about those who have grown old and lingered away in this estate, I don't yet know.

In addition to this Paul speaks very openly concerning the priests. He says demons have forbidden them to marry.[4] Since the voice of Paul is the voice of the Divine Majesty, I do not doubt that it must be trusted in this matter. Therefore even if they have consented to the devil's prohibition at the time of their initiation, then now, knowing the true state of the case and with

---

[1] This letter is a fragment; therefore there is no address, salutation, or signature. On Melanchthon as recipient of this letter, and on the date, see p. 284 and *WA*, Br 2, No. 424, Introduction. On Melanchthon, see p. 77, n. 3.

[2] Perhaps a reference to a letter which Melanchthon may have added to the material mentioned in note 3; this letter is not extant.

[3] Luther is referring to Karlstadt's (see p. 79, n. 12) theses which were the subject of two academic disputations conducted under Karlstadt's direction on June 21 and July 19; see *WA*, Br 2, No. 424, Introduction. The theses of June 21 dealt with clerical and monastic celibacy, those of July 19 with the Lord's Supper (see pp. 143 f.). With this material Karlstadt apparently wanted to prepare the way for the reforms he planned; see note 24. When Luther wrote the present letter, he must have had only a copy of the minutes of the disputations. When he wrote the next letter (No. 92), he had received and carefully studied two sets of printed sheets of the edition of Karlstadt's theses of June 21, which dealt with celibacy.

[4] I Tim. 4:1 ff. (Vulgate).

whom they made their pact, the contract should be boldly broken.

God's Word clearly establishes that the prohibition [of marriage] originates with the devil; this puts me under considerable pressure and compels me, therefore, to approve of the deed of the "bishop" of Kemberg.[5] For God does not deceive or lie when he says that this prohibition is of the devil. But if a pact has been made with the devil, it cannot be binding since it was made in an impious error against God, and with God's disapproval and condemnation. For [God] expressly calls those who are the authors of this prohibition "spirits of error." [6]

Why then do you hesitate to yield to this statement of God, even against the gates of hell? [The vow of celibacy] is not the same as the oath the children of Israel swore to the Gibeonites.[7] For they were commanded both to offer peace and accept it if offered them, and to gain proselytes [who] would comply with their religious observances. All this took place with the Gibeonites. Nothing happened there which was against the Lord or at the instigation of the "spirits of error." Although the [Israelites] murmured in the beginning, they finally accepted it.[8]

Moreover, celibacy is merely a human institution. Man, who has instituted it, can also abolish it; therefore any Christian can abolish it. I would say this even if it had been instituted by a good man instead of by demons.

I have no such declaration of God concerning the monks; therefore it is not safe to make the same assertion about them. I myself would not dare to comply with it;[9] therefore I will not counsel anyone else to do so. If only we could achieve that henceforth no one would become a monk, or that a monk would not withdraw in the years of physical desire. We must avoid offense, even in the things that are permitted,[10] unless we have a clear word of Scripture on our side.

---

[5] I.e., the marriage of Bartholomew Bernhardi, who was not really a bishop but a pastor at Kemberg; see p. 115, n. 21; p. 231, n. 19.
[6] I Tim. 4:1 ff.
[7] Joshua 9.
[8] Josh. 9:16-18.
[9] I.e., that the vow of monastic celibacy is to be abolished.
[10] On "permitted things," see p. 259, n. 15.

That excellent man Karlstadt[11] quotes from Paul that younger widows are to be rejected, and widows of the age of sixty to be chosen.[12] I only wish that this could settle the matter! For it would be so easy for someone to say that the Apostle was commanding this in regard to those who would be widowed in the future; the Apostle, however, calls those who have been widowed in the past "condemned" because they have [violated their previous pledge not to marry].[13] And thus this authority[14] will vanish and will not be a rock on which a man's conscience can faithfully rest; but that is what we are seeking.

Concerning the argument that it is better to marry than to burn, or that they should enter the estate of matrimony in the sin of a broken promise in order to avoid the sin of fornication[15] —what is this other than quibbling rationalization? We are looking for a word of Scripture and a testimony of the divine will. Who knows if he who "burns" today will "burn" tomorrow?

I would not have allowed priests to marry merely because of the "burning" if Paul did not call the prohibition of marriage erroneous, demonic, hypocritical, and condemned by God.[16] Thus even without the "burning" he compels us to give up celibacy for the sake of the fear of God. But it will be good to argue this matter at somewhat greater length. For I, too, would want to help the monks and nuns more than anything else, so greatly do I pity these wretched men and boys and girls who are vexed with pollutions and burnings.

Concerning "both kinds" in the Eucharist,[17] I am not arguing on the basis of the example [of the early church] but of the word of Christ. He[18] did not show that those who receive only

[11] In the theses mentioned in note 3.

[12] To understand Luther it is necessary to read I Tim. 5:3-16. Karlstadt saw a parallel between the case of the younger widows whom Paul considered eligible for marriage, and the case of the priests and monks who also should be allowed to marry.

[13] Literally: ". . . they have made the previous faith void."

[14] I.e., I Tim. 5:3-16.

[15] Both arguments were among Karlstadt's June 21 theses and were based on I Cor. 7:9 and 7:2; see *WA*, Br 2, No. 424, Introduction.

[16] I Tim. 4:1 ff.

[17] See pp. 143 f.

[18] The subject of this sentence is not clear. It could be Christ or it could be Karlstadt. Probably it is Karlstadt, however, since at this point Luther

the "one kind" either have or have not sinned. But it is important that Christ did not require either kind, just as he does not absolutely require baptism, when a tyrant or the world prevent the use of water. The violence of persecution puts asunder a husband and wife (whom God has forbidden being put asunder),[19] but they do not consent to the separation. In the same way pious hearts do not consent to being deprived of the "other kind." Who will deny, however, that they who do consent to it and approve of it—I mean the papists—are not Christians and are guilty of sin?

Since, then, Christ does not absolutely require "both kinds," and the tyrant prevents them, I do not see how those who receive only the "one kind" commit sin. For who can take the "other kind" by force, against the will of the tyrant?[20] We are under no compulsion here, therefore, except that of reason, which declares that Christ's institution is not being observed; Scripture, however, does not make any decision, and without a word of Scripture we cannot declare it[21] sin. The Lord's Supper is Christ's institution, to be used in freedom, and it cannot be imprisoned in whole or in part. For what would happen in a situation similar to that of the martyr Donatus,[22] when some could not partake of the wine because the chalice was broken and the wine spilled, and no other wine was at hand? And I could quote many similar cases. In summary: since Scripture does not force [us to say]

began the discussion of the second set of Karlstadt's theses (from the disputation of July 19, which dealt with the problem of the withdrawal of the cup from the laity), in one of which it is stated, "He who eats only the bread sins, in my opinion"; see *WA*, Br 2, No. 424, Introduction.

[19] Matt. 19:6.

[20] The translation of the last lines, beginning with "I do not see . . . ," is based on the earliest printed editions of this letter. The extant manuscript copy of this letter has a text which perhaps could be translated: ". . . them should you not see the tyrant [or the tyranny]?" The rest of the text is omitted. The (Latin) dative case of "tyrant," however, does not agree with the verb; the manuscript copy of the text cannot be used as the basis of the translation since its text suggests that some words are missing. The earliest printed edition, therefore, seems to offer the correct text, which perhaps was based on the autograph, which is no longer extant.

[21] I.e., the withholding of the cup.

[22] Luther is referring to a legend from the *Legenda aurea* (see p. 17, n. 5). While the martyr Donatus was celebrating the Lord's Supper, one of his deacons broke the chalice. Since it could not be replaced, Donatus picked up the pieces, and by his prayers they were miraculously joined together and the chalice could be used again. See *WA*, Br 2, 373, n. 12.

that [communion with] only "one kind" is sin, I cannot claim it.

I am greatly pleased, of course, that you are restoring Christ's institution.[23] I had especially intended to work for this, had I returned to you; for now we recognize this tyranny and can resist it, and are no longer forced to receive only "one kind."[24] But I also[25] will never say another private mass[26] in all eternity. Let us pray to the Lord, I beseech you, that he hasten to give us a larger portion of his Spirit, for I suspect that the Lord[27] will soon visit Germany, as its unbelief, impiety, and hatred of the gospel deserve. But of course this plague will then be charged to us on the grounds that we heretics have provoked God, and we will be scorned by men and despised by the people.[28] [The papists], however, will find excuses for their sins, and will justify themselves; [God will thus prove][29] that the wicked cannot be made good, either by kindness or by wrath, and that many will be tempted to do evil. The Lord's will be done.[30] Amen.

If you are a preacher of grace, then preach a true and not a fictitious grace; if grace is true, you must bear a true

---

[23] I.e., the giving of bread and wine to the communicants.

[24] Major reforms in church life were soon introduced in Wittenberg under the leadership of Karlstadt (see p. 79, n. 12) and Gabriel Zwilling (see p. 39, n. 3). In October the Augustinians of Wittenberg ceased to celebrate mass. The Lord's Supper in "both kinds" was administered to the people at the city church as early as the end of September. Karlstadt's ideas on celibacy and monastic vows were enthusiastically received by the Augustinians, and Gabriel Zwilling became one of the most violent and eloquent defenders of abandoning monastic life. Thus Karlstadt's theses of June and July contributed indirectly to the Wittenberg disturbances of 1521/22. See Bainton, pp. 197 ff.; see also in this volume, p. 386, n. 1.

[25] The conjunction is missing in the manuscript copy of this letter but is found in the earliest printed edition.

[26] *Missa privata,* i.e., a mass celebrated for its own sake, that is, as a sacrifice only, whereby the priest alone communes; no congregational communion is administered. For more details, see J. Jungmann, *The Mass of the Roman Rite* (New York), I (1951), 215 f. For Luther's criticism of the private mass, see his *Babylonian Captivity of the Church* (*WA* 6, 512 ff.; *LW* 36, 35 ff.), his *Misuse of the Mass* (*WA* 8, 482 ff.; *LW* 36, 128 ff.), and letter No. 99, p. 317; see also pp. 324 f.

[27] "Lord" is missing in the manuscript copy of this letter but is found in the earliest printed edition.

[28] Ps. 22:6.

[29] The manuscript copy of this letter offers a text which has to be translated: "so that they [the papists] prove [demonstrate]."

[30] The earliest printed edition of this letter repeats the "will be done."

and not a fictitious sin. God does not save people who are only fictitious[31] sinners. Be a sinner and sin[32] boldly,[33] but believe and[34] rejoice in Christ even more boldly, for he is victorious over sin, death, and the world. As long as we are here [in this world][35] we have to sin. This life is not the dwelling place of righteousness,[36] but, as Peter says,[37] we look for new heavens and a new earth in which righteousness[38] dwells. It is enough that by[39] the riches of God's glory we have come to know the Lamb that takes away the sin of the world.[40] No sin will separate us from the Lamb, even though we commit fornication and murder a thousand times a day. Do you think that the purchase price that was paid for the redemption of our sins[41] by so great a Lamb is too small? Pray boldly—you too are a mighty sinner.[42]

August 1, 1521

---

[31] The translation here is based on the text offered by the manuscript copy of this letter; the printed editions have a text which can be translated as: "only fictitiously sinners."

[32] The manuscript copy of this letter has the following text: "*et peccaris,*" "and you will have sinned," which makes little sense; therefore the translation is based on the text offered by the earliest printed edition.

[33] Passages such as this were misunderstood and used as main arguments against Luther. Luther was interpreted as encouraging laxity and licentiousness. When the Peasants' War broke out, this opinion was strengthened. Erasmus, for instance, constantly suspected that Luther was stimulating discontent and even rebellion with his ideas and work. For the proper understanding of this statement, see W. H. T. Dau, *Luther Examined and Re-examined* (St. Louis, Mo., 1917), pp. 111 ff. See also pp. 12 f.

[34] The phrase "but believe and" is missing in the manuscript copy of this letter but is found in the earliest printed edition.

[35] The word "here" is missing in the manuscript copy of this letter but is found in the earliest printed edition.

[36] The manuscript copy of this letter offers instead *animae,* i.e., "of the soul"; the translation is based on the earliest printed edition.

[37] II Pet. 3:13.

[38] The manuscript copy offers instead *anima,* i.e., "soul"; the translation is based on the earliest printed edition.

[39] The manuscript copy offers a text which has to be translated: "that we have come to know the riches of God's glory"; the translation is based on the earliest printed edition.

[40] John 1:29.

[41] See I Cor. 6:20 and I Pet. 1:18-19. The printed editions of this letter offer a text which has to be translated: "think that the price and the redemption [paid and] completed for us by . . . is too small?" The translation is based on the manuscript copy of this letter.

[42] So according to the manuscript copy of this letter. The printed editions offer a text which has to be translated: "for you are a mighty . . . ."

92

To Philip Melanchthon
Wartburg, August 3, 1521

In this letter Luther deals at great length with Karlstadt's June 21 theses on celibacy and monastic vows (see p. 277, n. 3). He approves of Karlstadt's efforts, but he points out weaknesses in Karlstadt's arguments, especially in the exegesis of Lev. 18:21, 20:2, and I Tim. 5:3 ff. While criticizing Karlstadt's position, Luther continues (see pp. 277 ff.) to discuss monastic and clerical vows. Though he is certain that there should be "an easy solution" to some of the problems involved, he is careful about reaching any conclusion. Luther also promises to fulfil Spalatin's wish for a thorough exposition of John 20:23, which is to be added to On Confession (see p. 246, n. 10). Joining Spalatin in lamenting the slowness of the Wittenberg printers, Luther urges that good work be done on the Postil (see pp. 237 ff.); he also discusses the possibility of a literary attack on the Sorbonne, and turns over to Melanchthon Spalatin's request to draw up plans for a reorganization of the University of Wittenberg.

On Philip Melanchthon, see p. 77, n. 3.

Text in Latin: WA, Br 2, 373-376.

To my friend Philip Melanchthon

Jesus

Greetings. I have studied the two sets of printed sheets of our Karlstadt's work on celibacy,[1] which were just now delivered to me. I highly approve of his effort and diligence, of course, although I rather wish that he had not twisted that passage about the "seed" which was sacrificed to Molech [2] into a reference to the emission of semen. [Our] enemies will ridicule the distortion of

[1] Luther is referring to Karlstadt's *Super coelibatu, monachatu et viduitate* (*On Celibacy, Monastic Life, and Widowhood*) (Wittenberg: N. Schirlenz, June 29, 1521), which developed out of the June 21 theses; see p. 277, n. 3.
[2] Lev. 18:21; 20:2; see pp. 293, 300.

this passage since it is clearer than light that it refers to the sons and daughters who were being sacrificed as a burnt offering to the idol. I also do not like the fact that the passage of Paul to Timothy[3] is treated so unclearly; it seems that it does not so much regulate celibacy as the support of the widows of the church. [Paul] says the congregation should not be burdened with [young widows], and it certainly is a disgrace if they want to marry afterward, when they have become wanton while supported by the congregation. [Paul] does not wish the conclusion to be drawn from this that he has excluded the younger persons from celibacy. For he talks only about widows, and excludes those who are young and wanton[4] from [receiving] congregational support.

Again—and this is contrary to what I have written in the previous letter[5]—it seems that Paul warns of future things but does not make things of the past void. This passage,[6] therefore, says absolutely nothing concerning virginity and celibacy. There is a difference between a congregation supporting a widow whose husband has died and whose other friends have abandoned her, and a congregation supporting virginity and celibacy. I say this because I don't want [you at Wittenberg] to be publishing anything based on obscure and ambiguous Scripture passages, since the light which is demanded of us has to be brighter than the sun and all the stars—and even then [our enemies] hardly see!

Who wants to insist that the statement, "I want the younger to marry,"[7] refers to [younger] widows? Is it not rather a general exhortation to all young women (except those condemned widows),[8] in the same way as when [Paul] said before, "[Treat] the younger [women] as sisters"?[9] Paul does not say [that he wanted] the younger widows to marry, since he had condemned those who did want to marry.[10] I am hard pressed by the fact

---

[3] I Tim. 5:3 ff.; see pp. 279, 293 f., 302.
[4] I Tim. 5:6 ff.
[5] See p. 279; what Luther meant here is not clear.
[6] I Tim. 5:6-7.
[7] I Tim. 5:14 (Vulgate).
[8] I Tim. 5:12.
[9] I Tim. 5:2.
[10] In the autograph this sentence is written in the margin.

that he says these younger widows are condemned because they have broken their pledge.[11] I doubt whether this difficulty can be resolved satisfactorily. One thing is certain: the pledge did bind these younger widows, no matter how young they might have been, if they are condemned [by Paul] for [having broken] it. On the other hand it might have been that these were widows who were not selected because of a personal vow but by a common vote of the congregation. For he says, "Let no widow be selected."[12] Here would be a place [to mention] the power of rejecting those whom it seemed wise to reject; but those who were selected as widows had no choice of refusing their selection.[13]

The very strict passages of the Old Law concerning the release from the fulfilment of vows do not move me at all.[14] It is impossible that they can refer or be applied to the vow of chastity[15] since everyone knows that they were given to people who under threat of the worst punishment of curse and shame were not permitted to remain unmarried—much less to take vows not to marry. I am absolutely convinced that it is impossible to prove from Scripture, either from a law or by an example, that chastity can be classified as a vow. There remains only I Corinthians 7; here it is left up to the individual [whether he wishes to marry or not]. This decision cannot be regulated by laws and statutes of men, except by an insinuation of Satan. Of this I am certain—come what may. It is dangerous, therefore, to vow chastity. But who would claim that there is no value in unmarried life? Especially since, following the counsels and examples of Scripture, one may freely live unmarried.

Although I am taking various things under consideration, I see that Peter (in Acts 15 [:10-11]), in the freedom of the Spirit, also cast off from himself and from all the other men the unbearable burden of the Law to which he had still been subordinated.

---

11 I Tim. 5:12.

12 I Tim. 5:9 (Vulgate). The "selection" refers to the status of widowhood to be supported by the congregation.

13 From "but those" to "selection" was apparently added by Luther after he had otherwise finished the letter; *WA*, Br 2, 376, n. d.

14 Deut. 23:21-22; Num. 30:2-3.

15 I.e., celibacy.

The only reason he gave [for doing this] was the impossibility of fulfilling [the Law], and the whole church agreed with him; and after this he himself ate with the Gentiles.[16] On the other hand the value of this action is jeopardized [insofar as our discussion is concerned] by the fact that he did nothing on the basis of his own authority but had a commandment from heaven to consider nothing unclean, that is, that the Law would not be necessary for the Gentiles.[17] But he concluded without a revelation that the Law was not necessary either for him or the Jews. Thus, on the basis of the example of the Gentiles, he who was burdened by the Law claimed freedom for himself also. I think also of Christ, who on the Sabbath healed a daughter of Abraham who had been bound for eighteen years.[18] What if also [the Jews] were here "bent double"[19] by Satan, so that at least the majority of those alive, having not yet tested the Spirit, vowed [to maintain the Sabbath law], either from their own or Satan's passion?[20]

I am absolutely certain that there is quite an easy solution to all these problems, even though we don't as yet see what it is. For if Christ were here, I do not doubt that he would dissolve these chains and would annul all vows. He would not allow anyone to be oppressed by an unbearable or involuntary burden, since he is Savior and Bishop of all souls.[21] Therefore it almost seems to me that at this point one has to use the freedom of the Spirit and has to break through whatever is in the way of the salvation of souls. For Christ has not yet made known by any oracle, sign, or witness that he is pleased with this vowing business. It might be quite dangerous to follow something of which it is not at all certain that Christ approves, especially since we see that so many souls perish unavoidably and against their will.

[16] The food laws (see Leviticus 11) made it impossible for Jew and Gentile to eat together; see also Deut. 7:2 ff.
[17] Acts 10:9 ff.
[18] Luke 13:11 ff. Luther wrote "eighty" years.
[19] Like the crippled woman who was bent over, whose paralysis Jesus ascribed to the work of Satan; see Luke 13:16.
[20] The conjectures in brackets show that the text does not make it clear of whom Luther was thinking. Another conjecture would be "the monks" and "to live in celibacy."
[21] I Pet. 2:25 (Vulgate?).

Under different circumstances such souls could have been successfully counseled if this vow of uncertain merit[22] didn't exist. Aren't we running for an uncertain goal? Aren't we beating the air? Why don't we rather slow down in our race?[23] How I wish that we could discuss these things together personally! Maybe Christ would give us more of the Spirit and a greater knowledge and then also more freedom. I pray that in the meantime the Spirit may enlighten all of you more.

I have still another strong argument regarding all this. A vow is never approved among men if it is made under the age of fourteen; this means that a vow for the whole life is not permitted. Who makes certain that a vow made after the age of fourteen is valid for the whole life? God is silent and man does not know. We miserable creatures, who are thus carried away with uncertainties and follow them as dependable goals! For this reason too, it seems that [taking vows] is impudent and does not please God, for he is a God of counsel and knowledge[24] and not a God of unfounded opinion, ignorance, and uncertainty. You see what great unrest disturbs me! Nevertheless I cannot as yet decide anything positive in these matters; I only wish to be helpful to all of you in your attempt [to understand this matter].

At times I stood[25] without scruples for abolishing those vows that were made under the age of twenty. I still would abolish them, since everyone sees that they were made without counsel and insight into the matter. I took this stand, however, only on the vows of those people who had not yet changed their status or dress.[26] Concerning those who have become priests in the monasteries, however, I haven't attempted to do anything yet, even if they took their vows before the age of twenty. I don't know what phantom of pomp and human opinion is plaguing me here. May the Lord Jesus instruct us and bring us by his mercy to our freedom. We are certainly a people on whom no law should be imposed—especially not for the whole of life—but to whom every-

---

[22] I.e., the vow of celibacy.
[23] An allusion to I Cor. 9:24 ff.
[24] Isa. 11:2.
[25] Probably in private discussions.
[26] I.e., have been ordained to the priesthood; see pp. 277, 301.

thing should be left free. It is to be feared that whatever is done differently is not done in a proper spirit. But enough of this.

Spalatin asks for the second time [27] that I explain in greater detail the word of Christ in John: "Whose sins you retain, they are retained," [28] in the treatise *On Confession*.[29] I am astonished if I didn't explain it, since I had in mind especially to deal with it because of [our] enemies. [Spalatin] may be disturbed by what disturbs all of you, namely, that this passage is so obscure. But now it will be hard for me to send you an addition, since I do not have the preceding and following pages. Yet if it is really necessary to send you something, I shall try, so that you may insert it at a fitting place, if possible, after you make the necessary changes.

[Spalatin] is also complaining to me about the slowness with which you people proceed to publish. Therefore I reprove and censure you whether I am right or wrong. Now look, what else should I do? You have six presses, I hear. As I figure it, I alone keep four presses busy, and your *Loci*[30] and Karlstadt keep the other two busy. Yet I really wonder why my *Magnificat* [31] is not yet finished. Of course I want the *Postil* [32] to be printed in a good and correct type face.[33]

I don't want you all to be concerned about my health;[34] should I find out that you are worried, I shall confess nothing further with regard to it. Who knows whether this should not be the end of my ministry? Have I not stirred up enough disturbance singlehandedly? I have not lived in vain. May God grant that I lived pleasingly in his eyes. I see that all of you grow in spiritual matters, so it seems to me that I could decrease.[35] I am proud of this, and I wish I would become nothing and you would be every-

---

[27] George Spalatin; see pp. 8 f. Neither letter is extant.
[28] John 20:23; see p. 294.
[29] Which Luther had sent to Spalatin in June, asking him to have it printed; see p. 254.
[30] See p. 232, n. 21.
[31] See p. 225, n. 17; p. 254, n. 4.
[32] See pp. 237 ff.
[33] Since Grünenberg was supposed to print the *Postil*, and since Luther had reason to be unhappy with Grünenberg's work (see p. 19, n. 8), Luther wanted to be sure the *Postil* was printed well.
[34] See p. 217, n. 15.
[35] An allusion to John 3:30.

thing. Only pray for me that my faith in the Lord does not fail.[36]

Please reply whether it would be wise for me to answer the Oakes and Bedes of the Sorbonne.[37] I am concerned that I, too,[38] launch an attack against them, and [wonder] whether a more extensive defense of the truth isn't called for. For I know I have to get advice [on this] from you all.

Spalatin has also written to me regarding the organizational plan of a Christian university; but I have answered that this is beyond my strength, that is, beyond the strength of a single man.[39] You people try to help him out on this. If you wish, you may send this letter to Spalatin to read.

Farewell.

August 3, 1521 Yours,

MARTIN LUTHER

93

To George Spalatin
Wartburg, August 6, 1521

Luther expresses his opinion of Karlstadt's work on celibacy. Sending the manuscript of his translation of Melanchthon's Defense (see p. 258, n. 7), he authorizes Spalatin to postpone the printing of certain of his own works. He expresses his impatience that the

[36] Luke 22:32.

[37] Luther planned to translate and annotate Melanchthon's *Defense* (see p. 258, n. 7) against the theologians of Paris. Now it seems that he also intended to write against them himself to defend his work. According to *WA*, Br 2, 377, n. 26, "Oakes and Bedes" is derived from the names of two outstanding members of the Paris Faculty. One of them, Noel Bedier, also known as Natalis Beda, was the *syndicus* (or official receiver, or perhaps business manager); the other one was Guillaume Duchesne, also known as William a Querco, or William Oak, a professor of theology. On Beda, see Allen 6, 1571, Introduction; on Oak, see Allen 4, 1188, n. 29.

[38] The position of this conjunction makes two interpretations possible: ". . . I, too . . . ," i.e., as Melanchthon had done with his *Defense* (see note 37); or ". . . that I launch an attack also against [the Sorbonne] . . . ," i.e., as Luther had attacked Cologne and Louvain; see p. 155, n. 6.

[39] See p. 269, n. 3; p. 275, n. 4.

Magnificat is not yet printed and his surprise that his exposition of Psalm 119 is apparently lost. He comments briefly on his health.

On George Spalatin, see pp. 8 f.

Text in Latin: WA, Br 2, 377-378.

To my friend George Spalatin

Jesus

Greetings. I received from my host[1] the dialogues[2] and two sets of printed sheets of Karlstadt's [work].[3] Good Lord! Will our people at Wittenberg give wives even to the monks? They will not push a wife on me! The author of the dialogues did not have enough talent or learning. And I wish that Karlstadt's writings, too, would be clearer, since they are full of talent and learning.[4]

I do not intend that everything I send should be published. I wish [the printing of] this *Defense* of Philip's[5] postponed until such time as the presses are idle, unless you think otherwise. The same should have been done with Psalm "*Exsurgat*,"[6] because there are other things [to be printed] that are more necessary and urgent. For goodness' sake, is my *Magnificat* not yet finished?[7] I am surprised that Psalm 119 is lost. I am certain I added it at the end of the treatise *On Confession*, so that a part of it was written on the same sheet of paper on which the last part of the treatise was written. If the Psalm is lost, then necessarily the treatise *On Confession* would also be incomplete.[8] The rest of the Psalm I sent separately with the other package.[9] Maybe you people don't search carefully enough. Put into its place

[1] Hans von Berlepsch; see p. 255, n. 15.

[2] It is not certain which dialogues Luther means. For possibilities, see *WA*, Br 2, 378, n. 1.

[3] See p. 283, n. 1.

[4] See pp. 283 f.

[5] See p. 258, n. 7; Luther is including the manuscript of his translation. For the text, see *WA* 8, 266 ff.

[6] Reference to the exposition of Psalm 68 (Psalm 67 according to Vulgate numbering), which begins: "*Exsurgat Deus*," i.e., "Let God arise." Luther had sent the manuscript to Melanchthon in May; see p. 229, n. 5.

[7] See p. 225, n. 17; p. 254, n. 4.

[8] See p. 246, n. 10; p. 254, n. 8.

[9] Perhaps with the "other things" of No. 88, p. 271, n. 3.

the part of my *Answer to Catharinus* I am herewith returning, for I have a complete copy of it.[10]

My constipation[11] seems to be permanent, so far as I can see, and must always be relieved with medication. Only every fourth, sometimes even fifth day, I have elimination. What a terrific stomach!

Farewell, and pray for me. Watch out that you, too,[12] do not marry, so that you don't run into worldly troubles.[13]

August 6, 1521 MARTIN LUTHER

94

To George Spalatin
Wartburg, August 15, 1521

Luther sharply criticizes Grünenberg's work on the treatise On Confession (see p. 246, n. 10) but is pleased with Lotther's work on Against Latomus (see p. 229, n. 3). He discusses Karlstadt's way of arguing the case against celibacy (see pp. 283 ff.). Reporting

---

[10] Luther is returning some extra sets of printed sheets of his *Ad librum eximii Magistri nostri Ambrosii Catharini . . . Responsio Martini Lutheri* (*Martin Luther's Reply to the Book of Our Outstanding Teacher Ambrose Catharinus*) (Wittenberg: M. Lotther, June, 1521). *WA* 7, 705 ff. Lancellotto de' Politi, or Ambrosius Catharinus of Siena, O. P. (1484-1553), studied and taught philosophy, theology, and canon and secular law in his native Siena and obtained the doctor's degree in 1500. Having joined the Dominicans in 1515 as a result of the influence of the writings of Savonarola (see *O.D.C.C.*, p. 1219), he was commissioned by his superiors to reply to Luther's attacks against the primacy of the pope. In February, 1521, he published a major work on this subject (for bibliographical information, see *WA* 7, 698 ff.), to which Luther replied with the work mentioned above. Although a strict Thomist, Catharinus soon became a controversial figure in the Dominican Order due to his stand on Immaculate Conception and predestination. It seems that Cardinal Cajetan (see p. 73, n. 3) was especially antagonistic to Catharinus. To avoid difficulties, the nature of which is not altogether clear, it seems that Catharinus lived for some time in exile in France. Despite his outspokenness he was made bishop of Minore in 1546 and archbishop of Conza in 1552 and served as theological advisor at the Council of Trent. See *O.D.C.C.*, pp. 247 f.

[11] See p. 217, n. 15.

[12] Like Bartholomew Bernhardi; see p. 231; p. 342, n. 20.

[13] I Cor. 7:28.

on a hunt and reflecting on it, Luther hopes that he is not a burden to the castellan of the Wartburg. He sends Spalatin a manuscript of the Postil and gives directions for its arrangement and printing; he also includes the exposition of John 20:23 for insertion in the treatise On Confession.

On George Spalatin, see pp. 8 f.

Text in Latin: WA, Br 2, 379-381.

Mr. George Spalatin, my friend in the Lord

Jesus

Greetings. My Spalatin: I have received the second and third set of printed sheets of the book *On Confession* from you;[1] I had previously received them from Philip, too,[2] along with the first set. I cannot say how unhappy and disgusted I am with the printing. I wish I had sent nothing in German![3] It is printed so poorly, so carelessly and confusedly, to say nothing of the bad type faces and paper. John the printer is always the same old John and does not improve.[4] For goodness' sake, under no circumstances let him print any of the German *Postils!*[5] What I have sent of them should be stored away, or rather returned to me so that I may send it somewhere else. What good does it do to work hard if such sloppiness and confusion causes other printers [who may reprint from this first edition] to make more mistakes that are worse? I do not want the Gospels and Epistles[6] to be sinned against in this way; it is better to hide them than to bring them out in such a form. Therefore I am sending you

---

[1] See p. 246, n. 10; Grünenberg's edition. On the reasons for Luther's unhappiness with Grünenberg's work, see p. 19, n. 8. The edition of Luther's letter to the Imperial Estates (see p. 203), which he had seen while returning from Worms and which was "full of mistakes" (see p. 255), was also probably the one put out by Grünenberg; see WA, Br 2, 356, n. 17.

[2] Philip Melanchthon; see p. 77, n. 3. Luther had received the printed sheets of *On Confession* containing the text of *WA* 8, 138-158; see *WA*, Br 2, 381, n. 1.

[3] Luther was dissatisfied with Grünenberg's work in general (see p. 19, n. 8), but particularly with Grünenberg's German publications.

[4] Luther here used a popular saying which is roughly similar to the English, "You can't teach an old dog new tricks." See also *WA*, Br 2, 381, n. 3.

[5] See pp. 237 ff.

[6] I.e., the *Postil.*

nothing now, although I have finished almost ten large manuscript sheets of the [*Postil*]. I shall send nothing more until I have seen that these sordid money-grubbers, in printing books, care less for their profits than for the benefit of the reader. For what does such a printer seem to think except, "It is enough that I get my money; let the readers worry about what and how they will read it"?

Philip has sent me three sets of printed sheets of the *Latomus*,[7] which I like very much.

How I wish that Karlstadt had tried to refute celibacy with more fitting Scripture passages![8] I am afraid he stirs up quite a lot of talk for himself and for us. What kind of exegesis is this: the giving of seed to Molech is the same as becoming unclean by a natural emission of semen?[9] Everyone knows that in this passage "seed" means the same as "children" or "offspring," just as in Psalm 77 and 106 [:27].[10] Why does he not use the words of Scripture which call [such] evil "unchastity" and "uncleanness" as the Apostle [Paul] does?[11] Any opponent will be able to refute even the way that Karlstadt twists the passage in Timothy on the widows who are to be rejected[12] as referring to celibacy. The cause he has undertaken is important, and an excellent endeavor, but I wish it were also done in an outstanding, skilful, and successful way. For you see what great clarity and strength our enemies demand of us, since they misrepresent even the most evident and fitting [of our] statements.[13] We

---

[7] Printed sheets of Luther's work *Against Latomus* (see p. 229, n. 3; p. 270), which was published by M. Lotther in Wittenberg. Melanchthon must have sent them, together with the printed sheets of *On Confession.*

[8] In reference to Karlstadt's work on celibacy; see p. 283, n. 1.

[9] Lev. 15:16-33; 18:21; 20:2; see pp. 283 f.

[10] The Vulgate interprets the Hebrew word for "seed" or "semen" as "offspring" or "children." In referring to Psalm 77 (Vulgate numbering), Luther is not correct, since this Psalm does not speak of sacrifices of humans or interpret "seed" as "children." Perhaps Luther confused this Psalm with Ps. 37:25, which in the Vulgate has *semen*, or "seed," meaning children.

[11] Reference to I Cor. 6:9; Gal. 5:19. These passages have to be seen against the background of the Old Testament passages referred to in note 9, and Gen. 38:9. Basing his argument on this biblical material, Luther considers such emission of semen either immoral (onanism) or unclean (nocturnal emission).

[12] I Tim. 5:3 ff.; see pp. 279, 284 f., 302.

[13] See p. 284.

are a spectacle to the world;[14] how much more, therefore, do we have to be careful that our word is blameless, as Paul teaches.[15] Perhaps I am concerned about things that are not my business. But they are not things beyond my concern, if Karlstadt succeeds in his attempt. For what is more dangerous than to incite such a big crowd of unmarried people[16] to matrimony on the basis of such unreliable and uncertain Scripture passages, only to have them harassed afterward with continual anguish of conscience, worse than the cross they now have to carry.[17] I too wish to see celibacy made a matter of choice, as the gospel requires.[18] I do not see clearly yet how to accomplish this. But my warning is in vain. Maybe [Karlstadt] does not want to be held back in his course. Therefore one has to let him continue.

I am enclosing a brief exposition of the passage of John, as you wished.[19] It will be up to you to insert it at an appropriate place, because I do not remember the entire treatise. I believe that I had treated this passage at sufficient length previously, however, so that this additional material would perhaps not have been necessary.

Don't be concerned that I have to bear this exile. For it makes no difference to me where I am, if only in the long run I am not a burden and inconvenience to the people here, since I wouldn't want anyone to be burdened with me. Yet I definitely believe I am here as a guest and at the expense of our Sovereign.[20] Otherwise I would not remain one hour, if I thought that I were consuming the property of this man here,[21] although he serves me cheerfully and freely in all things. You know, if anyone's wealth is to be wasted, it has to be that of those who rule, because to be a ruler and not to a certain degree also a robber is not at all—or hardly—possible. The greater the ruler, the bigger the robber. You would do me a favor if you would definitely inform

---

[14] I Cor. 4:9.
[15] Titus 2:7-8.
[16] I.e., the priests, monks, and nuns.
[17] See pp. 279, 287, 311, 337 f.
[18] Matt. 19:11 ff.; I Cor. 7:25 ff.
[19] See p. 288. This insert can be found in *WA* 8, 162.
[20] Elector Frederick; see pp. 49 f.
[21] The castellan of the Wartburg, Hans von Berlepsch; see p. 255, n. 15.

me on this matter, because I can learn nothing from this kind man except that he sustains me from the Sovereign's purse. But it is my nature to fear being a burden where perhaps I am not a burden; but an honorable man ought to have such scruples.

Last Monday I went hunting for two days[22] to see what this bittersweet[23] pleasure of heroes is like. We caught two hares and a few poor partridges—a worthy occupation indeed for men with nothing to do. I theologized even among the snares and dogs. However great the pleasure may be from these things, the mystery of pity and pain mixed into it is equally great. For what else does this picture [of a hunt] signify if not the devil, who hunts innocent little creatures with his ambushes and his dogs—that is, with the ungodly teachers, bishops, and theologians? This very sad comparison with simple, faithful souls was only too clearly at hand. A still gloomier allegory followed. By my efforts we had saved a little live rabbit. I had rolled it up into the sleeve of my cloak and left it alone for a while. In the meantime the dogs found the poor rabbit and, biting through the cloak, broke its right hind leg and killed it by choking it. Thus pope and Satan rage to destroy even the souls that have been saved, and care nothing about my efforts. I am sick of this kind of hunting. I consider more pleasant a hunt in which bears, wolves, boars, foxes, [which like] wicked teachers, are pierced with spear and arrow. Yet it consoles me that the secret meaning is an allegory of salvation: hares and innocent creatures are captured by people rather than by bears, wolves, and hawks of prey and those like them—that is, by bishops and theologians—and this signifies that they are here[24] consigned to hell, but there[25] to heaven. I tell you this jokingly in a letter, so that you may know that in paradise you courtiers who are lovers of game will also be game which Christ, who is the best hunter, can hardly catch and save in spite of all his great efforts. A game is played with you folks while you play around hunting.

22 August 12 and 13.
23 Luther used a Greek word here.
24 I.e., when caught by the bishops who don't care for them.
25 I.e., when captured by people who care for them. The original construction of the last portion of this sentence is rather ambiguous; the translation is as literal as possible.

I have changed my mind and am sending the rest of the *Postil.*[26] I think that since the printing of my previous shipments may have been started already,[27] the work cannot be postponed or stopped. But I do want it to be printed on folio paper[28] with Lotther's type faces,[29] since it will be a large book. I would divide it into four parts of the year, from quarter to quarter, so that it will not be too heavy and expensive.[30] But I know my wish doesn't count, since what will be done is what the press wants and not what I want. Whatever does or does not happen, please take care that those manuscripts of mine are guarded carefully or returned to me. I know the Satan who plots against them.

I wonder if my *Magnificat* will ever be finished.[31]

Farewell and pray for me.

August 15, 1521 MARTIN LUTHER

95

To Philip Melanchthon
Wartburg, September 9, 1521

Luther congratulates Melanchthon on the Loci (see p. 232, n. 21). He continues the discussion of the problem of monastic vows (which he had begun in No. 91 of August 1) and comes to some definite conclusions which he formulates in enclosed theses. He comments briefly on the problem of "unforgivable sin."

On Philip Melanchthon, see p. 77, n. 3.

Text in Latin: WA, Br 2, 382-386.

Mr. Philip Melanchthon, disciple and instrument of Christ, minister of the congregation at Wittenberg

---

26 See pp. 238, 240 ff.; see also above.
27 Whether or not the printing had already begun could not be determined. On Luther's previous shipments of *Postil* manuscripts, see p. 271, n. 3; p. 276.
28 Or in large quartos; see *WA*, Br 2, 382, n. 20.
29 On the printing of books in Wittenberg, see p. 19, n. 8.
30 On this arrangement, see pp. 242 ff.
31 See p. 225, n. 17; p. 254, n. 4.

Greetings. I am most pleased with your *Loci*;[1] there is no way my poverty could criticize your wealth; continue as effectively, and rule.

I wish I could be with you to settle the question of the vows.[2] It is not good to debate in a letter. While one writes quite verbosely about something the other person already knows only too well, one omits what the other person is most interested in, as for instance happened with regard to the question of confession.[3] If I can, I shall arrange for a secret meeting between us at some place, since I am vèry concerned about this matter.[4] In the meantime I shall continue to talk to the wind.

You write[5] that you have reached the point where you believe that a vow should be nullified if one is not able to keep it, so that the vow is not maintained in sin.[6] For goodness' sake, isn't this a completely unintelligible statement? Aren't you talking as if you wanted to say that a vow should not be binding since it is impossible to fulfil it? Following this line of reasoning, you would also have to concede that the divine commandments are to be abolished.

Or does it make a difference that the commandments are imposed upon us but a vow is taken voluntarily? What else does this prove than that [the vow] is to be nullified not because it is impossible to fulfil but rather because it is taken voluntarily. But that which is taken voluntarily has already become a law of God, since Scripture says, "Make your vows and perform them."[7] Do not follow reason at this point, but Scripture, and abrogate the vow a priori and not a posteriori; that is, refute the principle of the vow and its custom. It is over this matter that I am now sweating. Whether or not a vow can be fulfilled doesn't bother

---

1 Luther had finally received the first set of printed sheets of Melanchthon's *Loci;* see p. 232, n. 21.

2 See pp. 277 ff., 283 ff., 293 f., 310, 329 ff.

3 This statement could not be verified, unless one considers it to be a reference to the exposition of John 20:23 in Luther's *On Confession* and to Spalatin's twofold demand that Luther explain it in more detail; see p. 288. Cf. p. 314.

4 I.e., the validity of the monastic vows.

5 This letter is not extant; for a glimpse of its content, see Luther's discussion below.

6 I.e., with a heart that breaks the vow.

7 Ps. 76:11.

me; on this point you will accomplish nothing with me. For this way you could also make divorce acceptable, if the marriage partners simply cannot get along. It seems to me that the salient point of our discussion has to be whether or not a vow is binding.

Your *Loci* states [8] very well that the slavery of the vows is strange to the gospel and contrary to the freedom [9] of the Spirit. But here we really debate vows and not the slavery of vows. You know precisely what such freedom and such slavery are and where they exist: not in the vows themselves but in one's attitude [toward them]. For he who is free can, just as the Apostle Paul,[10] submit himself to all laws, and to the dominion of all men, in the same way in which St. Bernard [11] and others who were monks in the truest sense of the word surrendered themselves to [living under] a vow.[12]

It is part of evangelical liberty that one can submit oneself to a vow and to laws. The Law of God does not come from faith, says the Apostle [Paul]; [13] it certainly does not have its origin in freedom and it is contrary to the gospel, and yet we live under it in freedom. Consequently, many have lived as free under the slavery of the vows. If this were not so, your syllogism would be perfect: Whatever is contrary to the freedom of the gospel has to be abolished under the threat of an eternal curse; and the obligation to keep the vows is of this kind, therefore, etc.[14] What a fortunate and desirable conclusion!

What now? No law or slavery is positively abolished just because it is harmful and adverse but rather because it should be a free matter; all laws are even confirmed because we estab-

[8] *Loci communes,* 1521 (see note 1). *Melanchthon,* Studienausgabe 2, I, 52, 28 f.

[9] A manuscript copy of this letter has a note in the margin which reads: "slavery [dominion]."

[10] E.g., Acts 16:3; 21:22 ff.; I Corinthians 8.

[11] St. Bernard, O. Cist (1090-1153), abbot of Clairvaux; see *O.D.C.C.*, pp. 160 f.

[12] See Theses 76-78 of Luther's *Theses on the Vows* (see note 36). *WA* 8, 326.

[13] Gal. 3:12.

[14] This conclusion, attributed by Luther to Melanchthon, could not be identified verbatim. Melanchthon might have stated it in the letter which is not extant; see note 5. On the other hand it can be deduced from the thoughts which Melanchthon expressed in the passage to which note 8 refers.

lish the Law by faith. Therefore the law of vows will stand together with the freedom of the gospel, indeed, it will even be made firm by it.

I wasn't satisfied with what I wrote in my last letter,[15] except with what I said concerning the passage of Paul in I Timothy 5 [:3-16], where he condemns the widows who have broken their pledge. But I wanted to give you an opportunity to concentrate on the root, that is, on the law of the vow, and not on the fruit, or the consequence of the vow. How far I myself have progressed on this point, I shall write to you [now].

I think we can use no other counsel here than the one—as we see—Paul uses in Galatians and elsewhere[16] with regard to the abrogation of the Law. Don't you think that the Galatians circumcised themselves with a true heart, as if they were serving God by it and because they thought they were obligated to do it?[17] Didn't they submit themselves to the Law for the sake of God? Didn't they offer themselves to God by this in the same way as when someone offers himself to God through a monastic vow? But why does Paul draw them away from this? [He does not criticize] them for submitting themselves [to the Law] but rather for submitting themselves to it with an enslaved conscience. [He made them realize] that this is the greatest sacrilege against the grace of Christ and his Spirit.

I think one must show some courage here and must reformulate [your] syllogism in the following way: Whoever has taken his vow with a spirit which is contrary to evangelical liberty has to be released from it and his vow condemned; he who has taken his vow with the intention of seeking salvation or righteousness through it belongs in this category; therefore, etc., [his vow has to be annulled].[18] Since, however, almost the whole crowd of those who say their vows do it with this intention, it is obvious that their vows are godless, sacrilegious, and contrary to the gospel; therefore their vows have to be completely nullified and come under the anathema.[19]

[15] Of August 3, 1521; see pp. 283 ff.
[16] Gal. 3:19 ff.; I Corinthians 6—10.
[17] Gal. 5:1 ff.
[18] Luther is rephrasing Melanchthon's conclusion mentioned in note 14.
[19] See *Theses on the Vows*, Nos. 45, 46. *WA* 8, 325.

How many do you think would have said the vow had they known that they would acquire neither righteousness nor salvation through this vow? [20] Therefore almost all [of them] have this enslaved conscience in one way or another; even more, they vow for this very reason, in the hope that by so doing they will be pleasing to God and become righteous and be saved. What else (they say to themselves) should I do in the monastery? [21] Since they say the vows with such a conscience, they are really saying nothing but this: See, God, I pledge to you ungodliness and idolatry for my whole life.[22] They vow that they will become good through these works, but they don't think even once of the justifying faith. This error does not concern a temporal matter; besides this it destroys legitimate marriages. It is absolutely intolerable, because it sins against the salvation of souls and brings about ungodliness as opposed to godliness. Therefore [this error] has to be completely corrected.

But how can this error be corrected unless such a vow is either repealed, or a completely new vow taken,[23] that is, a vow which is undertaken in the spirit of freedom? Would the ungodly Manasseh, who had made a vow to sacrifice his son to God through the idol Molech [24] in order to imitate Abraham, whose freedom he did not have,[25] still have vowed to do this had he known that his action was ungodly and sacrilegious? [26]

Certainly those who take their vow in this way pledge themselves not to the living God but to a lie and to their idol.[27] For a vow of this kind, they deserve the sharpest censure. It is beyond question that they should be obliged to keep such a vow. I am sure, had I known this when I made my vow,[28] I would never have done so, although I am uncertain with what kind of an

[20] See *ibid.*, No. 43. *WA* 8, 325.
[21] See *ibid.*, No. 44. *WA* 8, 325.
[22] See *ibid.*, No. 34. *WA* 8, 324.
[23] See *ibid.*, No. 58. *WA* 8, 326.
[24] II Kings 21:6; 23:10.
[25] I.e., the freedom (from the law not to sacrifice humans) which was given to Abraham when he was ordered to sacrifice Isaac; see Deut. 12:31; 18:10.; Lev. 18:21; 20:2-5; Gen. 22:1-20.
[26] See *Theses on the Vows*, No. 36. *WA* 8, 325.
[27] A manuscript copy of this letter offers this text instead: "*idolo cordis sui*," i.e., "to the idol of their hearts."
[28] See pp. 301, 331 f.; Bainton, pp. 42 f.

attitude I took my vow. I was more overpowered than drawn [by considerations]. God wanted it this way. I am afraid that I, too, may have taken my vow in an impious and sacrilegious way.

Therefore I think one must not only suggest but instruct our Galatians[29] confidently to trample upon their vows and grieve over the ungodliness and sacrilege [in which they had become involved]; nothing should delay them, even if in the meantime they were bewitched and fooled into taking holy orders[30] (as they call them). This freedom, even necessity, applies especially to those who said their vows as young people or children. For they really have never learned what faith is, or law, and have been trapped like a flock of stupid birds in a net. Therefore they are to be freed and rebuked for their thoughtlessness and foolishness.

There can be no rule established for others by which we may know whether someone said his vow with a sacrilegious attitude or not. This has to be left to their consciences, as has to be done with every other good work. For who, besides the spirit of man which is in him, could know[31] in what attitude a man takes a vow or does a good work? A work of the law or of the slavery of the vow is not judged on the basis of the work itself but on the basis of the attitude of the heart, by Him who weighs the spirits and commands us to judge in the same way.[32]

I remember when I made my vow, my earthly father was terribly angry with this; after he was reconciled to the idea, I had to listen to the following: Let's hope that this was not a delusion from Satan.[33] This word took such deep root in my heart that I have never heard anything from his mouth which I remembered more persistently. It seemed to me as if God had spoken to me from afar, through my father's mouth—it was late, yet it was enough to punish and admonish me.

---

[29] Here the monks are compared with the Galatians, since the consciences of both were enslaved by legalism.

[30] I.e., the ordination into the priesthood; see pp. 277, 287; *Theses on the Vows*, No. 112. *WA* 8, 328.

[31] I Cor. 2:11.

[32] I John 4:1.

[33] See pp. 331 f.; Bainton, pp. 42 f.; *WA*, TR 1, Nos. 623, 881; 3, No. 3556.

On this basis [34] I feel justified in having all vows annulled, or at least in having them renewed [in a different attitude]. Being content with this notion, I shall look for nothing else. For in this matter it is absolutely obvious that such vows, if they are taken in the attitude which I have mentioned, are taken and kept in opposition to the whole First Table,[35] in opposition to faith and to the gospel, and as highest idolatry. If you have said your vow, however, in a free and evangelical attitude and have made yourself a slave voluntarily, then it is right that you keep your vow and fulfil it. Yet I would not want to affirm that an evangelical heart ever would dare or has dared to do this, except by self-deception.

I am sending you theses on this subject; [36] if you want to publish them I may add very short explanations [37] and dedicate them to the congregation at Wittenberg. For I think that this clear and sound logic, which is sufficiently based on Scripture, can hold out against light and publicity. What can the statements of the Law on vows prove against this? [38]

That leaves only that passage of Paul concerning the widows.[39] I shall not admit that this passage is contrary to this basic opinion concerning Law and faith, and I shall make no concession to it. I shall rather say that it is not clear; or I shall understand it in this way: these widows have made their vows [40] in the freedom of faith, which was then so new and well understood, just as Demas and all in Asia relinquished [this freedom].[41] But our people now are a heathen people who have never been taught anything about faith.

---

[34] I.e., all the reasons Luther has so far set forth in this letter.

[35] I.e., the first three Ten Commandments, referring to duty toward God.

[36] I.e., the *Themata de Votis* (so in Luther's September 9 letter to von Amsdorf; see *WA*, Br 2, 390; p. 310), the *Theses on the Vows,* from which Luther had quoted above; for the text, see *WA* 8, 323 f.

[37] For the time being Luther postponed this plan of writing "very short explanations" of the *Theses on the Vows.* On the same day he promised von Amsdorf to send "other theses" in which the problem of the vows would be debated in greater detail.

[38] See p. 285.

[39] I Tim. 5:3 ff.; see pp. 279, 284 f., 293 f.

[40] To remain unmarried.

[41] II Tim. 1:15; 4:10. The conjecture could also read "this faith," or, if one uses the text offered by one of the available manuscript copies, "Paul."

You write me what you think and conclude on this matter, for I am afraid these things are already old stuff for you.

This further proves the stupidity of the vows, that one makes a solemn promise of poverty and obedience. These two things are either a fiction or were once instituted only for children who should receive their first education. It seems, therefore, that the whole vowing business was nothing but some kind of discipline to guide children during their younger days. Now grown-up men vow, and that for all eternity—men who should serve others voluntarily, out of love.

What now? Am I myself already free and no longer a monk? Do you think that you should be a Demas for me, and finally fix up this Micio with a Sostrata, in order to get even with me for having given you a wife, as they say?[42] But I shall be quite careful with you, that you don't succeed!

I am not saying anything about the sin against the Holy Spirit,[43] since you are more learned and filled with the Spirit than I am.[44]

---

[42] Reference to characters in the *Adelphi* of the Roman playwright Terence (2nd century B.C.). Demas persuaded Micio that he should marry Sostrata; see *O.C.D.*, p. 884. Melanchthon had been married since November, 1520; see p. 166, n. 5.

[43] Matt. 12:31-32.

[44] This must be a reply to questions asked by Melanchthon in a not extant letter, perhaps the one mentioned in note 5. The problem concerning the sin against the Holy Spirit was raised by John Bugenhagen in an open letter which was published in the fall of 1521; see *WA*, Br 2, 387, n. 32.

John Bugenhagen of Pomerania (1485-1558) matriculated in the Theological Faculty of Wittenberg University in 1521; he was graduated as Doctor of Theology in 1533 and became a professor of theology at Wittenberg in 1535. In 1523 he was appointed the pastor of the city church, a position he held to the end of his life, in spite of many calls to high positions in other territories. Bugenhagen's deep feeling for the pastoral and episcopal office and his talents for organizing the work of the church made him one of the truly great men of the Reformation, though he and his writings are unfortunately little known. He was responsible for creating the superintendent's office, which was supposed to oversee doctrine and discipline within the congregations. He guided the organization of the church of the Reformation in many northern German territorial states and in the kingdom of Denmark, and he dedicated his efforts to establishing many schools and universities. Bugenhagen, who was Luther's pastor, had a very close friendship with him. He assisted in the translation of the Bible and translated Luther's German Bible into a Low German dialect. He gave Luther pastoral counsel in the many spiritual distresses the Reformer had to endure. See *O.D.C.C.*, p. 205.

The [problem of the] "burning,"[45] however, which you do not want to have minimized,[46] I in the meantime have reduced to even less importance,[47] because I think it is only the fire of a burning desire. The Apostle [Paul] calls the pollutions uncleanness, as you know.[43] And in II [Cor. 11:29] he says, "Who is made to fall and I do not burn?" It will be difficult for you to prove any worse burning than this.

In the meantime I shall ponder the sin of blasphemy, for this is the only sin Christ considers to be against the Holy Spirit and unforgivable.[49] It seems to me that neither Peter nor Paul ever committed this sin.[50] Up to now I think—with the same simplicity with which you yourself argue—that there is some kind of sin which is unforgivable compared with others. John calls it "sin unto death,"[51] and Paul, in Titus 3 [:10-11, Vulgate], calls it "heresy."

Farewell for now, and pray for me. I wish you would be burdened ten times as much, so little sympathy do I have for you. You are so often admonished not to load yourself down with so many burdens.[52] Yet you refuse to listen and despise all well-meant admonitions. The time will come, and then it will be too late, when you will condemn this your stupid zeal, with which you are eager to carry everything alone, as if you were made of iron or stone.

From the wilderness,[53] September 9, 1521

MARTIN LUTHER

---

[45] I Cor. 7:9.

[46] Apparently also in the (not extant) letter mentioned in note 5, in reply to Luther's statements in his letter of August 1; see p. 279.

[47] See p. 279 f.

[48] Gal. 5:19; Eph. 4:19; see p. 293, n. 11.

[49] See notes 43, 44.

[50] I.e., not even Peter by denying Christ, or Paul by persecuting the Christians.

[51] I John 5:16.

[52] For similar statements, see p. 119, n. 10.

[53] See p. 263, n. 36.

96

To George Spalatin[1]
Wartburg, September 9, 1521

Luther expresses his reaction to certain statements made by Erasmus and Capito, and he criticizes them both for what he thinks is cowardice on their part. He is delighted that Wittenberg prospers in spite of his absence. Concerned for the proclamation of God's Word in Wittenberg, however, he urges Spalatin to intervene with the city council so that Melanchthon may be called as a lay preacher.

On George Spalatin, see pp. 8 f.

Text in Latin: WA, Br 2, 387-389; translation based on S-J 2, 56-59.

Jesus

Greetings. Neither Capito's[2] nor Erasmus'[3] opinion moves me in the least.[4] They are only doing what I have suspected. Indeed

[1] The addressee is missing in the autograph. Since the earliest printed editions it has generally been assumed that the letter was addressed to Spalatin. That this assumption is quite correct can be seen from the contents, especially from the statement explained in note 11.

[2] Wolfgang Fabricius Capito (1478-1541) studied medicine, law, and theology in Freiburg/Breisgau, where he also taught theology. From 1515 to 1520 he was a preacher in the town of Basel and a close friend of Erasmus of Rotterdam. In 1520 he was appointed cathedral preacher in Mainz and became chancellor to Archbishop Albrecht (see pp. 44 f.), a position in which he tried hard to mediate between Luther and Albrecht. Due to the basic influence of Humanism, Capito was broad-minded in his attitude toward the theological issues existing between Luther and Rome. As a result he could not understand Luther, and they disagreed violently; see pp. 372 ff. In 1523 Capito was appointed provost of the St. Thomas Chapter in Strassburg. Here he committed himself wholeheartedly to the Reformation. Theologically he represented the Reformed branch of the Reformation. This became especially obvious during the eucharistic controversy. Compared with Bucer, who was the theological leader of Strassburg, Capito was of little importance, although he was superintendent of Strassburg until his death. See *O.D.C.C.*, p. 234.

[3] Erasmus of Rotterdam; see pp. 116 f.

[4] The following letters and events apparently are the background of this statement: the "opinion of Capito" refers to a (not extant) letter written by Capito to Spalatin sometime in the summer of 1521 in an attempt to bring about a truce between Luther and the Archbishop of Mainz (in whose service Capito was at that time). In this letter Capito must have voiced his unhappi-

I have been afraid that someday I should have some trouble with one or the other of them.[5] For I saw that Erasmus was far from the knowledge of grace,[6] since in all his writings he is not concerned for the cross but for peace. He thinks that everything should be discussed and handled in a civil manner and with a certain benevolent kindliness. But Behemoth[7] pays no attention and nothing improves by this. I remember when [Erasmus] said in his preface to the New Testament, [and he must have been thinking] of himself, "The Christian easily despises glory."[8] I thought in my heart: Erasmus, I am afraid you deceive yourself. It is a great thing to despise glory. But his way of despising glory was to think lightly of it, not to bear the contempt that others put upon him. Despising glory, however, is nothing if it is only in words; it is even less than nothing if only in thought. The kingdom of God consists in power, says Paul.[9] Therefore up to now I have not dared to boast about anything and am unable to do so, except about the Word of truth which the Lord has given to me. Their[10] writings accomplish nothing because they refrain from chiding, biting, and giving offense. For when the popes [and bishops] are admonished in a civil manner they

---

ness with some of Luther's statements, and perhaps even criticized Luther's sharp attacks on the Roman hierarchy. Spalatin must have shown this letter to Melanchthon, who in turn wrote to Capito that if he (Capito) had something to criticize in Luther's teachings, he should discuss it with him, Melanchthon; see *C.R.* 1, 456. Luther must have heard of Capito's letter. The "opinion of Erasmus" apparently refers to two letters of Erasmus: one to George Spalatin (July 6, 1520; Allen 4, 1119), the second to Louis Ber, a professor of theology at the University of Basel (May 14, 1521; Allen 4, 1203); perhaps a third letter should be added, namely one to William Warham, the archbishop of Canterbury (August 23, 1521; Allen 4, 1228). These letters could have been available to Luther—or his friends—either directly (as in the case of Allen 4, 1119) or indirectly, through circulation as manuscript copies or as unauthorized prints (as in the case of Allen 4, 1203, 1228); see Allen 5, 1262; *WA*, Br 2, 389, n. 1. In these letters Erasmus openly disapproved of Luther's thought and conduct.

[5] See p. 185.

[6] See pp. 40, 53.

[7] Job 40:15 ff. Luther follows Jerome in understanding Behemoth as "devil"; see also *WA*, DB 3, 513.

[8] According to *WA*, Br 2, 398, n. 4, this statement cannot be located; however in the letter of dedication of the Greek edition of the New Testament (see p. 116), there are certain phrases from which such a statement could be deduced; see Allen 2, 373.

[9] I Cor. 4:20.

[10] Capito's and Erasmus'.

think it is flattering and keep on as if they possessed the right to remain uncorrected and incorrigible, content that they are feared and that no one dares to reproach them. These are the kind of people pictured in your Plutarch's little book on flattery.[11] But Jeremiah speaks more gravely and dreadfully of them: "Cursed is he who does the work of the Lord deceitfully."[12] Here the Prophet speaks of the work of the sword against God's enemies. I, too, am very afraid, and my conscience troubles me because I yielded in Worms[13] to your advice and that of [our] friends, held my spirit in check, and did not show myself as an Elijah to those idols.[14] They would hear other things, if I would come before them again. But enough of this.

Duke John the Elder[15] at last knows where I am; so far he has not known. My host[16] has revealed it to him confidentially. But [the Duke] should keep it quiet. I am fine here, but I am growing sluggish and languid and cold in spirit, and am miserable.[17] Today, on the sixth day, I had elimination with such difficulty that I almost passed out. Now I sit aching as if in labor confinement, wounded and sore, and shall have no—or little—rest this night. Thanks be to Christ who has not left me without any relic of the holy cross.[18] I would have been healed from all soreness if the elimination had moved more easily. But whatever heals in four days is wounded again by elimination.[19] I write this not for sympathy but that you may congratulate me, praying[20] that I may be worthy to become fervent in the Spirit.

Now is the time to pray against Satan with all our strength; he is threatening Germany with some fatal tragedy. And in spite of my fear that the Lord will allow him to bring it about,

---

11 Spalatin had translated into German Plutarch's (Greek biographer and philosopher; A.D. 46?-120?) book on *How to Distinguish Between a Flatterer and a Friend;* it was published in 1520; on Plutarch, see *O.C.D.*, pp. 706 f.

12 Jer. 48:10 (Vulgate).

13 I.e., at the diet of 1521; see pp. 201 f., 215.

14 I Kings 18:17 ff.; perhaps also 21:17 ff.

15 Duke John; see p. 269, n. 8; see also p. 273, n. 8.

16 The castellan of the Wartburg, Hans von Berlepsch; see p. 255, n. 15.

17 See p. 28, n. 10.

18 For a similar statement, see p. 387.

19 See p. 217, n. 15; p. 257, n. 4.

20 The text does not make it clear who the subject of "praying" is, Luther or Spalatin; this editor thinks Spalatin is the subject.

until now I have been sleepy and lazy, both in praying and resisting [Satan], so that I am angry at myself, and am a burden to myself. Perhaps it is because I am alone and you are not helping me.[21] I beg you, let us pray and watch that we do not enter into temptation.[22] I have nothing else to write just now. You people in Wittenberg know everything about everyone.

I rejoice that Wittenberg's prestige is increasing, especially that it grows while I am absent, so that the wicked man sees it and grumbles, and his desire perishes.[23] May Christ complete that which he has begun!

I really wish Philip[24] would also preach[25] to the people somewhere in the city on festival days after dinner to provide a substitute for the drinking and gambling.[26] This could become a custom which would introduce freedom[27] and restore the form and manners of the early church.[28] For if we have broken all laws of men and cast off their yokes, what difference would it make to us that Philip is not anointed or tonsured[29] but married?[30] Nevertheless he is truly a priest and actually does the work of a priest, unless it is not the office of a priest to teach the Word of God. In that case Christ himself would not be a priest, for he taught now in synagogues, then in ships, now at the shoreline, then in the mountains. In a word, [Christ] was always and everywhere all things to all people at all times. Since, therefore, Philip is called by God and performs the ministry of the Word, as no one can deny, what difference does it make that he is not called by those tyrants—who are bishops not of churches but of

---

21 For similar statements, see pp. 216, 256, 257, 267, 319, 323 f.

22 Matt. 26:41.

23 Ps. 112:10.

24 Philip Melanchthon; see p. 77, n. 3.

25 On Luther's concern that Wittenberg be well supplied with preachers, see p. 221, n. 8; see also p. 236, n. 61; p. 311.

26 In the autograph the phrase beginning "to provide" is written in the margin.

27 I.e., freedom for the laity to preach and freedom from the domination of the clergy; this is a reference to the priesthood of all believers.

28 When the clergy held no position of spiritual monopoly.

29 I.e., ordained to the priesthood by a bishop. Anointment and tonsure were parts of the ordination ceremony prescribed by Canon Law; see *O.D.C.C.*, pp. 58, 1366 f.

30 Melanchthon had been married since November, 1520; see p. 166, n. 5.

horses[31] and courtiers. But I know that man's[32] mind. He will not yield to my persuasions. Therefore he has to be called and driven [to preaching] by the order and pressure of the whole congregation. For if the congregation demands and requests it, he ought not and cannot say no. Were I present, I would by all means work on the city council and the people so that they would ask Philip to lecture to them privately in German on the Gospels as he has begun to lecture in Latin, so that little by little he would become a German[-speaking] bishop, as he has already become a Latin[-speaking] bishop. I wish you would do what you can to bring this about, because what the people need above all things is the Word of God. Since he is incomparably rich in the Word, you can see that it is our duty to call him and not let the Word be cheated of its fruit; in addition the conscience urges this and God requires it. You will be able to have this passed by the city council quite easily with the help of Lucas[33] and Christian.[34] May Christ compensate for my absence and silence with Melanchthon's preaching and voice, to the confusion of Satan and his apostles. Origen[35] taught women privately. Why should Melanchthon not undertake something similar, when he can and ought to do it? And this especially since the people are thirsty and in need of such a thing. Please don't be moved too easily by his excuses! He will hide behind the most beautiful fig leaves,[36] as is becoming to him. For he ought not to seek such a duty, but he must be urged and called by the congregation, even begged to serve and to do not what is useful only for himself but rather what is profitable for many. I beg you, work on this most diligently, before all other things. Consult with friends who will help you to push this.[37]

[31] Due to the interweaving of state and church in the medieval and sixteenth century society, most bishops were also secular sovereigns; if not they at least held great secular wealth. Consequently they spent more time on secular projects, such as hunting, riding, and, as was the case in the High Middle Ages, even as warriors in combat.

[32] Melanchthon's.

[33] Lucas Cranach; see p. 201.

[34] Christian Düring; see p. 42, n. 8.

[35] Origen; see *O.D.C.C.*, pp. 991 ff.; *Patrology*, pp. 223 ff.

[36] An allusion to Gen. 3:7.

[37] Spalatin did intervene with the city council, which in turn requested that Melanchthon be appointed preacher at the city church; see *WA*, Br 2, 390, n. 24.

Farewell, and remember me before the Lord.
From the wilderness,[38] *September 9, 1521*

Yours,
MARTIN LUTHER

97

To Nicholas von Amsdorf
Wartburg, September 9, 1521

Luther is sending some theses on monastic vows. Announcing that he would send further material on this very important question (see Nos. 91, 92, 94, 95), he continues to elaborate on his disagreement with Karlstadt concerning the interpretation of celibacy. Since the people of Wittenberg were not to expect his return, Luther suggests that they call Melanchthon to preach and to teach.

On Nicholas von Amsdorf, see p. 218.

Text in Latin: WA, Br 2, 390-391.

To Nicholas Amsdorf, Licentiate of Theology [1] and a canon at Wittenberg

Jesus

I am enclosing theses on the vows.[2] Although there is nothing new among them for which you people might be looking, still they will be new and shocking to [our] enemies if they are published. Philip [3] relies on the argument that a vow should be nullified because of the impossibility of keeping it. I did not deal with this point; and thus far I do not believe that this point can be handled in a way that consciences could rely on it confidently and surely; and it is this for which we are looking.[4]

---

38 See p. 263, n. 36.
1 On this degree, see p. 264, n. 3.
2 *Themata de votis;* see p. 302, n. 36; perhaps a copy.
3 Philip Melanchthon; see p. 77, n. 3; p. 297.
4 See pp. 277 ff., 297 ff., 310 f., 321, 331 ff., 337 f., 354, 357 ff.

Here I have used material which is reliable and sufficient to assure consciences and liberate them from their vows. [That is, I have discussed the issue of whether or not a vow was made] in a godly or an ungodly way. I shall send other [theses][5] in which the question of a legitimate and pious vow is discussed in greater detail, that is, under what circumstances vows are to be kept. But this is also argued on the same basis, [namely, whether or not a vow was made] in a godly or an ungodly way.

I am grieved because of Karlstadt.[6] He can easily be refuted,[7] but an occasion would [thereby] be given to our enemies to boast over our internal disagreement; this would be a great stumbling block for the weak.

I have written to Spalatin that he should push the idea of our Philip lecturing to the people in German on the Gospels; Philip should do it on festival days and in some place like a lecture hall.[8] Thus it would gradually come about that [in Wittenberg] the gospel would be preached in the old manner.[9] You have a fitting answer if someone wants to object that a layman should not preach the gospel in a corner; answer that [Melanchthon] is doing it under the auspices of the University,[10] and ex officio. Who could

---

[5] Luther had changed his original plan. Instead of writing "very short explanations" of the *Themata de votis* (see note 2), as he had promised Melanchthon on September 9 (see p. 302), he now promises to send a second set of theses on monastic vows (based, however, on the *Themata*). This second series was entitled: *An liceat perpetuum vovere votum* (*Whether It Is Permitted to Take a Vow Intended to be Permanently Binding*). *WA* 8, 330 ff. It was published along with the *Themata* as Part II of: *Iudicium Martini Lutheri de votis* (*Martin Luther's Opinion on Vows*) (Wittenberg: M. Lotther, October, 1521). *WA* 8, 323 ff.

[6] Andrew Karlstadt; see p. 79, n. 12. Luther is expressing a concern similar to that expressed in his August 15 letter to Spalatin; see pp. 293 f.

[7] I.e., Luther, realizing the weakness of Karlstadt's argument, is convinced that he and others could show where Karlstadt was wrong and thus put an end to Karlstadt's agitation for abandoning monastic vows. Yet Luther also realizes that this might stir up trouble and even strife among the people of Wittenberg. The Wittenberg disturbances of 1521/22 (see p. 386, n. 1) and the clash between Luther and Karlstadt cast their shadows.

[8] See pp. 308 f. Luther apparently did not think that Melanchthon should preach in the city church but rather in a lecture hall or elsewhere.

[9] I.e., as was customary in the apostolic church, when the exposition of God's Word was not restricted to the actual worship service, and the right to preach was not restricted to "ordained" clergy, an institution of the second century.

[10] Luther wrote *loco studii*, i.e., on behalf of the University or in place of the University.

prohibit him from speaking in German, and common men and women from listening to him? Who could object if in some way the whole town listened to his lectures—if the town understood Latin, or if he lectured in German?

I hope you will not ignore this advice, especially since there is no hope of my returning to you. Who knows what God intends to accomplish through stupid me?

Farewell and pray for me. Thank you for the song.[11]

September 9, 1521

Yours,
MARTIN LUTHER, D.

98

To George Spalatin
Wartburg, September 17, 1521

During a visit to the Wartburg, Duke John of Saxony (see p. 269, n. 8) requested that Luther write an exposition of the Gospel concerning the ten lepers (Luke 17:11 ff., especially vs. 14). Since the Franciscans at Weimar had tried to prove auricular confession on the basis of Luke 17:14, the Duke was especially interested in Luther's opinion on this passage. In this letter Luther sends Spalatin the exposition to be forwarded to the Duke and makes suggestions concerning the future treatment of the manuscript. He briefly mentions a satire against the Faculty of the Sorbonne and comments on some political developments of which he has heard.

On George Spalatin, see pp. 8 f.

Text in Latin: WA, Br 2, 391-392.

Master George Spalatin: *Personal*

---

[11] *Cantilena,* i.e., "song," "old song," "old story," "gossip." Whatever Luther meant could not be identified.

Jesus

Greetings. Duke John [1] was confronted with the passage in Luke about the ten lepers.[2] He was told that because they were sent by the Lord to the priests, one has to believe in confession.[3] When he was here,[4] he requested through my host [5] that I explain this passage so that he would have something to answer to those gray Pharisees and hypocrites.[6] They want to anticipate my little book *On Confession* [7] and try to win over the Duke beforehand and alienate him from us through this passage, for they have heard that the treatise *On Confession* is in the press. Therefore I have arranged to send this [exposition] to you, so that you may have it carefully copied by someone who can write well, for you have a crowd of secretaries available who have nothing to do, and [anything in] my handwriting must be kept secret. Therefore please return this manuscript to me, since I have no other copy, and

---

1 Duke John of Saxony; see p. 269, n. 8.

2 Luke 17:11 ff.

3 Jesus' command that the lepers go to the priest and show themselves as having been cleansed was used in traditional theology (Peter Lombard, Gabriel Biel) and popular religious instruction (sermon literature) to prove the necessity of private or auricular confession and, even more, to demonstrate that Christ himself had instituted confession; for documentation, see *WA* 8, 152, n. 1; 336 f. For Luther's stand on this issue, see *WA* 6, 546 ff.; *LW* 36, 86 f., and the work mentioned in note 9.

4 This visit of Duke John to the Wartburg could not be verified. It must have taken place shortly before September 9, for on that day Luther wrote to Spalatin that the castellan of the Wartburg had told Duke John of his (Luther's) presence at the Wartburg; see p. 307. Since the Duke did not see Luther, for reasons unknown to us, his request for the exposition of the Gospel pericope of the ten lepers came to Luther through the castellan.

5 The castellan of the Wartburg, Hans von Berlepsch; see p. 255, n. 15.

6 I.e., the Franciscans, who at that time wore gray cowls, differing from the brown cowls worn at present; see *O.D.C.C.*, pp. 590, 523 f. In Weimar, one of the residences of the Electoral Saxon court, the Franciscans had the privilege of serving the people as confessors. (James Vogt, who was the Elector's father confessor, was a Franciscan; see p. 33, n. 5.) Disturbed by the consequences Luther's little book *On Confession* (see p. 246, n. 10) might have, they apparently petitioned the Electoral court to stop its printing. In personal interviews with the Duke, they must have based their arguments on Luke 17:14. On August 15 the Franciscans of Weimar informed Elector Frederick that they had the Pope's specific order to oppose Luther's heresies; they asked whether or not the Elector would support them in this task. See O. Clemen (ed.), *Supplementa Melanchthoniana*, 6, I, 154.

7 See p. 246, n. 10.

since it could not be given to anyone else for copying, lest I be betrayed. Although I have treated this passage in the little book on confession,[8] yet I had such a low opinion [of the arguments of our opponents] that a careful refutation seemed unnecessary to me. I did not believe that anyone could be so stupid that he would seriously want to prove confession from this passage. And so I have now treated this passage carefully and in detail, and I have refuted their nonsense. If you think it should be printed,[9] then furnish it with the preface[10] I am including and dedicate it in my name to whomever you want, either Haugold von Einsiedel,[11] or to someone else, as you see fit[12]—only by no means to the Duke; you can see the reason for this. The main reason why I would allow it to be printed is the support it can give to the treatise *On Confession,* and also because it contains almost a summary of Christian faith and fully depicts a pious life, so that the Germans would receive a foretaste of the *Postil.*[13] I would have added what Philip[14] misses in the treatise [*On Confession*], but I cannot understand what he means. If you do not think it should be printed, then destroy the preface and hand the rest over to Duke John. Please return the manuscript to me.

I believe you have heard how the Parisians have mocked

---

[8] See *WA* 8, 152.

[9] This exposition was published as *Evangelium von den zehn Aussätzigen* (*The Gospel Concerning the Ten Lepers*) (Wittenberg: M. Lotther, 1521). *WA* 8, 344 ff.

[10] See *WA* 8, 340 ff.

[11] Haugold von Einsiedel studied philosophy, theology, and canon and secular law at the University of Leipzig in 1476/77. Dissatisfied with the instruction he received, he left Leipzig and matriculated in the University of Ingolstadt in 1484, where he was tutored by the famous Humanist and jurist John Riedner. Haugold's ambition to round out his Humanistic education through a trip to Italy did not materialize due to his father's insistence that he settle down. After 1489 he held various ecclesiastical benefices. Having obtained papal dispensation from celibacy, Haugold married and entered the full-time administrative service of Electoral Saxony. Apparently he died in the late summer of 1522. See *ARG* 8 (1911), 1 ff.

[12] Spalatin dedicated this exposition to three Electoral Saxon officials who were stout supporters of Luther's cause: Haugold von Einsiedel (see note 11), Hans von Dolzig, the master of the court and marshal of Saxony (see *ARG* 7 [1910], 404 ff.), and Berhard von Hirschfeld (see p. 33, n. 2).

[13] See pp. 237 ff.

[14] Philip Melanchthon; see p. 77, n. 3. What Melanchthon had in mind could not be determined; see also p. 297.

their own sophists on my account.[15] This priesthood of Baal and Peor,[16] which is condemned by the Lord through the voice of Paul,[17] is beginning to be despised. God be praised.

The plans of the Pope and Emperor are not yet fully developed.[18] God leads both as they deserve, and where they should be led. In the meantime, however, they don't care for this until the iniquity of the Amorites is completed.[19] I rejoice and wish the Emperor this good fortune,[20] but only because of God's hidden plans.

Farewell and pray for me.

September 17, 1521

MARTIN LUTHER
Augustinian

99

To George Spalatin
Wartburg, October 7, 1521

Acknowledging a shipment from Spalatin, Luther reports that he is once again in good health. He comments briefly on some correspondence matters and urges that Melanchthon leave Wittenberg, should the plague break out there. He tells Spalatin that he will

15 Luther is referring to a satire supposedly written by the University of Paris as a rebuttal to Melanchthon's *Defense* (see p. 258, n. 7); for bibliographical information, see *WA* 8, 264. The real author, who is unknown, must have been among Luther's followers. He ridiculed the Sorbonne Faculty and its proceedings against Luther by taking Melanchthon's *Defense* apart in a way similar to the way the Sorbonne had dealt with Luther, but let the Parisians state that they did this without biblical basis, and so on. According to Luther's statement above, he must not have been aware that this satire had originated among his followers, but believed that it originated among the Parisians themselves.

16 Num. 25:3; Ps. 106:28; Hos. 9:10.

17 It is not possible to establish the identity of the scriptural reference Luther had in mind.

18 Luther is probably referring to the alliance between Pope Leo X (see p. 100) and Charles V (see pp. 175 f.) of May 29, 1521, which was intended to guarantee a united front between the Emperor and the Pope against France.

19 Gen. 15:16.

20 I.e., the alliance with the Pope, whereby the Emperor hoped to gain the Pope's support, not realizing the Pope's true motives.

not be restrained from attacking the Archbishop of Mainz for the sale of indulgences at Halle. In a postscript Luther voices his opinion of private mass.

On George Spalatin, see pp. 8 f.

Text in Latin: WA, Br 2, 395.

To my friend George Spalatin, a servant of Christ

Jesus

Greetings. Thanks for your last shipment.[1] At last my behind and my bowels have reconciled themselves to me.[2] Therefore I need no further medication,[3] and I am again completely healthy as before. Thanks be to God!

I could not send a letter to Gerbel[4] with this messenger, since he was in such a great hurry, also not to Taubenheim.[5] I had to absorb your material and pour out this letter in one and the same hour. I shall write in greater detail at another time. I implore you not to let Philip[6] stay in Wittenberg if the plague breaks out there.[7] That head must be preserved, so that the Word, which the Lord has entrusted to him for the salvation of souls, may not perish.[8]

I shall not let myself be restrained from privately and publicly attacking the idol at Mainz[9] with regard to his "brothel" at Halle.[10] Farewell in the greatest hurry.

October 7, 1521 MARTIN LUTHER

[1] This "shipment" could not be verified. Perhaps Gerbel's letter was enclosed; see below and p. 318, n. 2. Perhaps Spalatin sent Luther some communication about Capito's visit; see note 10.

[2] See p. 217, n. 15.

[3] See p. 268.

[4] Nicholas Gerbel; see pp. 317 f.

[5] John von Taubenheim; see p. 163, n. 3.

[6] Philip Melanchthon; see p. 77, n. 3.

[7] In the fall and early winter of 1521 the plague broke out in Wittenberg, so that on November 20 Elector Frederick (see pp. 49 f.) ordered the evacuation of the University; see *WA*, Br 2, 395, n. 2.

[8] For a similar statement, see p. 119.

[9] I.e., Cardinal Albrecht, archbishop of Mainz; see pp. 44 f.

[10] The Archbishop of Mainz, in a desperate attempt to bolster his finances, exhibited the relics kept in a church in Halle in mid-September, 1521, and invited the people to obtain the rich indulgences promised to those who visited the exhibition. Soon it became known that Luther would make a

There is a priest in the castle here who daily celebrates mass with great idolatry, I am afraid, if nothing worse.[11] If only he and all such private mass[12] celebrants were at least restricted, if [their office] can't be completely abolished immediately. It is a crime for the mass to be celebrated privately, since it is called *Synaxis*[13] and communion. The order of Christ and Paul[14] commands that it should be celebrated often in public and with a congregation gathered for the proclamation of the Word, that is, in remembrance of [Christ]. O Antichrist![15]

100

To Nicholas Gerbel
Wartburg, November 1, 1521

This is a long overdue letter in which Luther expresses his appreciation not only for Gerbel's friendship but also for his interest in Luther's work. Replying to Gerbel's inquiry about his literary work, Luther gives a detailed report on his writings.

Nicholas Gerbel of Pforzheim (1485?-1560) studied theology at the University of Cologne and at the Dominican college of the University of Tübingen. In October, 1514, he was graduated by

public protest. At the end of September the Archbishop sent Wolfgang Capito (see p. 305, n. 2) to Luther's friends in Wittenberg, to Spalatin, and to Elector Frederick (see pp. 49 f.) to ask their help in preventing Luther's attack. Capito had already established contact with Spalatin through an earlier letter; see p. 305, n. 4. Although while in Saxony Capito must have received assurance that there would be an attempt to stop Luther, he was not too satisfied with his visit, as can be seen from his October 14 letter to Erasmus of Rotterdam; see Allen 4, 1241. Luther must have heard of this visit; perhaps Spalatin had written about it (see note 1).

[11] This postscript is not a part of the autograph but is found on a separate sheet of paper and was written with a different pen. Although the *WA*, Br editor concedes the possibility that this postscript could belong to another letter written from the Wartburg, he nevertheless added it to this letter.

[12] See p. 281, n. 26.

[13] Greek word for "assembly," which was, especially in the Greek-speaking Early Church of the East, the traditional term for the Eucharist; see *O.D.C.C.*, p. 1314.

[14] Luke 22:14 ff. and parallels; I Cor. 11:26 ff.

[15] See p. 114, n. 16.

the University of Bologna as a Doctor of Canon Law. Although he was drenched in traditional Scholasticism, he became an admirer of Reuchlin (whom he supported against the University of Cologne; see p. 10, n. 11) and of Erasmus (whom he visited in Basel in the fall of 1516 for the purpose of assisting in correcting the proofs of the Greek text of the New Testament; see p. 23). In 1515 Gerbel came to Strassburg and worked as critic, corrector, and editor for the Schürer publishing house. He also practiced law and was a legal consultant to the bishop, the cathedral chapter, and the city council. It is not clear when his friendship with Luther began, but as early as May, 1521, he had already sent several letters to Luther. For a while Gerbel acted as a liaison man between Luther and the clergy and the city council of Strassburg, although he stayed mainly in the background. In the eucharistic controversy between Luther and Zwingli, Gerbel openly supported Luther; this was exceptional if one realizes that Strassburg was almost completely under Zwingli's influence, at least at the beginning of the controversy. He spent his later years studying history and geography.

Text in Latin: WA, Br 2, 396-398.

To Nicholas Gerbel, distinguished by education and Christian piety, a lawyer, and my most faithful friend in Christ

Jesus

Greetings in Christ. Your letter, my kindest Gerbel, which you wrote to me on the vigil of Pentecost,[1] reached me finally on St. Michael's Day,[2] and I write this letter to you today, on All Saints' Day. For goodness' sake,[3] when will it reach you? Maybe at another Pentecost, or maybe not at all![4] Thus you see the reason

[1] On the term "vigil," see p. 76, n. 18. Gerbel's letter was dated May 18; see *WA*, Br 2, No. 411.

[2] September 29. Perhaps Spalatin had forwarded Gerbel's letter in the "shipment" Luther acknowledged on October 7; see p. 316.

[3] Some printed editions have *nescio*, i.e., "I don't know."

[4] Luther wrote *Calendas Graecas*, i.e., "to the Greek Calends." In the Roman calendar, the Calends is the first day of the month. However in the Roman calendar there was no month by the name of "Greek"; and the Greek calendar did not use the term "Calends" to designate a specific day. Consequently the day "Greek Calends" does not exist. On the term

for my silence; it is evident that you may ascribe my silence to fate, that is, to the hidden will of God.

Yet I believe that in the meantime you found out from other people about the state of my affairs, which you ask about[5] with such great anxiety and friendship. I have withdrawn from the public and thus obeyed the advice of friends.[6] I have done this against my will, and I am uncertain whether with this action I have done something which is pleasing to God. I certainly thought I should expose my neck to the public fury;[7] but [my friends] were of another opinion.[8] Upon their suggestion, armed horsemen captured me along the way in a fake attack, and placed me in a safe spot where I am now treated in the kindest way.[9]

But you may believe me, in this leisurely solitude I am exposed to a thousand devils.[10] It is so much easier to fight the devil incarnate—that is, people—than the spirits of iniquity in heavenly places.[11] Often I fall, but the right hand of the Most High raises me again. Therefore I yearn again and again for companionship.[12] But I do not want to go back unless the Lord has called me back.

It is not safe for me[13] to send my little books to you, but I have written on this matter to Spalatin, asking him to take care of it.[14] In the meantime a little book on the Antichrist,[15] *Against Catharinus*, has come off the press,[16] one *Against Latomus* at

---

"*Calendae Graecae*" and the explanation drawn from passages of classical authors recorded in Erasmus' *Adagia*, see Clericus 2, 214, B f.

[5] In his letter of May 18; see note 1.

[6] See pp. 201, 215, 307.

[7] See pp. 125, 201, 215, 221, 228, 232, 249.

[8] See p. 201, n. 3.

[9] See pp. 255, 294, 357.

[10] See p. 28, n. 10.

[11] Eph. 6:12.

[12] Luther used a word which can also mean "life in public"; if one is aware of his statements concerning his life in public, however (see p. 119, n. 7; p. 308, n. 21; pp. 232, 267), then it is obvious that Luther meant companionship here.

[13] The translation is based on a text variation offered by some printed editions of this letter.

[14] See p. 323.

[15] See p. 114, n. 16.

[16] See p. 291, n. 10.

Louvain,[17] one in German *On Confession*,[18] also the 67th Psalm explained in German,[19] the [*Magnificat*] of Mary explained in German,[20] and the 36th Psalm explained as comfort for the congregation in Wittenberg.[21] Philip[22] has published a *Defense* in my behalf against the Parisians, to which I have added a German preface. It is already out; [and that takes care of that].[23] He also has the theological *Loci*[24] in the press, a book worthy of Philip. My German exposition of the Epistles and the Gospels for each Sunday of the church year[25] is being printed. I have also completed a public rebuke of the Cardinal of Mainz, because he has again erected the idol of indulgences, [and this time] at Halle.[26] The explanation of the Gospel concerning the ten lepers is also ready.[27] All this is in German. I am born for my Germans, whom I want to serve.[28] I am eager to launch a public attack against the universities, but I have not yet made definite plans.[29] I have made up my mind not to write a commentary on the Gospel of St. Matthew.[30] In Wittenberg, however, I had begun to preach to the people from the pulpit on both Testaments, starting at the beginning of each; in Genesis I had progressed to chapter 32, in

---

17 See p. 229, n. 3; in some of the printed editions of this letter, this work is not mentioned.
18 See p. 246, n. 10.
19 See p. 229, n. 5.
20 See p. 225, n. 17; p. 254, n. 4.
21 See p. 252, n. 10.
22 Philip Melanchthon; see p. 77, n. 3.
23 See p. 258, n. 7. Luther apparently has abandoned the idea of writing against the Sorbonne, which he had considered in his August 3 letter to Melanchthon (see p. 289, n. 37); see also note 29.
24 See p. 232, n. 21.
25 See pp. 237 ff.
26 Luther is referring to his *Against the Idol at Halle;* for details, see p. 316, n. 10; pp. 344 ff.
27 See p. 314, n. 9.
28 About a month later Luther decided to translate the Bible; see *WA*, DB 6, XL.
29 What Luther meant here is not clear. Having abandoned his idea of writing against the Sorbonne (see note 23), Luther was perhaps thinking of a general rebuttal of the universities that had condemned him.
30 This was written in reply to Gerbel's May 18 letter (see note 1), in which he expressed his wish that Luther would complete a commentary on the Gospel of St. Matthew. Somehow Gerbel was of the opinion that in the spring of 1521 Luther had been working on such a commentary; see *WA*, Br 2, 343.

the Gospels to the voice of John the Baptist.[31] There my voice was silenced.[32] Now you know everything about which you asked.

I received your previous letter, which you sent to me at Worms, only after a long time in this solitude.[33] I have been extremely pleased with the bride, and also with the bridesman who has adorned her for me and presented her to me. She has borne to me the children I mentioned above.[34] You will judge whether the offspring are similar to the mother.[35] She[36] is still fertile and highly pregnant. Christ willing, she will give birth to a son[37] who will destroy the papists, sophists, monks,[38] and Herodians with a rod of iron.[39] For Philip and I have a powerful conspiracy concerning the vows of monks and priests; they have to be abolished and made void.[40] Oh, that blasphemous Antichrist and his armor! How Satan has devastated all the mysteries of Christian piety through him!

Please greet your wife; may she love you and in turn be loved by you. You lucky man, that you have by an honorable marriage conquered that unclean celibacy which is reprehensible[41] because

---

[31] For these sermons on Genesis and Matthew, see *WA* 9, 320 ff. Perhaps it can be assumed that the *Shorter Postil*, which Luther asked Spalatin for on June 10 (see p. 237), contained material for some of these sermons.

[32] Due to the trip to Worms (see p. 197), Luther had had to interrupt these sermons.

[33] Luther received this (not extant) letter from Gerbel about May 12; see p. 222.

[34] The "bride" was Gerbel's edition of the Greek text of the New Testament which Gerbel must have sent with the letter mentioned in note 33. The "bridesman" was Gerbel, who gave away this "bride" to Luther. On Gerbel's edition, see *WA*, DB 6, XL. The "children" that came of Luther's "marriage" with the "bride" Gerbel had given to him are the writings listed above.

[35] I.e., the "bride" mentioned in note 34. The text is unclear here. One of the printed editions offers this text: *"an proles sit nostri similis,"* i.e., "whether the offspring are similar to us." Some editions instead offer this text: *"an proles sit matri similis,"* i.e., "whether the offspring are similar to the mother."

[36] I.e., the "bride" mentioned in note 34.

[37] I.e., the next "child" expected from Luther's union with the "bride," i.e., his study of the New Testament. On the basis of the following sentence it is clear that Luther is thinking of his attacks against monastic vows; see p. 302, nn. 36, 37; p. 311, n. 5; p. 331, n. 5.

[38] Luther wrote *religiosistae*; since *religiosi* is a common term for monks, it is adopted here.

[39] Ps. 2:9.

[40] See p. 328.

[41] One of the printed editions of this letter offers a text which has to be translated: "that you have recently [instead of "unclean"] conquered by an honorable marriage that celibacy which is reprehensible."

it causes either a constant burning or unclean pollutions. Suffer whatever this way of life brings, since it is instituted by God, and be grateful to him. That most miserable celibacy of young men and women daily presents such great horrors to me that even now nothing sounds worse to my ears than the words "nun," "monk," and "priest." I consider marriage to be a paradise, even if it has to endure greatest poverty.

Greet also the others whom you have mentioned to me, Otto Brunfels,[42] Caspar Uringer,[43] Luke Bathod,[44] and all who agree with you in the gospel and condemn the "worship of the angels," as the Apostle [Paul] says.[45] Farewell, stay very happy, and pray for me.

From my wilderness,[46] *1521*[47] MARTIN LUTHER

---

[42] Otto Brunfels of Mainz (1488?-1534) was a Carthusian who in the fall of 1521 left the Carthusian house outside Strassburg, due to difficulties which originated in his sharp criticism of the papal church. He stayed in Strassburg for a short time. He had in mind to go to Wittenberg (see *WA*, Br 2, 398, n. 30) but abandoned this plan to enter the service of von Hutten (see p. 163, n. 1). After a period of restless wandering he finally settled down in Strassburg in 1524, where he was made headmaster of the town school, and where he studied medicine and botany. He was deeply attached to von Hutten, whom he defended in a sharp attack on Erasmus. Although he had some connections with Melanchthon and Luther, he openly supported the Reformed branch of the Reformation. With Zwingli's help he was appointed physician in Bern, where he died in 1534. See *WA*, Br 2, 160, n. 3; Allen 5, 1405, Introduction.

[43] One of Gerbel's friends in Strassburg, of whom little is known; see *WA*, Br 2, 344, n. 5.

[44] A priest and teacher in Strassburg who later was in charge of charities there; see *WA*, Br 2, 344, n. 7. Apparently he had brought Gerbel's letter (see note 33) to Luther in Worms; since Luther had already left, he delivered the letter to Spalatin, who in turn forwarded it to the Wartburg. The letter finally reached Luther about May 12; see p. 222; *WA*, Br 2, 341.

[45] Col. 2:18.

[46] See p. 263, n. 36.

[47] One of the printed editions of this letter has 1522 as the date; the content of the letter, however, makes it obvious that this date is incorrect. On the date November 1, All Saints' Day, see p. 318.

101

To George Spalatin
Wartburg, November 1, 1521

Luther asks for Spalatin's help in handling some correspondence matters, and for Spalatin's prayers that Christ not desert him in his struggles against many demons.

On George Spalatin, see pp. 8 f.

Text in Latin: WA, Br 2, 399.

To my dearest friend, George Spalatin, a servant of Christ, and friend

Jesus

Greetings. Please take care, excellent Spalatin, that the [enclosed material][1] is forwarded to Philip.[2] Also I am finally sending my letter to Gerbel.[3] You see[4] that he would like to have my books;[5] in this we need your help and effort. I cannot do it myself. I have drawn up an index for him of all [the books that are completed];[6] if you would like to, you may take care of the rest.[7] Please forward the letter to Taubenheim, too.[8]

At the moment I have nothing else to write. So it is up to you, who are out in the world, to write to me—since I am now finally and really a monk.[9] Yet I am not actually a monk, because

[1] See pp. 345 ff.
[2] Philip Melanchthon; see p. 77, n. 3.
[3] See pp. 317 ff. The text does not make it clear whether Luther enclosed the letter for Spalatin to forward to Gerbel, or whether he sent it directly to Gerbel; see p. 328, n. 19.
[4] I.e., Spalatin could see this when he read the letter to Gerbel, if Luther had enclosed it. He also could have read it in Gerbel's May 18 letter (see p. 318, n. 1), in which Gerbel asked for Luther's books (see *WA*, Br 2, 343), and which apparently had reached the Wartburg via Spalatin; see p. 322, n. 44.
[5] See p. 319; *WA*, Br 2, 343.
[6] See pp. 319 f.
[7] I.e., ship the books to Gerbel; see p. 319.
[8] John von Taubenheim; see p. 316; p. 163, n. 3; this letter apparently is not extant.
[9] I.e., a hermit.

I have many evil and astute demons with me; they "amuse" me, as one says, but in a disturbing way.[10] Do pray that Christ does not desert me in the end.

Farewell.

November 1, 1521 MARTIN LUTHER

102

To the Augustinians in Wittenberg Wartburg, November, 1521

In this letter Luther is dedicating his November, 1521, book against the mass to the Augustinians in Wittenberg. It is available in a Latin and a German version, both prepared by Luther himself: De abroganda missa privata Martini Lutheri sententia (Martin Luther's Judgment on the Abrogation of the Private Mass) (Wittenberg: M. Lotther, January, 1522). WA 8, 411 ff. The Latin version of the letter of dedication was signed on November 1 (see WA 8, 412). The Latin version of the book was completed on November 11; see p. 327. The German edition is entitled: Vom Missbrauch der Messen (On the Abuse of the Mass) (Wittenberg: J. Grünenberg, January or February, 1522). WA 8, 482 ff. The German letter of dedication was signed on November 25.

In his early writings Luther concentrated primarily on the abuses of the Roman church in connection with the sacrament of penance. From 1519 on his attention was also directed to the Lord's Supper. He especially criticized the idea of the mass as a sacrifice (see WA 6, 365 ff.; LW 35, 94 ff.; WA 6, 512; LW 36, 35 f.) and the withholding of the cup from the laity; see pp. 143 f. At that time, however, Luther was not yet ready to draw any conclusions from his criticism and apply them to reorganizing the communion liturgy. He still hoped that this could be worked out in co-operation with the officials of the church, once a new understanding was agreed upon. After the Diet of Worms Luther realized that the hierarchy of the Roman church not only would

10 For similar statements, see p. 28, n. 10.

never co-operate but would attempt to suppress both his basic understanding of the Lord's Supper and the necessary liturgical reforms. During the days at the Wartburg his ideas ripened, and on August 1, 1521, he and Melanchthon discussed reorganizing the communion liturgy, favoring communion in "both kinds." At the same time he affirmed that he would never again celebrate a private mass; see pp. 280 f., 317. During his absence from Wittenberg some of Luther's colleagues (especially Andrew Karlstadt; see p. 277, n. 3) and some Augustinian friars under the leadership of Gabriel Zwilling (see p. 39, n. 3) took the initiative and refused to celebrate mass in the traditional way; consequently the prior of the monastery, Conrad Helt (see p. 125, n. 9), entirely stopped the celebration of the mass in the Augustinian monastery; see p. 281, n. 24. The liturgical reforms began with abolishing private mass (see p. 281, n. 26) and giving both elements to all communicants. This is the background of this letter.

See WA 8, 398 ff. For Luther's thoughts on liturgical problems, see Jaroslav Pelikan, "Luther and the Liturgy," More About Luther ("Martin Luther Lectures," Vol. II [Decorah, Iowa, 1958]), pp. 3 ff.; U. S. Leupold (trans.), V. Vajta's Luther on Worship (Philadelphia, 1958).

For the translation of the German version of the letter of dedication (WA 8, 482 f.) by F. C. Ahrens, see LW 36, 133-135.

103

To George Spalatin
Wartburg, November 11, 1521

Luther sharply criticizes Spalatin and the Elector for their timidity; affirming his determination to attack the Archbishop of Mainz for the part he had in the indulgence sale at Halle (see p. 316, n. 10), Luther orders Spalatin to turn over his (Luther's) manuscript of the attack against the Archbishop to Melanchthon. Luther also encloses his manuscript On the Abrogation of Private Mass (see p. 324), and refuses to write anything in the nature of a spiritual consolation for the Elector. He informs Spalatin of the work on the book on monastic vows (see p. 331, n. 5).

On George Spalatin, see pp. 8 f.

Text in Latin: WA, Br 2, 402-403; translation based on S-J 2, 63-65.

Mr. George Spalatin, disciple of Christ, my friend in the faith

Jesus

Greetings. I have hardly ever read a letter that displeased me more than your last one.[1] Not only did I put off my reply, but I had decided not to answer you at all. To begin with, I will not put up with your statement that the Sovereign[2] will not allow anything to be written against Mainz[3] or anything that could disturb the public peace. I would rather lose you, the Sovereign himself, and the whole world [than be quiet]. If I have resisted [the] creator, the pope, why should I yield to his creature?[4] Your idea about not disturbing the public peace is beautiful, but will you allow the eternal peace of God to be disturbed by the wicked and sacrilegious actions of that son of perdition?[5] Not so, Spalatin! Not so, Elector![6] For the sake of the sheep of Christ, we must resist that most atrocious wolf[7] with all our strength, as an example to others. Yes, I put out the little book against him.[8] It was already completed when your letter arrived. The letter has not influenced me to change anything in it, though I had in mind to leave it to Philip's[9] judgment to change it as he saw fit. Be sure to give the book to Philip and do not dissuade him from

[1] This letter is not extant; one may only guess at its content from Luther's answer here. The letter apparently was the result of Capito's visit to Electoral Saxony (see p. 316, n. 10) and the insight Spalatin had gained into *Against the Idol at Halle* (see note 8).
[2] Elector Frederick; see pp. 49 f.
[3] Cardinal Albrecht, archbishop of Mainz; see pp. 44 f.
[4] The pope had "created," i.e., appointed Albrecht to his position.
[5] I.e., Albrecht; see note 3. He disturbed God's eternal peace with the sale of indulgences at Halle; see p. 316, n. 10.
[6] Elector Frederick.
[7] I.e., Albrecht; see note 3.
[8] *Against the Idol at Halle;* see pp. 316, 344 ff.
[9] Philip Melanchthon; see p. 77, n. 3; pp. 344 ff.

publishing it. This question is settled, and I will not listen to you.

The fact that we and our friends have a bad reputation with our opponents or with those who have too much worldly wisdom in divine things ought not disturb you. For you know that Christ and the Apostle [Paul] were not men-pleasers. I haven't heard our party being accused of any crime as yet, but only of despising impiety and false doctrines. Of course I do not like the conduct of the students who received the legate of the Antonian Order in such a terrible way.[10] But who can hold everyone in check everywhere and at all times? Are [our opponents] to do no wrong at all? Even the disciples had to endure the disgrace of Judas Iscariot, and the wicked are tolerated all the time in the communities. Of us alone is it required that [among us] no dog growl. For goodness' sake, do you expect me to apologize to everyone who will be displeased with Wittenberg? What would be more impossible?

It will not destroy the gospel if a few of our people sin against propriety. As for those who are alienated from the Word because of this, they have not been adherents of the Word in the first place, but of the glory of the Word. He who adheres to the Word for the sake of the Word will not be torn from it—not even by the gates of hell.[11] He who is alienated, let him be alienated. Why does he not look at those things among us which are better and stronger? Why does he look only at those things which are worse and weaker? Does anybody blame Philip and his friends for this offense?[12] Then why condemn all because of a part? It is a smaller sin to hiss at an impious preacher than to accept his doctrine; but the latter is praised [by our enemies], the former is pronounced unforgiveable. And do you fear these judges and their judgments and think the gospel will be destroyed because of such foolish talk?

In the little book I am sending, I approve the abrogation of the [private] masses.[13] I have not been able to prepare a con-

[10] In October the students of Wittenberg rioted against the Lichtenberg delegation of the Hospital Brothers of St. Anthony (see *O.D.C.C.*, p. 65); see *WA*, Br 2, 403, n. 2.
[11] Matt. 16:18.
[12] See note 10.
[13] See p. 324. Luther is now sending the manuscript of the Latin version.

solation,[14] nor do I see the necessity for it, since I have already dealt with this subject in the *Tessaradecas*.[15] Why don't you give him [16] that, or even better, why don't you urge him to read the Gospels and the Passion of Christ, for there is no better consolation than that? Do I have to write a new consolation for every case that may arise? What will [our] opponents say [about this weakness]? While saying this, I am hoping that Philip's consolation [17] will suffice. I think [the Elector's] illness of soul will have passed away in the meantime, so that my consolation would come too late anyway, and so be useless. Also there is no danger that the Elector will fall into impiety, for were that the case it would not be safe to put off the matter or neglect it. The [theme] on which I am now working, however, concerns the perdition of souls. For I have decided to attack monastic vows and to free the young people from that hell of celibacy, totally unclean and condemned as it is through its burning and pollutions.[18] I am writing partly because of my own experience and partly because I am indignant. May you take this in good spirit. For I have not just one Satan with me, or rather against me; sometimes I am alone, sometimes I am not alone.

Farewell for now, and greet all our friends! I had already written to Gerbel before I received your last letter,[19] and it was all closed up and sealed.

November 11, 1521

Yours,
MARTIN LUTHER

---

[14] Spalatin must have asked Luther (perhaps in the [not extant] letter mentioned in note 1) for a letter or little book of spiritual consolation for Elector Frederick (see note 2).

[15] *Tessaradecas consolatoria* (*The Fourteen of Consolation*); see p. 134, n. 10.

[16] Elector Frederick.

[17] Spalatin originally asked Melanchthon to write a little book of spiritual consolation. Melanchthon in turn suggested to Spalatin that it would be better to approach Luther for it; see *C.R.* 1, 455. It seems that this consolation was never written.

[18] See pp. 321 f.; p. 331, n. 5.

[19] See p. 323; perhaps Spalatin had asked Luther to extend greetings to Gerbel. On the basis of this statement, one could argue that Luther sent the letter to Gerbel directly, and not via Spalatin (see p. 323, n. 3). Apparently Spalatin had asked Luther to extend greetings to Gerbel; since the letter was already sealed, the greetings could not be included, and the letter was sent off from the Wartburg without Spalatin's greetings. Had Luther sent the

104

To Hans Luther
Wartburg, November 21, 1521

With this letter Luther dedicates his book On Monastic Vows to his father Hans Luther. Discussing his entrance into the monastery in the light of the Fourth Commandment, Luther shows how monastic vows are contrary to Scripture. He emphasizes that the authority of parents is nullified only when it conflicts with the authority and calling of Christ, which is not the case, Luther says, when a monastic vow is taken against the will, or without the consent, of the parents.

On Luther's family, Schwiebert (p. 102) says, "All attempts at tracing the ancestral heritage of Martin Luther have ended in failure because of the scarcity of existing sources." The Luders, Ludhers, or Lutters, lived as Erbzinsleute in Möhra/Thuringia, south of Eisenach; they were free peasants who owned their land for the payment of the Zins or ground-rent. To insure continuous holding of the undivided Bauernhof or farming-estate in the same family, the youngest son by custom and law was heir to the estate. In about 1480 Luther's grandfather Heine Luther is known to have been farming in Möhra. He had at least four sons: Gross-Hans, Luther's father; Klein-Hans, Veit, and Heinz, Luther's uncles. Gross-Hans married Margareth Lindemann of Eisenach,[1] and they had ten children. Since Gross-Hans could not inherit the estate, he moved to Eisleben to work in the copper mines; here Martin was born. In 1484 Luther's parents moved to Mansfeld where they stayed for the rest of their lives. Gross-Hans died on May 29, 1530.

---

letter to Spalatin to forward to Gerbel, Spalatin could have included the greetings himself.

[1] On Luther's mother, see *Theologische Studien und Kritiken*, LIV (1881), 684 ff.; *Archiv für Sippenforschung*, 1935. The maiden name of Luther's mother has been controversial for some time; she is also called a Ziegler. The Zieglers were an old family in Möhra; it was assumed that "Ziegler" was a professional name meaning brick manufacturer, and that her real maiden name was Margaret, the daughter of the Ziegler Lindenmann. H. Bornkamm (in: J. W. Doberstein, T. G. Tappert [trans.], H. Boehmer's *Road to Reformation* [Philadelphia, 1946], pp. 4 f.) suggests that this could be a confusion with Luther's grandmother, so that Heine Luder would have been married to a Ziegler.

In Mansfeld, which was at that time the heart of the copper mining industry, the Luders sought their fortune in mining and made it. Through hard work, thriftiness, and honesty Gross-Hans made his way from hired mine hand to renter, co-owner, and owner of mines and furnaces, and from an immigrant to the city to a position comparable to a present-day alderman. By 1508/09 the Luders had gained the respect of their fellow-citizens and some wealth.[2]

A web of legends and assumptions cloud Martin's childhood and his relationship to his parents. Much has been written about the strictness in which he was raised, and how this could have influenced him. A recent study[3] *even uses psychoanalysis in an attempt to explain Luther's life and thought and sees in a "split father-image" and an "anti-mother complex" the key to many thoughts and phenomena in the Reformer's life. Exciting as such an undertaking may be, the sources are too scarce and too ambiguous to justify it from a historical basis. All that can be said is that Martin was raised in a poor, pious, stern, and thrifty home, where pennies counted*[4]*—and where a college education was considered a luxury far beyond the means available. And yet Gross-Hans sent his son to college instead of putting him to work in the mines, a fact which might show the high regard he had for him. On the basis of the few remarks that are available, Luther held his father in high regard throughout his life.*

On Gross-Hans, see Zeitschrift des Harz-Vereins 39 (1906), 169 ff.

Text in Latin: WA 8, 573-576; translation based on S-J 2, 65-71.

To Hans Luther, my Father, I, Martin Luther, your son, send greetings in Christ

---

[2] It seems doubtful, however, whether one can call Luther's parents capitalists or big business people of a small town as Schwiebert (pp. 107 f.), Erikson (see note 3), and others do.

[3] E. H. Erikson, *Young Man Luther: A Study in Psychoanalysis and History* (New York, 1958).

[4] Bainton (pp. 22 ff.) gives a good evaluation of the home in which Luther grew up.

This book[5] I have decided to dedicate to you, dearest Father. [I do not intend to make] your name famous in the world and to glory in the flesh, which would be contrary to the teaching of St. Paul.[6] Rather my purpose is to recall, in a short preface, what took place between you and me in order to indicate to the pious reader the argument and the content of this book, together with an example.

To begin with, I wish you to know that your son has reached the point where he is altogether persuaded that there is nothing holier, nothing more important, nothing more scrupulously to be observed than God's commandment.[7] But here you will say, "Have you been so unfortunate as ever to doubt this, and have you only now learned that this is so?" Most unfortunately indeed I not only doubted it, but I did not at all know that it is so; and if you will permit me, I am ready to show you that this ignorance was common to both of us.

It is now almost sixteen years since I became a monk,[8] taking the vow without your knowledge and against your will. In your paternal love you were fearful about my weakness because I was then a youth, just entering my twenty-second year (that is, to use St. Augustine's words, I was still "clothed in hot youth"),[9] and you had learned from numerous examples that this way of life turned out sadly for many. You were determined, therefore, to tie me down with an honorable and wealthy marriage.[10] This fear of yours, this care, this indignation against me was for a time implacable. [Your] friends tried in vain to persuade you that if you wished to offer something to God, you ought to give your dearest and your best. The Lord, meanwhile, was dinning in your ears that Psalm verse: "God knows the thoughts of men, that they

---

5 *De votis monasticis Martini Lutheri iudicium* (*Martin Luther's Opinion on Monastic Vows*) (Wittenberg: M. Lotther, February, 1522). *WA* 8, 577 ff.

6 Gal. 6:13.

7 In this case the Fourth Commandment.

8 Luther entered the monastery in July of 1505; see p. 3.

9 St. Augustine's *Confessions* (see *Patrology*, pp. 499 f.), II, 3. *MPL* 32, 677.

10 As far as this editor can see, this seems to be the only reference from which the marriage plans his father had for Luther can be deduced. These plans seem to be quite in agreement with the father's ambition to see young Martin in the important and influential position of a legally-trained administrator; see Fife, p. 67.

are vain";[11] but you were deaf. At last you desisted and bowed to the will of God, but your fears for me were never laid aside. For I remember very well[12] that after we were reconciled and you were [again] talking with me, I told you that I had been called by terrors from heaven and that I did not become a monk of my own free will and desire, still less to gain any gratification of the flesh, but that I was walled in by the terror and the agony of sudden death and forced by necessity to take the vow. Then you said, "Let us hope that it was not an illusion and a deception." That word penetrated to the depths of my soul and stayed there, as if God had spoken by your lips, though I hardened my heart against you and your word as much as I could. You said something else too. When in filial confidence I upbraided you for your wrath, you suddenly retorted with a reply so fitting and so much to the point that I have hardly ever in all my life heard any man say anything which struck me so forcibly and stayed with me so long. "Have you not also heard," you said, "that parents are to be obeyed?" But I was so sure of my own righteousness that in you I heard only a man, and boldly ignored you; though in my heart I could not ignore your word.

See, now, whether you, too, were not unaware that the commandments of God are to be put before all things. If you had known that I was then in your power, would you not have used your paternal authority to pull me out of the cowl? On the other hand, had I known it, I would never have attempted to become a monk without your knowledge and consent, even though I had to die many deaths. For my vow was not worth a fig, since by taking it I withdrew myself from the authority and guidance of the parent [to whom I was subject] by God's commandment; indeed, it was a wicked vow, and proved that it was not of God not only because it was a sin against your authority, but because it was not absolutely free and voluntary.[13] In short it was taken in accordance with the doctrines of men and the superstition of hypo-

---

[11] Ps. 94: 11 (Vulgate).

[12] The following is a recollection of what took place between father and son at the celebration of Luther's first mass; see pp. 3 f., 300 f.; Bainton, pp. 39 ff.

[13] I.e., the vow was said under the pressure of external circumstances (the lightning near Stotternheim; see Bainton, pp. 21 ff.) and thus with the wrong motivation.

crites, none of which has God commanded. But behold how much good God (whose mercies are without number and whose wisdom is without end)[14] has made to come out of all these errors and sins! Would you now not rather have lost a hundred sons than not have seen this good?

I think that from [the days of] my childhood Satan must have foreseen something in me [which is the cause] of his present suffering. He has therefore raged against me with incredible contrivings to destroy or hinder me, so that I have often wondered whether I was the only man in the whole world whom he was seeking. But it was the Lord's will, as I now see, that the wisdom of the schools and the sanctity of the monasteries should become known to me by my own actual experience, that is, through many sins and impieties, so that wicked men might not have a chance, when I became their adversary, to boast that I condemned something about which I knew nothing. Therefore I lived as a monk, indeed not without sin but without reproach.[15] For in the kingdom of the pope impiety and sacrilege pass for supreme piety; still less are they considered matters for reproach.

What do you think now? Will you still take me out of the monastery? You are still my father and I am still your son and all the vows are worthless. On your side is the authority of God, on my side there is nothing but human presumption. For that continence of which they boast with puffed-up cheeks is valueless without obedience to God's commandments. Continence is not commanded but obedience is, yet the mad and silly papists will not allow any virtue to be equal to continence and virginity. They extol both these virtues with such prodigious lies that their very craze for lying and the greatness of their ignorance, singly or together, ought to cast suspicion on all they do or think.

What kind of intelligence do they show when they distort the word of the Sage, "No balance can weigh the value of a continent mind,"[16] to mean that virginity and continence are to be preferred to everything else and that vows of virginity cannot be commuted or dispensed with? It was a Jew who wrote these words to Jews

[14] Ps. 147:5.

[15] For similar statements, see *WA* 38, 143.

[16] Ecclus. 26:15 according to the Septuagint numbering and the RSV, 26:20 according to the Vulgate and Luther's Bible.

about a chaste wife; among the Jews virginity and continence were condemned. Thus, too, they apply to virgins that eulogy of a modest wife: "This is she who has not known a sinful bed."[17] In a word, although the Scriptures do not laud virginity but only approve it, these men,[18] who are so ready to inflame men's souls to lives that endanger their salvation, dress it up in borrowed plumes, so to speak, by applying to it the praises the Scriptures bestow on a chaste marriage.

But isn't [the value] of an obedient soul also beyond all measure? For that reason indeed a continent soul (that is, a chaste wife) defies every measure, not only because [such a soul] is commanded by God but also because, as the well-known proverb says, there is nothing in the world more desirable than a chaste wife.[19] But these "faithful" interpreters of Scripture [take] everything that is said about the continence which is commanded [and] apply it to that type of continence which is not commanded, and [thus] make a human evaluation the measure of God's judgment. Thus they grant dispensations from everything, even from obedience to God, [but they grant no dispensation from continence],[20] even from that forbidden continence which is entered upon against the authority of one's parents. O worthy and truly picayunish papistic doctors and teachers! Virginity and chastity are to be praised, but in such a way that by their very greatness men are frightened off from them rather than led to them. This was Christ's way. When the disciples praised continence and said, "If such is the case of a man with his wife, it is expedient not to marry," he at once set their minds straight on the matter and said, "Not all men can receive this precept."[21] The precept must be accepted, but it was Christ's will that only a few should understand it.

But to come back to you, my Father; would you still take me out of the monastery? But that you would not boast of it, the Lord has anticipated you, and taken me out himself. What difference does it make whether I retain or lay aside the cowl and tonsure?[22]

---

[17] Wisd. of Sol. 3:13.

[18] I.e., the papists.

[19] This is either a popular saying (which could not be traced) or an allusion to Prov. 12:4; 31:10, 30.

[20] I.e., the monastic and clerical vow of celibacy.

[21] Matt. 19:10-11.

[22] See p. 308, n. 29.

Do [they] make the monk? "All things are yours, and you are Christ's," says Paul.[23] Shall I belong to the cowl, or shall not the cowl rather belong to me? My conscience has been freed, and that is the most complete liberation. Therefore I am still a monk and yet not a monk. I am a new creature, not of the pope but of Christ. The pope also has his creatures,[24] but he creates puppets and straw-men, that is, masks and idols of himself. I myself was formerly one of them, led astray by the various usages of words, by which even the Sage confesses that he was brought into the danger of death but by God's grace was delivered.[25]

But am I not robbing you again of your right and authority? No, for your authority over me still remains, so far as the monastic life is concerned; but this is nothing to me anymore, as I have said. Nevertheless [God], who has taken me out of the monastery, has an authority over me that is greater than yours; you see that he has placed me now not in a pretended monastic service but in the true service of God. Who can doubt that I am in the ministry of the Word? And it is plain that the authority of parents must yield to this service, for Christ says, "He who loves father or mother more than me is not worthy of me." [26] Not that this word destroys the authority of parents, for the Apostle [Paul] often insists that children should obey their parents;[27] but if the authority of parents conflicts with the authority or calling of Christ, then Christ's authority must reign alone.

Therefore—so I am now absolutely persuaded—I could not have refused to obey you without endangering my conscience unless [Christ] had added the ministry of the Word to my monastic profession. This is what I meant when I said that neither you nor I realized that God's commandments must be put before everything else. But almost the whole world is now laboring under this same ignorance, for under the papal abomination error rules. So Paul also predicted when he said that men would become disobedient to parents.[28] This fits the monks and priests exactly, espe-

[23] I Cor. 3:22-23.
[24] For a similar statement, see p. 326.
[25] Ecclus. 34:12-13.
[26] Matt. 10:37.
[27] Eph. 6:1; Col. 3:20.
[28] II Tim. 3:2.

cially those who under the pretense of piety and the guise of serving God withdraw themselves from the authority of their parents, as though there were any other service of God except the keeping of his commandments, which includes obedience to parents.

I am sending [you] this book,[29] then, in which you may see by what signs and wonders Christ has absolved me from the monastic vow and granted me such great liberty. Although he has made me the servant of all men, I am, nevertheless, subject to no one except to him alone. He is himself (as they say) my immediate bishop,[30] abbot, prior, lord, father, and teacher; I know no other. Thus I hope that he has taken from you one son in order that he may begin to help the sons of many others through me. You ought not only to endure this willingly, but you ought to rejoice with exceeding joy—and this I am sure is what you will do. What if the pope should slay me or condemn me to the depths of hell! Having once slain me, he will not raise me up again to slay me a second and third time,[31] and now that I have been condemned[32] I have no desire ever to be absolved. I trust that the day is at hand when that kingdom of abomination and perdition will be destroyed. Would that we were worthy to be burned or slain by him[33] before that time, so that our blood might cry out against him all the more and hasten the day of his judgment! But if we are not worthy to bear testimony with our blood, then let us at least pray and implore mercy that we may testify with deed and word that Jesus Christ alone is the Lord our God, who is praised forever. Amen.

Farewell [in the Lord], my dearest Father, and greet in Christ my mother, your Margaret,[34] and our whole family.

From the wilderness,[35] *November 21, 1521*[36]

---

[29] See note 5.
[30] I.e., the diocesan bishop to whom the individual church member was subordinate.
[31] For a similar statement, see p. 147.
[32] See p. 210; p. 179, n. 1; p. 192, n. 3.
[33] I.e., the pope, or Satan.
[34] See note 1.
[35] See p. 263, n. 36.
[36] Although the dedication letter was signed on November 21, the treatise did not come off the press until early 1522. The signature is missing, since the *WA* text is based on a copy of the printed edition of *On Monastic Vows* in which the letter appears as the preface.

105

To George Spalatin
Wartburg, November 22, 1521

This is a covering letter for some manuscripts ready for publication. Luther discusses rumors about the Augustinian monastery at Wittenberg and expresses his wish that the Elector dissolve the All Saints' Chapter.

On George Spalatin, see pp. 8 f.

Text in Latin: WA, Br 2, 404-405.

To my dearest friend, George Spalatin

Jesus

Greetings. Please see to it, my Spalatin, that these two prefaces—the German one should precede the Gospels,[1] the Latin one should precede the little book *On Monastic Vows*[2]—are carefully kept with you or Philip[3] so that they don't get lost before I have finished the rest of the *Postil* on which I am now working.

From a vague and indefinite report I have learned that some of our people have disposed of the cowl.[4] I have been afraid that perhaps they might have done this with a conscience not sufficiently strong. This fear has wrested out of me this little book,[5] so that on the authority of my name, if it has any, they[6] might receive support among pious and good people and be encouraged

[1] The letter with which Luther dedicated the *Wartburg Postil* to Count Albrecht of Mansfeld (see p. 145); see pp. 237 ff.; *WA* 10^{I,1}, 1 f. This is one of the Wartburg letters omitted in the present edition. It is addressed to Count Albrecht of Mansfeld and was signed on November 19.

[2] See pp. 329 ff.; p. 331, n. 5.

[3] Philip Melanchthon; see p. 77, n. 3.

[4] Zwilling's (see p. 39, n. 3; p. 281, n. 24; pp. 324 f.) and Karlstadt's (see p. 79, n. 12; p. 277, n. 3; p. 283, n. 1) agitation showed further results. On November 12 the prior of the Wittenberg Augustinian monastery, Conrad Helt (see p. 129, n. 9), reported to Elector Frederick that thirteen monks had left the monastery and thrown away the cowl; according to another source fifteen had left the monastery by November 30. In both cases Zwilling was, either directly or indirectly, made responsible for this exodus. See *WA*, Br 2, 405, n. 4; see also pp. 293 f.

[5] *On Monastic Vows;* see note 2.

[6] I.e., the monks who had abandoned their monastic life.

to have more confidence in themselves. It is certain that the monastic vow must be condemned now, if only for this one reason: the Word of God is not treated in the monasteries and only unadulterated lies of humans rule there.

May God grant that our Sovereign[7] also abolish his Beth-aven at Wittenberg;[8] after the present residents[9] have died he may distribute the income[10] among the poor, of which we have quite a number around here, even among the nobles, as you know. This kind of generosity would be worthy of the Sovereign, and would open the eternal kingdom to him. What good does this ungodliness do, which is only strengthened by him?[11]

Other matters at another time.

Farewell in the Lord.

From the wilderness,[12] *November 22, 1521*

MARTIN LUTHER

---

[7] Elector Frederick; see pp. 49 f.

[8] In Old Testament times Beth-aven was the place of idolatrous worship; see Hos. 4:15; 10:5. This is a reference to the All Saints' Chapter at the Castle Church of Wittenberg. This chapter, richly endowed with real estate and benefices in the country around Wittenberg and highly privileged by the Roman church, was in charge of the famous relic collection of Wittenberg. One of the most important privileges (granted to the chapter in 1398) was the right to offer the so-called *Portiuncula* indulgence to those who would come to view the relics. This indulgence business and the obligation of the canons of the chapter to celebrate mass in the Castle Church were the reasons Luther called the chapter "Beth-aven." Luther held the Elector responsible for this "Beth-aven" because of the Elector's interest in the relic collection and his position as territorial lord. For more details, see Fife, pp. 133 f.; Schwiebert, pp. 259 f.; *O.D.C.C.*, p. 1092.

[9] E.g., Justus Jonas (see p. 275, n. 3), Andrew Karlstadt (see p. 79, n. 12), and John Dölsch (see p. 202, n. 14).

[10] Apparently Luther was thinking of the current income from the indulgences, mass celebrations, and confessions, since the major part of the income from endowments (real estate, benefices, and privileges) went to the University treasury; see Schwiebert, pp. 257 f.

[11] Luther wanted a basic reform of the All Saints' Chapter because of the idolatry involved and because certain members (e.g., Jonas and Karlstadt; see note 9) openly supported the Reformation. Why should they, why should Wittenberg, have to put up with the idolatry of those canons who were still faithful to the papal church? Luther did not succeed with this plea, which is understandable considering Elector Frederick's conservatism. Consequently between 1521 and 1524 Luther, supported by Jonas, worked for a reform of the chapter from within.

[12] See p. 263, n. 36.

106

To Cardinal Albrecht, Archbishop of Mainz
Wartburg, December 1, 1521

Luther issues an ultimatum to the Archbishop of Mainz to make, within fourteen days, a public statement on the sale of indulgences at Halle and to put an end to it. He also warns the Archbishop to stop harassing priests who had married or intended to do so.

The address is missing on the manuscript copy of this letter; but the content makes it clear to whom Luther was writing.

For the background of this letter, see p. 316, n. 10. On Cardinal Albrecht, see pp. 44 f.

Text in German: WA, Br 2, 406-408.

To begin with, Most Reverend and Most Gracious Lord,
Your Electoral Grace may be assured of my willing service

No doubt Your Electoral Grace has a clear and vivid recollection of the fact that I have twice written in Latin to Your Electoral Grace. The first time was at the beginning of that mendacious indulgence which was issued under Your Electoral Grace's name.[1] In that letter I faithfully warned Your Electoral Grace and opposed in Christian love the wild, seductive, and greedy preachers, and the heretical, superstitious books.[2] Had I preferred arrogance, I could have directed the whole attack against Your Electoral Grace as the one who undertook this sale in full responsibility and knowledge, as was written in the printed titles of those heretical books. But instead I have spared Your Electoral Grace and the ruling family of Brandenburg.[3] I thought Your Electoral Grace might have acted in ignorance and inexperience, led astray by lying whisperers; so I attacked only them. It is well known to Your Electoral Grace how much trouble and danger this caused me.

---

[1] See pp. 43 ff.
[2] This is a reference to the Archbishop's *Instruction*, issued for the use of the indulgence commissioners; see p. 47, n. 16.
[3] Albrecht was a member of the Hohenzollern family, which ruled Brandenburg, among other territories; see p. 56, n. 3.

My faithful admonition was mocked, however, and received ingratitude instead of thanks from Your Electoral Grace. Therefore I wrote most humbly a second time;[4] I expressed my willingness to receive instruction from Your Electoral Grace. I received a harsh, improper, unepiscopal, and un-Christian answer;[5] for the purpose of obtaining instruction I was referred to higher powers.

These two letters accomplished nothing; yet I still do not give up. According to the Gospel,[6] I am sending Your Electoral Grace the third warning, too, and this time in German; maybe such superfluous warning and entreaty, which is beyond the call of duty, will do some good.

Your Electoral Grace has now again erected at Halle that idol [7] which robs poor simple Christians of their money and their souls. With this [Your Electoral Grace] has publicly confirmed that all the stupid outrage committed by Tetzel [8] was not his alone but was also due to the insolence of the [Arch]bishop of Mainz, who disregarding my attempt to spare him insists on taking all the blame on himself. Perhaps Your Electoral Grace thinks I am now out of action and that you are safe from me, and that the monk is well under the control of His Imperial Majesty.[9] This may be so; but Your Electoral Grace should nevertheless know that I shall do what Christian love requires, even the gates of hell notwithstanding,[10] to say nothing of the unlearned, the popes, the cardinals, and bishops. I will not put up with or be silent about the fact that the [Arch]bishop of Mainz pretends he knows nothing, or that it is none of his business to give instruction when a poor man seeks it from him; but on the other hand he certainly knows and proceeds with impudence if it could bring him money. I cannot be fooled; one has to behave differently.[11]

My humble supplication to Your Electoral Grace is, therefore,

---

[4] Martin Luther to Cardinal Albrecht: February 4, 1520. *WA*, Br 2, No. 248; *S-J* 1, 281 f.

[5] Cardinal Albrecht to Martin Luther: February 26, 1520. *WA*, Br 2, No. 259; *S-J* 1, 292 f.

[6] See Matt. 18:17.

[7] I.e., the sale of indulgences; see pp. 43 ff.; p. 316, n. 10.

[8] John Tetzel; see p. 45.

[9] Through the Edict of Worms; see p. 210; p. 216, n. 7; p. 220, n. 12.

[10] Matt. 16:18.

[11] Literally: "one has to sing differently about this, and hear [of it]."

that Your Electoral Grace refrain from leading the poor people astray and from robbing them, and present yourself as a bishop and not as a wolf. It is sufficiently well known that indulgences are nothing else but knavery and fraud and that Christ alone should be preached to the people. Therefore Your Electoral Grace cannot be excused on the ground of ignorance.

Your Electoral Grace will please remember the beginning,[12] and what a horrible fire was kindled by ignoring this little spark. The whole world was then surely of the opinion that one poor friar was too unimportant to receive the pope's attention and was undertaking an impossible task. But God decided to give the pope and all his followers more than enough to do. Over and against the opinion of the whole world, God directed the game to the point where the pope will hardly be able to straighten out this affair any more; in addition the pope's situation is daily growing worse, so that one may see the hand of God in this. Let no one doubt that this God still lives and also knows how to withstand a cardinal of Mainz, even if four emperors would support him. God also takes special pleasure in breaking the lofty cedars[13] and humbling the proud, hardened pharoahs.[14] I beg Your Electoral Grace not to tempt or ignore Him; God's knowledge and power are without measure.

Your Electoral Grace should not at all think that Luther is dead. He will so gladly and joyfully rely on that God who has humbled the pope and will start a game with the Cardinal of Mainz such as few people expect. Get together, dear bishops; you may remain nobles, but you will not silence this spirit, or deafen it. If you unexpectedly become a laughingstock from this,[15] however, then I will herewith have warned you.

Therefore be it finally made known in writing to Your Electoral Grace: if the idol[16] is not taken down, my duty toward divine

---

[12] Of the controversy on indulgences, i.e., in 1517/18.
[13] Isa. 2:12-13.
[14] E.g., Exod. 4:21; 7:3, 13.
[15] The text does not make it clear to what "this" refers. It could be the fact that the bishops remain nobles, or the game which will be played with the Cardinal. The latter possibility seems the most probable.
[16] I.e., the sale of indulgences at Halle; see p. 316, n. 10.

doctrine[17] and Christian salvation is a necessary, urgent, and unavoidable reason to attack publicly Your Electoral Grace (as I did the pope); then I shall have to oppose freely such an undertaking, to blame all the previous abomination of Tetzel on the [Arch]bishop of Mainz, and to show to all the world the difference between a bishop and a wolf. Your Electoral Grace may decide how to react and what to do.

If I am despised, another will come who will despise the despiser, as Isaiah says.[18] I have admonished Your Electoral Grace enough. Henceforth, according to St. Paul's teaching, it is the time to accuse, ridicule, and punish publicly all the obvious offenders before the whole world, so that the cause of the offense may be driven out of God's kingdom.[19]

Moreover I beg Your Electoral Grace to restrain yourself and to leave in peace those priests who have married to avoid unchastity,[20] or intend to do so. Do not rob them of their God-given rights.[21] For Your Electoral Grace cannot show any authority, reason, or law to do this; wrongdoing that is simply wanton ill becomes a bishop.

What do you bishops accomplish by resorting so insolently to force and by embittering hearts against you while you will not and cannot show reason or law for your conduct? Who do you think you are? Have you all become nothing but giants and nimrods from Babylon?[22] Don't you poor people know that as soon as the pretense [of their right] is gone, wrongdoing and tyranny [on anyone's part causes] the loss [of the privilege of] the common prayer of Christians, and cannot exist for long? Why do you hasten like madmen to your own destruction? It will come all too soon for you.

Let Your Electoral Grace be aware that if this[23] is not stopped,

---

17 See p. 6, n. 5; p. 49, n. 23.

18 Isa. 33:1.

19 I Cor. 5:13.

20 Apparently Luther is referring to the fate of Bartholomew Bernhardi (see p. 115, n. 21; pp. 231, 378) and some other pastors who had married and were therefore persecuted by the Archbishop. See *WA*, Br 2, 409, n. 16.

21 I.e., to marry; on celibacy, see pp. 277 ff., 283 ff., 293 f., 297 ff., 329 ff.

22 Gen. 10:8 ff.

23 I.e., either the persecution of the priests who had married or the arbitrary rule of the hierarchy.

due to the gospel a roar will arise proclaiming that it would become the bishops to tear first the beams out of their own eyes,[24] and that it would be just if bishops would first do away with their harlots[25] before they separate devout wives from their husbands.

I beg Your Electoral Grace, in your own interest, to give me a possibility and chance to be silent. I have no joy or pleasure in Your Electoral Grace's shame and dishonor. But if there is no end to the disgracing of God and the dishonoring of his truth, I and all Christians are obligated to hold fast to God's honor, though the whole world—to say nothing of one poor man, a cardinal—be put to shame by it. I shall not be silent; and even if I may not be successful, still I hope that you bishops will not finish your song with joy. You haven't yet wiped out all whom Christ has raised up against your idolatrous tyranny.

I beg and expect Your Electoral Grace's definite and speedy reply to this letter within fourteen days; if after this appointed fortnight no public answer should appear,[26] my little book *Against the Idol at Halle* will be released.[27] Should this letter be intercepted by Your Electoral Grace's councilors [28] and not reach you, I will not hold off for that reason. Councilors should be faithful; a bishop should organize his court so that whatever should reach him actually gets through to him. God give Your Electoral Grace his grace to have a right mind and will.

Written in my wilderness,[29] *December 1, 1521* [30]

Your Electoral Grace's willing and dedicated
MARTIN LUTHER

---

24 Matt. 7:5.

25 On Albrecht's harlots, see *WA* 30II, 338, n. 3.

26 In the form of a public proclamation by the Archbishop; a private letter could not reach Luther, whose whereabouts were secret.

27 This is Luther's *Against the Idol at Halle;* for details, see pp. 344 ff.

28 Perhaps Luther was thinking of the possibility that some of the Archbishop's councilors (maybe Capito, whom he did not trust at this point anyway; see pp. 305 f.; p. 316, n. 10; pp. 326 f.) might intercept the letter and not turn it over to the Archbishop in an attempt to avoid further complications, such as a violent reaction on the part of the Archbishop.

29 See p. 263, n. 36.

30 On the date, see pp. 345 ff.

Excursus

Luther had worked on *Against the Idol at Halle* since the end of September or the beginning of October, when he had heard of the indulgence sale at Halle. On the basis of Luther's statements in the ultimatum and in his correspondence (see pp. 316, 341 f.), it must be assumed that this book dealt with the sale of indulgences at Halle; perhaps it can also be assumed that Luther dealt with the persecution of married priests too; see pp. 342 f. It could not be definitely determined whether this book was written in Latin or German. The latter can be assumed, however, if one applies Luther's statement in his November 1 letter to Gerbel that "all this is in German" [i.e., all the books mentioned] to *Against the Idol at Halle;* see p. 320. On questions of language and content of this book, see below. Albrecht, anticipating Luther's attack, had sent Capito to Electoral Saxony at the end of September in an attempt to have the Electoral government and Luther's friends stop any such attack. Luther was determined, however, to go ahead with his rebuke of the Archbishop; therefore on October 7 he informed Spalatin that he would not be restrained from privately and publicly attacking the Archbishop for his part in the sale of indulgences at Halle; see p. 316.

Thus Luther envisioned from the very beginning of this controversy two forms of communication which his criticism of the Archbishop would take: one private, i.e., letter No. 106; one public, i.e., the book *Against the Idol at Halle.* On November 1 the manuscript of this public rebuke of Albrecht was completed; see p. 320. Luther apparently included the manuscript with the "material" he sent Spalatin on November 1 for forwarding to Melanchthon; see p. 323. As Luther mentioned in his November 11 letter to Spalatin, he left it up to Melanchthon to change the manuscript wherever Melanchthon saw fit, or even to delete any statements that were too sharp; see pp. 326, 353. In spite of the Elector's attempt to prevent Luther from publishing *Against the Idol at Halle* (see p. 326, n. 1), on November 11 Luther firmly expressed his determination to publish this work, saying he would rather lose Spalatin's friendship and the Elector's good will than be silent; see pp. 326 f.

At the beginning of December when Luther secretly went to Wittenberg (see p. 350), he found that Spalatin, most likely upon orders from the Elector, had refrained from forwarding to Melanchthon the manuscript of *Against the Idol at Halle,* as well as manuscripts of other works. Luther vehemently insisted that Spalatin follow his orders (see pp. 350 f.), and his sharp words had results. Before December 12 Spalatin forwarded to Melanchthon the manuscripts he had retained: that of *On Monastic Vows* (see p. 331, n. 5, sent by Luther to Spalatin either on November 22 or shortly thereafter; see p. 337) and that of *On the Abrogation of the Private Mass* (see p. 324, sent by Luther to Spalatin on November 11; see p. 327). See *WA*, Br 2, 410, n. 1. It can easily be understood why Spalatin did not forward this material to Melanchthon for publication if one considers the situation in Wittenberg (see pp. 324 f.; p. 337, n. 4) and the Elector's attempt to prevent any further trouble within Wittenberg and with Mainz. Why add oil to the fire by publishing Luther's sharp statements on controversial subjects? Spalatin must also have forwarded to Melanchthon letter No. 106 (to the Archbishop of Mainz), for Melanchthon sent it off to Mainz via Capito on December 11; see p. 305, n. 4; p. 316, n. 10; *C.R.* 1, 492; *WA*, Br 2, No. 442, Introduction. Luther's order of about December 12 to Spalatin to turn the letter (No. 106) and the manuscript of *Against the Idol at Halle* over to Melanchthon was at least partially unnecessary. Spalatin, however, apparently still retained the manuscript of *Against the Idol at Halle,* since it was not before January 13, 1522, that Luther thought Melanchthon had received it; see p. 372. In his letter of about December 12, Luther consented to postponing its publication, but insisted that the letter to Mainz be sent immediately (see p. 353), which of course had already been done. It could not be determined whether the manuscript of *Against the Idol at Halle* ever reached Melanchthon. Luther believed that it did (see p. 372), and it is possible that it finally did reach Melanchthon, who, according to Luther's January 13 request (see p. 372), may have filed it away for the time being.

In the reconstruction of these events there are three unclear points which the editor of *WA*, Br 2, overlooked: (1) Luther's shipment of November 1 (see p. 323), (2) the date of letter No. 106, and (3) certain statements concerning the manuscript of *Against the Idol at Halle* in Luther's November 11 letter to Spalatin. Did Luther on November 1 send to Spalatin for forwarding to Melanchthon both the manuscript of *Against the Idol at Halle* and No. 106? Or only one of these documents? Or none of them? To what does the "material" mentioned in No. 101 refer? The *WA*, Br editor assumes the first possibility when he identifies the "material" of No. 101 with No. 106 and the manuscript of *Against the Idol at Halle.* This identification would also make it necessary to assume a change of the date of No. 106 from December 1 to November 1. Thus he contradicts himself when he states in the introduction to the letter to the Archbishop (No. 106) that Luther sent the letter to Spalatin *alsbald,* i.e., soon after December 1; see *WA*, Br 2, 405. Therefore his assumption cannot be upheld that the material Luther sent to Spalatin on November 1 for forwarding to Melanchthon included both the letter to the Archbishop (No. 106) and the manuscript of *Against the Idol at Halle* (see *WA*, Br 2, 399, n. 1).

Could it not have been that Luther sent *only* the manuscript of

Against the Idol at Halle on November 1, and not yet the letter? Perhaps Luther reconsidered his sharp statements of November 11 (see pp. 326 f.) and tried to settle the case with the ultimatum in No. 106, thus completing his original plan of approaching the Archbishop both privately and publicly (see p. 316). No. 106 would then have had to be written on December 1, the date the *WA*, Br editor gives, not realizing that his footnote to *WA*, Br 2, No. 436 (see in this volume, p. 323) would make a change in date necessary. Luther wrote No. 106 on December 1 and sent it off to Spalatin. While Luther was in Wittenberg (see p. 350) he found out Spalatin had retained the material sent from the Wartburg (see p. 350, nn. 3, 4; p. 351, n. 5). In his indignation and hurry he forgot to mention No. 106 when, in No. 107, he ordered Spalatin to release the manuscripts. Therefore about December 12 he made a special point to Spalatin that No. 106 was finally to be forwarded to Mainz, not knowing that this had already been done; see above.

This interpretation necessitates identifying the neuter accusative plural *ista* or the "material" of No. 101 of November 1. On the basis of the material mentioned in No. 107 (in which Luther listed the manuscripts in an order just the reverse of the order in which he had sent them; see above and p. 350, nn. 3, 4; p. 351, n. 5) and in the letter to Gerbel, in which Luther mentioned that the public rebuke of the Archbishop of Mainz had been completed (see p. 320), it seems certain that Luther enclosed the manuscript of *Against the Idol at Halle*. But what else did he enclose that would justify the plural *ista*? He could not have sent the manuscript of *On the Abrogation of the Private Mass* (see p. 324), since he shipped this on November 11; see p. 327. Nor could it have been the manuscript of *On Monastic Vows,* since Luther said on November 11 that he was working on it; see p. 328. Perhaps it was a final shipment of the Christmas portion of the *Wartburg Postil;* see pp. 237 ff.; on November 22 Luther sent the letter of dedication for this work; see p. 337, n. 1. Or perhaps one should understand the *ista* to refer to something like *ista folia,* and translate it as "these [manuscript sheets of *Against the Idol at Halle,* which will be with you]."

Luther's statements concerning the manuscript of *Against the Idol at Halle* in his November 11 letter to Spalatin seem to confuse the issue even more; see pp. 326 f. There Luther wrote: ". . . *mitto libellum in eum* [the Archbishop] *iam paratum, cum venissent tuae litterae, quibus nihil motus sum, ut aliquid mutarem . . .*"; see *WA*, Br 2, 402. Since *mittere* means "to send off," this passage would have to be understood to mean that Luther was enclosing the manuscript of *Against the Idol at Halle,* which had been completed before Spalatin's letter (see p. 326, n. 1) arrived at the Wartburg, and in which manuscript he would make no changes in spite of Spalatin's letter. This understanding would completely nullify the identification of the "material" of No. 101 given by the *WA*, Br editor.

There are three possibilities of interpreting Luther's statement quoted above: (1) Adopt the translation of *mitto* as "I send." This would mean that Luther did not send Spalatin the manuscript of *Against the Idol at Halle* on November 1 (see p. 323) but enclosed it on November 11. Further, if one does not want to assume, due to the differences in the dates (see above), that Luther included the letter to the Archbishop (No. 106) in his November 1 letter to Spalatin, one is faced with the problem of identifying the "material" of this letter (see p. 323). It seems to this editor that this possibility has to be eliminated in view of the complications which would arise concerning the identification of this "material." And even more important, the assumption of this possibility would raise the question: how did Spalatin know of *Against the Idol at Halle,* even in detail, so that shortly before November 11 he could have written to Luther and characterized this work as something which would disturb the peace? See pp. 326 f.; p. 326, n. 1. Spalatin must have seen this work before November 11. The problem would then be whether or not before November 11 Spalatin had seen the whole work or only a portion of it. This raises a second possible interpretation of Luther's statement quoted above: (2) Maintain the literal meaning of *mitto* and argue that Luther enclosed in his November 11 letter to Spalatin the final portion of his manuscript of *Against the Idol at Halle,* of which he had sent a first instalment on November 1. This first instalment gave Spalatin and the Elector a good look at this work, and they were aghast at the reaction they knew would come. Spalatin (in his letter which Luther answered on November 11; see p. 326, n. 1) then tried to stop Luther, or at least make him change some of it. Spalatin's letter, however, came too late: Luther had already finished the manuscript and could not be influenced to change any of it. Luther enclosed the last part of the manuscript of *Against the Idol at Halle* on November 11 and ordered Spalatin not to retain it but to turn it over to Melanchthon at once; see p. 326. In spite of the fact that this reconstruction seems somewhat artificial, many elements speak for it: Spalatin's attempt to stop Luther is clear if one considers that he had knowledge of the contents of the book; Luther's November 11 statement that he was enclosing a work which already had been completed is also understandable; the "material" of November 1 can at least be partially identified as *Against the Idol at Halle* (or completely if one conjectures *folia;* see above); and Luther's November 11 statement that he had left it to Melanchthon to make changes makes sense if it refers to his letter to Spalatin of November 1, when he had shipped the first instalment of the work, although he did not make this reference explicit.

A third possibility is to supply a different interpretation of *mittere;* it can mean "to send off," but it can also mean "to put out" or "to release." This would mean that on November 11 Luther affirmed his determination to publish *Against the Idol at Halle* in spite of Spalatin's protests. It would leave open, however, when the manuscript was sent to Spalatin. Luther's additional statement, "it was already completed," suggests, however, the same circumstances presented in (2), namely, that Luther was then sending the final part.

This editor is inclined, as a result, to reconstruct the events which occurred between November 1 and the beginning of December as follows: contrary to the opinion of the *WA*, Br editor, it seems that on November 1 Luther sent Spalatin only a first instalment of the manuscript of *Against the Idol at Halle,* which was to be forwarded to Melanchthon. Although Luther did not say so, he intended to leave any changes to Melanchthon's discretion. Shocked by what he read in the first instalment and perhaps ordered by the Elector, Spalatin tried to intervene with Luther. Luther totally rejected Spalatin's attempted intervention. On November 11 he informed Spalatin that the manuscript was completed (and thus it may be assumed that he enclosed the last portion of it), that he would change nothing in it in spite of Spalatin's requests, and that he was determined to have the book published, even if this cost him the friendship of Spalatin and the support of the Elector. Having perhaps reconsidered his sharp statements and returning to his original plan of approaching the Archbishop both privately and publicly (see p. 316), Luther wrote letter No. 106, on December 1, issuing his ultimatum to the Archbishop. Maybe it would do some good (see p. 340), but if not, then *Against the Idol at Halle* (which Luther thought was already in Melanchthon's hands, ready to go to press) could and would be published.

How disappointed and angry Luther must have been when he learned during his visit to Wittenberg at the beginning of December that none of the material he had sent to Spalatin from the Wartburg in the last weeks had been sent on to Melanchthon! Letter No. 107 reflects this disappointment and anger on Luther's part. It is interesting to observe that through Spalatin's fearful procrastination, Capito's mission (see p. 316, n. 10) was successful after all, at least in part, since Luther's public rebuttal of the Archbishop was temporarily postponed. Although Luther was suspicious of Albrecht's answer to his ultimatum (see pp. 365, 373 f., 376 ff.), nevertheless on January 13 he abandoned his idea of publishing *Against the Idol at Halle* until others, like the Archbishop, would go "insane" with the sale of indulgences and/or the persecution of the married priests; see p. 372.

Luther was obviously of the opinion that his manuscript of *Against the Idol at Halle* had finally reached Melanchthon. Whether or not this was the case, and what happened to the autograph, could not be determined. It apparently was never published in Luther's time. Perhaps some light is shed on the fate of this work, as well as some insight gained into its content, through an autograph fragment of a German text in the Bodleian Library in Oxford. See *WA* 10^{II}, 93 ff. This fragment in Luther's handwriting shows corrections (perhaps in Melanchthon's handwriting, as is suggested in *WA* 10^{II}, 94) which alter direct references to the Archbishop of Mainz and substitute general statements for them. The fragment is edited in *WA* 10^{II}, 121 ff., col. 1. A printed text which apparently is identical with the corrected text of the Bodleian fragment (disregarding minor discrepancies) is available in Luther's *Wider den falsch genannten geistlichen Stand des Papstes und der Bischöfe* (*Against the Wrongly Named "Spiritual" Estate of the Pope and of the Bishops*) (Wittenberg: N. Schirlenz, July, 1522). *WA* 10^{II}, 105 ff. Based on this fact as well as the corrections which can be found in the Bodleian fragment, the *WA* editors drew the following conclusions: Realizing that the corruption with which he had charged the Archbishop of Mainz in *Against the Idol at Halle* was typical of the Roman hierarchy as such, Luther did not wait until any particular bishop went "insane" (see p. 372) but published, in July, 1522, a general indictment of the Roman hierarchy, i.e., *Against the Wrongly Named . . . .* For this work Luther used *Against the Idol at Halle;* to do this only the direct references to Albrecht of Mainz had to be replaced with general statements. According to the *WA* editors, the Bodleian fragment precisely fits this situation. Consequently, the *WA* editors argue, the Bodleian fragment is a portion of the autograph of *Against the Idol at Halle;* further, the text of *Against the Wrongly Named . . .* is the text in which Luther finally—after Melanchthon(?) had made corrections—issued *Against the Idol at Halle.*

Exciting as this argument is and as convincing as it sounds, it raises certain problems which the *WA* editors overlooked. First of all, the Bodleian fragment is in no way clearly designated as a fragment of *Against the Idol at Halle;* unimportant as this may be, it has to be pointed out. Secondly, one has to ask: does the text of *Against the Wrongly Named . . .* still reflect the circumstances (sale of indulgences, persecution of married priests) with which *Against the Idol at Halle* must have dealt? And if so, does it do this in such a way that one recognizes them, or, are indulgence sales and the persecution of married priests just some among many points, so that one is not compelled to think of a specific issue involved? Thirdly, could not the Bodleian fragment be a part of the (not extant) autograph of *Against the Wrongly Named . . . ?* Could the references to the sale of indulgences and to the persecution of married priests only be a trace of the past controversy with Albrecht of Mainz? In summary, one has to ask, do the corrections in the Bodleian fragment demand the interpretation given by the *WA* editors as well as justify the assumption that it is a fragment of the autograph of *Against the Idol at Halle?* If the Bodleian fragment really is a part of *Against the Idol at Halle* (which cannot be confirmed or denied in this excursus) which was used for *Against the Wrongly Named . . .* , then the relationship between both works has to be shown in greater detail than the *WA* editors did. Did Luther incorporate a part of *Against the Idol at Halle* (namely, the Bodleian fragment) into *Against the Wrongly Named . . . ?* Or did he enlarge and change certain statements, so that *Against the Wrongly Named . . .* would be, so to speak, a second edition of *Against the Idol at Halle?* These questions would have to be answered, at least in part, before one could confirm the *WA* editors' assumption that the Bodleian fragment is part of the autograph of *Against the Idol at Halle.*

107

To George Spalatin
Wittenberg, about December 5, 1521[1]

While making a brief secret visit to Wittenberg at the beginning of December, 1521, Luther sends greetings to Spalatin. He expresses his disappointment and near anger that the manuscripts he had recently sent to Spalatin from the Wartburg were not forwarded to Wittenberg as he had requested. Luther orders Spalatin to release the manuscripts immediately. He tells of his worries about the improper conduct of certain of "our" people and promises to write a public exhortation on that subject.

On George Spalatin, see pp. 8 f.

Text in Latin: WA, Br 2, 409-410; translation based on S-J 2, 78-79.

To my George Spalatin, a servant of Christ and a friend

Jesus

Greetings. I have sent you, along with letters,[2] the [manuscripts of the] little books on vows,[3] on the masses,[4] and against the tyrant

[1] On the dating of this letter, see *WA*, Br 2, No. 443, Introduction.
[2] See notes 3, 4, 5.
[3] See p. 331, n. 5. The covering letter is not extant; perhaps it is No. 105.
[4] See p. 324. No. 103 is the covering letter; see p. 327.

of Mainz.[5] I had hoped that they all were given to the proper people. Now, since I find everything different, I have to draw my own conclusions. I fear, namely, that the material might have been intercepted on the way or have been lost in some other way by the messenger. There is nothing that would disturb me more at this moment than to know that [these manuscripts] had reached you and that you were holding them back, since I have dealt in these little books with themes that require the greatest possible haste. Therefore if you have them, for goodness' sake curb that moderation and prudence of which I suspect you, for you accomplish nothing by rowing against the stream.[6] What I have written I want published, if not in Wittenberg then certainly somewhere else. If the manuscripts have been lost or if you have kept them, I will be so embittered[7] that I will write more vehemently than ever on these points. Whoever destroys lifeless paper will not also quench the spirit. I came to Wittenberg and amid all the delight of being with my friends again[8] I found this drop of bitterness, namely, none of them has ever heard of or seen my little books and letters. Judge for yourself whether I should not consider [my] disappointment justified.

Everything else that I hear and see pleases me very much. May the Lord strengthen the spirit of those who want to do right! Nevertheless I was disturbed on the way by various rumors concerning the improper conduct of some of our people,[9] and [there-

[5] See pp. 344 ff. Nos. 101 and 103 are the covering letters for the two parts in which (in the opinion of this editor) the manuscript was sent to Spalatin.
[6] This seems to be an allusion to a statement made by Seneca (*Epistolae* 122); see *WA*, Br 2, 410, n. 2. For a similar statement, see Erasmus' *Adagia*. Clericus 2, 748, A.
[7] Literally: "my spirit will become embittered"; this is an allusion to Ps. 106:33.
[8] Literally: "among the sweetest sweetnesses of friends."
[9] It is not clear to what Luther is referring. It certainly cannot be the events which took place in Wittenberg (see p. 281, n. 24; pp. 324 f.; p. 337, n. 4), since he endorsed them (see pp. 281, 327, 337 f.) and now says that he is pleased with everything. The reference apparently is not to a single event but rather to the general tense atmosphere Luther encountered on his journey from the Wartburg to Wittenberg. As early as May 26 Luther expressed his fear that the tyrannical rule of the clergy, by which the gospel was suppressed, would cause a reaction among the people that might be explosive; see p. 233. Rumors, perhaps reports of individual accidents (such as the one to which p. 327, n. 10, refers), and the general tension only confirmed Luther's fear. See *WA* 8, 670 f.

fore] I have decided to issue a public exhortation [10] on that subject as soon as I have returned to my wilderness.[11]

More at another time. Commend me to the Most Illustrious Sovereign,[12] from whom I want to keep my arrival in Wittenberg and my departure a secret. You well enough realize the reason for this.

Farewell.

Wittenberg, in Amsdorf's [13] *house, in the company of my Philip.*[14] *1521*

MARTIN LUTHER

Philip will provide you [15] with a Latin Bible [16] which you should send me; please assume [this task] and handle it with your [usual] trustworthiness.[17]

---

[10] See p. 355, n. 18.

[11] See p. 263, n. 36.

[12] Elector Frederick; see pp. 49 f.

[13] Nicholas von Amsdorf; see p. 218. While in Wittenberg Luther did not stay in his old quarters, the Augustinian monastery, for obvious reasons (see p. 359); instead he stayed with his friend von Amsdorf. At one time during this visit Lucas Cranach must have portrayed Luther as a knight; see p. 228, n. 33. On von Amsdorf's house, see *WA*, Br 8, 662.

[14] Philip Melanchthon; see p. 77, n. 3.

[15] Luther wrote *apud te*, which in classical Latin would mean "with you" or "at your place," but this would make little sense here. Consequently this postscript is ambiguous and is interpreted differently by different editors; see *WA*, Br 2, 410, n. 6. It seems to this editor that Luther used *apud* to mean *ad*, i.e., "to." This is a rare use of *apud* but occasionally is found in writings of the period 200 B.C. to A.D. 120, in the Vulgate, and in medieval documents; see Lewis and Short, *A Latin Dictionary* (New York, 1958), p. 147; E. A. Gooder, *Latin for Local History* (London, 1961), p. 103. Thus it seems justifiable to understand this passage as meaning that Melanchthon would send a Bible to Spalatin, who in turn was to forward it to the Wartburg.

[16] The purpose of Luther's visit to Wittenberg was probably to discuss work on the translation of the Bible, a plan which must have evolved during the early fall of 1520. In addition Luther wanted to find out what was going on in Wittenberg, and to be with his friends again. It is not clear what type of Bible Luther means. Since it seems dubious that Luther needed a Vulgate, the *WA*, Br editor has suggested that this Bible was a copy of one of the medieval German translations of the Vulgate; see p. 363, n. 26; *WA*, Br 2, 410, n. 6.

[17] Luther wrote *fide tua*. The translation here expresses sarcasm, stemming from Luther's disappointment about Spalatin's action, or lack of action. *Fides* can also be a technical term, however, connoting the credit rating of a person. Thus one could also translate it: "and take care of it with your credit," i.e., financially; thus the *WA*, Br editor (*WA*, Br 2, 410, n. 6) suggests that Spalatin should assume responsibility for the Bible; financial, if Spalatin bought the Bible; personal, if he borrowed it.

108

To George Spalatin[1]
Wartburg, about December 12, 1521

In the aftermath of his visit to Wittenberg (see p. 350) Luther permits the publication of Against the Idol at Halle to be postponed, insisting, however, that his letter to the Archbishop of Mainz (see pp. 339 ff.) be immediately forwarded to Melanchthon. Reproaching Spalatin for being too much involved in the affairs of the court, Luther gives his reaction to the latest moves of the Archbishop. He also includes the manuscript of the Exhortation, returns a spare set of printed sheets of Melanchthon's Loci, asks for other sets he lacks, and sends a Greek New Testament to be forwarded to Melanchthon.

On George Spalatin, see pp. 8 f.

Text in Latin: WA, Br 2, 412.

Greetings. I will allow the publication of the little book against the man of Mainz[2] to be postponed, so that it doesn't seem as if I never give in to you. But I wish you to turn it over to Philip,[3] whom I have requested to delete any statements which may be too sharp.[4] I definitely want the letter,[5] however, to be forwarded to [the Archbishop of Mainz], and I shall send him another letter via my own messenger.[6]

I am satisfied with what you write concerning [the Archbishop's] preaching in the future.[7] You are right not to judge

[1] The address is missing in the printed editions of this letter. That Spalatin was the recipient of this letter is clear from the contents. On the dating, see *WA*, Br 2, No. 444, Introduction.

[2] Cardinal Albrecht, archbishop of Mainz; see pp. 44 f., 344 ff.

[3] Philip Melanchthon; see p. 77, n. 3.

[4] See pp. 326, 344. This concession seems to be somewhat more far-reaching than Luther had originally intended. Perhaps it was the result of a discussion concerning *Against the Idol at Halle* which Luther might have had with Melanchthon during his short visit to Wittenberg at the beginning of December; see p. 350.

[5] See pp. 339 ff.

[6] It is not clear what Luther means here.

[7] In Spalatin's (not extant) answer to letter No. 107 he apparently told Luther that the Archbishop had promised to reform and preach the gospel in order to prevent Luther's onslaught; he also must have written that the married

rashly, but you are wrong not to believe me at least once. I know Satan's designs, my Spalatin, but nothing [can be done] against the plans of the Lord. I even know there will be more action on Satan's part; he may attack us with a greater show than this one, but not even this will cause me to fear him. For the Lord lives, whom you people—as is becoming to courtiers—do not trust unless he arranges his works according to your way of thinking, so that faith would no longer be necessary. Nothing offends me more in this court [8] than the unbelief which neither believes that all events are due to the will of God alone, nor approves of anything else but what we can hope to complete by our own power. All the experiences and examples we have had haven't thus far accomplished anything at all, even in this particular case.[9] You write that the priests [10] were released by them,[11] as if this release were not seven times more cruel than captivity or immediate homicide, since they forced those poor men to perjure themselves and deny the truth of God.[12] These are the very people of whom you boast that they have returned to the straight path; these are the very people whom you expect to preach the gospel from the heart at one time or another.

For goodness' sake, if it is the truth that celibacy and monasticism are condemned by God, which is without doubt the case, why should one not be free to try to follow the opposite course? [13] Or should one continue only to debate about the Word of God and forever refrain from action? But why do I talk to the deaf? [14] Your mind does not believe; it is too much occupied with the

---

priests who had been imprisoned by Albrecht were being released. With this news Spalatin must have tried to justify the fact that he had retained *Against the Idol at Halle;* see pp. 350 f. Spalatin's source for this news could not be verified. For more details, see *WA*, Br 2, No. 444, Introduction.

[8] I.e., the Electoral Saxon court; see also pp. 383 ff.

[9] I.e., the controversy with the Archbishop of Mainz concerning the sale of indulgences at Halle and the persecution of the married priests; see pp. 342 f., 344 ff.

[10] See p. 342, n. 20.

[11] I.e., the officials of the Archbishop of Mainz; see p. 377, n. 27.

[12] See pp. 377 f.

[13] For the development of Luther's stand on celibacy and monasticism, see pp. 277 ff., 283 ff., 293 f., 297 ff., 310, 329 ff.

[14] This saying (drawn from the statements of classical authors) was recorded by Erasmus in *Adagia;* see Clericus 2, 178, C.

affairs at court, that is, it is both too sophisticated and too timid. I shall believe that the bishops will preach the gospel when I have seen that they have given up their dioceses and have dedicated themselves to the Word of God;[15] before that I shall not believe it. In the meantime I shall not fear the designs of Satan, who blasphemes this office[16] with sacrilegious pretense.[17] I finally see that in this case the counsels of men must be overcome. Up to now I was hindered by them in many ways; but they vainly fear that heaven will go to pieces. If nothing should be done differently than we have previously done, then also one should never have taught anything else [than what had previously been taught].

I am sending the German *Exhortation* to you.[18] I want it to be published as soon as possible in order to counteract those rough and foolish braggarts who boast of our name. I have this extra set of "G" of the printed sheets of Philip's *Loci*.[19] But I lack the last three sets, "Q," "R," and "S," which you will please supply at your convenience. Also, please turn over the Greek New Testament to Philip.[20]

Farewell to you and the whole court. May Christ one day bring this court to a true and sincere[21] faith.[22] Amen.[23]

Yours,
MARTIN LUTHER

---

[15] See p. 47; p. 309, n. 31; pp. 376 ff.
[16] I.e., the office of preaching the gospel.
[17] Luther considers the Archbishop's willingness to reform to be nothing more than a maneuver of Satan; see also pp. 376 ff.
[18] Luther had just promised to write this exhortation; see p. 352. *Eine treue Vermahnung Martin Luthers an alle Christen, sich vor Aufruhr und Empörung zu hüten (A Sincere Admonition by Martin Luther to All Christians to Guard Against Insurrection and Rebellion)* (Wittenberg: M. Lotther, 1521/22). *WA* 8, 676 ff.; *LW* 45, 57 ff.
[19] See p. 232, n. 21; p. 297.
[20] Since Luther had Gerbel's Greek New Testament at the Wartburg (see p. 321, n. 34) he did not need this one. It probably belonged to Melanchthon and may have been used as a basis for the discussions on the translation of the Bible which took place during Luther's visit in Wittenberg; see p. 350. Luther must have forgotten to return it; see *WA*, DB 6, xxxv f.
[21] Luther used a Greek word here.
[22] I Tim. 1:5.
[23] One of the early printed editions adds here: "*Anno MDXXIIII*," i.e., "in the year 1524." The content of this letter, however, makes it clear that this date is wrong.

109

To John Lang
Wartburg, December 18, 1521

Karlstadt's literary work (see p. 283, n. 1), Luther's own stand on monasticism (see p. 302, n. 36; p. 311, n. 5; p. 331, n. 5), and Zwilling's agitation in Wittenberg (see p. 337, n. 4) caused many monks and nuns to abandon their monastic life. In this letter Luther criticizes the disorderly departure of monks from the monasteries. He also mentions his intention to stay at the Wartburg until Easter and his work on the translation of the New Testament.

On John Lang, see p. 14.

Text in Latin: WA, Br 2, 413.

To my dearest friend John Lang, Augustinian friar, ecclesiast at Erfurt, from Martin Luther

I do not approve of that tumultuous exodus, for the monks could have parted from each other in a peaceful and friendly way. You will be at the next chapter meeting;[1] see to it that you favor and defend the evangelical party.[2]

I shall be hiding here until Easter.[3] In the meantime I shall finish the *Postil*[4] and translate the New Testament into German, an undertaking our friends request.[5] I hear you are also working on this.[6] Continue as you have begun. I wish every town would have its interpreter, and that this book alone, in all languages, would live in the hands, eyes, ears, and hearts of all people.[7]

---

[1] A special chapter meeting of the Reformed Augustinians (see p. 6, n. 3; p. 171, n. 7) was to be held in Wittenberg in January, 1522; this meeting was to deal with the drifting away of the friars from monastic life.

[2] Among the Augustinian Eremites.

[3] April 20, 1522.

[4] This is a reference to the Advent portion of the *Wartburg Postil;* see pp. 237 ff.

[5] According to Luther's later statement, it was Melanchthon who advised him to translate the Bible; see *WA*, DB 6, xxxii. It is most probable that this was done during Luther's secret visit to Wittenberg at the beginning of December, 1521; see p. 350; p. 355, n. 20.

[6] Lang translated the Gospel according to St. Matthew; see *WA*, DB 6, xxxii, n. 1.

[7] Erasmus of Rotterdam made a similar statement in *Paraclesis* (one of his

You will hear about other things from the people of Wittenberg.[8] Physically I am healthy and well cared for, but I am also thoroughly buffeted by sins and temptations.[9] Pray for me, and farewell.

From the wilderness,[10] *December 18, 1521*

Yours,
MARTIN LUTHER

110

To Wenceslas Link
Wartburg, December 18, 1521

Summarizing his stand on celibacy (see pp. 277 ff., 283 ff., 297 ff., 329 ff.), Luther discusses the unrest among the Augustinians and their desertion of monastic life. He urges Link, the vicar general of the Order, to direct the upcoming chapter meeting so that it passes a resolution which would make the abandoning or maintaining of monastic life a matter of personal choice. Luther also asks Link to extend greetings to von Staupitz.

On Wenceslas Link, see pp. 169 f.

Text in Latin: WA, Br 2, 414-415.

To the excellent Christian man, Wenceslas Link, vicar of the Augustinian congregation,[1] my superior in Christ

Greetings. I glory in the Lord, excellent Wenceslas, that you like my *Catharinus*,[2] because I rely heavily on your judgment. But look (so I may deal directly with you), they say, "Whosoever agrees with the premises of a sound statement cannot deny its conse-

introductions to the Greek text of the New Testament; see p. 23); see Clericus 6, 3 verso.

[8] I.e., the Wittenberg Augustinian delegation to the chapter meeting.

[9] See p. 28, n. 10.

[10] See p. 263, n. 36.

[1] Link had been vicar general of the Augustinians since August, 1520; see p. 171, n. 7.

[2] Luther had dedicated his *Answer to Catharinus* to Link; see p. 291, n. 10.

quences."[3] And the consequence is what you now see in the monastery.[4] If it is contrary to the gospel to declare the [particular] usages of food, place, person, time, and other things to be sin, where then will the vows, the monasteries, the rules, and the statutes remain? For all these things are contrary to the gospel.[5] And so it is as true that it is contrary to the gospel to make sins out of these things as it is certain that the gospel is the gospel. What will you do now? Whom will you force into obedience? Whom will you call back, once he has left [the monastery]? Whom will you accuse of being an apostate if you will teach, as you ought to, that we are free here—and are not involved in any sin? You may perhaps want some advice from me; indeed you don't need my counsel. I am certain you will not do or allow anything to be done which would be contrary to the gospel, even if all the monasteries would have to perish.

I am, of course, displeased with that tumultuous exodus of which I have heard.[6] They[7] should have separated from one another by mutual consent and in peace.[8] Maybe this[9] is a punishment for a vow taken in an evil and impious way—so that what was constituted[10] in impious unanimity is now being dissolved in disorder. I would not, however, consider it right and correct that they should be called back, even though they themselves may have acted incorrectly and improperly. I also think you cannot hinder any others who may want to leave a monastery. Therefore it would be best to arrange during your coming chapter meeting,[11] by means

---

[3] See L. Schütz (ed.), *Thomas Lexikon: "antecedens."*

[4] Luther is obviously referring to the events in Wittenberg; see p. 337, n. 4. In the following lines Luther is trying to convince Link of the correctness of his own stand on monastic vows; see pp. 283 ff., 297 ff., 310, 329 ff. Link, as vicar general, called a chapter meeting of the Order to meet in Wittenberg early in 1522. This meeting was to deal with the problem of monastic vows, especially since Luther's, Karlstadt's, and Zwilling's opposition to monasticism had had such drastic results. See also *ARG* 6 (1909), 402 ff.

[5] One of the printed editions of this letter offers a text which has to be translated: "All these things are contrary to our gospel."

[6] See p. 356.

[7] I.e., the monks who have abandoned monastic life.

[8] See p. 356.

[9] I.e., the disturbances that accompanied the departure of the monks from monastic life.

[10] I.e., the monastic community.

[11] See note 4.

of a public proclamation, that freedom be given to those who wish to leave—according to the example of Cyrus.[12] No one should be delayed or forced to remain in a monastery against his will. Meanwhile you, like Jeremiah, should remain in the service of Babylon,[13] for I, too, shall remain in this cowl and manner of life, if the world does not change. Under no circumstances do I see that you could act differently in this case. I do not want you to rule over ungodliness or become a leader in it. If you read my little book on vows,[14] you will understand my opinion.

I was at Wittenberg, but was not allowed to enter the monastery, so that I would not betray myself.[15] Hence it is up to you to dare something in this matter, since you see that time and the word of God demand this. I admit that these things were heretofore unheard of, but at the same time [one has to admit] that they cannot be refuted. I have become convinced by what I saw.[16] You have Philip[17] and others whom you may consult.

I was pleased that you summoned this chapter meeting to Wittenberg. I do not know where our dearest Father Staupitz is.[18] I hear, however, that he is now a man of the court and stays with the "idol" of Salzburg,[19] which makes me sad about this excellent man. Please greet him, for I believe that on the basis of my little books he will understand who I am and what I am doing. Presently I am working on a *Postil*[20] and the translation of the Bible into German.[21]

Farewell from the wilderness.[22]

December 18, 1521

Yours,
MARTIN LUTHER

---

12 II Chron. 36:22-23; Ezra 1–3.
13 Jer. 40:5-6.
14 See p. 331, n. 5.
15 See p. 350.
16 It is not clear whether Luther is referring to his experiences during his recent visit to Wittenberg or to his life as a monk.
17 Philip Melanchthon; see p. 77, n. 3.
18 John von Staupitz; see p. 64, n. 1; pp. 72, 138.
19 I.e., the archbishop of Salzburg, Matthew Lang; see p. 99, n. 14; p. 191, n. 2.
20 The Advent portion of the *Wartburg Postil;* see pp. 237 ff.
21 See p. 352, n. 16; p. 356, n. 5.
22 See p. 263, n. 36.

111

To Nicholas von Amsdorf
Wartburg, January 13, 1522

The major part of this letter deals with eschatological questions. Replying to Amsdorf, Luther discusses the question of the whereabouts of departed souls and the nature of purgatory. In addition while contrasting his work on the translation of the Bible with previous translations, and voicing his concern that the translation on which he is working be done well, Luther informs von Amsdorf that he is thinking of coming to Wittenberg for help on the project. He also comments briefly on the "Zwickau prophets."

On Nicholas von Amsdorf, see p. 218.

Text in Latin: WA, Br 2, 422-423.

To the Right Reverend Mr. Nicholas Amsdorf,
Licentiate of Sacred Theology,[1] canon at Wittenberg, etc.

Jesus

Concerning your "souls," I have not enough [insight into the problem] to answer you.[2] I am inclined to agree with your opinion that the souls of the just are asleep and that they do not know where they are up to the Day of Judgment. I am drawn to this opinion by the word of Scripture, "They sleep with their fathers."[3] The dead who were raised by Christ and by the apostles testify to this fact,[4] since they were as if they had just awakened from sleep and didn't know where they had been. To this must be added the ecstatic experiences of many saints. I have nothing with which I could overthrow this opinion. But I do not dare to affirm that this[5] is true for all souls in general, because of the ecstasy of Paul,[6]

[1] On this degree, see p. 264, n. 3.
[2] In a letter which is not extant von Amsdorf apparently asked Luther for his opinion on the whereabouts of the souls of the departed, as well as for his understanding of purgatory.
[3] II Sam. 7:12; I Kings 2:10.
[4] I.e., that the departed are asleep and that they do not know where they are.
[5] See note 4.
[6] II Cor. 12:2.

and the ascension of Elijah [7] and of Moses [8] (who certainly did not appear as phantoms on Mount Tabor).[9] Who knows how God deals with the departed souls? Can't [God] just as well make them sleep on and off (or for as long as he wishes [them to sleep]), just as he overcomes with sleep those who live in the flesh? And again, that passage in Luke 16 [:23 ff.] concerning Abraham and Lazarus, although it does not force the assumption of a universal [capacity of feeling on the part of the departed],yet it attributes a capacity of feeling to Abraham and Lazarus, and it is hard to twist this passage to refer to the Day of Judgment.

I think the same about the condemned souls; some may feel punishments immediately after death, but others may be spared from [punishments] until that Day [of Judgment]. For the reveler [in that parable] confesses that he is tortured;[10] and the Psalm says, "Evil will catch up with the unjust man when he perishes." [11] You perhaps also refer this either to the Day of Judgment or to the passing anguish of physical death. Then my opinion would be that this is uncertain. It is most probable, however, that with few exceptions, all [departed souls] sleep without possessing any capacity of feeling. Consider now who the "spirits in prison" were to whom Christ preached, as Peter writes:[12] Could they not also sleep until the Day [of Judgment]? [13] Yet when Jude says concerning the Sodomites that they suffer the pain of eternal fire, he is speaking of a present [fire].[14]

---

[7] II Kings 2:11.

[8] An assumption based on Deut. 34:5-6, which is supported by pseudepigraphical literature.

[9] Matt. 17:3. According to tradition this took place on Mount Tabor; see *WA*, Br 8, 662.

[10] Luke 16:24.

[11] Ps. 140:11 (Vulgate, but RSV numbering).

[12] I Pet. 3:19.

[13] The translation here is based on the manuscript copy of this letter. The *WA*, Br editor conjectures the text to be as follows: *"annon et illi dormire in eum usque diem potuerint?,"* i.e., "couldn't they [the departed souls] also have slept up to this day [when Christ preached to them]?" It seems to this editor that the text offered by the manuscript copy has to be retained. The "Day of Judgment" in the sentence here (the "fire" in the future, so to speak) seems to be the contrast required by the conjunction *autem*, i.e., "yet," with which the reference to Jude is introduced, which speaks of a "present fire."

[14] Jude vs. 7.

On purgatory I have this opinion:[15] I do not think, as the sophists[16] dream, that it is a certain place, nor do I think that all who remain outside heaven or hell are in purgatory. (Who could assert this, since [the departed souls] could sleep suspended between heaven, earth, hell, purgatory, and all else, just as could happen with the living, when they are in a deep sleep?) I think purgatory is that punishment[17] which they call a foretaste of hell and under which Christ, Moses, Abraham, David, Jacob, Job, Hezekiah, and many others suffered. This punishment is similar to hell, yet restricted in terms of time; it is purgatory for me regardless of whether this punishment takes place emotionally[18] or physically,[19] since we attribute such punishment to purgatory. Yet while it is declared that this punishment takes place physically, and that this is certain, it also cannot be denied that [this punishment] takes place emotionally, although this cannot be proven. Consequently you are by no means in error, whatever you may believe here. Even if you deny purgatory, you are no heretic, since you do not deny that the punishment [of purgatory] can be felt physically and emotionally, but you deny only that purgatory is a definite place and that it has been proven that such punishment is felt emotionally.[20] This I deny too. For they who feel that

[15] For the development of Luther's understanding of purgatory, see *WA* 1, 555 ff.; *LW* 31, 125 ff. (1518), and the *Smalcald Articles,* II, 2 (1536/37). *WA* 50, 204 ff.

[16] This is the term Humanists and Reformers generally applied to Scholastic theologians. Since the doctrine concerning purgatory was developed by the pre-Scholastic theologians, however (especially St. Gregory the Great, 540?-604, and even St. Augustine, 354-430), this term has to be applied here to all the theologians of the papistic church who dealt with this subject. The Council of Lyons (1274) and of Florence (1439) defined the official teaching of the Roman Catholic Church in terms which Luther rejected in his discussion with von Amsdorf. See *O.D.C.C.*, pp. 1125 f.; Denzinger, No. 693. For Thomas Aquinas' opinion on this subject, see *Summa Theologica,* Suppl., ques. 69.

[17] The manuscript copy of this letter offers a text which has to be translated: "[I do think] . . . purgatory to be their punishment [i.e., of those who are departed]," whereby the "I do think" has to be supplied on the basis of the second sentence of this paragraph.

[18] I.e., that the punishment can be felt by man's conscience as pangs of hell.

[19] Luther wrote: "*extra corpus . . . in corpore,*" i.e., "outside of the body . . . in the body." This is a reference to II Cor. 12:2 according to the Vulgate.

[20] Were von Amsdorf's letter available, this passage would be clearer. It seems that he rejected the concept of purgatory as a definite place and also

punishment physically are actually no longer in the body, but dead, as far as life itself [and the senses] are concerned. And so it is not possible for you to deny that this punishment can be felt this way, that is emotionally.[21] This is how I see it. If you have something else to say, let me know.

Karlstadt's wedding makes me very happy. I know the girl.[22] May the Lord strengthen him as a good example to fight and to lessen the papistic unchastity.[23] Amen. I shall deliver my small present in due time, after Easter.[24] In the meantime I shall translate the Bible,[25] although I have here shouldered a burden beyond my power. Now I realize what it means to translate, and why no one has previously undertaken it who would disclose his name.[26] Of course I will not be able to touch the Old Testament all by myself and without the co-operation of all of you. Therefore if it could somehow be arranged that I could have a secret room with any one of you, I would soon come and with your help would translate the whole book from the beginning, so that it would be a worthy translation for Christians to read. For I hope we will give a better translation to our Germany than the Latins have.[27] It is a great and worthy undertaking on which we all should work, since it is a public matter and should be dedicated to the common good. Reply what hope there is concerning this idea. I do not aim to hide myself all the time, since this is impossible, [but I

---

rejected the idea that it could be proven that the pains of purgatory can be felt (only?) emotionally. Thus it seems that he wanted Luther to give a clear definition of what purgatory actually is. Luther agrees with von Amsdorf, at least in part, since in the concluding sentence of this paragraph he obviously affirms the idea that the pains of purgatory can be felt emotionally.

21 Even though this cannot be proven; in this Luther agreed with von Amsdorf.

22 Andrew Karlstadt (see p. 79, n. 12) got engaged to a certain wealthy Anna von Mochau in December; they were married on January 19, 1522; see *WA*, Br 2, 424, n. 12.

23 See pp. 321 f., 328, and the discussion concerning the vow of celibacy on pp. 277 ff., 283 ff., 293 f., 297 ff., 310, 329 ff.

24 Luther apparently intended to return to Wittenberg in April; see p. 356.

25 On the translation of the Bible, see p. 352, n. 16; p. 356, n. 5.

26 Luther was familiar with anonymous translations of the Bible which had been published before he began to work on his project. The best-known German Bible before Luther's was printed by G. Zainer in Augsburg in 1475 in an edition of about one thousand to fifteen hundred copies. See p. 352, n. 16; *WA*, DB 6, 595 ff.

27 Reference to the Vulgate.

wish it] to be known that I prefer to hide and not have people think I wish to show up in public. I believe that this way the timid and the evil would be satisfied when they find out that I want to hide.

The "Zwickau prophets" should not disturb you too quickly.[28] You have Scripture passages (Deuteronomy 13 [:1 ff.] and I John 4 [:1]) which assure you that you do not sin when you delay a decision on their case and first test the spirits, whether they are from God. Meanwhile the Lord will show what is to be done. At first glance I am highly suspicious of their boasting that they have conversations with God in his majesty. More on this to Philip.[29]

Farewell and pray for me.

January 13, 1522

Yours,
MARTIN LUTHER

112

To Philip Melanchthon
Wartburg, January 13, 1522

Luther comments on the latest development of his controversy with the Archbishop of Mainz and Wolfgang Capito (see pp. 344 ff.). He also makes suggestions for dealing with the "Zwickau prophets" (see below, note 28), especially with their understanding of baptism. Promising to deal with this subject further upon his

[28] Toward the end of December, 1521, the "Zwickau prophets," i.e., Nicholas Storch, Thomas Drechsel, and Mark Stübner, came to Wittenberg from Zwickau (a small, highly industrialized town in the southern part of Saxony and a "hotbed of religious revolt" [Schwiebert, p. 538]). They claimed to be prophets of God and to have received revelations directly from God. When they arrived in Wittenberg that city was on the verge of religious anarchy: the Augustinians were abandoning monastic life and private masses were being abolished; see p. 281, n. 24; pp. 324 f.; 337. The religious enthusiasm and social fanaticism of the "Zwickau prophets" only added fuel to the fire and touched off the Wittenberg disturbances. See p. 386, n. 1; *O.D.C.C.*, p. 1491.

[29] Philip Melanchthon; see p. 77, n. 3; pp. 365 ff.

return to Wittenberg (necessary due to his work on the translation of the Bible), Luther asks Melanchthon to prepare some quarters for him there.

Some of the printed editions of this letter offer a great number of text variations. Since they do not seem to influence the basic meaning of the text, however, the translation is based on the text offered by one manuscript copy of this letter made available by the WA, Br edition.

On Philip Melanchthon, see p. 77, n. 3.

Text in Latin: WA, Br 2, 424-427.

To Philip Melanchthon, Christ's servant and faithful steward, my brother

Greetings. Had the letter of the man of Mainz come alone, it would have won.[1] Now, however, since this one by Fabricius [2] was added to it, both letters betray guile and deceit, and therefore I am extremely displeased with Fabricius. I wanted to put an end to ungodliness. Now that orator [3] takes up the cause of ungodliness and teaches the [Arch]bishop to confess his personal sins, believing that this way Luther is fooled in a neat way. I shall restrain myself and not treat that man as he deserves—at least in the first letter. But I shall show him that I am alive.[4]

Now let me deal with the "prophets." [5] Before I say anything else, I do not approve of your timidity, since you are stronger in

---

[1] Cardinal Albrecht to Martin Luther: December 21, 1521. *WA*, Br 2, No. 448; *S-J* 2, 80 f. This was the answer to No. 106. The Cardinal promised in this letter to behave in a way becoming to a pious sovereign and bishop of the church. He also pointed out that Luther really had no reason to complain, since the idol at Halle (see p. 316, n. 10) had been abolished long ago.

[2] The Archbishop's letter was forwarded to Wittenberg by Wolfgang Fabricius Capito (see p. 305, n. 2; p. 316, n. 10), who added a letter of his own; see *WA*, Br 2, No. 447; Luther replied to Capito's letter with No. 113.

[3] I.e., Capito.

[4] Literally: ". . . that there is breath in the nostrils of the son of man." This is an allusion to Isa. 2:22.

[5] See p. 364, n. 28. The letter to Luther in which Melanchthon gave his opinion of the "prophets" is not extant, but it must have shown that Melanchthon was deeply impressed by them. See *WA*, Br 2, 428, n. 4.

spirit and learning than I.[6] First of all, since they bear witness to themselves,[7] one need not immediately accept them; according to John's counsel, the spirits are to be tested.[8] If you cannot test them,[9] then you have the advice of Gamaliel that you postpone judgment.[10] Thus far I hear of nothing said or done by them that Satan could not also do or imitate. Yet find out for me whether they can prove [that they are called by God], for God has never sent anyone, not even the Son himself, unless he was called through men or attested by signs. In the old days the prophets had their authority from the Law and the prophetic order, as we now receive authority through men. I definitely do not want the "prophets" to be accepted if they state that they were called by mere revelation, since God did not even wish to speak to Samuel except through the authority[11] and knowledge of Eli.[12] This is the first thing that belongs to teaching in public.

In order to explore their individual spirit, too, you should inquire whether they have experienced spiritual distress and the divine birth, death, and hell.[13] If you should hear that all [their experiences] are pleasant, quiet, devout (as they say), and spiritual, then don't approve of them, even if they should say that they were caught up to the third heaven.[14] The sign of the Son of Man is then missing,[15] which is the only touchstone[16] of Christians and a certain differentiator between the spirits. Do you want to know the place, time, and manner of [true] conversations with

[6] This probably refers to Melanchthon's request, made in the not extant letter (see note 5), that Luther deal directly with the "Zwickau prophets," an opinion Melanchthon also voiced to Spalatin and to the Electoral government; see *ARG* 6 (1909), 324 f., 385 f., 390 f.; *S-J* 2, 81 ff.

[7] John 5:31-32; 8:13-14.

[8] I John 4:1.

[9] I.e., the spirits of the "Zwickau prophets." This sentence is missing in some of the printed editions of this letter.

[10] Acts 5:34-35.

[11] I.e., that Eli had commanded Samuel to listen.

[12] I Sam. 3:4 ff.

[13] Luther is using the terminology of the German mystics (see p. 36, n. 16). He means that only he who has suffered the pangs of hell (i.e., has experienced to the final degree the fact that he is a sinner) can come to faith and be reborn. See Bainton, pp. 54 ff.; G. Rupp, *The Righteousness of God: Luther Studies*, pp. 85 f., 142 ff., 188 ff.

[14] II Cor. 12:2.

[15] By this term Luther apparently understands the cross; see Matt. 24:30.

[16] Luther used a Greek word here.

God? Listen: "Like a lion has he broken all my bones";[17] "I am cast out from before your eyes";[18] "My soul is filled with grief, and my life has approached hell."[19] The [Divine] Majesty (as they call it) does not speak in such a direct way to man that man could [actually] see it; but rather, "Man shall not see me and live."[20] [Our] nature cannot bear even a small glimmer of God's [direct] speaking. As a result God speaks through men [indirectly], because not all can endure his speaking. The angel frightened even the Virgin,[21] and also Daniel.[22] And Jeremiah pleads, "Correct me [O Lord] but in just measure,"[23] and, "Be not a terror to me."[24] Why should I say more? As if the [Divine] Majesty could speak familiarly with the Old Adam without first killing him and drying him out so that his horrible stench[25] would not be so foul, since God is a consuming fire![26] The dreams and visions of the saints are horrifying, too, at least after they are understood. Therefore examine [them][27] and do not even listen if they speak of the glorified Jesus, unless you have first heard of the crucified Jesus.[28]

You will say, what does this have to do with the case? After all, it only refutes others, and does not establish our position. But how can I speak of our position when I am absent and do not know what they may present against it? If they do not appeal to anything but this passage, "He who believeth and is baptized shall be saved,"[29] and to the fact that children cannot believe on their own account, that does not disturb me at all. For how will these "prophets" prove that children do not believe? Perhaps by the fact that children do not speak and express their faith. Fine!

[17] Isa. 38:13 (Vulgate).
[18] Ps. 31:22 (Vulgate, but RSV numbering).
[19] Ps. 88:3 (Vulgate, but RSV numbering).
[20] Exod. 33:20.
[21] Luke 1:29.
[22] Dan. 8:16-17.
[23] Jer. 10:24.
[24] Jer. 17:17.
[25] Exod. 5:21 (Vulgate).
[26] Deut. 4:24.
[27] I.e., the "Zwickau prophets."
[28] Literally: ". . . listen to the glorified Christ, unless you have first seen the Crucified [in them]."
[29] Mark 16:16.

On that basis [we have to ask] how many hours [of the day] even we are Christians, in view of the fact that we sleep and do other things? Can't God in the same way keep faith in small children during the whole time of their infancy, as if it were a continuous sleep? Fine, you say. This confutes the opponents in the question concerning faith already infused.[30] It is enough for now that they are shown to be the kind of people who can prove nothing and are moved by a false spirit.

What do you say concerning faith which is to be infused? [Here] nothing else is left but extrinsic faith;[31] if we cannot uphold this, then there is nothing else to be debated, and baptism of small children simply has to be rejected.

You say, aren't the examples for extrinsic faith weak? I reply that there is nothing stronger. These "prophets," or all the devils, should show one weak example of extrinsic faith! You quote the passage where Samuel prays for Saul,[32] but this has nothing to do with it. Samuel grieved for Saul, he did not pray [for him]; or if he prayed, he did not pray in faith, that is, he did not believe he would obtain that for which he was praying but placed the outcome [of his prayer] in doubt and left it to the arbitrariness of God. It was the same as when David prayed for his little son,[33] or when many other people pray for many other things. If he had been certain he would receive, he surely would have, because the promise of Christ in Matthew 21 [:22] stands fast, "Whatever you may ask for, believe that you will receive it and you shall receive it." And in Matthew 18 [:19], "If two on earth," etc. This fact cannot be shaken: it is impossible that that for which one prays will not happen if one believes that it will happen. Otherwise the whole doctrine of faith would waver, and personal faith, which

---

30 Luther is using the Scholastic term *"fides infusa"* (a term parallel to *gratia infusa*), i.e., faith which is infused by God through baptism. See pp. 156 ff.; *O.D.C.C.*, pp. 491 f.

31 *Fides aliena,* i.e., faith of transsubjective character. For Luther this means that faith originates in God, outside the individual. He believed that God creates faith in the individual through the Holy Spirit (who works through Word and sacrament), thus fulfilling His plan of salvation; in this plan the faith of the neighbor who intercedes on behalf of the individual is an important factor.

32 I Sam. 15:35.

33 II Sam. 12:16 ff.

is based on [Christ's] promise, would be of no value. Indeed [the faith in which my neighbor intercedes on my behalf] [34] belongs to me personally but is really also someone else's faith,[35] so far as my neighbor is concerned; nevertheless it is necessary that [that for which the neighbor intercedes] in faith should happen in him [on whose behalf the neighbor makes the intercession.][36] All the examples from the gospel pertain to this. For Christ has never rejected a single man who was brought to him through someone else's faith, but accepted all.[37] What more should I say? The testimonies and examples of the whole Scripture are on the side of extrinsic faith, that is, on the side of personal faith, which attains faith and whatever is desired for someone else.[38]

Now one point remains unresolved, which is whether the church believes faith is infused into infants. This question might perhaps arise in connection with the discussion of the [nature of the] church, rather than of extrinsic faith and its efficaciousness. What extrinsic faith is able to do is not subject to discussion, since all things are possible to him who believes.[39] [The question of the church], however, is one of reality and not of theory.[40] We cannot debate whether the church has to believe that faith is infused

---

[34] *Fides aliena;* see note 31.

[35] See note 34.

[36] This sentence, beginning "but is really . . .," can also be translated as follows: ". . . is really someone else's faith, notwithstanding the fact that it is necessary that that which the neighbor believes happens [also] in himself."

[37] E.g., Mark 2:3 ff.

[38] With reference to infant baptism, Luther means in this paragraph that the faith of the parents and godparents who intercede on behalf of the infant is extrinsic faith in relation to the infant, and is the basis for the "personal faith" of the infant, which is necessary for baptism (see note 31 and Mark 16:16). This should not be understood, however, as meaning that the faith of parents and godparents would qualify the child for baptism and that this faith of parents and godparents would be the basis for infant baptism, or that someone can vicariously believe for someone else. Throughout his teaching Luther insists that God himself creates faith in the infant; the parents and godparents only present the infant in obedience to God's Word, believing that God will create faith in the infant, and interceding that he do so. The extrinsic faith becomes personal faith, i.e., part of the individual, whether child or adult, only through God's action. See *WA* 11, 452 f.; *WA* 15, 710; *WA* 17^{II}, 82; *WA* 26, 156, 163 f.; *WA* 30^{I}, 219. On Luther's understanding of baptism, see R. Prenter, "Luther on Word and Sacrament," *More About Luther* ("Martin Luther Lectures," Vol. II), p. 81 ff.

[39] Mark 9:23.

[40] Luther wrote: "*de facto . . . de iure.*"

into infants, since the church has the authority not to baptize infants at all, nor is there any Scripture passage which could force the church to believe this,[41] as there are Bible passages for other tenets.

What should we do here? Do we not approve of the theory? Who can see faith? Therefore we have to proceed to the [question of] the confession of faith, since confession for salvation is made with the mouth.[42] What does the church confess that it believes in this article?[43] Is it not this, that children also participate in the benefits and promises of Christ? One may object here, however: what if Augustine and those whom you call the church, or whom you believe are the church, have erred at this point? Who will make us certain that the church has to believe this,[44] since we cannot prove it? This objection should be contradicted as follows: there may be no law, but there is the fact that this[45] is believed in the church. For who can be sure that Augustine believed in the Trinity if one does not trust his confession? I am certain that [Augustine's] confession agrees with Scripture,[46] but I do not know whether he believes what he confesses. But I see it as a special miracle of God that the article that infants are to be baptized is the only one which has never been denied, not even by heretics. No one's confession opposes it; on the contrary the constant and unanimous confession of the whole world supports this argument.[47] To deny, however, that this is the confession of the true and legitimate church, I consider tremendous ungodliness. This seems to me to be the same as if one were to deny the existence of the church. If this were not so, no doubt the church would have issued some contrary statement at least once, since the faith of the church has never ceased, and

---

41 I.e., that faith is infused into infants.

42 Rom. 10:10.

43 Luther is referring to the Nicene Creed, which in the concluding paragraph reads: "I confess one baptism for the remission of sins," which does not *exclude* infant baptism, as Luther argues here.

44 I.e., infant baptism.

45 I.e., infant baptism. For a different interpretation of this sentence, see *WA*, Br 8, 662.

46 On Augustine, see *De Genesi ad litteram*, 10, 23, 39 (*MPL* 34, 426); *Epistolae* 98; 166, 7, 21; 185, 9, 39; 187, 8, 26; *Ennar. in Psalmos*, 106, 3.

47 For infant baptism.

since the church was never without confession of its faith. You, as an understanding man, will deduce further conclusions from this.

To present a child for baptism is nothing else but to offer it to Christ, who is present on earth and opens [his] hands of grace [toward the child]; Christ has shown throughout his entire life that he accepts whoever is brought to him. Why should we then have any doubts at this point? This one thing, at least, we have taken away from these "prophets," namely, that they could prove their ideas, since they lack example and testimony; but we have both, and their testimony does not withstand ours. For who will argue this way: One has to believe and be baptized,[48] therefore infants are not to be baptized?[49] [The "prophets"] certainly cannot draw this conclusion from this passage, since it does not prove that children do not believe. They presuppose this, and have to prove it on some other basis; but they are unable to do this. What is not against Scripture is for Scripture, and Scripture is for it. On the basis of that same sophistry, they could also take away circumcision, saying: small children do not have Abraham's faith,[50] therefore they should not have the sign of this same faith. We are certain that circumcision had the same power as baptism. Therefore I do not see why, only on the basis of God's authority and of this example,[51] children shouldn't be baptized. There is only one difference: baptism is free and not compulsory like circumcision. It was therefore not necessary that baptism be bound to any certain times, ages, places, or other externals, since it is completely free in itself. Therefore what was then commanded to one people concerning the eighth day is now said to all people of every age: "He who believes . . . ," etc.[52]

More on this when I see you.[53] I have always expected Satan to touch this sore, but he did not want to do it through the papists. It is among us and among our followers that he is stirring

[48] On the basis of Mark 16:16.

[49] Because they cannot have faith of which they can be conscious and which they can express in word or deed.

[50] Gen. 12:1 ff.; 17:10 ff.; Rom. 4:1 ff.

[51] I.e., the argument concerning circumcision.

[52] Mark 16:16; see also note 50.

[53] On Luther's intention to return to Wittenberg, see pp. 356, 363.

up this grievous schism, but Christ will quickly trample him under our feet.[54]

I would also like to know how you understand that passage in I Corinthians 7 [:14], "Otherwise your children would be unclean, but now they are holy" [Vulgate]. Do you want to have this understood only of adults, or of the sanctity of the flesh [in general]? I wish it would be demonstrated from this passage that according to apostolic custom, and in the time of the apostles, small children were baptized. Although I see what could be said concerning this sanctification, yet I would also like to have your opinion. Why should the Apostle [Paul] say this only of children, since all things are holy to the holy, and to the clean all things are clean? [55]

Keep the little book against the [Arch]bishop of Mainz,[56] so that it can go out [one day] and serve as a general censure, should others go insane like that.[57] Please prepare a lodging for me, since the translation [of the Bible] will compel me to return to Wittenberg.[58] Pray the Lord that this may be done in agreement with his will. I wish, however, to stay hidden as much as possible;[59] meanwhile I shall proceed with what I have begun.

Farewell.

January 13, 1522 Yours,

MARTIN LUTHER

113

To Wolfgang Fabricius Capito Wartburg, January 17, 1522

Following his controversy with Cardinal Albrecht, archbishop of Mainz (see pp. 344 ff.), Luther in this letter answers a letter from Wolfgang Fabricius Capito, one of the Archbishop's officials.

[54] Rom. 16:20.
[55] Titus 1:15.
[56] See pp. 348 ff.
[57] And sell indulgences and/or persecute the married priests; see pp. 344 ff.
[58] See note 53.
[59] For a similar statement, see pp. 363 f.

Pointing out that true Christian love does not ignore faults and sins, not even those of high officials, but rather reproves them, Luther charges Capito with hypocrisy. Although in the realm of faith sin has to be reproved, Luther argues, in the realm of love it can be endured after it has been reproved and the reproof has been humbly accepted. Challenging the Cardinal's reply to the ultimatum Luther issued on December 1, 1521 (see p. 339), Luther demands that the Cardinal document his willingness to reform by his actions: the Cardinal should resign his office in the papistic church and become a faithful parish priest; he should immediately cease the persecution of parish priests who had married, and nullify any actions taken against them.

Capito was greatly disturbed by this letter. He therefore came to Wittenberg in the spring of 1522 to seek a reconciliation with Luther. He was able to regain Luther's friendship. Soon after this visit Capito asked to be discharged from the service of Albrecht of Mainz, and by July he had settled in Strassburg, where he openly supported the Reformation.

The text variations of this letter (which is only available in printed editions) are so numerous that they could be noted only occasionally. The translation is based on the text made available to the WA, Br editor; it is assumed that his text comes as close to Luther's original as possible.

On Wolfgang Fabricius Capito, see p. 305, n. 2.

Text in Latin: WA, Br 2, 430-434.

Martin Luther to Wolfgang Fabricius Capito
Greetings in the Lord

As much as your Cardinal's [1] letter [2] brought me joy,[3] so much your letter [4] made me downcast, my Fabricius. This sad and unfriendly beginning may perhaps disturb you. But it is your own fault, since you destroyed the credibility and weight of the Cardinal's letter by

[1] The cardinal referred to in this letter is Albrecht, archbishop of Mainz; see pp. 44 f.
[2] See p. 365, n. 1.
[3] See p. 365; cf. pp. 353 ff.
[4] See p. 365, n. 2.

your inopportune rhetorics. Among the many things that concerned me was especially the fact that you write that you have set out on another way than ours to further the [cause of the] gospel.[5] What else can this mean but that either your way or ours is to be condemned? Yet the ministry of the Spirit ought not have any [internal] discrepancy at all! Paul commends Timothy to the Corinthians since they both walked the same way.[6] Due to my friendship for you, I certainly would have qualified your statement concerning the "other way" if you yourself had not forced me, through your own interpretation, to the following understanding: the [cause of the] gospel is being furthered by glossing over the actions of sovereigns, sparing them criticism, excusing their actions, and (as your words say) by not insolently provoking them to a fight.[7] This is your way of behaving; according to our opinion, this is plain flattery and a denial of Christian truth.[8] I would not even want my enemies to be content with this type of opinion; it lacks so much that I cannot even wish that the gospel were helped by this approach. There is nothing that I would avert more. May Christ grant that you accomplish something, but may he preserve you, and us, so that you may do no harm.

I know you demand gentleness and kindness. But what do a Christian and a flatterer have in common? Christianity is something direct and simple. It looks at things as they are, and it speaks accordingly. Even the pagans wish evil to those who flatter their friends about their vices.[9] How, then, could the truth of Christ flatter evil and ungodliness?

Nevertheless we shall expound to you also our way of promoting the cause of the gospel and expose it confidently to your judgment and the world's. We are not afraid that the crowds will be offended by this "biting," as you write. For whom did Christ not offend? Whom did he not reprove? The Spirit of truth

---

[5] *WA*, Br 2, 416.
[6] I Cor. 16:10.
[7] *WA*, Br 2, 419.
[8] One of the printed editions offers an addition which has to be translated: ". . . and exactly that partiality [a Greek word is used here] which Scripture detests so vehemently that there is nothing more vehemently [detested in Scripture than this]."
[9] This is a reference to Plutarch's work on flattery; see p. 307.

reproves [10] and does not flatter. He [11] reproves not just some people, however, but the whole world. Therefore we think that everything ought to be straightforwardly censured, reproved, confounded, and that nothing should be spared, bypassed, or excused, so that the unshackled, pure, and clear truth remains victoriously among us.

To continue, it is a totally different thing to accept, endure, and assist with greatest gentleness those whom you have rebuked. This belongs to the realm of love and service, and not to the ministry of the Word. Even Christ, when he has reproved all people with the greatest severity, wishes then to be like a hen to them and gather them under his wings.[12] Love bears all things, endures all things, hopes all things.[13] Faith, however, or the Word, endures nothing but rather reproves and consumes, or as Jeremiah says, plucks out, destroys, and overthrows, and, "Cursed be he who does the work of the Lord in a cheating way." [14]

There is a difference, dear Fabricius, between praising evil or minimizing its importance, and healing it with kindness and gentleness. Before all else one has to say what is right and what is wrong. When your listener has accepted this, then he has to be endured, and, as Paul says, he who is weak in faith is to be accepted.[15] Your way, however, brings about a situation in which truth is never recognized, and yet it is nevertheless assumed that evil is corrected by such flattery and false kindness. Thus the word of Jeremiah is fulfilled, "They have healed the wounds of my people [lightly saying, 'Peace, peace, where there is no peace]," and again, "They strengthen the hands of evildoers so that no one turns from his wickedness." [16]

I also hope that we never behaved in such a way that one could accuse us of having lacked charity in accepting and enduring the weak. We do not lack gentleness, kindness, peace, and joy with someone who agrees with our word yet cannot be perfect at

---

[10] John 16:8.
[11] I.e., Christ or the Holy Spirit.
[12] Matt. 23:37.
[13] I Cor. 13:7.
[14] Jer. 1:10; 48:10 (Vulgate).
[15] Rom. 14:1.
[16] Jer. 8:11; 23:14.

once. We are content that he has meanwhile recognized truth and has not resisted or condemned it. Whatever follows is [done on the basis of] love, in which he is admonished to act according to what he has recognized to be true. Had your Cardinal written this letter with a sincere heart—for goodness' sake, with what great joy and humility would I kneel before his feet, not considering myself worthy of kissing the dust of his feet! Are we not also unclean and filled with sin as a bag is filled with waste? [17] Let him only accept the Word of God, and we shall be his slaves.

There is, however, no grace, no love, no kindness for those who condemn or despise doctrine itself and the ministry of the Word, or persecute it cunningly—or rather, it is the highest kind of love to resist their fury and ungodliness with all strength and in every possible way.

Yet if your Cardinal has shown himself to be such a tremendous hypocrite due to your influence (which I suspect), then you yourself can very well see that this should not move us in any way. You people could not fool us since we are not ignorant of Satan's designs;[18] we can both justify and condemn anyone on the basis of his words.[19] Your Cardinal writes that by God's grace from now on he wants to do what is fitting for an official of the church.[20] If he says this in all honesty, and you have not suggested it to him, then he is certainly ready to take off the mask of a cardinal and the pomp of a bishop and dedicate himself to the ministry of the Word. Yet who will make us believe this? It is impossible that he should thus [21] be able to administer even a small parish. And it would be hard for him to resign and become a parish priest. [You object here:] who will dare to require this of him? I reply: how can you be sure if you do not reveal this truth [22] to him? After this is done, then be kind to him and overlook [any faults he may have]. But he has to know where he is sinning and where he is

[17] Luther wrote *sentina*, i.e., the lowest part of a ship where the bilge water is.
[18] See p. 354; see also II Cor. 2:11.
[19] Matt. 12:37.
[20] *WA*, Br 2, 421; *S-J* 2, 80; see p. 365, n. 1.
[21] One of the printed editions offers a text which has to be translated: ". . . that he [i.e., the Cardinal] be on the way of salvation as long as he is bishop of so many churches, since he is hardly able to administer. . . ."
[22] I.e., that he has to become a faithful parish priest.

not sinning. Then work so that he does not sin; or if he has sinned, sustain him in love. But do not tolerate it or bypass it either out of Christian [modesty] or human propriety if he goes astray in an ungodly way. For this is what is accomplished by that cruel flattery which pretends to be either Christian or human moderation.

How can I believe that what you write is true,[23] that the married priest is freed?[24] How can I believe what the Cardinal writes, that the reasons which led me to write my little book had already been removed a long time ago?[25] This is a fine liberation! As if it would not have been better to kill [the priest]![26] You forced him to abjure his wife,[27] contrary to his conscience, and this now causes him great grief. For goodness' sake, do you people also tempt the Holy Spirit?[28] Is it not that you persist in rejecting the marriage of priests until you nullify the renunciation to which you forced this man and [renounce] the violence with which you have brought about the divorce? You say she was a whore.[29] Excellent orator! This should have been investigated in advance. And even if she really were a whore, why do you rage against him alone but constantly bypass your brothels in Halberstadt, Mainz, and Magdeburg and the other innumerable ones,[30] as if your ears were closed? You see, Fabricius, your rhetoric is no good in this case. You people should certainly have been satisfied when he stated that she was his wife, or you should have refuted Paul, who most clearly condemns that celibacy by calling it a demonic doctrine.[31] If he lied in saying that she was his wife, it would have been his own danger, and you would not have been responsible.

You argue that this new marriage would have had to end in

---

23 *WA*, Br 2, 419; see p. 365, nn. 1, 2.
24 The Cardinal put certain priests in prison because they had married; see note 27; p. 342, n. 20.
25 *WA*, Br 2, 421; S-J 2, 80, regarding *Against the Idol at Halle;* see pp. 344 ff.; p. 316, n. 10.
26 See p. 354.
27 Capito was present when Balthasar Zeiger, pastor of Vatterode, a small town near Mansfeld, had to abjure his marriage; apparently Luther is thinking of him. See *WA*, Br 2, 435, n. 22.
28 Acts 5:9.
29 *WA*, Br 2, 419.
30 See p. 343, n. 25.
31 I Tim. 4:1 ff.; see pp. 277 f.

divorce, if he got disgusted with the hardships of marriage.[32] I think you don't believe that yourself! For how does it affect the rightness of a doctrine that the wicked abuse good institutions? We do not require of you people that you make available to us marriages without all hardships, but only that you not condemn the teaching and practice [of marriage for priests].[33] Concerning the marriage of priests, we affirm only that according to God's Word priests may marry. The Provost of Kemberg[34] is a man about whom all things are praiseworthy. He lacks anything that anyone might possibly call instability, unless perhaps men would be unstable just because you are afraid they will be. Nothing changes just because of your fear or our hope, nor do people's actions change, to say nothing of the words of God. Otherwise this fear would prevent us from attempting to follow any of the divine commandments.

You see, my Fabricius, how I am disturbed by these great arguments, so that I cannot believe that your Cardinal wrote this letter with a sincere heart. Of course I say nothing of the tremendous tyranny with which he[35] so ignominiously removed Andrew Kauxdorff[36] from his pulpit in Magdeburg; your Cardinal has hardly anyone who can compare with him. One day you people will be sorry for this.

For goodness' sake, my Fabricius, do you think this Luther is a man who would ignore all that if only he is coaxed with a flattering letter—in spite of the fact that your actions are abominable? Are you people not content that we are willing to forgive and endure in love? Do you even demand that we also justify [your actions], that is, that we deny true doctrine itself and replace it with ungodliness? Excellent Fabricius, you tempt me enough,

---

[32] *WA*, Br 2, 418.

[33] One of the printed editions offers a text in which a sentence is added which has to be translated: "Dispute it with God, who decrees these things which, due to man's instability, are so badly observed."

[34] Bartholomew Bernhardi; see p. 342, n. 20.

[35] One of the printed editions offers a text which tries to modify this and has to be translated: "you people."

[36] Andrew Kauxdorff of Torgau had studied theology at the University of Cologne and the University of Wittenberg. He was cathedral preacher in Magdeburg and had to leave his office in September, 1521, due to the Cardinal's pressure. On Kauxdorff, see *WA*, Br 2, 435, n. 29.

and more than enough! And I am answering you in a very kind way, even more than kindly. You deserved a far sharper reply! You people not only do not do [anything about my demands], but so often mock them and ridicule them with what seems to you excellent camouflage, but to me seems utterly absurd. We [37] shall defend the godly doctrine with all the strength at our command, even if it should offend heaven or hell.

Thus you have a most obedient servant in Luther, as you have always had, if only you are a friend of piety—but an outspoken despiser if you and your Cardinal should continue to trifle with what is a holy matter. Summarizing: [I am] ready to die for you; but whoever touches faith touches the apple of my eye.[38] My love you have completely at your disposal, to mock or to honor as you are pleased. We want you to have reverence for the faith and the Word and hold it as the Holy of Holies. Expect everything from our love, but fear our faith at all times.

I am not answering your Cardinal since I could not safely walk the middle of the road, neither praising him nor censuring him regarding his sincerity or hypocrisy. Through you, however, he will understand Luther's attitude. As soon as I am convinced of his sincerity, I shall not hesitate to throw myself humbly at his feet.

Farewell, my Fabricius; do not doubt that I am honest with you. As you realize, this matter is very important and sacred. We have to live up to this, so that we do not love our brothers and sisters more than Christ.[39]

From my wilderness,[40] *January 17, 1522* [41]

---

[37] One of the printed editions offers a text which replaces "we" with a long insert.
[38] Literally: "the pupil of [my] eye," an allusion to Ps. 17:8.
[39] Matt. 10:37.
[40] See p. 263, n. 36.
[41] The signature is missing since the text is based on printed editions in which Luther's name appears in the title.

114

To George Spalatin
Wartburg, January 17, 1522

Luther confirms receipt of a shipment from Spalatin. Informing Spalatin that he will leave the Wartburg "in a short time," Luther specifies that this is not because of the "Zwickau prophets" (see p. 364, n. 28). He also comments briefly on the latest move of Duke George of Saxony against the Reformation.

On George Spalatin, see pp. 8 f.

Text in Latin: WA, Br 2, 443-444.

Mr. George Spalatin, secretary to the Elector of Saxony,
my dearest friend in the Lord

Jesus

Greetings. I have received everything, my Spalatin, even the bag, yet that later than the rest.[1]

I do not come to Wittenberg, nor do I change my quarters, because of the "Zwickau prophets,"[2] for they don't disturb me. Yet I do not want them jailed, especially not by those who praise our cause.

Anything new concerning the sacramental practice at Eilenburg[3] either has been forced on the people or is a false rumor.[4] A little while ago I was disturbed by such rumors, so much that I even went to Wittenberg to see for myself;[5] but now I daily hear wilder things. The Lord willing, I shall definitely return in a

[1] This shipment could not be identified; according to *WA*, Br 2, 444, n. 1, it was a mailbag containing books and letters.
[2] See p. 364, n. 28.
[3] Eilenburg, founded in 1150, today is a highly industrialized town, about sixty miles south of Wittenberg; at Luther's time it was a center of the Electoral Saxon district administration.
[4] Having abandoned monastic life, Gabriel Zwilling (see pp. 324 f.; p. 337, n. 4) went to Eilenburg at Christmas, 1521, where he introduced a radical form of reformation, and on New Year's Day celebrated a communion service in which both elements were given to the communicants; see *WA*, Br 2, 444, n. 4; *ARG* 9 (1912), 347 ff.; 10 (1913), 51 ff.
[5] See p. 350.

short time;[6] if I don't stay in Wittenberg I shall certainly stay somewhere else, or wander around.[7] The cause itself demands it. I do not want the Sovereign [8] to worry about me, although I wish he had my faith and I his power!

I do not doubt that we could easily make a laughingstock out of those two stumps of smoldering firebrands [9] without resorting to the use of bloodshed and sword. Duke George,[10] the unhappiest of all people, is doing in this affair only what has been decreed for him by [God], who is terrible in his plans for the children of men. It is hatred, a hatred [Duke George] has nourished toward us for some time, but he does not realize that it is hatred.[11] May the Lord have mercy upon him, if he be worthy of it. I can't do anything else. Please see to it that our Sovereign does not stain his hands with the blood of these new "prophets" from Zwickau.

Farewell and pray for me. I am satisfied with neither the [Arch]bishop's letter nor Capito's, because of their miserable and only too obvious deceit.[12] I have replied to Fabricius, but not to the [Arch]bishop.[13] I shall wait until I know what he really thinks.

From the wilderness,[14] *January 17, 1522*

MARTIN LUTHER

I am waiting impatiently for the Bible, since I am responsible for it.[15]

---

[6] On Luther's plans to return, see pp. 356, 363 f., 371.
[7] For similar statements, see pp. 88, 90, 94, 274.
[8] Elector Frederick; see pp. 49 f.
[9] Isa. 7:4, with reference to the "Zwickau prophets" (see p. 364, n. 28). The *WA, Br* editor suggests that Luther was thinking of Storch and Stübner.
[10] Duke George of Saxony; see p. 110, n. 20.
[11] Duke George had complained to Duke John (see p. 269, n. 8) about the Wittenberg disturbances (see p. 386, n. 1) and asked why the Elector did not intervene. When Duke George arrived in Nürnberg on December 28, 1521, and met Hans von der Planitz, the Electoral Saxon ambassador to the Council of Regency (see p. 70, n. 1), he informed von der Planitz at once that he would approach the Council of Regency and demand that it put an end to the innovations in Wittenberg and to the Lutheran heresy. See E. Wülcker, H. Virk (eds.), *Des Kürsächsischen Rathes Hans von der Planitz Berichte aus dem Reichsregiment in Nürnberg, 1521-1523* (Leipzig: Teubner, 1899), Nos. 26, 27, 31, 33.
[12] See p. 365, nn. 1, 2; pp. 376 ff.
[13] See pp. 365, 372 ff., 379.
[14] See p. 263, n. 36.
[15] Apparently the Bible Luther mentioned in the postscript to No. 107, p. 352.

115

To George Spalatin[1]
Wartburg, January 22?, 1522

This letter was written in behalf of Michael Kreuz, a priest who wanted to exchange his recently acquired mass-benefice for a parish where he would not have to celebrate mass. Spalatin, considering the priest's wish to be due to instability, had refused to intervene with the Electoral government. Luther criticizes Spalatin for his lack of understanding in this case and explains the principles which should govern brotherly admonition and correction among Christians.

On George Spalatin, see pp. 8 f.

Text in Latin: WA, Br 2, 445-447.

Jesus

Grace and peace in Christ

I have seen the letter [2] you wrote to Amsdorf [3] regarding the parish for Kreuz, etc.[4] I am deeply grieved, not so much for the sake of Kreuz but for your sake. You are so imbued with a courtly state of mind and immersed in it that you think and write of your brother in an almost un-Christian way. You say you will be more careful in the future and that you do not want to be mixed up in the instability of other people, and I do not know what other grandiose things. As a result you have forced me to write this letter to you,

---

1 Although the address of this letter is missing, the fact that Luther speaks directly to Spalatin and calls him by name makes it obvious to whom the letter was written. On the date, which is doubtful, see WA, Br 2, No. 453, Introduction.

2 This letter is not extant.

3 Nicholas von Amsdorf; see p. 218.

4 Michael Kreuzen, or Kreuz, a young priest whom, upon Luther's recommendation, the Elector appointed to a parish in the spring of 1521; see WA, Br 2, 283. It seems that the reformers' attacks on the mass (see pp. 324 f.) made it impossible for Kreuz to continue to hold his position because it involved the obligation of celebrating mass. He wanted to exchange his position with one which would not have involved such responsibility. See WA, Br 2, 284, n. 1.

certainly as a brother to a brother.[5] Therefore I ask you for the sake of Christ also to accept it with a brotherly heart. If you don't intend to do so, tell me, and I will be more mute than a fish.[6]

If you had considered the whole affair in the proper light, then you would certainly know that this man is not a bad person. You would also know that his wish to leave his parish is not motivated by levity and instability but rather by the greatest exigency and demand of conscience (than which there is nothing greater in any creature), unless you don't know in what great tyranny and ungodliness such parishes are held and must be administered, and how difficult it is to get one. I admit he had previously obtained this parish with our help,[7] not knowing what he would get into. Now, having recognized the matter and understood the danger, he retreats, and intends to leave. You ought to approve of this by showing him greatest kindness and praise and commend him for it. You, however, accuse him of vacillating and condemn him; this you do with such great violence that you even vow not to help anyone else in the future. If you think and teach this way at court, then it would be better if you would be mute unto eternity. What I always have suspected in regard to this court becomes obvious now; I also understand now why the court rejected Pfaffenbeck so completely.[8] But this court covers up the secret evil of revenge and the ignorance of that charity found in Christ and most highly praised in all the letters of St. Paul, which is slow to revenge—even if one is justly provoked to it.[9] Do you perhaps think that it is not revenge if you don't inflict any harm [on someone] but withdraw your brotherly service [from him] so that he cannot overcome or check evil, which with your help he might avoid? My dear Spalatin, don't err! God is not mocked,[10] not even by the court, however hypocritical the court may be. You wouldn't want someone to do to you what you are considering doing to this man. You

---

[5] Matt. 18:15.
[6] See Erasmus, *Adagia*. Clericus 2, 192, D f.
[7] Luther to Spalatin: March 7, 1521. *WA*, Br 2, 283.
[8] Luther had previously intervened on his behalf, without success (see *WA*, Br 2, No. 468; *S-J* 2, 117 f. Luther's letter is not extant, and the background of it could not be established.
[9] Rom. 2:7; Gal. 5:22; Eph. 4:2; Col. 3:12; I Tim. 6:11.
[10] Gal. 6:7.

are sinning against the entire law and against love; I cannot permit you to perish in this sin. Therefore it is certainly brotherly anxiety that compels me to admonish you. Your boasting is not good.[11]

You reply that rashness and instability have to be punished, so that there is no occasion for a bad example. Right, but first one has to see whether it is rashness or rather piety which would be censured here, in order to avoid any possibility of any evil example by punishing innocence and piety. In this case it is piety, however, since he does not dare to take upon himself or administer the ungodliness of the masses. Now this may be rashness and should certainly be punished, but in such a way that it is set right and corrected, and not left uncorrected and the brother deserted in his misery. If you pursue that matter with such great harshness, then you will not only deprive the man of a parish, but you will also put him into the hands of his superiors, which would be the greatest danger [for him] and extremely harmful. In short you would have ruined him. For goodness' sake, will you who teach the gospel nevertheless dare to call this a punishment of rashness? I cannot believe this about you.

But be that as it may, you cannot act differently, since this is the custom of the court and the Sovereign's [12] way of thinking, I [can] hear [you saying]. But what are you then doing at court as a man of the gospel? Your task is to press forward on the basis of the Word to the end that this custom and way of thinking no longer exist, or at least not for you. That means "you will tell the ungodly about his sin and so save your life," as Ezekiel writes in chapter 3 [:19]. You know what strong words you courtiers have so often used to admonish me about my harshness. But now look, I ask you, what must one think about you people? Isn't it more salutary to fight ungodliness, even if it offends many people, than to flatter men in order to preserve peace and quietness? [13] Since you are so slow to castigate the thinking [of those] at court, which is incomparably worse than even the "fickleness" of this man, are you not then caught as an unjust judge? For I don't believe that

[11] I Cor. 5:6.
[12] Elector Frederick; see pp. 49 f.
[13] For similar statements, see pp. 326 f., 373 ff.

you would thunder against a lapse on the part of the Sovereign as you thunder against the "fickleness" of this man. Why do you deal differently with him than with those [at court]? It's only because you don't consider the merits but rather the persons involved. You therefore either have to receive this man with the same patience and kindness with which you accept the faults of the men at court, or know that you have repudiated Christ.

What miserable people we are, that we fool ourselves with our urbane courtesies and pretenses and do not see that secretly we omit Christian love! We treat the problems of the brethren in a cold, even ungodly way. Why? Because we act as if they were the problems of others and not our own. Love, however, cares for the problems of others as if they were one's own, as it is written, "Bear one another's burdens";[14] and again, "Let no one consider his own interests but the interests of others."[15] Love reproves faults but does not desert [him who falls]. This special vice of [the men at] this court has often offended me very much: claiming that they do not harm those who have only given offense once (and therefore boasting of not being bloodthirsty), they persistently undermine such poor people by withdrawing their help from them. It would sometimes be better to suffer at the hands of the bloodthirsty than at the hands of those who ["only"] withdraw [their help]. Whoever wishes to praise this may do so; I condemn it as being diametrically opposed to Christian patience. Be careful, therefore, that in detaching yourself wisely (as you think) from other people's instability, you don't on the other hand unwisely (as I think) involve yourself in other people's cruelty.

May God grant that you accept this [admonition] in a brotherly and grateful attitude. I wish you would see what a great and magnificent thing it is to teach the ungodly and to discuss the Word of God with them—and how few there are who are doing this openly and plainly.

I therefore plead with you that if you are able to help this Kreuz, you would not only not be offended but would also see to it that the Sovereign does not become even more ungracious toward him. Also, if this is possible, [I ask] that he may exchange

14 Gal. 6:2.
15 Phil. 2:4.

his parish for another one where it would not be necessary to celebrate mass. If you cannot do this [I beg you] at least to treat this man with gentleness and kindness. For we are brothers and he has done no evil, but he wants to act in a pious and Christian way; and in his attempt to do this, we have to help him. If you do not want to help him, then I have at least fulfilled my obligation to you and to him by writing this letter, and my conscience will be clear. See to it that you [not only] teach Christ but also recognize Christ in [this your] brother, and treat [him as such].

Farewell in the Lord; may he give you light and set you on fire with his knowledge. Amen.

January 22, 1522 MARTIN LUTHER

116[1]

To Elector Frederick
Wartburg, about February 22, 1522[2]

Luther congratulates the Elector on the acquisition of his new relic. He also announces his imminent return.

On Elector Frederick, see pp. 49 f.

Text in German: WA, Br 2, 448-449. The following translation, with minor changes, is by Theodore G. Tappert and is used by permission from Luther: Letters. LCC 18, 139-140. Published 1955, The Westminster Press.

---

[1] Letters No. 116 through 118 have to be seen against the background of the disturbances which took place in Wittenberg in December of 1521 and January/February of 1522. Karlstadt's and Zwilling's ideas and reforms caused restlessness among the people of Wittenberg and led finally, due to the agitation of the "Zwickau prophets," to disturbances and violence in the city. Asked by the people of Wittenberg to return (see p. 395), Luther left the Wartburg and came to Wittenberg to restore order in the city, to fulfil his pastoral responsibility for his congregation, and to prevent the Word of God from being distorted by a false understanding. On the origin and development of the Wittenberg disturbances, see p. 281, n. 24; pp. 324 f.; p. 364, n. 28; p. 366, n. 6; p. 381, n. 11; pp. 388 ff., 401 f.; Bainton, pp. 203 f.; Schwiebert, pp. 535 ff.; *ARG* 6 (1909), 161 ff., 261 ff., 385 ff.; 7 (1910), 185 ff., 233 ff., 353 ff.; 8 (1911), 1 ff.

[2] On the dating of this letter, see *WA*, Br 2, No. 454, Introduction.

TO ELECTOR FREDERICK, ABOUT FEBRUARY 22, 1522

To my most gracious Lord, Duke Frederick,
elector of Saxony: *Personal*

Jesus

Grace and joy from God the Father on the acquisition of a new relic!

I put this greeting in place of my assurances of respect. For many years Your Grace has been acquiring relics in every land, but God has now heard Your Grace's request and has sent Your Grace without cost or effort a whole cross, together with nails, spears, and scourges. I say again: grace and joy from God on the acquisition of a new relic![3]

Your Grace should not be terrified by it; stretch out your arms confidently and let the nails go deep. Be glad and thankful, for thus it must and will be with those who desire God's Word. Not only must Annas and Caiaphas rage,[4] but Judas must be among the apostles and Satan among the children of God. Only be wise and prudent, and do not judge according to reason or outward appearances. Do not be downhearted, for things have not yet come to such a pass as Satan wishes.

Your Grace should have a little confidence in me, fool though I am, for I know these and other similar tricks of Satan. I do not fear him [because I know] that this hurts him. Yet all of this is only a beginning. Let the world cry out and pass its judgments. Let those fall away who will—even a St. Peter [or persons like] the apostles. They will come back on the third day when Christ rises from the dead. This word in II Corinthians 6 [:4, 5] must be fulfilled in us, "Let us prove ourselves in tumults," etc.[5]

I hope that Your Grace will take this letter in good part. I am in such haste that my pen has had to gallop, and I have no

---

[3] The Elector was especially concerned with the collection of relics entrusted to the All Saints' Chapter at the Wittenberg Castle Church (see p. 46, n. 1; p. 388, n. 8). He did not hesitate to overcome difficult situations (see pp. 33 f.) or spend large sums of money (although he was generally thrifty) to enlarge this collection. Luther compares the Wittenberg disturbances to a relic of Christ's cross. The Elector had received this relic without having sought it. How lucky he was to be presented with such a relic!

[4] Matt. 26:57; John 18:12-13.

[5] This quotation is written in Latin.

time for more. God willing, I shall soon be there. But Your Grace must not assume responsibility in my behalf.

Your Grace's humble servant,
MARTIN LUTHER

117

To Elector Frederick
Borna, March 5, 1522

Immediately upon receiving Luther's letter No. 116, Elector Frederick sent a special message to his official at Eisenach, who in turn was to inform Luther of its contents; see WA, Br 2, No. 454, Document II; S-J 2, 90 ff. In this message the Elector requested Luther not to come out of hiding, at least not for the time being. The Elector also asked Luther's counsel regarding the disturbances at Wittenberg (see p. 386, n. 1). The Elector's message reflects his grave concern about the situation in Wittenberg and the latest moves of the Imperial government. Duke George's agitation against Electoral Saxony (see p. 381, n. 11) resulted in the issuance of a mandate by the Imperial government on January 20, 1522, in Nürnberg, demanding that all innovations concerning religious practices be suppressed or nullified under threat of punishment. See Akten und Briefe 1, No. 288.

Luther decided to return to Wittenberg in spite of the Elector's wish that he stay at the Wartburg. This letter, written by Luther on his way back to Wittenberg, is a reply to the Elector's message to him and an explanation that he is returning to Wittenberg because he has to obey God rather than any secular government.

On Elector Frederick, see pp. 49 f.

Text in German: WA, Br 2, 454-457; the following translation, with minor changes, is by Theodore G. Tappert and is used by permission from Luther: Letters. LCC 18, 318-321. Published 1955, The Westminster Press.

To the Most Serene, Noble Sovereign and Lord, Sir Frederick, duke of Saxony, elector of the Holy Roman Empire, landgrave of Thuringia, margrave in Meissen, my Most Gracious Lord and Patron

Jesus

Grace and peace from God our Father and from our Lord Jesus Christ, and my most humble service.

Most Serene, Noble Elector, Most Gracious Lord: Your Electoral Grace's kind letter and opinion reached me Friday evening [1] as I was preparing to depart the next day.[2] I need not say that I know Your Electoral Grace has the very best of intentions, for I am as certain of it as a man can be. On the other hand I am convinced by more than human means of reckoning that I too have good intentions. But this does not get us anywhere.

I take the liberty of supposing on the basis of Your Electoral Grace's letter that Your Electoral Grace was somewhat offended by that part of my letter in which I wrote that Your Electoral Grace should be wise.[3] Yet this impression of mine is canceled by the confidence I have that Your Electoral Grace knows my heart better than to suppose that I would sneer at Your Electoral Grace's well-known wisdom in such unseemly terms. I hope that it will always be that I have a thoroughly unaffected love and affection for Your Electoral Grace above all other sovereigns and rulers. What I wrote was done out of concern to reassure Your Electoral Grace, not for my own sake (of that I had no thought at the time) but for the sake of that untoward movement introduced by our friends in Wittenberg to the great detriment of the gospel.[4] I feared that Your Electoral Grace would suffer great inconvenience from it. Moreover, I myself was so overwhelmed by the calamity that had I not been certain that we have the pure gospel, I would have despaired of [our] cause. Whatever I have suffered hitherto

[1] February 28.
[2] March 1. The "letter and opinion" is a reference to the instruction mentioned in the Introduction.
[3] See p. 387; *WA*, Br 2, No. 454, Document II.
[4] The Wittenberg disturbances; see p. 386, n. 1.

for this cause has been nothing compared with this. I should willingly have averted the trouble at the cost of my life if that had been possible. We can answer neither to God nor to the world for what has been done. And yet it is blamed on me and, what is even worse, on the gospel. This pains me deeply.

Accordingly, Most Gracious Lord, my letter concerned only the action of these men,[5] not my own, in order that Your Electoral Grace should not pay attention to the ideas of the devil now unfolding in this drama [at Wittenberg]. Although such admonition may have been unnecessary for Your Electoral Grace, yet it was necessary for me to write it.

As for myself, Most Gracious Lord, I answer this: Your Electoral Grace knows (or, if you do not, I now inform you of the fact) that I have received the gospel not from men but from heaven only, through our Lord Jesus Christ,[6] so that I might well be able to boast and call myself a minister and evangelist, as I shall do in the future. I offered to appear for hearings and trial[7] not because I had doubts about [my mission] but out of excessive humility, in order to persuade others. But since I now see that my excessive humility abases the gospel, and that if I yield an inch the devil will take a mile, I am compelled by my conscience to act otherwise. I have served Your Electoral Grace well enough by staying in hiding for this year to please Your Electoral Grace. The devil knows very well that I did not hide from cowardice, for he saw my heart when I entered Worms. Had I then known that as many devils were lying in wait for me as there were tiles on the roofs, I should nevertheless have leaped into their midst with joy.[8]

Now Duke George is still far from being the equal of one devil.[9] Since the Father of infinite mercies[10] has by the gospel made us daring lords [with power] over all devils and over death and has given us such an abundance of confidence that we may

---

[5] The agitators in Wittenberg: Karlstadt, Zwilling, and the "Zwickau prophets"; see p. 386, n. 1.
[6] Gal. 1:11-12.
[7] See pp. 249 f.
[8] See p. 198.
[9] Duke George of Saxony; see p. 381, n. 11.
[10] II Cor. 1:3.

venture to call him our dearest Father,[11] Your Electoral Grace can see for yourself that it would be a great insult to such a Father not to trust him enough to take the measure of Duke George's wrath.

I know myself well enough to say that if the condition that exists in Wittenberg existed in Leipzig,[12] I would go to Leipzig even if (Your Electoral Grace will excuse my foolish words) it rained Duke Georges for nine days and every duke were nine times as furious as this one. He takes my Lord Christ to be a man of straw. My Lord and I can suffer that for a while.

I shall not conceal from Your Electoral Grace that I have more than once prayed and wept for Duke George, that God might enlighten him. I shall pray and weep once more and then cease forever. I beg Your Electoral Grace also to help in praying and to have others pray that the judgment which (O Lord God!) moves in on him without let-up might be averted. I would slay Duke George with a single word[13] if I knew that this would settle the matter.[14]

I have written this so Your Electoral Grace might know that I am going to Wittenberg under a far higher protection than the Elector's. I have no intention of asking Your Electoral Grace for protection. Indeed I think I shall protect Your Electoral Grace more than you are able to protect me. And if I thought that Your Electoral Grace could and would protect me, I should not go. The sword ought not and cannot help a matter of this kind. God alone must do it—and without the solicitude and co-operation of men. Consequently he who believes the most can protect the most. And since I have the impression that Your Electoral Grace is still quite weak in faith, I can by no means regard Your Electoral Grace as the man to protect and save me.

Since Your Electoral Grace wishes to know what to do in this matter and thinks that you have done too little, I humbly answer that Your Electoral Grace has already done far too much and should do nothing at all. God will not and cannot tolerate your

---

[11] Rom. 8:15-16; Matt. 6:9.

[12] Leipzig was located in the domain of Duke George; see p. 63, n. 24.

[13] Of prayer.

[14] I.e., avert the judgment threatening the Duke or solve all problems or bring the Duke to true faith or disarm the devil.

worrying and bustling, or mine. He wishes the matter to be left [in his hands] and no one else's. May Your Electoral Grace act accordingly. If Your Electoral Grace believes, then Your Electoral Grace will be safe and have peace. If Your Electoral Grace does not believe, I at least do believe and must leave Your Electoral Grace's unbelief to its own torturing anxiety, such as all unbelievers have to suffer.

Inasmuch as I do not intend to obey Your Electoral Grace, Your Electoral Grace is excused before God if I am captured or put to death.[15] Before men Your Electoral Grace should act as an elector, obedient to the authorities and allowing His Imperial Majesty[16] to rule in your cities and lands over both life and property, as is his right according to the Imperial constitution; Your Electoral Grace should by no means offer any resistance or request such resistance or any obstruction on the part of others in case [His Imperial Majesty] wants to capture me or put me to death. For no one should overthrow or resist authority save him who ordained it; otherwise it is rebellion and an action against God. But I hope they will have the good sense to recognize that Your Electoral Grace occupies too lofty a position [to be expected] to become my executioner. If the representatives [of the Imperial government] themselves or their deputies come to capture me and Your Electoral Grace admits them and upholds their Electoral safe-conduct, then Your Electoral Grace will have done enough in the way of obedience. They can ask no more of Your Electoral Grace than that you do not hold Luther back. [I can be taken prisoner] without causing Your Electoral Grace trouble, work, or danger. For Christ has not taught me to be a Christian at another's expense. If they are so unreasonable as to command Your Electoral Grace to lay hands on me, I shall at once tell Your Electoral Grace what to do. [In any case] I shall see to it that Your Electoral Grace suffers no harm and danger in body, estate, or soul on my account, whether Your Electoral Grace believes this or not.

Herewith I commend Your Electoral Grace to the grace of God. If necessary we shall speak further of the matter very soon.

---

[15] On account of the Edict of Worms; see p. 210.
[16] Charles V; see pp. 175 f.

I have written this letter in haste so that Your Electoral Grace may not be disturbed at hearing of my arrival [in Wittenberg], for if I would be a true Christian I must be everyone's consoler and do no harm to anyone. It is Someone other than Duke George whom I have to consider. He knows me rather well, and I have some real knowledge of Him too. If Your Electoral Grace believed, you would see the glory of God. But because you do not believe, you have not yet seen. Love and praise to God forever. Amen.

Written at Borna, [in the house of] the official escort,[17] *March 5, 1522*

Your Electoral Grace's humble servant,
MARTIN LUTHER

118

To Elector Frederick
Wittenberg, March 7 or 8,[1] 1522

Luther returned from the Wartburg excommunicated by the church and under the ban of the Imperial government. This could have had important consequences, had the Imperial government insisted that the Edict of Worms (see p. 210) be enforced, or had it had the military power to execute it even against the Elector's will. Elector Frederick apparently was willing and courageous enough to deal with this problem. Nevertheless he wanted to be careful so that he (still confessing the faith of the Roman church)

---

17 Michael von der Strassen of Dresden; see *ARG* 8 (1911), 36 f.; *WA*, Br 2, 457, n. 40. He had studied in Wittenberg in 1503/04 and was *Gleitsmann* at Borna from 1511 on. In this position he supervised the collection of taxes at Borna (center of an administrative district south of Leipzig in Electoral Saxony) and was the Elector's official representative there; he also functioned as an escort for the Elector, government officials, and official guests. Because the court valued him for his thriftiness and ability to manage public funds, he was often entrusted with buying supplies for the Electoral household. He died in 1531. In spite of the fact that he was well versed in financial matters, he did not acquire private wealth. After his death Luther apparently tried several times to obtain scholarships for one of his sons.

1 On the dating of this letter, see p. 398, n. 17.

did not publicly permit a heretic and outlaw to live in his territory. The Elector apparently felt that there was a great difference between tolerating Luther and his work (and protecting him from unfair treatment), and giving Luther explicit permission to return to public life in the Electoral domain.

Upon receiving Luther's letter (pp. 388 ff.), the Elector commissioned Jerome Schurf of Wittenberg (see p. 219, n. 2) to meet with Luther at once. Schurf was to request a letter from Luther "in which he [Luther] sets forth the reasons and motivations for his return to Wittenberg and the fact that this was without our permission; he is also to state his willingness to exercise some self-restraint and to say that he does not wish to give anyone any trouble; and the letter is to be formulated so that we can forward it to some of our men [i.e., apparently the Electoral Saxon delegation to the Imperial government as a possible answer to the January 20 mandate; see p. 388], in order to maintain our honor." See WA, Br 2, No. 455, Document II; S-J 2, 96 f. Jerome Schurf apparently met with Luther on March 8 (see WA, Br 2, No. 456, Introduction), and this letter, No. 118, is the result of this meeting.

On Elector Frederick, see pp. 49 f.

Text in German: WA, Br 2, 459-462.

Jesus

Grace and peace from God our Father and our Lord Jesus Christ, Amen; and my humble service.

Most Serene, Noble Sovereign and Most Gracious Lord: I have very carefully considered that it truly would be a burden for Your Electoral Grace if I would return to Wittenberg again without Your Electoral Grace's wish and permission, particularly since it seems that this would cause great danger for Your Electoral Grace, the whole country, and all the people, but especially for myself, banned and condemned by papal and Imperial law as I am, and expecting death at any moment.

What should I do? There is urgent reason for my return and God compels and calls me. Therefore it has to be this way and will be so; so let it be in the name of Jesus Christ, the Lord of life and death.

In order that Your Electoral Grace is not ignorant, however, regarding the reasons for my return, I will explain to Your Electoral Grace those [which I consider most important]. To begin with, I am returning not out of contempt for the authority of the Imperial Majesty [2] or of Your Electoral Grace or of any other government. Human authority is not always to be obeyed, namely, when it undertakes something against the commandments of God;[3] yet it should never be despised but always honored. Christ did not justify Pilate's verdict; but he did not depose him or the emperor, nor did he show any contempt for him.[4]

The first reason [for my return]: I am called by the whole congregation at Wittenberg in a letter filled with urgent begging and pleading.[5] Since no one can deny that the [present] commotion [6] has its origin in me, and since I must confess that I am a humble servant of the congregation to which God has sent me, I had no way of refusing [this call] without rejecting Christian love, trust, and obedience. Many may consider this commotion something demonic, many may criticize and condemn it; no doubt they don't consider this to be a reason for my return and instead might consider it only just that Wittenberg and the work that was begun there should be left to perish. This does not excuse me, however, because God will not judge me according to the belief or disbelief of others, be they many or few, but according to my own conscience. I know that what I have to say and what I have begun does not originate in me but in God; no death or persecution will teach me differently. It seems to me that one has to leave it this way.

The second reason [for my return]: on account of my absence Satan has intruded into my fold at Wittenberg.[7] The whole world shouts it abroad—and it certainly is true—that Satan has injured

---

[2] Emperor Charles V; see pp. 175 f.
[3] Acts 5:29-30.
[4] John 19:11.
[5] The letter is not extant. See p. 366, n. 6; p. 371; *WA*, Br 2, 462, n. 4.
[6] I.e., the reformation of the church, especially the disturbances which it caused in Wittenberg.
[7] The Wittenberg disturbances; see p. 386, n. 1; see also p. 401. As early as June, 1521, Luther worried about the possibility that during his absence "wolves" might enter his sheepfold; see p. 248.

some [sheep] which I cannot heal with any writing. I have to deal with them personally via mouth and ear. My conscience will no longer allow me to yield or procrastinate. Therefore I have to disregard not only Your Electoral Grace's pleasure or displeasure but even the whole world's wrath or good will. [The congregation at Wittenberg is,] after all, my fold, entrusted to me by God; they are my children in Christ. There has been no time for doubting whether I should or should not return. I owe it to them to lay down my life for them, as Christ requires, John 10 [:11], and by God's grace I will do that willingly and joyfully. Had I been able to help things by writing letters, as I did until now, so that it would not have been necessary to be called back, why should I not willingly consent to stay away from Wittenberg even for good, since it is also my duty to die for my neighbor's sake?

The third reason [for my return]: I am rather afraid (and I worry that unfortunately I may be only too right) that there will be a real rebellion in the German territories, by which God will punish the German nation. For we see that this gospel[8] is excellently received by the common people; but they receive it in a fleshly sense; that is, they know that it is true but do not want to use it correctly.[9] Those who should calm such rebellion only aid it.[10] They attempt to put out the light by force, not realizing that they are only embittering the hearts of men by this and stimulating them to revolt. They behave as if they wanted themselves, or at least their children, destroyed. No doubt God sends this as a punishment.

The spiritual tyranny has been weakened, and this was the only purpose of my writings. Now I see that God will go further and may deal [with us] as he dealt with Jerusalem and its two authorities.[11] I recently learned that not only spiritual but also

---

[8] I.e., the way the reformers preach it.
[9] See pp. 214, 233; p. 351, n. 9.
[10] Perhaps a reference to the agitators of the Wittenberg disturbances (see p. 386, n. 1) or to the opponents of the Reformation; see also pp. 224 f.
[11] I.e., the chief priest and the king. Thinking apparently of II Kings 25, Luther draws a parallel between the capture of the royal family and the temple officials which climaxed the destruction of the Judean commonwealth, and the fate to which he is afraid secular and ecclesiastical authorities of his own time may be exposed.

worldly authority must yield to the gospel, be it voluntarily or not, as is clearly indicated in all the stories of the Bible. Now God has commanded, through Ezekiel, that we set ourselves before him as a wall of protection for the people.[12] Therefore I—and my friends—have considered it necessary to act upon this, to see whether we might turn away or defer God's judgment. Even if I could not accomplish anything in this affair, and even if I seem ridiculous to my enemies when they hear of it, I have to do what I see and know I must do.

Your Electoral Grace should know and rely with security on the following: something absolutely different was decided in heaven than at Nürnberg.[13] Unfortunately you will see that they who think they now are gourmandizing the gospel have [14] not yet even begun to eat.

There are certainly more reasons [for my return]; I do not yet consider them urgent enough, however, to point them out or think about them thoroughly.[15] One reason is more than sufficient, namely, the [cause of the] gospel is in need, and therefore I could not take human matters into consideration.

With this I beg Your Electoral Grace to be gracious to me and not to hold against me my present stay in Your Electoral Grace's city; I know that this stay is without Your Electoral Grace's knowledge or consent. Your Electoral Grace is lord only of earthly goods and bodies, but Christ is also lord of souls. To these he has sent me and for this [purpose] he has raised me up. I cannot abandon them. I trust my Lord Christ is stronger than our enemies and certainly can protect me from them if it is his will. If he does not wish to do this, then his blessed will be done. I cer-

---

[12] Ezek. 13:5; 22:30.

[13] A reference to the Imperial mandate issued on January 20 at Nürnberg; see p. 388.

[14] From here to the end of the sentence reads literally, "have not yet said the *Benedicite* [i.e., grace]." The subject of this last sentence is unclear; it has to be either the Elector or the enemies who "will see." Depending on the interpretation of the word *leider*, i.e., "unfortunately," and its position in the sentence, this sentence may also be translated: "They [i.e., the enemies] will see to their sorrow that those who think . . . ." Although in this interpretation the sense requires enemies to be the subject, structurally the original text leaves the subject ambiguous.

[15] It is not clear of what additional reasons Luther was thinking.

tainly know, however, that I shall not suffer danger or harm from Your Electoral Grace.[16]

I commend Your Electoral Grace to God's mercy.

Wittenberg, March 8, 1522 [17]

Your Electoral Grace's dedicated servant,
MARTIN LUTHER

Postscript

Should Your Electoral Grace be dissatisfied with the form of this letter,[18] then I humbly ask that Your Electoral Grace have one drafted which will be satisfactory to you, and have it forwarded to me.[19] I am not afraid of having my last letter to Your

---

[16] The original text could perhaps also support the following translation of this sentence: "But I certainly know that Your Electoral Grace will not be exposed to any danger or harm on account of me."

[17] Luther wrote: "*Freitag ante Invocavit,* 1522," i.e., "Friday before Invocavit [i.e., the first Sunday in Lent, named after the first word of the Introit in Latin], 1522." According to the *WA*, Br editor this was March 7. The *WA*, Br editor has convincingly shown, however, that Luther predated this letter to pretend that he wrote it immediately upon his return to Wittenberg on March 7; it also seems that the meeting with Schurf (see p. 394) did not take place before March 8, so that one is justified in assuming March 8 as the date on which this letter was actually written. Together with Schurf's official report, it was forwarded to the Elector by Schurf on March 9; see *WA*, Br 2, No. 456, Introduction, and Document II.

[18] On the Elector's request for this letter, see p. 394.

[19] On March 11 Elector Frederick answered Schurf's official communication of March 9 (see note 17) and enclosed a draft of a letter, as Luther had suggested. This draft was prepared by Spalatin. Although Luther did not like the way Spalatin had altered his letter (pp. 394 ff.), he yielded and copied and signed it on March 12. A comparison of Luther's original version (letter No. 118) with the more diplomatically phrased final version (the March 12 letter) shows definite differences in style and argument, though the content is the same. Were the sample draft by Spalatin also available, one could see whether or not Luther followed it verbatim. It may be assumed, however, that Luther did so, in view of his unhappiness with the March 12 letter; he expressed his criticism of Spalatin's draft and the final (March 12) version of letter No. 118 in his March 13 letter to Spalatin, which is the covering letter for the final version. Luther gave Schurf the March 12 letter to the Elector, together with the March 13 covering letter to Spalatin. On March 15, in the early morning, Schurf forwarded both documents (to which he added his own report; see *WA*, Br 2, No. 458, Document II) to the Electoral Saxon court in Lochau, where they arrived late in the afternoon. Elector Frederick had Luther's March 12 letter copied at once, and had the copy forwarded via Duke John (see p. 269, n. 8) to the Electoral Saxon delegation at the Council of Regency in Nürnberg (see p. 381, n. 11; p. 394). On March 16 the Elector issued a special instruction to Hans von der Planitz, the Electoral Saxon ambassador to the Council of

Electoral Grace[20] get out into the public. From now on I do not want to undertake anything of which I would be ashamed should others see me doing it during the day. I was not afraid of rebellion;[21] thus far I have taken it quite lightly, thinking it was directed only against the clergy. Now I am worried, however, that it might also surge against the government and, like an epidemic, involve the clergy [in its violent rush]. Yet this will not and should not happen until the gospel is persecuted and put down, as has always been the case in the past.

119

To Nicholas Hausmann
Wittenberg, March 17, 1522

Luther returned from the Wartburg to restore peace to Wittenberg and prevent the Word of God from being distorted. In this letter he comments on the "Zwickau prophets" and gives a theological evaluation of the radical changes brought forth by the Wittenberg disturbances; see p. 386, n. 1. He points out principles which should underlie any change in religious practices.

Nicholas Hausmann of Freiberg/Saxony (1478?-1538) was a close friend of Luther, although he is one of the lesser known men of the Reformation. A pastor in Zwickau since 1521, he was confronted with great difficulties there. First he had to face the enthusiasts (see p. 364, n. 28) and later he had to deal with the Zwickau city council, which was attempting to meddle in the affairs of the church. The controversy between Hausmann and the city council is important in understanding the relationship of the Reformation churches to secular power. In these difficulties Luther

Regency; the Elector requested that von der Planitz show Luther's March 12 letter to everyone who might want to cause trouble to Electoral Saxony because of Luther's return to Wittenberg. On March 21 von der Planitz received a copy of Luther's March 12 letter, and the next day he reported to the Elector that he had turned over the copy to the Council of Regency. See WA, Br 2, 473.

20 See pp. 388 ff.

21 See pp. 98, 152, 192, 223, 233, 245, 281, 307.

was Hausmann's faithful friend, and on Hausmann's behalf he wrote some of his sharpest letters.[1] *Recommended by Luther, Hausmann was called in 1532 to be court chaplain to the dukes of Anhalt in Dessau, a position he held until 1538, when he accepted a call to his home town of Freiberg. There he died of a stroke suffered while preaching his installation sermon. His primary interest was the development of an order or constitution for the congregations and a form of worship; both were to reflect the understanding of the gospel the Reformation had brought forth. Thus Hausmann was involved in the liturgical changes Luther worked out, and was primarily responsible for the visitations conducted in Electoral Saxony (and later in other territories), which led to the organization of the territorial church.*

Text in Latin: WA, Br 2, 474-475.

To the faithful evangelist of the congregation in Zwickau, Mr. Nicholas Hausmann, my dearest brother in Christ

Jesus

Greetings. My Nicholas, [my friend] in Christ: Although I am in the midst of such great commotion and am occupied with various tasks [because of it],[2] yet I could not skip writing to you, espe-

---

[1] According to K. Aland (ed.), *Martin Luther: Die Briefe* (*"Luther Deutsch,"* Vol. X [Stuttgart: E. Klotz Verlag, 1959]), p. 412.

[2] The Wittenberg disturbances; see p. 386, n. 1. From March 9 to 16 Luther preached his famous eight *Invocavit Sermons;* see *WA* 10^{III}, 1 ff.; *LW* 51, 70 ff. Through these sermons he restored peace to the minds of the people and order in the city. The impression these sermons made on the public is reflected in a letter of one of the Wittenberg students, who listened to them: "On March 6 Martin Luther returned to Wittenberg in equestrian habit, accompanied by several horsemen. He came to settle the trouble stirred up by the extremely violent sermons of Karlstadt and Zwilling. For they had no regard for weak consciences, whom Luther, no less than Paul, would feed on milk until they grew strong. He preaches daily on the Ten Commandments. As far as one can tell from his face the man is kind, gentle, and cheerful. His voice is sweet and sonorous, so that I wonder at the sweet speaking of the man. Whatever he does, teaches, and says is most pious, even though his impious enemies say the opposite. Everyone, even though not Saxon, who hears him once, desires to hear him again and again, such tenacious hooks does he fix in the minds of his auditors. In short there is nothing lacking in that man which makes for the most perfect Christian piety, even though all mortals and the gates of hell may say the contrary." S-J 2, 115.

cially since the occasion demanded it, and this friend, the carrier of the letter, requested it. I hope you are strong in faith and are growing daily in the knowledge of Christ.[3] The "prophets"[4] who came from your [town] are striving for peculiar things; they are pregnant with monstrosities I do not like. If these should be born, they will cause no small damage. Their spirit is extremely deceitful and specious. The Lord be with us. Amen.

Satan attempted to do so much damage here in my fold that it was hard to oppose him without causing offense to both sides. By all means see to it that you don't permit any innovations, either on the basis of a common resolution[5] or by force. Only with the Word are those things to be fought which our people tried to accomplish by force and violence; with the Word they are to be overthrown, with the Word they are to be destroyed! It is Satan who has driven them to their actions.

I condemn the idea that masses are considered sacrifices or good works;[6] but I do not want to lay hands on the unwilling or unbelieving, or curb them by force. I condemn only with the Word; he who believes, let him believe and follow—he who does not believe, let him disbelieve and be dismissed. No one should be forced to faith and to what belongs to faith, but he should be drawn by the Word so that, willingly believing, he may come of his own accord.

I condemn religious symbols,[7] but with the Word; they should not be burned, but trust should not be put in them as was done before and is still done today. They would fall by themselves if people were taught and knew that before God symbols are nothing.

---

[3] Col. 1:10.

[4] See p. 364, n. 28.

[5] I.e., a resolution of the people. On the other hand, however, Luther saw the possibility that the resolution of the community could abolish old customs, as well as abuses in the field of religion; see *WA*, Br 2, 491. As a result, in the passage here the emphasis has to be on the "force," i.e., on the tumultuous circumstances under which such common resolutions were brought forth.

[6] See pp. 324 f.

[7] Literally: "images." References to the iconoclasm which had taken place in Wittenberg in January, 1522, under the leadership of Karlstadt and the "Zwickau prophets," who thought religious symbols were contrary to God's commandment in Exod. 20:4-5.

Likewise I condemn the pope's laws on confession,[8] communion,[9] prayer, and fasting—but I condemn with the Word, so that I may liberate consciences from these laws. When the consciences have been freed, then of course people can use all these things [10] for the sake of the weak who are still entangled in them; when the weak have become firm, then these things may be discontinued. This way love will rule with regard to these external works and regulations.[11]

Now nothing is more disgusting to me than our mob of people here who have abandoned Word, faith, and love and can only boast that they are Christians because before the very eyes of the weak they can eat meat, eggs, and milk,[12] receive the Lord's Supper in "both kinds," [13] and neither fast nor pray.

I plead that you too take up this [my] way of teaching. Everything has to be exposed to the Word, but hearts must be driven slowly,[14] like Jacob's flock,[15] so that first they take up the Word of God voluntarily, and when they have finally become strong, do everything. Perhaps it is unnecessary to tell this to you because you know this [already]; but it was the solicitude of love that prompted it.

Farewell in Christ, and support the [cause of the] gospel with your prayers.

Wittenberg, March 17, 1522

Yours,
MARTIN LUTHER

---

[8] See p. 246, n. 10.
[9] See pp. 324 f.
[10] I.e., religious symbols.
[11] I Corinthians 8; Rom. 13:8-9; 14, 15. For Luther's thoughts on the subject outlined in the last paragraph, see the *Invocavit Sermons* (see note 2) and his work *The Freedom of a Christian*. *WA* 7, 20 ff., 49 ff.; *LW* 31, 343 ff.
[12] I.e., on days of fast.
[13] See pp. 143 f., 324 f.
[14] In the autograph the word is illegible; the translation is based on the conjecture and interpretation made by the *WA*, Br editor on the basis of the context.
[15] Gen. 33:13.

INDEXES

INDEX OF NAMES AND SUBJECTS

[References to biographical sketches are in boldface type.]

INDEX TO SCRIPTURE PASSAGES